WILL IT LIBERATE?
Questions About Liberation Theology

Michael Novak

PAULIST PRESS
New York/Mahwah

In homage to
Carlos Rangel
Mario Vargas Llosa
and all who work tirelessly in Latin America
for liberty

Library of Congress Cataloging-in-Publication Data

Novak Michael.
    Will it liberate?

    Bibliography: p.
    Includes index.
    1. Liberation theology—Controversial literature.
2. Theology, Doctrinal—Latin America. 3. Latin America—Social conditions. 4. Latin America—Church history. 5. Latin America—Economic conditions.
I. Title.
BT83.57N69   1986   230   86-18754
ISBN 0-8091-0385-0

Published by Paulist Press
997 Macarthur Boulevard
Mahwah, New Jersey 07430

Printed and bound in the
United States of America

CONTENTS

ACKNOWLEDGMENTS

Six of the longest chapters below appear for the first time in this book. Four of the others, although previously published in journals or magazines, appear here in a new and considerably longer version. Although some unavoidable repetitions and differences in tone remain, I have worked hard to shape the whole by the standards of the book-writer's craft, rather than solely by the standards proper to the essayist.

This book goes substantially beyond my earlier writings on liberation theology. In *The Spirit of Democratic Capitalism* (1982), the reader will find three chapters on Latin America, which supply statistical data of relevance to the present inquiry. (These were later condensed in the *Atlantic Monthly* under the title "Why Latin America Is Poor.") The reader may also wish to consult two volumes I have edited at the American Enterprise Institute: *Latin America: Dependency or Interdependence?* (1985) and *Liberation Theology and the Liberal Society* (1987). Other volumes in that series may also be of interest.* In addition, Chapter 10 of *Freedom with Justice* (Harper & Row, 1984), "Liberation Theology in Practice," should also be consulted.

I am particularly grateful to the following publishers and editors for their permission to reprint, usually in revised and enlarged versions, material first appearing in their pages. Among these are *The New York Times Sunday Magazine,* for a shorter version of Chapter One (published October 21, 1984, under the title "The Case Against Liberation Theology"); the *Notre Dame Journal of Law, Ethics and Public Policy* (1986) for earlier and shorter versions of Chapters Two and Three; and *Commentary* magazine, for a somewhat different version of Chapter Four (June 1979). Seven chapters are new for this book.

In particular I want to thank Robert Sirico, C.S.P. of St. Paul's College in Washington, D.C., who proposed the idea for this book, and

Capitalism and Socialism: A Theological Perspective (1979); *Democracy and Mediating Structures: A Theological Inquiry* (1980); and *The Corporation: A Theological Inquiry* (1981).

Dr. John Farina of the Paulist Press for his able and dedicated editorial assistance. I am thankful, too, for the research assistance that Scott Walter and James Muldoon have lent to my otherwise poorer efforts; their work on the endnotes was herculean. Gayle Yiotis has for several years done immense amounts of word-processing, with an uncanny ability to read my original handwriting and (too often) my mind. Judy Shindel kept our office functioning and good-spirited during the friendly chaos entailed in meeting multiple and conflicting deadlines. Even those who take exception to portions of what I write have always made plain how much they admire Karen Laub-Novak, as the redeeming influence in my life, which she is. To her, too, public thanks.

Washington, D.C.
February 2, 1986

The overthrow by means of revolutionary violence of structures which generate violence is not *ipso facto* the beginning of a just regime. A major fact of our time ought to evoke the reflection of all those who would sincerely work for the true liberation of their brothers: Millions of our own contemporaries legitimately yearn to recover those basic freedoms of which they were deprived by totalitarian and atheistic regimes which came to power by violent and revolutionary means, precisely in the name of the liberation of the people. This shame of our time cannot be ignored: While claiming to bring them freedom, these regimes keep whole nations in conditions of servitude which are unworthy of mankind. Those who, perhaps inadvertently, make themselves accomplices of similar enslavements betray the very poor they mean to help.

> Congregation for the Doctrine of
> the Faith—"Instruction on
> Certain Aspects of the 'Theology of
> Liberation' "

Introduction

TOWARD A THEOLOGY FOR THE WESTERN HEMISPHERE

It is a special pleasure to bring these *quaestiones disputatae* to the public through a Press whose origins go back to Isaac Hecker, the founder of the Paulists and a great Americanist. When many years ago I was thinking about the priesthood, Isaac Hecker's love for the "experiment" of the United States drew me toward the Paulists. (I ended up spending twelve years with the Congregation of Holy Cross, beginning at Notre Dame, Indiana.) As a grandchild of very poor immigrants, I knew through family memory the liberations the United States could bring: political, from tyranny; economic, from grinding poverty; moral and cultural, from the repression of conscience, information, ideas, and expression. Liberation theology is a very American idea; for my family, the Statue of Liberty was a first symbol of "liberation theology," North American style. With Orestes Brownson, Jacques Maritain and John Courtney Murray, S.J., and with Archbishops Ireland and Hughes, and Bishop Spalding, Isaac Hecker saw clearly that the citizens of the United States are the heirs of a great religio-political experiment that would one day invigorate Catholicism around the world.

When I first started writing in the 1950s, "liberal Catholics" warmly accepted the positive vision of American life heralded by Hecker. My first non-fiction book, *A New Generation: American and Catholic,* signalled that my own lifetime intention was to explore the twin inheritance of being Catholic and being American—and to do so in a fairly sustained and systematic way. Looking back after thirty years—over books on belief, radical politics, Vietnam, the experience of nothingness, ethnicity, the presidency, the three great sports of America (invented by Americans for Americans), the founding of the United Mine Workers, and political economy—I can fairly say that I have accomplished the first part of what I wanted to do.

When I first began writing, the great slumbering complacence of the United States during the 1950s seemed in need of stirring. Today, by contrast, an entire generation has been prepared to think harshly of the United States. In some circles, the overpowering reflex is to "blame America first." Students today often face this instinct, less in themselves than in some of their professors, who came of age during the 1960s. The North American idea of liberation is neglected.

Still, a large part of my subject in the essays that constitute this book is that other and more recent "liberation theology"—that of Brazil and Argentina, Nicaragua and Peru, and the other nations of Latin America. There is much in Latin American liberation theology to admire. There can be no question that great revolutions in political economy are necessary in Latin America, if that great and much-blessed continent is to fulfill its full human destiny. That in so many places the human rights of its citizens are abused, and that so many of its peoples live in wretched poverty, are conditions undoubtedly in need of change. It is a hopeful sign, however, that swift and thorough change is possible. Such recently impoverished and war-broken nations as Japan, South Korea, Taiwan, Singapore and Hong Kong—in 1939, considerably poorer than several nations of Latin America—have not doubled, or trebled, but ten times over multiplied their national wealth during the past twenty years, rapidly raising up their poor. Building on sound ideas of order, Latin America can swiftly do the same. In natural resources, Latin America is perhaps the richest of all the continents. In its Jewish-Christian heritage, it is a swirling ocean of powerful humanistic currents.

There is much to praise in Latin American liberation theology. What I admire most about it is its intellectual ambition. "Philosophy," writes Enrique Dussel in *The Philosophy of Liberation*, "the exclusive patrimony of, first, the Mediterranean world and then of Europe, now finds an origination that allows it to be authentically worldwide for the first time in the course of history."[1] Dussel intends to overthrow the whole Western tradition, pivoting philosophy (and theology) upon a new fulcrum. Compared to sentiments such as his, North American theologians seem both timid and spiritually dependent upon Europe; they are often even as "anti-American" as European intellectuals are wont to be. Liberation philosophy is, writes Dussel, "like the alienated child who protests the overbearing father; the child is becoming an adult." When will North American theology become adult?

For it seems to me the true case that in our time the theology of the entire Western Hemisphere—the theology of the Americas—is coming of age. It is not only Latin America that has a liberation theology. North America does, too. North American liberation theology

is, however, buried in institutions, practices and habits; it exists much
more powerfully in reality than in books. North American liberation
theology has hardly yet begun to achieve self-consciousness. Jacques
Maritain writes:

> You are advancing in the night, bearing torches toward which
> mankind would be glad to turn; but you leave them envel-
> oped in the fog of a merely experiential approach and mere
> practical conceptualization, with no universal ideas to com-
> municate. For lack of an adequate ideology, your lights can-
> not be seen.[2]

By contrast, Latin American liberation theology exists at present much
more powerfully in books than in reality. In reality, it has entered the
lives of only a few million of Latin America's 406 million inhabitants.

What North American theologians owe profoundly to Latin
American theologians is the intellectual challenge to make them articulate the self-consciousness of the Americas. The founders of the
United States knew that the *novus ordo seclorum* of the New World was
unlike anything known in Europe. No nation in Europe was built on
principles like those on which the United States was constituted. Theologians—a few exceptions such as Isaac Hecker and John Courtney
Murray, S.J., aside—have, however, failed to articulate a theology
commensurate with the novelty of the New World. Latin Americans,
given their intense contemplative and speculative tendencies, as opposed to the practical, empirical temper of North Americans, have
risen to this theoretical challenge in an admirable fashion. They challenge North Americans to do the same.

The most stark contrast between North American and Latin
American liberation theologies, however, lies in their judgment upon
economic activism, commerce, invention, discovery, entrepreneurship, enterprise, investment—in a word, capitalism. For centuries now,
Latin American humanism has been hostile to commerce and to economic dynamism, which it considers vulgar, low, of little esteem, and
more than a little tainted with evil. Latin American humanism prefers
the mode of the aristocratic spirit on the one side, and the simplicity
of the rural peasant, on the other. Its basic enlivening vision is feudal,
whereas that of North America is post-feudal. Mark Twain in 1876 was
the first writer in history to submit a manuscript typed on a typewriter,
the first model of E. Remington & Sons. Just so, North America de-
lights in economic inventions: among them, the invention of Scotch
tape, the stapler, the telephone, the electric light, the refrigerator, the

sewing machine, the dishwasher, the electric fan, air-conditioning, and hundreds of other humble instruments of daily life, in all their tumbling profusion.

This is not to say that North American culture is "better" or even "more advanced." It is only to say that cultures do choose (by billions of daily decisions) to differentiate themselves. North Americans caught the fundamental idea of economic liberation—that the way out of poverty is invention—and established institutions, customs, habits, and educational methods that encouraged practical inventiveness by every means possible.[3] Latin America, by contrast, remained humanistic in a more ancient Mediterranean way: courteous, genteel, often dashing, flirtatious, playful and even festive; but also relatively changeless, impressed with power (and especially the power of the state), family-centered, suspicious of the individual, less concerned with material advance than with noble feelings and a sense of culture. There are many beautiful aspects—marks of superiority, even—in the Latin American way.

Comparisons between cultures, of course, are inherently invidious. One cannot truly compare dissimilars. And when the dissimilarities have to do with values and ends, as invariably they do (for values and ends shape, as it were, the "cult" in culture), there is no neutral Archimedean point on which to stand to compare them. Nonetheless, one cannot understand the traditional antipathy toward commerce and enterprise of large segments of Latin American culture, especially in its educated humanistic classes, an antipathy inherited by liberation theology, without attempting to grasp the quite different cultural histories of Latin America and North America.

Often in Latin America I have been told by journalists, lawyers, academics, and others that I must learn to understand what it has been like to live one's whole life apart from the genuine consent of the governed. Latin American history, they remind me, displays several generations under tutelage to foreign thrones; later generations under the tutelage of political elites over whom there was very little popular control; too many decades under cruel dictatorships; and still other periods under fragile democracies, in which rights to dissent, the principle of a loyal opposition, and the acts of practical compromise in favor of the imperfect but achieveable second-best were scarcely honored. Even the word "liberty" has a different ring, therefore, in Latin America. North Americans understand this term in the light of law, historical institutions, and unself-conscious habits. Latin Americans, having a different history in all these respects, must imagine what they have scarcely experienced.

In Latin America, the government—the state—and often enough the military have played roles analogous to those played by the traditional colonial powers as agents of Spain and Portugal. The tradition of reliance upon the state is in Latin America at least as strong as it has been in modern France, perhaps much stronger. Typically, in Catholic Europe, especially in Latin Europe, Communist parties are larger and stronger than in Northern Europe. Those who are not Communist tend also to be attracted to socialist approaches in economics. These trends are also powerful in Latin America. That is why many astute observers of Latin American politics believe that socialism, in one version or another, is a likely or even natural outcome in Latin America.[4]

Liberation theology says that Latin America is capitalist and needs a socialist revolution. Latin America does need a revolution. But its present system is mercantilist and quasi-feudal, not capitalist, and the revolution it needs is both liberal and Catholic. The present order is not free but statist, not mind-centered but privilege-centered, not open to the poor but protective of the rich. Large majorities of the poor are propertyless. The poor are prevented by law from founding and incorporating their own enterprises. They are denied access to credit. They are held back by an ancient legal structure, designed to protect the ancient privileges of a pre-capitalist elite.

This elite invents virtually nothing, risks virtually nothing, takes virtually no new initiatives. It is parasitic upon and distributes the goods and services of foreign enterprises, whose inventiveness and dynamism it does not emulate. Thus do the Latin American elites sit behind a thick wall of law, whose purpose is to prevent capitalism from arising. These elites fear economic competition. Their greatest preoccupation is the protection of ancient privilege. They are willing to buy and sell, but only behind protective walls, designed to keep others out. They are not creators. Too few were born among the poor.

The whole structure of economic law in Latin America needs to be shaken at its foundations, and built on new pediments. The elite needs to yield place to the talented millions among the poor who show greater imagination, initiative, inventiveness, and creativity. The economic talents of the poor—presently unrecognized in law—need to be legitimated, promoted, and given full scope. The "informals," now "outsiders," need to be brought "inside" the law. When law is aimed at liberating the poor for economic activism, *only then* has a capitalist revolution begun, against entrenched privilege and old hereditary elites. Until then, government officials continue to act as did the viceroys of the colonial period, restricting legal economic activities to their family and friends.

Furthermore, anti-capitalism is a motif in Latin American life that far antedates, and has deeper cultural roots than, liberation theology alone. What is distinctive about Latin American theology is that it offers a *Christian* re-interpretation of Marxism and socialism. Theology in Latin America used to be traditionalist, of a form compatible with the Holy Roman Empire and its worldview, and it maintained integral links to the traditional societies of Latin America. What has always been missing is a theology of enterprise, of commerce, of economic dynamism—in short, of capitalism. Indeed, some liberation theologians today think of economic growth, or (as they symbolize it) money, as "Mammon." Some associate capitalism with Death, in a kind of manicheism that assigns socialism the contrasting lightsomeness of Life.

This radical discontinuity between North American liberation theology and Latin American liberation theology—this disparity in the practical judgment rendered upon the free economy—should not blind the unwary to a powerful unity of aim. The aim both of democratic capitalism as the liberal societies of North America conceive of it, and of socialism as the liberation theologians of Latin America conceive of it, is to lift up the poor. The theology of both the Americas is "an option for the poor." The radical question is a practical one. Which sorts of economic institutions, in fact, do lift up the poor? On this, persons of good will often disagree. What works in one place, some argue, does not or will not work in another. The principle that all Christians are committed to—at least now, when the methods of attaining it have become so well known—is that the condition of the poor must be bettered. There is today no excuse for the sort of imprisonment inflicted on the poor by material destitution.

In a sense, then, the emerging theologies of both Americas stand as one in their commitment to ending poverty in the Western Hemisphere (indeed, in the entire world). Now that theologians are beginning to acquire economic consciousness, as earlier they acquired historical and political consciousness, however, the theological argument about economic practices is and should be lively.

A generation from now we may look forward, then, to a new self-consciousness in the theology of the Americas. This self-consciousness will almost certainly be pluralistic. Continent differs from continent, region from region, culture from culture. Latin Americans probably will continue to be attracted to state-centered solutions, in some form of socialism. Some North Americans will concur with them at least in part. Nonetheless, without question North America as a whole is moving in the direction of a dynamic, research-based, capitalist future. These differences in approach will eventually be narrowed by strict attention to results. History itself will teach lessons to those willing to learn from experimentation. The issue that separates us today is not precisely ideological, although ideas certainly have consequences, both good and bad. The issue that divides us is primarily practical. The common aim, after all, is not to be ideologically pure but to be of practical assistance to the poor. There is great urgency in more intense dialogue between North American liberation theology and Latin American liberation theology.

There is, furthermore, one clear point of convergence. In Latin America since 1979, eleven nations have entered upon the path of democracy. More and more liberation theologians are praising the democratic ideal. Whatever the faults of democratic governance, and these are many, they certainly represent a humane advance beyond cruel and barbarous dictatorships. Although Latin Americans and North Americans may well continue to disagree, then, about the economic institutions they wish to live under, they seem today to be in considerable concordance about the need for political democracy. Institutionally, no liberation theologian worthy of the name would be in favor of a state-controlled press, censorship of intellectual and literary work, abuses of human rights through torture or imprisonment without due process, suppression of free labor unions or unions of peasants, the persecution of churches or the restriction of minority populations, etc. There is a rough concordance, then, concerning democracy. About the economic system most compatible with democracy, most likely to assist democracy to flower, and most likely to help the poor no longer to be poor, there will continue to be vital argument. This is as it should be. Concerning spirituality, our differences are far fewer.

I begin this study, then, with admiration for what the liberation theologians of Latin America have already achieved. Rooted in an experience quite different from theirs, however, I have many questions about their methods of social—especially economic—analysis. In their judgment, no doubt, I am in error; in mine, theirs is the error. There is considerable hope, though, that argument about the proper first principles of political economy—particularly on the economic side—can be mutually beneficial, can lead to new ideas for all participants in the discussion, and can deepen a sense of mutual respect in one same Christian faith and one same allegiance to democratic principles.

*   *   *

Since 1948, the world has grown from 49 nations to 165. More than a hundred new experiments in political economy have been attempted. Ideologies projecting a "revolutionary" future have abounded, but few have brought anything like the promised results. To take ideologies seriously, then, is to question them. Most modern ideologies have offered glowing promises—many have even mimicked the Jewish and Christian Scriptures in their promises—only to turn out to be more murderous and more oppressive than regimes they replaced. Few of the scores of "revolutions" in modern times have brought genuine liberation.[5] Questions, then, must be addressed to liberation theology.

One of the fundamental practical questions to be addressed to liberation theology is: "But does it actually liberate?" What institutions will it put in place, *after* the revolution, to protect human rights? Through which institutions will it open its economy to the initiative, intelligence, and creativity of the poorest of its citizens?

The text that follows raises at least a few such questions. Philosophers and theologians ought to take liberation theology seriously, by arguing strenuously against it wherever they find it unconvincing, and by praising those elements in it which they find admirable. Merely to agree, without raising questions, is unworthy.

The argument of this book proceeds as follows. After introducing liberation theology in its Latin American form, even in its rather harsh condemnations of North America, I then try to explain my own vision of a society of freedom with justice, and thus place in contrast the socio-economic ideals of liberation theology with those of the liberal society. Neither version, it is now clear, promises to bring the Kingdom of God on earth, but only to press the imperatives of that Kingdom— truth, love, justice, liberty and beauty—into daily life as yeast in stubborn dough. As I see it, the most necessary and fruitful arguments now concern economic, rather than theological, disagreements.

All parties to the debate share one same Christian faith. Just the same, of course, theological methods, emphases, and favorite techniques of analysis differ, as is appropriate to our different histories, cultures, experiences, and purposes. While defending a pluralism of theologies, I hold that such theologies must engage in strenuous argument with one another, raising questions about each other, challenging one another to do better, pushing one another toward a high and civil mutual excellence.

Questions about economic matters, in addition, are subject to empirical tests—or at least to recognition that on such matters practical wisdom rules.

It is my hypothesis that the liberal society, built around a capitalist society that promotes discovery and entrepreneurship among the poor at the base of society, will succeed more quickly, more thoroughly, and in a more liberating fashion, than the socialist societies so far conceived of by liberation theologians. The liberation theologians, of course, hold the opposite hypothesis. Most opt for socialism. My own hypothesis is based on historical observation. It is subject to future disconfirmation. Their hypothesis is explicitly based upon hope and, as many of them admit, a kind of blind hope without much specificity yet concerning the concrete structures and economic institutions that will embody their socialism. In any case, the issue between us is empirical and will, accordingly, be settled by historical experiments. Thirty years from now our successors will judge which hypothesis was in error—or, at least, how much of the truth was on each side.

Because liberation theologians seem systematically to misunderstand the spiritual resources and economic dynamism of liberal societies, I take special pains to set forth my own theology of the liberal society in some detail, and to confront liberation theologians accordingly. To achieve genuine disagreement is an arduous task. There are a great many mutual misperceptions to cut through first, in order to dismiss false disagreements—disagreements based, not upon reality, but upon faulty perceptions or analyses. This is not to say that, in the end, there will be, or should be, complete agreement. On the contrary. A pluralism of theologies *entails* serious disagreements. But identifying those disagreements exactly—neither minimizing nor exaggerating them, neither misplacing nor distorting them—is by no means easy. To do this well requires each participant in the debate to "cross over" into the point of departure and dynamic of the other points of view, both with sympathy and with alert skepticism, but in the end with a painstaking desire to understand. To the extent that I have failed to present the positions of liberation theologians exactly, I hope to be fraternally corrected, just as I hope to prompt fraternal correction in their perceptions regarding the liberal society. If there is a better way for hemispheric dialogue to proceed, in a manner marked by charity, civility, and candor, I have yet to discover it.

I cannot pretend to have got everything exactly, or to have put things precisely as liberation theologians put them; their framework of experience is so different from mine that such translation defies one's best efforts. But I have tried to read them with seriousness and dogged inquiry. The point is to understand—and to raise further questions. I welcome further questions in return.

*   *   *

A final point. In 1971, Gustavo Gutierrez suggested the need for a new spirituality in Latin America, adapted to the immense social task facing that continent. "More than ten years were to pass," Henri J.M. Nouwen writes, "before Gustavo had the opportunity to develop this spirituality fully"—in *We Drink from Our Own Wells*.[6] The spiritual teaching in this book recalls many ancient teachings in all their interior power. There are many passages in it on St. John of the Cross (recalling for me some of the themes I dwelt on in my own meditation on St. John of the Cross, *The Experience of Nothingness*). In their spiritual teaching, the liberation theologians often combine the ancient with the contemporary in a fresh and fertile way. On conversion, gratuitousness, joy, spiritual childhood, solitude, and community, Gutierrez is quite eloquent. His spirituality is classic. It rings true. Thus it is important to say, once again, that it is not in its spirituality that one has difficulties with liberation theology; it is, rather, in its interpretations of economic and social realities.

LIBERATION THEOLOGY AND THE LIBERAL SOCIETY

One

LOOK NORTH IN ANGER

"Christ led me to Marx," bluntly declares Ernesto Cardenal, the Nicaraguan priest at whom Pope John Paul II wagged an admonishing finger at the Managua airport in 1983. "I do not think the Pope understands Marxism," says the world-famous poet, and the Sandinista Minister of Culture. "For me, the four Gospels are all equally communist." Cardenal summarizes his brief against the Pope: "I'm a Marxist who believes in God, follows Christ and is a revolutionary for the sake of his kingdom."[1]

Leonardo Boff, the Brazilian Franciscan summoned to Rome in 1984 to defend his vision of the Church today, wrote shortly afterward in the left-wing Rome newspaper *Paese Sera* that Pope John Paul II's view of Marxism is "a kind of caricature." Friar Boff says that the Vatican document, which endorses the Church's commitment to the poor while condemning Marxism, seems "to believe what is on the label of the bottle before trying the real contents." He sets aside Pope John Paul II's lifetime experience of Marxism, asserting: "Marxism is a principally European theme. In Latin America, the big enemy is not Marxism, it is capitalism."[2]

This debate between Pope John Paul II and such Latin priests as Father Cardenal and Friar Boff deeply involves the United States. For the main enemy of liberation theology, make no mistake about it, is the United States. So writes the founder of liberation theology, the Peruvian priest Gustavo Gutierrez:

> Liberation is a term which expresses a new posture in Latin America. . . . Among more alert people today, what we have called a new awareness of Latin American reality is making headway. They believe that there can be authentic development for Latin America only if there is liberation from the domination exercised by the greatest capitalist countries, especially the most powerful, the United States of America.[3]

13

Liberation theology is a method of defining Christian faith in the political context of underdevelopment, in a side-choosing spirit committed to action. It is not distinctive for wishing to apply Christian faith to social action. It is not more concerned about "the working class" or "the poor" than Pope Leo XIII, whose 1891 encyclical underlined Catholicism's responsibility to these groups. Nor can it be universally defined as Marxist. Yet it gains its excitement from flirting with Marxist thought and speech, and from its hostility to the "North."

A majority of the world's 800 million Catholics now lives in third world nations—in Hispanic Latin America and the Philippines predominantly, but also in the burgeoning church of Africa, and in the small but vital Catholic communities of many nations of Southeast Asia. If Marxism, even of a mild sort, grows in such lands, and if it were to be blessed by Catholicism, two powerful symbolic forces would then have joined hands. In such a world, what would be the fate of civil liberties?

Via U.S. missionaries, liberation theology reaches into the United States, too, not only among many Catholics in the Congress but right into the office of House Speaker Tip O'Neill. For example, Sister Jeanne Gallo of the Sisters of Notre Dame de Namur belongs to the Nicaragua Action Group in Cambridge, Massachusetts, O'Neill's home district. "We realized that Mr. O'Neill was key to what happened in the House," Sister Jeanne says. "The group decided to work on educating him about Central America." Another group member adds: "We've been very pleased that he listens to us. He is a good Catholic and trusts people in the church who give him information."[4]

Speaker O'Neill gives credit to another source of his education: "I have a connection with the Maryknoll Order." A beloved aunt of his was a Maryknoll nun until her death at 91 in 1981, and now there is Sister Peggy Healy, an ardently pro-Sandinista Maryknoller in Managua, who writes to the Speaker frequently. The Speaker tells the press: "I have great trust in the order. When the nuns and priests come through, I ask them questions about their feelings, what they see, who the enemy is, and I'm sure I get the truth. I haven't found any of these missionaries who aren't absolutely opposed to this [Reagan] policy."

Liberation theology has influenced not only the Maryknolls. Mr. Charles A. Sirey, Jr., a Quaker businessman from New York, visits Nicaragua "to see for himself" and writes: "The Jesuits of Nicaragua almost to a man are outspoken in their support of the Sandinistas."[5] The Jesuit Armando Arguello, former head of the Sandinista election commission, assures Mr. Sirey of the then upcoming election's "generous" provisions for the opposition.

Pope John Paul II is considerably less trusting than Mr. Sirey or House Speaker O'Neill, Ernesto Cardenal or Leonardo Boff. Before the entire world, on television, the Pope rebuked Father Cardenal for the priestly support his official role as Minister of Culture brings the Sandinista government in Nicaragua. And on September 3, 1984, in Rome, Joseph Cardinal Ratzinger, a longtime ally of the Pope and Cardinal Prefect of the Congregation for the Doctrine of the Faith, issued a firm denunciation of the red thread running through a great deal of the "theology of liberation."[6]

Truth to tell, liberation theology forms a tapestry much broader than its Marxist part and is woven of many colors. Marxist movements always hide in "popular fronts," and so forms of Marxist analysis do hide within liberation theology. But it would be a great mistake— which the Vatican was careful not to make—to think that all liberation theology is Marxist.* The condemnation of Marxist elements hiding in its folds will not bring an end to its long-term vitality.

Clear-eyed in his experienced analysis of Marxist popular fronts, Pope John Paul II is also a frequent critic of "rigid capitalism." In Canada in 1984, a nation which heavily regulates business activities, the Pope criticized "unfettered capitalism." He attacked those who ignore "the needs of the many in pursuit of profits for the few." In the rich nations, he discerned—using almost Leninist terms—economic "imperialism." According to one of his assistants in Canada, the Pope did not mean to condemn capitalism, only to criticize its excesses. Nonetheless, liberation theologians are clearly wrong if they think the Pope is soft on capitalism. Less trusting than they, however, he recognizes the disguises in which Marxists always hide their purposes.[7]

*   *   *

---

*In this volume, I wish to use "Marxist" in a precise sense. Even the liberation theologians who are most explicit in speaking of Marxism (such as Jose Miranda) reject (1) atheism and (2) materialism. By Marxism, I mean precisely four commitments: (1) that history is accurately characterized as a theater of struggle between social classes; (2) that this struggle entails passion, violence, and armed conflict, whose cessation will commence only in some future utopian social order; (3) the abolition of private property, as the key to class struggle; and (4) a theory of truth identifying truth with the cause of a particular social class in history. The dangers of such commitments have been made manifest in both Nazi and Marxist-Leninist movements in our century. Finally, I should note that over the past fifteen years, many liberation theologians have been progressively modifying their initial infatuation with Marxist analysis, in response both to real experiences and to public criticism. A certain fluidity is manifest, and public argument clearly plays a role in advancing the discussion.

In the writings of liberation theologians, nonetheless, the contradictions in Marxist theory and practice for a long time went unnoted. And this tells us something significant about some among the liberation theologians: some incline to Marxist analysis not by reason or by experience, but by faith. The great Marxist philosopher Leszek Kolakowski, who (like Pope John Paul II) has lived through the Marxist phenomenon in Poland, has observed: "Almost all the prophecies of Marx and his followers have already proved to be false, but this does not disturb the spiritual certainty of the faithful, any more than it did in the case of chiliastic sects: for it is a certainty not based on any empirical premises or supposed 'historical laws,' but simply on the psychological need for certainty. In this sense Marxism performs the function of a religion, and its efficacy is of a religious character."[8]

*   *   *

Gustavo Gutierrez is a short, mild-mannered professor, whose theological writings and lectures are influential far beyond his native Peru. By common acclaim, he is the father of liberation theology, which received its name from his electrifying book of 1971, *A Theology of Liberation*. Other leading intellectual lights of this school include Juan Luis Segundo, S.J. (*A Theology for Artisans of a New Humanity*, 5 vols.); José Míguez Bonino (*Christians and Marxists: The Mutual Challenge to Revolution*); Hugo Assmann (*Theology for a Nomad Church*); Alfredo Fierro (*The Militant Gospel*); the Mexican José Miranda (*Communism in the Bible* and *Marx and the Bible*); and the Brazilian Franciscan, Leonardo Boff, who became known to the world when the Vatican summoned him to Rome for a "dialogue" with Cardinal Ratzinger on September 7, 1985. Dozens of other authors, writing mostly in commentary on or in extension of the pioneers, also belong to the intellectual vanguard.

More significant, however, are some hundreds of activist priests and sisters who, as teachers and intellectual guides, form the teaching body of the new theology—and, of course, the hundreds of thousands who, in one way or another, have been inspired by it. Most of the intellectual leaders have been trained in Europe; few are European or North American missionaries. Latin American experts say that liberation theology affects only a minority of the clergy, even among theologians, and that the symbolic strength of the movement is exaggerated internationally by the fact that books and articles by liberation theologians are far more often translated into other languages than those by their critics.

Strong defenders of liberation theology, such as the carefully reasoning Arthur F. McGovern, S.J., of the University of Detroit, author
of *Marxism: An American Christian Perspective* (1980), point out that
there are very large differences among the major proponents of liberation theology.[9] McGovern says that most do not ground their theology in Marxism, as some critics contend, and they are generally
careful to modify concepts of class hatred, violence, and "class struggle." Their starting point is an awareness of the structural causes of
poverty; their faith commitment leads them to use the insights from
Marxist critiques of society. However, in the liberation theologians'
sharp critiques of the status quo, he says, their critics "hear" Marxism
even when they may be saying something quite different. What the
liberationists actually do mean by "socialism" will be examined in more
detail below in Chapters Eight and Nine.

*   *   *

The headquarters for liberation theology in the United States are
located near the Hudson River at Maryknoll, New York, international
center of America's most active missionary order, the Maryknoll Fathers and Sisters. In a recent bibliography of third world theologies,
32 of 82 titles were published by Maryknoll's Orbis Press. Founded in
1970, Orbis announced that it "draws its imperatives from and orders
its priorities on the fact that the majority of Christians live in the affluent countries of the North Atlantic community, which controls almost 80 percent of the world's resources but accounts for only 20
percent of the world's population. . . . Christians bear a heavy responsibility for a world that can annually 'afford' to spend $150 billion on
arms, but can scarcely scrape together $10 billion for economic and
social development." At the heart of the matter, according to the initial
Orbis release, was the need for a change in intellectual focus: "Total
development will demand the restructuring of oppressive political and
social orders wherever they exist, in Calcutta or Chicago, New York or
Recife. For this reason, the word *development* should be replaced by *liberation*."[10]

It is quite remarkable that the list of cities requiring liberation did
not include Cracow or Leningrad, Havana or Peking, Hanoi or
Prague. The complete Orbis catalogue (1982) of 141 titles maintained
this distinction intact. Thirty-nine titles are concentrated on Latin
America, a few on Africa and other places, none on Communist lands,
even though such lands were once the target of intensive missionary
effort.

The focus on Latin America is not accidental. Father Sergio Torres of Chile, lecturer at Maryknoll, describes his world view and that of his fellow Latin American theologians in this way:

What we understand is that we are at the end of a stage in the history of the world. Europe and Western society is no longer making the history of the world as it has been since the Roman empire. We understand that history is now being made by the peoples of the Third World. The oil crisis is getting that through here in the United States. . . . We in Latin America are the only continent that is both Christian and underdeveloped, so we are in a special place. We will start a new understanding of the faith because we belong to the churches, Catholic and Protestant, and are living in a situation which makes them functional to the system. . . . The process of colonization, liberation, and organization is best understood in Marxist terms.[11]

Father Miguel d'Escoto, today the Foreign Minister of Nicaragua, but then the director of communications at Maryknoll, wrote in those early days:

As Latin Americans, we know capitalism in a way young people here don't know it. We had no New Deal, no Roosevelt to come along and soften it up. Capitalism is intrinsically wrong at its base. The basic concept is that man is selfish, and being realistic, we should accept this and cater to it rather than change it.[12]

The chief systematizer of liberation theology, Father Juan Luis Segundo, whose five-volume treatise, *Theology for Artisans of a New Humanity,* had sold 64,000 copies by 1982, told a group of American Jesuits:

There is no perfect solution. The only way is for us to choose between two oppressions. And the history of Marxism, even oppressive, offers right now more hope than the history of existing capitalism. . . . Marx did not create the class struggle, international capitalism did.[13]

Distinguished bishops, like the Bishop of Cuernavaca, Arceo Mendez, and the Archbishop of Recife, Dom Helder Camara, have also been unambiguous in their preference of Marxism. Archbishop Camara, for example, addressed the University of Chicago's celebration of the Seventh Centenary of St. Thomas Aquinas in these terms:

> When a man, whether philosopher or not, attracts irresistibly millions of human beings, especially young people; when a man becomes the inspiration for life and for death of a great part of humanity, and makes the powerful of the earth tremble with hate and fear, this man deserves to be studied. . . . As the University of Chicago chose to take upon herself the responsibility of celebrating St. Thomas Aquinas's Seventh Centenary, we have the right to suggest that the best way to honor the centenary . . . should be for the University of Chicago to try, today, to do with Karl Marx what St. Thomas, in his day, did with Aristotle.[14]

The social and intellectual background of the liberation theologians is germane to their views. When I was studying theology in Rome at the Gregorian University in 1956–58, I deliberately spent as much time as I could with Latin American and Spanish seminarians, and several clear impressions about their political-theological culture fixed themselves in my mind. First, it was obvious that they chafed under the image of their own cultures that prevailed in the English-speaking world. They were, they felt, the victims of an Anglo-Saxon ethnocentric bias, a Protestant bias to boot, and a bias informed by a type of individualism, pragmatism, and materialism they found especially abhorrent. Some seemed, in fact, both to love and to hate the United States: to be attracted to it in admiration, but also to feel a great many resentments that no single list of grievances quite exhausted—a resentment from very deep sources, indeed.

Many of these bright young men studied not only in Rome but in Belgium, France, and Germany as well. There they shared in what was then known as *nouvelle theologie*—that contemporary reaction against Thomism, strong on scriptural studies and "salvation history," intensely preoccupied with the renewal of the Church from biblical and patristic sources (and rather patronizing toward the "outdated" theory of Christian democracy developed by Thomists like Jacques Maritain). On their return to Latin America, many of them became involved in the movements organizing peasants in credit unions and agrarian cooperatives. Much of their earlier training seemed far too theological, and they reacted with an almost Oedipal vehemence against their European teachers.

*   *   *

Put yourself in the place of an idealistic priest or sister during the 1960s, fresh from theological studies in Europe or North America, fired with a vision of social justice and the relevance of Christian teachings to this world, and sent to work among the poorest of God's poor in the *barrios* and *favelas* of Latin America's teeming cities. On unpaved streets, in shacks with no plumbing, among children badly clothed and poorly fed, most such priests and sisters arrived with political-social ideals formed by social democratic currents in Europe and North America. In Latin America, however, such currents lacked a broad, supportive middle class, with solid traditions of democracy and social action. The Christian Democratic parties of Latin America, by then at least a generation old, seemed to some of them far too weak a vessel for their hopes. They wanted, and felt they needed, faster action.

Such ardent spirits then encountered two solid cultural obstacles. First, folk Catholicism in Latin America had long emphasized personal, familial piety—but not much social action or public responsibility. If they listened solely to the people, they found that the fastest-growing religions, by far, were forms of pietism and Pentecostalism. Religion seemed traditionally to be confined to the "private" sphere, apart from responsibility for social action. Second, the traditional Church itself, not only its bishops but also its middle and upper classes (to which many liberation theologians belong), who support its schools, orphanages, and other good works, seemed in the light of secular social science to be part of the very establishment responsible for Latin America's social ills. These two powerful Latin Catholic traditions—a personal piety and traditional identification with elites—seemed to block progress for the poor.

*   *   *

Enter Gustavo Gutierrez. His *Theology of Liberation* announced a new approach to political problems, problems not identical to those found in Germany, Switzerland, or France, and therefore seldom directly treated by European (or American) theologians. With him, Latin Americans claimed that they were rediscovering a Jewish-Christian theme as old as the exodus itself, and also that they were declaring their intellectual independence from the prevailing theological models of Western Europe and North America. "I have delivered," the Jesuit Juan Luis Segundo writes, "a radical criticism of European theology, even the most progressive."[15]

Nonetheless, some European theologians, like the Protestant Jürgen Moltmann, have praised liberation theology but find in it little that has not been closely paralleled by Europeans who had learned their methods of political analysis from social democracy, from the Frankfurt school, and from the democratic socialist tradition springing in part from Marx (the "young, humanist" Marx, as many often took pains to emphasize).[16] What is so "new" about liberation theology? some asked. It will naively deliver Latin America to the Marxists, others said.

If this debate had been contained solely among intellectuals, perhaps not much would have come of it. But as the "economic miracle" claimed by Brazil in the 1960s seemed to fade and military rule commenced; as Allende was toppled in Chile, and was replaced by repression under General Pinochet; as a broadly based revolution in Nicaragua toppled Somoza; and as guerrilla movements became active in Peru, Bolivia, Colombia, El Salvador, Guatemala and elsewhere, liberation theology seemed to live less and less in books alone and to leap to life in armed insurrections and popular movements in many nations simultaneously.

*   *   *

Twenty years ago, beginning already at the Second Vatican Council (1962–65), the Latin American bishops had discovered a new continental unity—and through it resolved to attack the continent's sociopolitical problems head-on. Some bishops remained traditionalists of the old school. Many more grasped the challenge of social action in terms analogous to those of their brother bishops in Western Europe and North America. And some opted for yet more "radical" views. Meeting at Medellín, Colombia, in 1968, the entire episcopal conference of Latin America (CELAM) issued a letter that became the manifesto of a new church in Latin America, clearly committed to a much-needed, long-delayed social transformation of the continent.[17]

The new teaching of Medellín coincided with the rise of a new school of thought among secular social scientists, viz., "dependency theory." (See chapter seven, below.) For some, this theory articulated two commonsense observations. First, Latin American nations are disproportionately dependent on economic activities and decisions taken elsewhere (in the developed nations). Second, the highly visible inequalities in Latin America between the very rich and the very poor (with an unusually small middle class) are at least *analogous* to the "class struggle" posited by Marx between the proletariat and the bourgeoisie.

Much more than in North America, what Raymond Aron called "the Marxist vulgate" shapes the thinking of almost all intellectuals. For some *dependencistas,* Marxist ways of thinking are as natural as breathing air. But not all *dependencistas* are Marxists.[18]

These two movements—the birth of social conscience in the Church and the rise of secular theories of dependency—seemed to many to go hand in hand. There is no necessary reason why they should. Even if dependency theory is largely mythical, or false, as many even of its original propagators now believe, nonetheless, Catholic social thought retains its own validity.

Just the same, prominent Catholic leaders associated with liberation theology typically mixed these two streams of discourse. On the one hand, they tried to show at every opportunity that Catholic social thought has implications for the restructuring of unjust societies. And so it does. Ever since the encyclical letter of Pope Leo XIII, *Rerum Novarum,* in 1891, and Pius XI's sequel forty years later in 1931, "Toward the Reconstruction of the Social Order," this point has not been in dispute. In the declaration of Vatican Council II on "The Church in the World," and in the world famous encyclicals of John XXIII (*Mater et Magistra* and *Pacem in Terris*) and Paul VI (*Populorum Progressio* and *Octogesima Adveniens*), the Catholic Church has placed itself firmly on the side of human rights, economic development, and the defense of religious liberty.

On the other hand, in diagnosing the specific ills of Latin America, particularly in the economic order, Latin American church leaders sometimes appeared to identify Latin American societies as "capitalist" societies. Is this a correct analysis? The fact seems to be that Latin American economies are *pre*-capitalist, disproportionately state-directed. The three leading social classes are government officials, landholders, and the military. Yet it is precisely here, in its economic theories, that liberation theology most borrows from "Marxist analysis." Here is where most of the intellectual confusion arises.

Consider the following declarations. *Ernesto Cardenal* (after the conversion he experienced in Cuba): "It was like a second conversion. Before then, I saw myself as a revolutionary, but I had confused ideas. I was trying to find a third way, which was the Revolution of the Gospel, but then I saw that Cuba was the Gospel put into practice. And only when I converted to Marxism could I write religious poetry."[19]

Gustavo Gutierrez: "Class struggle is an actual fact and neutrality on this point is absolutely impossible. . . . What the groups in power call 'advocating' class struggle is really an expression of a will to abolish its causes, to abolish them, not cover them over, to eliminate the ap-

propriation by a few of the wealth created by the work of the many. . . .
It is a will to build a socialist society."[20]

Juan Luis Segundo: "Today the only thing we can do is to decide
whether we are going to leave to individuals and private groups, or
take away from them, the right to possess the means of production
which exist in our countries. That is what we call the option for capitalism or socialism."[21]

Is liberation theology Marxist? A reader of Gutierrez will find
scores of citations from Marxist social scientists; in most other writers,
many fewer. Most liberation theologians give little evidence of having
studied Marx, Marxist theoreticians, or Marxist experiments elsewhere. Yet some of their fundamental assumptions are Marxist.
"Given the pervasiveness of Marxist ideas in Latin America," the sympathetic commentator Arthur F. McGovern, S.J., admits, "one could
hardly analyze the problems of Latin America without at least implicit
use of Marxist ideas."[22] In summary form, Gustavo Gutierrez explains
his own progression as he worked with the poor of Lima:

> I discovered three things. I discovered that poverty was a des-
> tructive thing, something to be fought against and destroyed,
> not merely something which was the object of our charity.
> Secondly, I discovered that poverty was not accidental. The
> fact that these people are poor and not rich is not just a matter
> of chance, but the result of a structure. It was a structural
> question. Thirdly, I discovered that poor people were a social
> class. When I discovered that poverty was something to be
> fought against . . . it became crystal clear that in order to serve
> the poor, one had to move into political action.[23]

More to the point, perhaps, than a thoroughly grounded Marxism, many churchmen in Latin America, even those who are not liberation theologians, are profoundly anti-capitalist. In the nineteenth
century, the saying was *"liberalismo es pecado"*—liberalism is a sin.
Bishop Alfonso Lopez Trujillo, a critic of liberation theology, writes:
"We are convinced that capitalism is a human failure."[24] Even the conservatives are anti-capitalist. Between the traditionalist anti-liberals
and the anti-liberal liberation theologians, indeed, there is nearly an
anti-liberal concordance, at least on liberal economics if not on liberal
democracy. Thus, it was the Medellín Conference of *bishops* that first—
earlier than Gutierrez—gave the term "liberation" official sanction.
The bishops did so in the context of blaming North America and Europe for Latin America's ills.

The Medellín document speaks of "External Neocolonialism." It asserts that "the countries which produce raw materials—especially if they are dependent upon one major export—always remain poor, while the industrialized countries enrich themselves."[25] It describes the "neocolonial" situation of Latin America in extraordinarily dramatic terms: "institutionalized violence." While the bishops urge ways of non-violence and peace, their use of "liberation" in this context is charged with the energy of revolutionary expectation. Astonishingly, they conclude: "We wish to emphasize that the principal guilt for the economic dependence of our countries rests with [foreign] powers, inspired by uncontrolled desire for gain. . . ."[26] These few sentences, and others like them, seem to legitimate not only the reformist course they advocate but also revolution, the word preferred by many others.

It is not a long jump from Medellín to the judgment of one of the most explicitly Marxist of the liberation theologians, Hugo Assmann, that Latin Americans are "being *kept* in a state of underdevelopment."[27] "The theologians of liberation glory in Medellín," writes a critic, Fr. André-Vincent, O.P., in *Nouvelle Revue Théologique.*[28]

The judgments of Medellín most useful to liberation theologians are not its theological judgments; these are fairly classical. Rather, the bishops' judgments of the Latin American factual situation seem to legitimate this picture: Poverty—Dependency—Exploitation—Conscientization—Revolution.[29] Gutierrez carries this scheme further: "situation of dependence and oppression"; "Poverty, the result of social injustice . . ." (no other causes considered); "To opt for the poor man is to opt for one social class against the other."

Writing from São Paulo, Brazil, critic and theologian François Hubert Lepargneur condenses the message: "By casting all the blame for Latin American underdevelopment on the shoulders of international capitalism, these believers are too ready to excuse the responsibility of Iberian Christianity and of its Latin American clerical representatives."[30] He sees a radical manicheism in liberation theology: "We are the good guys, the oppressed. The others are bad, the oppressors. Who are they? Principally the United States when it is a question of economics and hence of imperialism; Europe, when it is a question of cultural power . . . *the guilty party is the other fellow.*"[31]

There is also a note of triumphalism in liberation theology. Before Vatican II, Latin American prelates were thought to be among the most arrogantly Catholic in the world, boasting that whereas in Europe and North America Catholicism encountered a world of unbelief, in Latin America the atmosphere was one of widespread belief in God through a patently Catholic sensibility. The new triumphalism claims that Latin America is the axial point of a new Christianity, a new man, a new future, and that Christianity has only now reached its true identity in the identification of faith with revolutionary praxis, the ending of all dualisms. "They say: This is a new way to do theology, with the newspaper in hand," Lepargneur acidly comments.[32]

In his book *Christians and Marxists,* the Argentinian Protestant theologian José Míguez Bonino quotes Fidel Castro as exclaiming in wonder that "the theologians are becoming communists and the communists are becoming theologians."[33] While elsewhere in the world Marxism as an intellectual current is on a death watch, in Latin America Marxism and the Church may each need the other. Eric Hobsbawm has written:

> The churches are now left free to move left, for neither the right nor the state can any longer protect them against erosion. Some Christians may thus hope to retain, or more doubtfully, regain the support of the masses believed to be identified with the left. It is a surprising development. Conversely, parties of the Marxist left, seeking to widen their support, are more inclined to abandon their traditional identification with active opposition to religion.[34]

It is of course not necessary to be a Christian to be a socialist. But in Latin America, socialists and Marxists must use Christianity to carry them to power and some Christians are all too willing to oblige.

There are serious factual problems with the theory of dependency, whence socialism in Latin America seeks to derive its legitimacy. First, countries such as Canada and the U.S. have become far larger exporters of raw materials—grain, lumber, coal, etc.—than all of Latin America put together. As John Kenneth Galbraith puts it, "If to be part of the Third World is to be a hewer of wood and a supplier of food and natural produce, the United States and Canada are, by a wide margin, the first of the Third World countries."[35]

Second, other regions of the world, specifically on the East Asia rim, are far poorer in natural resources than Latin America, and yet have in recent years been far more successful in conducting land reform, building highly intelligent and dynamic free economies, overcoming poverty worse in 1945 than that of Latin America today, providing literacy and opportunity to rapidly growing (and more densely crowded) populations, and inspiring industriousness, ambition and drive among their peoples. Dependency theory ill explains why Latin America is poor; poverty existed long before capitalism was a blight in Adam Smith's eye. Even more inadequately does it explain why Latin America has done so much worse with its own vast resources than such stellar performers as Japan, South Korea, Taiwan, Singapore, Hong Kong, and others have done with infinitely less.

There are, then, both theological and practical reasons for rejecting the main economic claims of liberation theology. Its single greatest flaw lies in combining two quite different methods of analysis in an effort to overcome "dualism." The monism of liberation theologians consists in rejecting European and North American distinctions between religion and politics, church and state, theological principles and partisan practice. Liberation theology says that truth lies in revolutionary praxis. So extreme is this position that Juan Luis Segundo can claim that the choice of socialism ("human life in society, liberated as far as possible from alienations") constitutes the highest real value, is *the* "theological crux," and that to say otherwise reduces the gospel to "no value at all."[36]

Needless to say, Catholic faith, whose chief guardian is the papacy, cannot accept such a claim. From the beginning of his pontificate, step by step, piece by piece, Pope John Paul II has built a theological case against "liberation theology" so conceived. The transcendence of religion beyond politics, the primacy of the spiritual, can be surrendered by no Christianity worthy of the name.

The British religious writer Peter Hebblethwaite puts very graphically the visible distortion liberation theologians introduce into Christianity:

> Would you go to Communion alongside General Pinochet (the Chilean ruler)? On the whole, they answer no. He is a class enemy. But if someone raises the objection that Christians are commanded to love their enemies, the theologians of liberation do not demur: but they go on to produce a whole casuistry which enables them to combine class war with, so to speak, a postponed love of enemies.[37]

Many defenders of liberation theologians deny that they reduce everything to revolutionary praxis. If true, this defense robs liberation theology of its most important claim to originality, its identification of theologizing with revolutionary action. A more moderate judgment seems to be that most liberation theologians *do* want to save the transcendent claims of Christianity, on the one hand, while on the other hand insisting too unguardedly that Christian faith demands "struggle" against class enemies. Most do not *reduce* Christianity to class struggle or to the commitment to socialism. Yet the common Marxist vulgate of so much Latin American intellectual life almost obliges them to *think* in terms of "Marxist analysis." Much is hidden in that term.

Several years back, the Father General of the Jesuits, Pedro Arrupe, warned the Jesuits that "Marxist analysis" incorporates within itself Marxist conclusions.[38] Some defenders of liberation theology say, in retort, that Marxism has been revised and is no longer Marxist in the older sense; and, in any case, the liberation theologians are not Marxist. It is sometimes hard to know whether they intend us to support the liberation theologians because they are Marxist—or because they are not.

Pope John Paul II lived his entire adult life in the bosom of "Marxist analysis," far more rigorously and cynically applied than anything Latin Americans have yet experienced (except in Cuba and Nicaragua). No Marxist thinker in Latin America has attained the stature, say, of the Pope's Polish compatriot, the Marxist philosopher Leszek Kolakowski. Cardinal Ratzinger, too, has experienced in Germany bitter ideological struggles among Stalinists, Trotskyites, democratic socialists, and social democrats. Such men know well the sociology of the "slippery slope": *principles* which one generation accepts provisionally, in the context of other cultural commitments, soon harden into icy dogmas for a generation brought up on nothing else. The Pope sees clearly enough that whoever accepts "Marxist analysis" sooner or later authorizes the bold and the ruthless to draw consequences for action. Marxist analysis is aimed at action. Those who employ it without drawing its inexorable consequences won the contempt of the young Marx of the Manifesto: "Christian socialism is but the holy water with which the priest consecrates the heart-burnings of the aristocrat."[39]

What no one clarifies is what is meant by "Marxist analysis." Liberation theologians have not yet been sufficiently self-conscious to tell us what they mean. The indications that they give are not consoling. Consider the following elements.

(1) *The new man, the new earth.* Gustavo Gutierrez:

The liberation of our continent means more than overcoming economic, social, and political dependence. It means, in a deeper sense, to see the becoming of mankind as a process of the emancipation of man in history. It is to see man in search of a qualitatively different society in which he will be free from all servitude, in which he will be the artisan of his own destiny. It is to seek the building of *a new man*. Ernesto Che

Guevara wrote, "We revolutionaries often lack the knowledge and the intellectual audacity to face the task of the development of a new human being. . . ."[40]

(2) *The utopian sensibility.* Juan Luis Segundo:

. . . the objective of left-wing radicalism is the permanent opening up of society to its future. In the sixteenth edition of the Brockhaus encyclopaedia, the following definition of the left appears: "the conquest of that which is still without form, of that which is still unrealized, of that which is still in a state of utopia." For that very reason the sensibility of the left is an intrinsic feature of an authentic theology.[41]

About these two themes, André-Vincent, O.P., has commented succinctly in *Nouvelle Revue Théologique:* "Only with the last day will come the final synthesis: *the classless society, the promised land, the new heaven.* Might one not say that the theologies of liberation are the South American echo of the theological utopias born in sad old Europe?"[42]

(3) *A naive vision of the state.* Juan Luis Segundo writes: "We give the name of socialism to a political regime in which the ownership of the means of production is removed from individuals and handed over to higher institutions whose concern is the common good."[43] Is there any historical record of higher institutions of the state showing concern solely for the common good, and not for the particular goods of the ruling elite? The trust shown by liberation theologians in state ownership shows how close they are to traditionalist Latin American conceptions of authoritarian control. Even today in most Latin nations, state authorities control more than fifty or sixty percent of the economy (including banks and many basic industries), and in some cases nearly eighty percent of all employment.[44]

(4) *No theory of wealth creation.* In Marxist analysis (which has as its precondition the successful creation of wealth by a capitalist society, which it despises), affluence is simply taken for granted and poverty is said to be caused solely by exploitation. Marxist analysis says nothing about creating new wealth, about invention, about entrepreneurship. Its assumption is that wealth creation is a zero-sum game, that my poverty is someone else's fault, and that its cure is to expropriate the expropriators. Dependency theory has been invented to apply this myth to pre-capitalist lands, whose residual widespread poverty (despite immense economic and social advances in Latin America since 1945) is said to be caused by others—chiefly, by the United States.

(5) *The abolition of private property.* In the *Communist Manifesto,* Marx and Engels wrote: "The theory of the Communists may be summed up in a single sentence: Abolition of private property."[45] The abolition of private property recurs as the crucial theme in virtually all liberation theologians. There is, to be sure, some confusion on this score. I once heard Paolo Cardinal Arns of Brazil say (I paraphrase from memory): "It is not for the Church to pronounce on capitalism or socialism. One thing is clear, however; we must reject capitalism, which is based on selfishness. We believe in the right of workers to own their own land and to keep their profits for themselves, and therefore we incline toward socialism." Surely, this inverts the North American meaning of capitalism and socialism. And it misses the fact that capitalism arose from the struggle between the new men of commerce and industry and the ancient landholding class.

(6) *Class struggle.* "Class struggle is an actual fact," Gutierrez has written, "and neutrality on this point is absolutely impossible." Gutierrez means by this the disparity of wealth and power between the very rich and the very poor in Latin America, not "class struggle" in the Marxist sense. Nor does Gutierrez preach hatred—quite the opposite. Nor does he see "class struggle" as the interpretive key to history. He means that the poor must be helped, that poverty is no longer either necessary or acceptable. But Adam Smith said as much. "Freedom from want" was one of the Four Freedoms of FDR and Harry Truman. And the Statue of Liberty beckoned to "the huddled masses yearning to breathe free . . . the wretched refuse of your teeming shores." One does not need "Marxist analysis" in order to liberate the poor.

(7) *The evils and corruptions accompanying private property, the profit motive, multinational corporations, international finance, and—in a word— capitalism.* Here, the liberation theologians, standing almost entirely outside the Anglo-American intellectual tradition, totally fail to grasp the genius, especially the moral genius, of the free economy in the free and pluralistic polity. They concede—at least, the less utopian among them concede—that sin endures under any and every social system. They tend to have a naive faith in socialism, despite scores of socialist experiments around the world since 1945, and an uncommon trust in the political elites to whom they intend to confide all economic (and other) decisions. They seem to be adamant in believing that selfishness, sin, and injustice *inhere in,* not only *accompany,* the institutions of a free economy. They do so despite abundant evidence that the freest communities on this planet, with the strongest (although inevitably flawed) institutions of human rights, are to be found in practice in societies with relatively free economies. They overlook the fact that, in

practice, a free economy seems to be a necessary, but not sufficient, condition for a free polity and a free cultural and moral life.

*   *   *

In short, while the Vatican has brilliantly diagnosed the ways in which some liberation theologians risk confounding authentic Catholic belief, my own objections are directed more centrally at the latter's flawed vision of political economy. Most liberation theologians are so intent upon revolution against injustice that they give very little thought to the shape of the institutions of political economy which they intend to put in place *after* the revolution. As Hannah Arendt points out in *On Revolution*,[46] most revolutions on this planet since 1776 and 1789 have made matters worse, not better, for those in whose name they were conducted: 16 million dead in Hitler's "final solution," 23 million dead in Mao's "cultural revolution," 65 million dead since Lenin's Terror was instituted to bring about a "worker's paradise." And then Cambodia, "the boat people," Mariel.

Cardinal Ratzinger's Instruction of September 1984 put this point, redolent with the experience not only of Pope John Paul II's Poland but also of Germany, quite succinctly:

> A major fact of our time ought to evoke the reflection of all those who would sincerely work for the true liberation of their brothers: Millions of our own contemporaries legitimately yearn to recover those basic freedoms of which they were deprived by totalitarian and atheistic regimes which came to power by violent and revolutionary means, precisely in the name of the liberation of the people. This shame of our time cannot be ignored: While claiming to bring them freedom, these regimes keep whole nations in conditions of servitude which are unworthy of mankind. Those who, perhaps inadvertently, make themselves accomplices of similar enslavements betray the very poor they mean to help.[47]

To the skeptical eye, liberation theology for all its good intentions promises a mirror image of the Latin American authoritarian societies of the past, but this time of the left rather than of the right. Once again, economic decisions will be state-controlled. Once again, theologians will identify Christianity with the Latin American state. To be sure, the liberation theologians intend this "new earth," for this "new man," to

be democratic and genuinely liberating. As in Cuba? As in Nicaragua?
We have heard all this before.

What is the missing link in liberation theology? *It has no concrete
vision of political economy.* It refuses to describe the institutions of human rights, economic development, and personal liberties that will be
put in place *after* the revolution. It shows no realism about institutions
that meet the tests of praxis, or about institutions (in Madison's words)
designed not for "angels" but for "men." Liberation theology seems to
trust its own fervent Christianity as a sufficient brake on tyranny. This
is naiveté indeed, unmasked already in Nicaragua.

On the contrary, a crucial condition for genuine liberation is that
no one group of men, arrayed with a panoply of all the coercive powers
of the state, gain all power over politics, over economics, and over mor-
als and culture. The absorption of all of life by politics, and of politics
by the state, is the Achilles' heel of existing socialist regimes. The separation of systems, the separation of powers—in short, the hard-won
lessons of liberal societies—do in fact achieve such splendid liberations
as humanity has ever yet achieved.

*   *   *

What is likely to happen? In 1984 Father Leonardo Boff left his
"dialogue" with Cardinal Ratzinger in Rome smiling, confident, and
cocky enough to continue upbraiding the Vatican for *its* alleged naiveté. Two Brazilian cardinals flanked him in Rome as "cardinal pro-
tectors." Liberation theologians busily began to show how the
Ratzinger declaration does *not* apply to them. In so doing, many in fact
seem to be becoming more "critical"—precisely the chief recommen-
dation of Ratzinger—about the vaguely Marxist thinking their works
have until now exhibited.

All this will be a gain. But if traditional Latin American societies
are not acceptable, and if Marxism is unacceptable, then what? De-
mographic facts based on children already born show that Latin America will need at least 76 million new jobs by 1999. Who will create these
new jobs, if not caudillos, landholders, or commissars? Even a little economic sophistication—learned perhaps from East Asia—will suggest
that Latin America needs an unprecedented burst of entrepreneurship and of industrial and commercial activity. Revolutionaries—in
Cuba and in Nicaragua, as in Vietnam and Eastern Europe—seem
mostly to create huge armies. Economic activists create jobs. Sooner or
later, liberation theologians will need to learn how to create new wealth
in a sustained and systematic way, in their resource-rich but econom-

ically repressed continent. Genuine liberation must include economic liberation, economic activism, economic invention.

Regrettably, liberation theologians never look northward except in anger. They will not concede that the United States, too, embodies a kind of liberation theology—liberal, pluralistic, communitarian, public-spirited, dynamic, inventive. Such a liberal society is not, has never promised to be, either a utopia or a sinless paradise. Especially regarding Latin America, our society has committed a full complement of sins. But mutual criticism does not presuppose mutual innocence. Let us hope that the Latin Americans can build free societies, uplifting all their poor, better than we have done. In any case, there are more liberation theologies in this world, committed to practice, to trial and error, and to self-reform, than the liberation theologians of the South have yet to dream of.

Thus, in the next two chapters, I would like to spell out the meaning—political, economic, and moral—to be attached to the word "liberation." Used in an incarnational way, this word refers not only to a personal, spiritual liberation from one's own sins—"salvation" in the precise theological sense and in the light of eternity—but also to those human *institutions* that, together, form an *order* or *system* of political economy. To ask whether a system is "liberating" is, in this sense, to ask about its institutional arrangements. I offer my own vision of the liberal ("liberated") society.

Such questions run deep. They involve, in the end, questions of political philosophy, social science and the daily arts of politics and economics. Deeper still, they eventually involve questions of a philosophy of being—questions about the nature and destiny of humans, a metaphysics. Toward the end of this book, I mean to attend to the latter. Toward the beginning, it seems wiser to attend first to more concrete matters, closer to worldly experience. Therefore, we turn in Chapter Two to basic institutional questions. In this world of flesh, what does "liberation" mean, institutionally? In Chapter Three, it seems useful to offer a short "catechism," concerning several disputed questions that typically arise during long evenings of argument, over brandy, in contexts such as this. Such as, What about United Fruit?—and the "robber barons"?

Two

BUT WILL IT LIBERATE?

One wishes to applaud liberation theology, in the first place, for raising the liberal question: How can human liberation be attained in practice, in the real world of flesh and blood, amid the ambiguity and contingency that constitute worldly history? Liberation theology begins by asking the right question. A next practical question then arises: Has liberation theology asked the right question *in the right way*? That is, are the teachings of liberation theology (at their present early stage of development) likely *in practice* to achieve what they hope? Liberation theology *intends* to liberate. But *does* it? What are its probable consequences?

There are two approaches to the theology of political economy, the utopian and the realistic. The utopian approach, frankly recommended by such liberation theologians as Juan Luis Segundo, S.J., argues from abstractions about a future that has never been.[1] Permit me to take an example from Bishop Tutu of South Africa, speaking of the liberation of South Africa. Asked by a journalist whether he is a socialist, Bishop Tutu unambiguously replies "absolutely, yes." Asked then to specify the concrete socialist model he would like South Africa to follow, the bishop demurs. We have not yet seen, he says, "the kind of society" he would recommend. And he adds: "But then we are visionaries. We hope we are visionaries. And we leave it to others to try and put flesh to the things we try to dream."[2] A better description of the utopian approach is hard to find. One encounters it frequently in socialist and Marxist writings. Grand moral principles are asserted. Bishop Tutu says: "And all I long for is a society that will be compassionate, sharing, and caring." He leaves the institutional questions—those that "put flesh to" his dreams—to others. This is one approach.

The other—the realistic approach—is quite different, not entirely different, but different in significant ways. The realistic approach, while clearly aware of its own ideals and of the open possibilities of the future, is concerned with concrete realities, proximate next steps, and comparisons based upon actual existents. Like the utopian approach, the realistic approach also has yet-unrealized ideals and, again like the utopian approach, it knows the importance of the idea of the future. But unlike the utopian approach, it takes care to use as its proximate standard of measurement the simple question: *Compared to what?* "The goal of liberation theology is a non-capitalist, socialist society," some will say; to which the realist asks: "Like what? Bulgaria? Cuba? Sweden? Identify your nearest concrete model." And if to this someone counters, "Liberation theology seeks a *new* form of society, unlike any other," the realist rejoinder is straightforward: "What concrete institutional design do you have for it? Like what? Explain to me how classic abuses will be prevented."

In suggesting that liberation theology in Latin America is not yet practical enough—does not yet offer a practical concrete model, toward whose realization institutional steps may be directed today—it is necessary for me to state the concrete ideal that informs my own thought. As a theology or philosophy of political economy, liberation theology is clearly at a pre-theoretical stage. It criticizes. It exhorts. It stimulates. But it has not yet spelled out its future *institutional* form. Until it does so, it is not yet political, but merely hortatory. Abuses of human rights are not curbed by exhortation but only by institutions functioning according to well-defined due process. Those of us who are skeptical about the claims of liberation theology must, therefore, press its thinkers to become more concrete. In doing so, we must spell out our own practical ideals of liberation.

I will accept the definitions of liberation theology that the various liberation theologians offer. It is fair to hear people out in their own terms and to accept their labels and their symbols on their terms. Insofar, though, as liberation theologians have a "preferential option for the poor," and seek to reduce "repression" and "human rights abuses," there is a fairly clear and stable standard that, in its own terms, liberation theology must meet: *Does it liberate?* Actually? In practice? Does it actually lift up the poor so that they are no longer poor? Does it actually institute new structures of human rights, so that citizens are not tortured and their other rights are not violated?

In this respect, the books of liberation theologians are disappointing. They say that they are interested in *praxis*. But one learns very little from them about the practical institutions they will put in place the day *after* the revolution that they seek. Institutionally, how will they protect human rights? Institutionally, how will they achieve the economic growth that raises up the poor? One will learn far more about how to prepare oneself for the praxis of actual liberation from reading *The Federalist* than from any volume of liberation theology written thus far.

That is why I turn now to the liberation theology native to North America, "the liberal society." The first persons to be called, and to call themselves, "liberals" were so named because they sought *three* liberations. The infant United States was among the first crucibles in which their experiment was tried. They sought liberation from tyranny and torture *in the political sphere;* liberation from the tyranny of poverty *in the economic sphere;* and liberty of conscience, information and ideas *in the religious, cultural, and moral sphere.*

Quite naturally, the *tri-couleur* was the symbol of the first liberal nations: one color for each liberation. True, some of the first liberals (especially on the Continent) were harshly anti-religious. The anti-clerical, anti-religious ferocity of French liberalism, for example, was one of the forces that drove some of the newly founded Pères de Saint Croix from France to found the University of Notre Dame in Indiana. Thus, *Liberalisme* achieved a bad name in the Catholic tradition. Often, too, its true import has not been grasped. Among early liberals, my favorites are those, perhaps better called Whigs, who grasped the importance of tradition, religion, liturgy, community and history in the liberal project: not only Lord Acton, but also Adam Smith and John Stuart Mill, Edmund Burke, and, above all, Alexis de Tocqueville. Tocqueville opposed the socialists of France on one side, the traditionalists on the other. He once said that the heart of the Christian faith is liberal. And he understood the originality of the American experiment.

When the people of France, a hundred years ago, wished to offer a proper symbol for the United States, they contributed the Statue of Liberty. That has ever been the proper symbol of the liberal society of North America. "Send me your tired, your poor," that Statue says, as if to underline the preferential option of this system for the poor. And most of our families did come here poor. I urge my readers to think back to their own families circa 1935 or earlier. Were they from a privileged class? Or were they poor? Generation after generation, the poor have streamed to America and been lifted out of poverty. *This* "liberation theology" actually does liberate. (Of course, I have always been glad my grandmother could not read English and therefore could not read those other, more ambiguous words of welcome on the Statue of

Liberty: "the wretched refuse of your teeming shores.") My family was not, I'm afraid, aristocratic. Nor were those of most Catholics in the United States.

In fact, as Gertrude Himmelfarb makes clear in her magisterial study, *The Idea of Poverty,* one of the great motivating drives of the first liberals, as distinct from the Malthusians, was their recognition that poverty is a form of tyranny, and that that tyranny can and should be broken.[3] Because they, particularly Adam Smith, had discovered the causes of wealth, they knew that poverty *could* be broken, systematically and in a sustained way. And if it could be, it must be. A new moral obligation thereby entered human history. Concerning poverty, resignation is not enough. Humans must act to diminish it. Underdevelopment is not good enough. There is a moral obligation to achieve development, along all its human axes. The motto of New York state expresses this: "Excelsior!" ["Higher!"]

Looking out at the world of 1800, the first liberals contemplated a world of some 800 million living souls, mostly living under tyranny, in poverty, in ignorance, in illiteracy, lacking in knowledge of basic hygiene and fundamental medicine, average age of death universally about 19. In perhaps the most developed nation, France, the average age of the oppressed sex at death was 27, the average age of death of the oppressor sex, 23. The condition of man in his natural state offered by Thomas Hobbes was taken to be reasonably descriptive of human life: "solitary, poor, nasty, brutish, and short."

As Pope John Paul II said recently, there are today 800 million hungry persons on this planet. That is a sad, but true, fact. The liberal task has yet to be completed. But what the Pope *didn't* say is that, 186 years after 1800, there are 4 billion people who are *not* hungry: that many more are living (because of giant strides of creativity in medicine, pharmaceuticals, immunizations, and the like), and now living to an average age worldwide of nearly 60.

Karl Marx described the bourgeois revolution as the greatest transformation ever experienced by the human race.[4] He wrote this in 1848, when he had not seen the half of it.

So the liberal society is not solely an abstract ideal, but a real flesh-and-blood system, full of its own sins and inadequacies, a system sin-laden and yet noble, that has dramatically altered human history. In particular, I want to consider the United States as it is, as one embodiment of the liberal society. If the U.S. is not democratic, which nation is? If the U.S. is not capitalist, which nation is? If the U.S. is not pluralistic and free in conscience, what place on earth is? Yet this actual, real system we live in is based upon an idea, a conception of order, painstakingly worked out by our Founders. (One can see the slow forging of these ideas in the Constitutional debates, *The Federalist,* and the private papers and correspondence of these practical visionaries.) They knew our system was unlike that of France, Great Britain, Italy, Morocco, or any other. They described it with full seriousness as *Novus ordo seclorum:* an *ordo,* an order rooted in a *new* conception, and "of the ages," a turning point in human history.

The Founders were the offspring of a biblical people. For a thousand years and more, devout readers of the Bible had reflected on its images of the person, the community, the nature and destiny of human beings, the common good, and an order worthy of what God had taught them about human dignity. They had learned of the inalienable dignity of every single person, of the need "to promote the general welfare," of the necessity for "republican virtue," and of the need to build "a new republic" worthy at last of human dignity. Jefferson, indeed, thought of the U.S. as "the second Israel."[5]

Parenthetically, it is here that the early drafts of the U.S. Catholic bishops' pastoral on the U.S. economy erred, precisely in the section on the Bible.[6] The early drafts summarized what contemporary biblical scholars find of interest in the Bible. But the current interest of the biblical scholars of this generation, whose wisdom will wither as the grass of the field, is not decisive. To accumulate biblical texts, written for a pre-democratic, pre-capitalist, pre-growth period of history, and then to leap from *that* context to today is a kind of fundamentalism. Of far more decisive importance is the impact of the Bible down the centuries, upon devout and practical persons who reflected upon it, trying by many and often bloody experiments to design institutions worthy of the human dignity affirmed in the Bible. One must see the Bible as it actually worked in the history of political economy, as yeast works in dough. One must study how it affected Catholic social thought from Augustine to Aquinas to Lord Acton and, above all, how it affected the social vision of the new American republic, in its political, economic and moral systems. The Bible was decisive for the invention of the system we enjoy in the U.S., mired in sin as every human system is, the system whose proper and most telling name is democratic capitalism.

Many Catholics miss the full impact of that concept. They think of "capitalism" alone, an "unfettered market," an "invisible hand," solely a "free enterprise" system, "libertarianism." This was never the American idea. (It was certainly not the idea of Adam Smith, who canonized the quite different term "political economy," or of John Stuart

Mill in *The Principles of Political Economy*.) In political economy, both the political system and the moral-cultural system possess crucial power.

For example, a cultural system rooted in Judaism and Christianity will insist upon concern for the poor. Through the political system, its citizens will seek "to promote the general welfare," to design a system of universal education, and to keep experimenting with a system of care for the poor. Such steps do not *contradict* a successful capitalist economy; on the contrary, they are indispensable to it. Similarly, a free market economy *requires* regulation and cannot function without it. Welfare for those too old, too young, the disabled, and the unfortunate is an altogether proper task for political economy, especially among peoples of Jewish, Christian, and humanist roots. Both in the world of theory and in the real world of practice, political economy is three systems in one: a political system, an economic system, and a moral-cultural system—all three mutually interdependent.

The most apt descriptive name for this system runs parallel to the phrase "political economy." Democratic in its political system, its economic system is properly designated capitalism. Further, this name, "democratic capitalism," implies respect for liberty of conscience, information, and ideas: in short, pluralism in its moral and cultural institutions. Such a tripartite system represents the three full "liberations" that are the inheritance of the liberal society.

This concept of social order is opposed both to the illiberalism of the Right and to the illiberalism of the Left. It is opposed both to traditionalism (e.g., of Latin American and other third world types) and to socialism (whether of the Soviet Union or of the Socialist International). In a large sense, social democratic and democratic socialist societies (such as Sweden) are variants of the democratic capitalist idea. They tilt toward the left or statist side. They lean to the "political" in "political economy," that is, to the state. There are important differences between social democratic and democratic socialist parties, on the one hand, and "liberal" parties, on the other hand. The political struggles that result are fruitful for pluralism, and serve to keep the tensions among the three constitutive systems (political, economic, and moral-cultural) lively and creative. Yet these are, in a sense, debates within the family. For example, social democrats and democratic socialists also allow for some autonomy to the economic system and to the moral-cultural system. They are not fully socialist. The full-blown democratic capitalist idea, by contrast, requires a dynamic and fluid balance among the three independent-interdependent systems. While recognizing important roles for the political system—for the state—it also insists upon due autonomy for the economic system and the moral-cultural system vis-à-vis the state.

Three biblical ideas, among others, lie behind the democratic capitalist reality. Without such ideas the latter could not have come into existence. As Jacques Maritain saw, the modern conception of democracy springs from centuries of meditation upon the biblical vision of humankind.[7] And as Max Weber saw, capitalism cannot be defined solely in terms of ancient and traditional social techniques such as private property, markets, profits, and incentives, since all these existed even in biblical times in such ancient cities as Jerusalem.[8] In Weber's eyes, capitalism brought something new into history, first seen near the end of the eighteenth century. Its originality lay less in technique than in the domain of the human *spirit*. (Thence the second half of his title: *The SPIRIT of Capitalism*.) This new thing, for which he reserves the name of "capitalism," consists of a new morality and a new set of moral obligations.[9] The three biblical ideas mentioned above led, during centuries of trial and error, to its invention. One can discern this originality in the differences of *ordo*, or system, in Latin America and North America.

Already in 1776, Adam Smith had predicted that Latin America would eventually end in poverty and tyranny (exactly as the liberation theologians of today describe). Why? Because the Latin American experiment consisted in reconstructing an ancient order, that of the Holy Roman Empire: a mercantilist view of wealth as gold and silver, an economy based chiefly upon a landed aristocracy, and the unity of church and state. By contrast, Smith saw, "the colonies" of North America were attempting a *new* experiment, based upon an original conception of social order, a *novus ordo*.

What made the *ordo* of the United States different from any in Europe or elsewhere? What was new about it? Three of its novelties were biblical in inspiration.

(1) *The Jewish-Christian notion of sin lay behind the fundamental division of systems, the division of powers in the political system, and a pervasive, systemic concern with checks and balances.* The Jewish-Christian conception of man is empirically based. It holds that every human being sometimes sins. Therefore, no person, class, or group may be entrusted with total power. Every human, even a saint or a philosopher-king, given total power, will sooner or later be tempted to torture others (for the common good). Therefore, one cannot trust political leaders with power over *conscience, ideas,* or *information.* The institutions of religion, intellectual life, and the press must be given

powers separate from those of the political system. This idea had been pioneered in the free cities and free republics of Europe since the Edicts of Toleration.

More original was the principle that political leaders should not be trusted with power over *economic* institutions. To an unprecedented degree, economic institutions in the United States were separated from the state. The result, as Oscar Handlin has pointed out, was that in 1800, in a nation of roughly four million persons, there were more private corporations in the U.S. than in all of Europe.[10]

The reality of human sinfulness, therefore, led to the invention of an unprecedented division of social systems, the separation of the American social system into three relatively equal, but quite different systems: political, economic, and moral-cultural. From this conception of order arises both a check upon human sinfulness, and a liberation of historical dynamism.

Madison had written that, in designing a new order, the Founders must build neither for angels nor for brutes, but for humans as we are. Any plausibly successful order must represent a political economy designed for sinners, the only moral majority there is. In *Federalist* 51, Madison wrote:

> But what is government itself but the greatest of all reflections on human nature? If men were angels, no government would be necessary. If angels were to govern men, neither external nor internal controls on government would be necessary. In framing a government which is to be administered by men over men, the great difficulty lies in this: you must first enable the government to control the governed; and in the next place oblige it to control itself. A dependence on the people is, no doubt, the primary control on government; but experience has taught man the necessity of auxiliary precautions.[11]

The motto on our coins expresses the Founders' concept quite well: *"In God We Trust."* That is, *"Nobody else."* Humans are sinners.

(2) *The Jewish-Christian concept, beginning in Genesis, that humans are made in the image of God the Creator, taught the early Americans that the vocation of Christians, Jews, and humanists is not merely to be passive, resigned, and reconciled to history but, on the contrary, to change history and to be creative, to pioneer, and to persevere in being inventors of a new order.* The short answer to Adam Smith's *Inquiry into the Nature and Causes of the Wealth of Nations* is: The cause of wealth is creativity. Not natural resources.

Not labor. Not planning. Rather, human wit, intelligence, inquiry, invention—in a word, the old *caput* (L.: head), from which the name for the system, "capitalism," is appropriately derived. Until Adam Smith, wealth (identified with gold, silver, and the like) was thought to be limited. It could not be created, only taken. "If the rich get richer, the poor get poorer." This traditional conception held that wealth is a zero-sum: if some gain, others must lose. Since until that time new wealth had only rarely been created by invention and discovery, this error had a long life. It thrives in intellectual backwaters even today. The classic villain was the miser, whose hoarded coins were withheld from the common use. After Adam Smith, a new morality came into play. If wealth can be created, then, seeing the tyranny and misery inflicted by poverty, human beings must discern a new moral obligation: the moral obligation of development, the moral imperative to raise every poor person in the world out of poverty. If new wealth can be created, the miser who hoards his gold is less a villain than a fool, and thus the miser disappeared from the ranks of literary villains. And a new moral obligation to end poverty on earth arose.

Three brief examples may make the power of this insight plain. First, a contrast between Brazil and Japan. Brazil is larger than the continental U.S. (excluding Alaska), and is perhaps among the top three nations in the world in natural resources. With an almost identical population (in 1980: about 118 million), Japan is roughly the size of Montana. It has almost no natural resources. Yet Japan produces seven percent of gross world product, Brazil under two percent. If natural resources were the cause of wealth, Brazil would be rich, Japan poor. In three ways, Japanese society is ordered to creativity: in the design of its system; in the organization of the Japanese personality by mind; and in inventiveness.

Secondly, a reflection on "natural resources." If we had sought down the centuries a metaphor for poverty, we would have said: "Poor as a Bedouin." Dwellers in the desert lacked even water and shade. Yet what do we say of such peoples today? "Oil-rich Arab nations." What made the difference? The invention of the piston engine, and the discovery of how to refine gasoline from crude oil. Invention turned oil from useless, noisome stuff to "black gold." So it is with almost everything today designated as a "resource." Most have become "resources" only in recent times. The stuff of nature becomes a "resource" only when creative intellect discovers a use for it. There are no pre-defined limits to the wealth the Creator has hidden in nature, waiting for humans to detect its clues.

Thirdly, as Adam Smith drew many of his central insights from "the colonies," arguing that Great Britain should learn from them, so also Americans after 1776 learned much from his *Inquiry*. One such lesson led to the Homestead Act, opening up the American Middle West to what Abraham Lincoln called "free labor—the just and generous, and prosperous system, which opens the way for all—gives hope to all, and energy, and progress, and improvement of conditions to all."[12] The principle is that there is more intelligence in millions of individual citizens than in any small band of central planners or government officials, however brilliant. Whereas the American "slave states" were built upon the Latin American idea of the large plantations of a landed aristocracy, the North American idea was free labor and an independent citizenry. The Congress further insisted upon land grant colleges in every new territory, on another Smithian principle: viz., that the cause of development is intellect.

(3) *The distinctive Jewish-Christian idea of community—based on neither birth nor kin nor territory nor religious unity, but on free and voluntary covenant—led to the American discovery of a new principle of the new science of politics: the principle of voluntary association.* There are three aspects to the new democratic-capitalist conception of community.

First, Adam Smith called his book, not *The Wealth of Individuals*, but *The Wealth of Nations*. His was the first vision of universal, worldwide development. His is preeminently a social vision. The vision of democratic capitalism will not be attained until a sound material base is placed under every single person on this planet.

Second, the chief institutional invention of democratic capitalist societies is not the individual (already magnified by the aristocracy) but the corporation and the association. These social forms provide a new way for human beings to organize themselves for voluntary social action, including economic action, in independence from the state.[13]

In addition, and quite paradoxically, the market system *obliges* individuals to be other-regarding, not necessarily from charity, but even from enlightened self-interest. As a systemic device, the market system enforces other-regardingness. No matter how good you think the product or the service you offer, you will get nowhere in a market system unless you actually serve the needs of others.

Third, democratic capitalist societies develop in their young a new type of personality, aptly called the communitarian personality.[14] We do not bring up our children to be "rugged individualists." On the contrary, we bring them up to be open to others, gregarious, active in many groups, skilled in association. My youngest daughter—not unlike the readers of this book—by the time she was seven already belonged to more organizations, attended more different meetings, and took part in more different activities than both my wife and I could drive her to. Democratic capitalist youngsters have a larger range of social skills than those developed in any socialist society. Even our most beloved sports—our public liturgies—are team sports.

*   *   *

In short, the liberal society, benefiting from centuries of reflection upon biblical themes such as sin, creativity, and a new conception of community (universal, associative, and communitarian), has set a benchmark for other social orders. The liberal society, to repeat, is based upon three liberations: liberation of conscience, ideas, and information (the institutions of pluralism); liberation from tyranny and from torture (democratic institutions); and liberation from poverty (capitalist institutions, in concert with moral-cultural and political institutions).

Liberation theology also claims to have a "preferential option for the poor." But, the day *after* the revolution, what sort of economic institutions does liberation theology plan to set in place that will actually help the poor no longer to be poor? What sort of institutions will it set up to block tyranny and to prevent torture? What sort of institutions will it set up to guarantee liberty of conscience, ideas, and information? If liberation theology succeeds in helping to construct such institutions as these, then it will meet the tests of the liberal society, and achieve genuine human liberation. Then we are all "liberation theologians." And if not, not.

Three

A SHORT CATECHISM

Several misunderstandings of the nature of democratic capitalism are so frequently encountered in the writings of liberation theologians that a short "catechism" may usefully clarify certain themes. Much more in terms of question and response—from both directions—needs to be done. Dialogue cannot be speech from one side only.

1. *Capitalism in the U.S. is morally bankrupt. It has been saved from itself by political and moral energies emanating from elsewhere.*

The American system, from the beginning, relied upon all *three* fundamental social systems: (1) *the institutions of the moral-cultural system:* churches, press, universities, families, and associations of all sorts, etc.; (2) *the institutions of the political system:* executive, legislative, judicial; parties, citizen organizations and movements; regulatory agencies of government, patent laws, and laws governing private property and voluntary contracts; and the welfare functions of localities, states, and federal government; etc.; (3) and *economic institutions:* including habits of enterprise and invention; corporations large and small; partnerships; unions; associations of employees, stockholders, consumers, professionals, industries, and commerce, etc.

Significant moral impulses, principles, habits, and important institutional protections are found in each of the three systems. No one of the three systems aims to cover the whole of life.

In particular, a liberal government provides many goods that the economic system alone does not, not only in protecting the legal bases of a commercial republic, and not only in the necessary regulation of commercial life, but also in its legitimate educational and welfare functions.

The legitimate functions of political and moral-cultural institutions are not *contrary* to a capitalist system, but its necessary adjuncts, supports, and counterbalance. The Homestead Act, the land-grant colleges, the patent and copyright laws, rural electrification, the many Highway Acts, and the like are a few among many examples of such legitimate functions. So also Social Security and the progressive income tax.

   2. In America, laissez-faire capitalism has been modified by socialist ideas, leading to the "mixed economy" of the "welfare state." Much that is good in the system is not due to capitalism, but to socialism.

   The expression "mixed economy" suggests that two incompatible ideals have been "blended." This is not an accurate rendering either of the original idea of the American experiment or of its historical unfolding. From the beginning, the Founders recognized the rights inhering in citizens as moral-cultural agents, as political agents and as economic agents. Their basic conception was "political economy." The economy and the polity were joined together from the start. Ours is not, then, an artificially "mixed economy." The original conception of "political economy" implies a legitimate role for each of three fundamental systems. The concept of "political economy" explains how the expansion of the "welfare state" since the 1930s could be justified as coherent with America's original premises, among them, "to promote the general welfare."

   3. Social democratic or democratic socialist regimes such as Sweden, the Netherlands, Israel, West Germany, and Great Britain are morally superior to the U.S. model, economically at least as dynamic, and politically democratic.

   The political economies of such regimes are most accurately classified as variants of the democratic capitalist ideal, somewhat more heavily tilted than the U.S. toward state controls. Their own socialist parties criticize them for being insufficiently socialist. The socialist bloc classifies them as "capitalist." Such regimes do, in fact, respect the principles of private property, markets, incentives, invention, and growth.

   Many of us prefer the U.S. model because it is more inventive and dynamic, and less burdened by statist regulation and controls. This difference leads some to think of the Western European nations as closer than the U.S. to the "socialist" ideal. But the West Germans, for example, strenuously insist that their "social market economy" is *not* socialist. Some analysts (myself included) think the greater role of the state in Western European nations is a defect, and that the burden of social spending they have inflicted upon themselves in the name of security is diminishing their economic and cultural vitalities. Since 1970, while the U.S. has created some 29 million new jobs (as of the end of

1985), such regimes have been losing jobs. In Sweden, many analysts rightly speak of the "crisis" of the welfare state, already committed now to absorbing 50 percent of GNP in taxes and by the year 2000 more than 60 percent.[1]

4. *In Latin America, capitalism has not worked.*

Latin American economies are not capitalist but *pre*-capitalist. They are heavily burdened by traditionalist state bureaucracies, which dominate the economy. To have markets, private property, and a private sphere is *traditional,* not in itself capitalist. Capitalist economies go beyond traditionalist economies in setting limits upon state activities in the economic sphere; in their attention to education, invention, and creativity; in the scope they allow to enterprise and private economic associations; in the public virtues they nourish; and in the balance they try to strike between the political system and the economic system. In addition, capitalist economies operate by a different "spirit" (Max Weber's shrewd word) than do traditionalist economies, by different virtues and habits, and by a different range of economic institutions. These institutions include: patents and copyrights; research and development; easy access to legal incorporation; incentives for growth; the availability of easy credit for the poor and underprivileged in order that they may launch enterprises of their own; reliance upon a large and constantly growing small business sector; bankruptcy laws, and the like. Latin America has not yet passed from a pre-capitalist, traditionalist system to a capitalist system.

5. *In the third world, capitalism offers no hope.*

On the contrary, those third world countries that follow the capitalist model soon join the ranks of "developed" nations, e.g., the capitalist nations of East Asia. Even in socialist countries, the movement is toward proven capitalist economic methods, as in the cases of Fabian India, Marxist China, Hungary, Yugoslavia, and even the U.S.S.R. itself. Socialism was not invented as a system designed to produce economic development. Its main historical purpose has been political control. The socialist ideal of economic organization is rapidly being modified by a thousand capitalist qualifications because of repeated historical failures in the one sphere and success stories in the other.

Wealth in a truly capitalist nation wells up from the bottom, especially in the small business and small farm sector, and in the entrepreneurial genius of many who were born poor.

6. *Capitalist economies are morally decadent, emphasize "having" rather than "being," and engender an epidemic of "loneliness" and "alienation," etc.*

These are empirical assertions. They must be demonstrated. Are moral and religious vitalities in the U.S. weaker, empirically, than in other nations? Are they weaker at universities such as Notre Dame and Brigham Young, for example? Capitalist economies allow for an immense range of free choices in the moral and religious sphere, e.g., concerning how young persons choose a way of life. The moral and religious vitalities of the people of the U.S.—and also the artistic vitalities, scientific and research vitalities, and vitalities of invention (as represented, e.g., in Nobel prizes)—do not seem weaker than those visible in traditionalist, in Soviet-style, or in social democratic systems.

Both freedom and the right to pursue happiness (alone or in association with others) are *inherently* terrifying. In free societies, one can blame no one but oneself for one's choices in life. A free life is not the life of a hive, herd, or flock. Each person is on the spot (as, in baseball, each individual, though in association with teammates, comes to the plate one at a time). The terrors of liberty (which I have elsewhere called "the experience of nothingness") are not a sign of alienation, but of authenticity.

As for loneliness, most Americans have a deserved reputation for gregariousness and openness, are up to their ears in associations of many kinds, and live as full a voluntary social life as any citizens on earth. Even our bumper-stickers say "smile," and both a communal impulse and public-spiritedness are immensely powerful. It may be doubted whether any people on earth attend as many meetings in a year, or are as active in as many associations as the citizens of the United States. We do almost everything we do with others. As for myself, I'm often dying to have a little more solitude, a little more "loneliness."

About a third of our working population works in the not-for-profit system. Becoming a saint, a mystic, a poet, a folksinger, a dropout—emphasizing "being" rather than "doing" or "having"—are options pursued by many Americans. Most, indeed, choose work in which they are happy, in preference to work in which they might be paid more and "have" more. In any case, there is ample room to choose to live as one wishes—and even to be supported by others in doing so.

7. *Who are the neo-conservatives, and why do they oppose liberation theology?*

A neo-conservative is a person brought up as a person of the left, who grew dissatisfied with the ideas and the spirit of the left. Typically, this dissatisfaction arose because the way of life of the left seemed to demand so many forms of false consciousness and, above all, a loathing for the American system. Most of us can recall in family memory our own real and urgent poverty. Yet America did liberate us from poverty, while other nations, to which members of our original lands of birth also migrated (such as Brazil, Argentina, etc.), did not succeed as well in the project of liberation. This difference is crucial to our self-identity. In this respect and others, the analyses of the left regularly involve the denial of one's own experience. The left also punishes anyone who begins to deviate and to dissent. Dissenters are excommunicated, verbally abused, driven out. That is why more and more young people, constantly exposed to leftist criticism, are becoming disillusioned with the left: in that sense, becoming neo-conservative.

The idea that will own the future is democratic capitalism. It works. Besides, not much is left of the left. A poster announcing a socialist meeting in New York City two years ago read: "What's left?"

8. Elaborate on what you said about "false consciousness."

A good deal of the support for liberation theology among middle-class North Americans comes from compassion and a desire to help. But some comes from false consciousness. A clear example of the latter occurs in the first chapter of a sympathetic introduction to liberation theology: *An Alternative Vision,* by Roger Haight, S.J. Father Haight explicitly disclaims expertise in economics, so as to treat liberation theology *theologically.*[2] But, of course, his material forces him to make judgments about economics, since liberation theology does. The very first presupposition he must deal with is the *experience of poverty,* which he takes care to define, not as the mere *fact* of destitution but rather as the *reaction* to destitution. Note that that is already an ideological step. Haight defines this reaction "as an experience all at once of outrage, of condemnation of this condition, and of guilt in allowing it to continue."[3] Encapsulated in this definition is the proposition that poverty is not the historical, inevitable condition of the human race, about which nothing can be done, but, rather, a condition that can be removed. In other words, the human race understands the causes of how to create such wealth as would render destitution unnecessary. The discovery of these causes is precisely the claim Adam Smith has to world fame. Capitalism made poverty eliminable. Haight assumes this to be the case, for he goes on: "This guilt implies human responsibility. There is a connection between wealth and poverty, a *causal* interrelationship between the extraordinary wealth of the developed sectors both inside and outside Latin America and the extensive poverty that prevails there" (emphasis added).[4]

Father Haight asserts a causal relationship, but he does not specify it. An error in specifying this point would falsify the whole enterprise of liberation theology. Yet Haight does not raise the crucial questions at all. Imagine two different cases. In one case, the destitution of many in Latin America is *caused* by the behavior of the few in Latin America. Perhaps the few in Latin America intend this, perhaps they do not, but in any case the causal relationship is plain. One can appropriately speak of "guilt," objective for certain, and subjective perhaps. In the other case, however, the picture is very different. Those nations that grasp the causes of wealth identified by Adam Smith, and construct economic systems accordingly, achieve two results: (a) they create wealth and (b) they raise up the vast majority of the poor, and even define "poverty" by levels of "decency" far above subsistence. Among such nations are Japan, the nations of the East Asian rim, Australia, Canada, the U.S., and the nations of Western Europe—in a word, the "developed" nations. Those nations that continue in pre-capitalist systems continue to suffer from the poverty and destitution virtually universal in the pre-capitalist era. In this second case, the *causes* of the destitution common to pre-capitalist states are clear. They lie in pre-capitalist systems that prevent the poor and the destitute from sharing in economic activism, from developing their own God-given talents and economic creativity, and from the sort of advance that the vast majority of the poor have experienced under capitalist conditions. In that case, North Americans may well feel outrage and condemnation. But it would be entirely false for them to feel guilt. The secrets of how to create wealth, and so to eliminate destitution, and the secrets of how to effect the *embourgeoisement* of the proletariat, are now well known. That is why Haight can say that there is a question of "human responsibility." The choice of an economic system to live under *is* a human responsibility. Those responsible for choosing a system that results in destitution—when other options that do not so result are available—are culpable. That is the situation, as I see it, in Latin America.

Latin Americans, beginning about 1950, *could* have chosen the same path as Japan, Singapore, Taiwan, and the others. They did not, in part because of the influence of Raul Prebisch, tradition, culture, and well-meaning Americans. They have reaped what they have sown. We ought to do our best to persuade them to do otherwise. It cannot be said that many North Americans *admire* the statism of Latin America. The systems of Latin America are abhorrent to most of us.

It is false consciousness to pretend to feel an inappropriate guilt. It is a further act of false consciousness to recommend for Latin Americans, and to abet, the construction of socialist systems of economy which we would abhor for ourselves, and whose consequences we abhor when we encounter them in Ethiopia, Tanzania, Cuba, the Vietnam of today, Eastern Europe, and the U.S.S.R.

9. But capitalism helps the rich, not the poor.

We were all—virtually all who read this book—born poor. Capitalism helped us, and billions of others. Capitalism did little for duchesses, who already had silk stockings, but much for the poor and working classes, who within two or three generations of the beginnings of capitalism *also* had silk stockings—and tea, coffee, pepper, spices, and many other goods once solely the prerogative of the rich.[5]

In the aristocratic literary tradition, and in the Marxist tradition, it is always asserted that capitalism is "exploitative." But was that, even in 1830 or 1897 or 1931, a fair picture of events? If so, why did our families migrate in such great numbers precisely toward the centers of capitalist activity? They well knew the exploitation of traditionalist societies. They found capitalist forms comparatively liberating.

Even the 28 million blacks in the U.S., arguably the worst-off of the U.S. population, have a cumulative income ($200 billion) larger than the gross domestic product of all but nine other nations of the world.[6]

This is not to say that the three liberations to which democratic capitalist societies are committed (political, economic, and moral) have been accomplished. There is much yet to do. But one must compare the *realities* of the liberal society to the *actual* historical alternatives. Secondly, one must compare the *ideals* of the liberal society to other active ideals.

In my judgment, the liberal society is superior in the realm of practice. And its ideals are also morally more attractive. Those ideals are the ideals of the future, both because they work and because they are most consonant with human nature itself. Thomas Jefferson succinctly stated the ideal of the liberal society: "The God who gave us life gave us liberty."[7] And the Catholic intellect who towers over the nineteenth century, Alexis de Tocqueville, observed quite correctly that the heart of Christianity discerns in human liberty the dignity of the child of God.[8] Few have stated more clearly the "Proposition" on which the United States is built than John Courtney Murray, S.J., when he wrote:

> The American Bill of Rights is not a piece of eighteenth-century rationalist theory, it is far more the product of Christian history. Behind it one can see, not the philosophy of the Enlightenment but the older philosophy that had been the ma-

trix of common law. The "man" whose rights are guaranteed
in the face of law and government is, whether he knows it or
not, the Christian man, who had learned to know his own personal dignity in the school of Christian faith.[9]

Ironically, the liberal society, some of whose first historical protago-
nists were anti-religious, owes its originating insights about the dignity
of the human person and the nature of community to Jewish and
Christian inspirations, and does not make ultimate sense apart from
biblical perceptions.

Not accidentally, perhaps, most of the prominent neo-conservatives are Catholic and Jewish, loyal to traditions older than modernity.

   *10. You speak about "growth." That notion is materialistic. A better ob-
jective is "joy," a "more abundant life."*
   It is not a purely materialistic measure to try to correct conditions
under which a citizen is unemployed, not receiving sufficient food for
a daily minimum level of nutrition, without shelter, and the like.[10]
True economic growth means the improvement of the conditions of
the poorest. It means the wealth that wells up from the bottom, not the
wealth that, it is supposed, "trickles down." The wealth of the United
States, e.g., welled up from the small farms and villages, long before
the age of corporations or great fortunes. Moreover, economic wealth
springs from the human spirit—from invention, from discovery and
also from the habits of punctuality, sound worksmanship, practical
know-how, and adaptability. It cannot be measured solely in material
terms. Thus, even though much of Western Europe was reduced to
rubble during the six long years of World War II, the habits and skills
of the European peoples became the major resource on which the "economic miracle" of European recovery was built.[11] So-called "human
capital"—constituted by the habits of the human spirit—is more important than physical capital. The recent debt crisis shows that billions
of dollars in financial capital can be used uncreatively, in ways that do
not create sufficient new wealth even to meet interest payments, let
alone new wealth in excess of the original investment. Thus, to be materialistic about the causes of wealth is to miss the point.
   One should not be materialistic, either, about the *ends* or *purposes*
of economic growth. Growth is not an end in itself. It is a means toward
liberation from poverty. It is a means toward freeing human beings
from the physical constraints of hunger, lack of shelter, and lack of
means for self-expression, in order that the domain of liberty and human choice may be enlarged. In Brazil, for example, it is sad to see how

sparse are the funds available for education, and how pitifully few of the nation's many millions of youngsters complete elementary schools.[12] For entire states as for individual persons, economic wealth is only a means to spiritual purposes. The primacy of the human spirit remains in force. To be sure, few human beings are saints. Many became ensnared in material pursuits. For better and for worse, free citizens unconstrained by binding poverty use their liberty as their own ideals move them: some admirably, some deplorably. Insofar as greater economic wealth enlarges the domain of free choice, it imposes greater human responsibilities. "It is as difficult for the wealthy to enter into the kingdom of heaven as for a camel to pass through the eye of the needle" (Mt 19:24).

Finally, whereas during the Industrial Revolution, growth usually meant larger, perhaps even dirtier, today the larger proportion of economic growth—in an age of electronics, computers, communications and services—lies in the direction of smaller, cleaner, cheaper, and more efficient. A cheap hand-held computer may have as much power as the huge, wall-sized computers of forty years ago. Electronic processes are cleaner and cheaper than mechanical processes, as one sees even in new automobiles. "Growth" does not always mean "larger"; it often means more inventive, less cumbersome, more direct, even—in a sense—more spiritual. The impulses of a word processor, for example, more closely approximate the workings of the human mind than the pen or the typewriter.

11. The evil of capitalism lies in the wage relation. "When you work for another person and come to depend not on work offered up to God but on work demanded by an employer for your daily bread, a kind of idolatry takes place. The institutionalization of this employee-employer relationship has resulted in the domination of one over another. Such domination is sin." (Enrique Dussel)[13]

In what sort of world would every human being work as a freelance, independent of all others? Authors could certainly not get their books published if they had to make the paper, ink, and presses, and then print their books by themselves, distributing and selling them alone. All human society under all economic systems requires for humane and liberating purposes a differentiation and coordination of labors. In socialist societies, every worker is an employee of the state. A Polish architect, fired for political reasons by his bosses, has no other employer for whom to work; he drives a taxi, unable to practice the craft that brought him joy. Indeed, the larger the number of employers, and the larger and more complex the economic possibilities, the higher the probabilities there are that every person will seek and find the form of work most pleasing to himself or herself.

It is true that those whose opportunities for employment are few, and whose skills are limited, are obliged at first "to take what they can get." Given a mobile and open economy, however, and opportunities to enlarge their skills, their own enterprise can lead them to move from job to job, seeking the rewards and the pleasure suited to their desires. Dussel seems to imagine a closed, rigid, unfree economy. One of the signs of a free economy, however, is how often citizens *quit* one job, in preference for another. In many developed economies, citizens do so many times during a lifetime. In any one year in the United States, about nine percent of all workers voluntarily do so—the turnover is immense.[14] Furthermore, nothing prevents a person from starting an enterprise of his or her own. During 1985, some 13,000 such new businesses were started in the United States *every week*, at a rate of about five or six every minute of every working day.[15]

And is it "domination"[16] to work for another? In some scheme of perfect and total human liberty, in which one does only what one wishes to do, one may imagine that having to go to work for someone else is to "submit to domination." But that is to imagine that life on earth is angelic, each human as self-sufficient as an archangel. The very concept "economy" entails that human beings need one another, necessarily cooperate together, and work in that differentiation of functions proper even to the Mystical Body.

In contemplating the future of the new states of the American West, Abraham Lincoln reflected on the contrast between free labor and slave labor:

> . . . there is not, of necessity, any such thing as the free hired laborer being fixed to that condition for life. Many independent men everywhere in these States, a few years back in their lives, were hired laborers. The prudent, penniless beginner in the world, labors for wages awhile, saves a surplus with which to buy tools or land for himself; then labors on his own account another while, and at length hires another new beginner to help him. This is the just, and generous, and prosperous system, which opens the way to all—gives hope to all, and consequent energy, and progress, and improvement of condition to all. No men living are more worthy to be trusted than those who toil up from poverty—none less inclined to take, or touch, aught which they have not honestly earned. Let them beware of surrendering a political power which they

already possess, and which, if surrendered, will surely be used to close the door of advancement against such as they, and to fix new disabilities and burdens upon them, till all of liberty shall be lost.[17]

12. I would tell a "big Mexican industrialist, a bread manufacturer," that the huge plant he has constructed from "nothing" is ill-gotten: "The only way you can acquire wealth is to buy cheap and to sell dear. You have no right to suppose that society accepted your self-enrichment . . . of its own free will, knowing that it remained subjected to the will and constraint of your capital." (José Miranda, Communism in the Bible)[18]

There are many ways to acquire wealth without buying cheap and selling dear. One can invent a new process, a new product, or a new service. Miranda's world is the world of the zero-sum, a world without invention or creative wit or cooperation. Two men, joining their labors in partnership, may decide that they can pool their efforts, to mutual benefit. Both may become wealthier without taking from anyone else. Indeed, they may enlarge the world's share of goods and services, to the benefit of others. Their own children will benefit, but so also may the children of others.

Miranda begins with the Marxist labor-theory of value and an angelic idea of "liberty without constraints." Like Dussel in the previous comment, he imagines a sort of liberty in which there are no constraints—a situation virtually unknown to human beings in any sphere. He attacks economic acts between consenting adults because neither party is wholly needless, and is thus "coerced" into consent. This is absurd. Economic life begins with the fact of universal human need. Each of us has needs for whose fulfillment we depend on others. As scholars, Miranda and I have needs for food that we do not grow for ourselves, upon its processing, and upon its delivery to markets near us. These needs make us quite vulnerable. We are not self-sufficient. To live we must have bread. Now what system will bring us bread at a lower price, in greater abundance, in greater variety of choice, and routinely? Miranda may believe that Marxist societies do so best. He is free to argue for that belief. Having visited and studied Marxist lands, I know he is wrong. More than that, even most Marxist and socialist theoreticians know he is wrong. The issue has been decided in the world of fact. It is Marxist and socialist societies today that are widening the scope of markets, private property and incentives, precisely on the ground that these better serve the common good than Marxist and socialist techniques.

Miranda holds that "the country folk" who sold their wheat to the bread manufacturer he addresses "had no alternative. Either they accepted the price you felt like offering, or their harvest would rot and they would die of hunger."[19] In Mexican cities I have visited, there seem to be many more than one baker or other purchaser of wheat. Surely, though, the practical answer to the harsh case posed by Miranda is that other manufacturers ought to enter the picture, giving the farmers several prices to choose from. "But objectively you cannot speak of freedom of contract when the only alternative is hunger and misery."[20] Neither the farmer nor the purchaser has complete freedom. If the purchaser desires long-term, steady suppliers of wheat—without which he cannot function—he will want to pay an attractive price, to ensure continued good will. Farmers may turn to other purchasers; to other crops; or may in extremity flee to other occupations. Miranda constructs an image of one single monopolist, able totally to control the market for wheat, and asks us to believe that this is typical. It *is* typical in state-controlled economies, in which the government is the sole purchaser of agricultural produce and in which the government sets prices low enough to keep urban populations happy, while bankrupting farmers. This is the classic disease of socialist agriculture and of agriculture in Africa and other societies under the influence of socialist ideas. Oddly, it is the only model Miranda can imagine.

But Miranda's intellectual difficulty runs deeper still. "The wealth you boast of," he tells his industrialist, "could, and can, be acquired only by millions of expressed or implied contracts: contracts of sale and purchase of the raw materials, contracts of sale and purchase of the labor, contracts of sale and purchase of the end product. *The only possible source of wealth is to make off with the difference*" (emphasis added).[21] But this is to imagine that wealth comes only from buying and selling. This absurd notion reduces capitalist activity to that of merchants. Has creative intellect in organizing production, in developing new products, or in conceiving of new systems of distribution nothing to do with creating new wealth? If Miranda's views were correct, there would never be new wealth. Wealth would simply be rearranged.

The views of Miranda are primitive, to say the least. "But the real question," he writes, "is whether a system ought to exist in which anyone *has* to take risks. . . ."[22] He thinks entirely in pre-capitalist, mercantilist terms, writing: "But in a mercantile economy, the market price is necessarily the one which allows capital to make a profit. Otherwise capital is not invested."[23] It does not seem to occur to him that new inventions—home computers, say—might or might not sell; or, at least, that those of one design might, and those of another might not;

and, therefore, that of twenty new firms building home computers, those who invest in fifteen of them may lose their entire investment— and that no investor knows in advance which will succeed. Like most Marxists (for such he calls himself), Miranda utterly underestimates skills in which he does not share. "The greater part" of the "mental work" of capitalism, he writes,

> contributes nothing to the effective production of goods, but consists in thinking up ways to 'kite' negotiables, ways to create artificial needs for the consumer, ways to squeeze more labor out of the work force, ways to carry on commerce more effectively, to drive out the competition, and the like.[24]

It never occurs to Miranda that in its economic views the Bible is a pre-capitalist document. The secrets of economic development were not discovered until the end of the eighteenth century. Before that, the world was locked in the zero-sum he describes. The only way to get rich was to take from others. New wealth could scarcely be created; at least, the secrets of how to do so in a sustained, self-conscious, systematic way were not yet known. Among the pioneers in the new discoveries that launched the modern age—self-consciousness about the causes of economic development is the distinctive modern contribution to social thought—were the Catholic writers in the Salamanca School, whose work became known to Adam Smith.[25] In ignorance of modern discoveries, Miranda writes of "the Spurious Origin of All Wealth," and adds that "the rich are historical heirs of the masters of a slave society."[26] No wonder Miranda is a self-described Communist. "Why communism?" he asks. "The response is unequivocal: because any other system *consists* in the exploitation of some persons by others. Just because of that."[27]

And communism? Miranda discounts the Soviet Union, speaking of the "failure of Russian communism . . . (what you now have in the Soviet Union is state capitalism)."[28] Miranda dreams of something entirely new. "Our revolution is directed toward the creation of the new human being . . . we seek to posit the necessary means for the formation of this new human being. And the indispensable means is a new social structure."[29] He calls this system "radical anarchism (not anarchy)."[30] And it is easy to see why. In his new society, there will be no employing of some by others, no risk, no investment or invention, no market prices, no recognizable organization at all. And he does not think that government will be necessary in a universe of persons loving one another as God would desire. Having identified evil with wealth, profit, and capitalism, he thinks to banish evil for all time.

> Where there is no differentiating wealth, where economic activity is directly for the purpose of the satisfaction of needs and not for trade or the operations of buying and selling for profit, government becomes unnecessary. By no means is this the invention of Marx and Engels, as can be seen from the biblical texts we have cited.[31]

It does not seem unfair to call such a vision utopian, even angelic, and radically devoid of the biblical sense of the pervasiveness and endurance of human evil in the human breast until the end of time. St. Augustine, St. Thomas Aquinas, and the traditional social teaching of the Church have been far more realistic.

    *13. "Every day, the capitalistic system itself commits aggression in Latin America, aggression far more evil than that committed by the police and the army led by dictators. Millions of children die in the world each year from simple malnutrition. And many more are mentally deficient all their lives from the same cause. And many millions of human beings have their lifetimes cut in half from the same cause. . . . Now, it is not as if the resources presently existing in the world were inadequate to produce sufficient nutrition for all. Technologically it is possible. What is happening is that capitalism as a system does not permit existing resources to be directed to the satisfaction of needs, because the purpose it imposes upon them is the augmentation of capital. Unless a demand of buying power is foreseen which makes a profit likely there is no production; but the world's most tragic and urgent needs are without buying power and consequently cannot translate into demand. Capitalism has seized the resources of humanity, and physically kills millions of human beings day by day with hunger, or leaves them lifelong mental defectives. Would it be more violent to shoot them than to prevent them from eating? Where did this definition of violence come from? The aggression is right here, right now, in the form of genocide, and it is constant." (*José Miranda, *Communism in the Bible*)[32]

    It is odd, in light of Miranda's views, that such "capitalistic systems" as the U.S., Canada, and the nations of Western Europe produce food in immense abundance, and lead the world both in the export of food for sale and in donations to the needy (the U.S. supplies about twenty percent of the food needs of Bangladesh, e.g.). It is odd, too, that existing socialist systems are all racked by intense agricultural crisis.[33] The Ukraine, once considered the "bread basket" of the world, no longer feeds itself (suffering since the Revolution, as the joke goes, under 69 straight years of bad weather). But most odd of all is that those nations initially inspired by socialist methods, but turning in recent years to capitalist methods of agriculture, vast nations such as India and China, have thereby immensely increased their capacity to feed themselves. China has the goal of trebling its per capita income by the year 2000 (from $300 to $900) by the use of such methods. Why, then, does Miranda blame capitalism for the sufferings in Latin America?

The economy of Mexico, his own country, is not capitalist. Some estimates place the proportion of Mexicans on the payroll of the state as high as seventy percent. The space for free economic activity is exceedingly narrow. To start a new corporation or partnership is fraught with obstacles and difficulties. Encouragement for enterprise is virtually nil. The middle class is not large and, such as it is, prudently encourages a disproportionate share of its young to seek government jobs. If Mexicans seek higher education, there are virtually only state universities to attend. Newspapers depend upon state subventions and government advertising. By every known standard, Mexico has a precapitalist, mercantilist, state-directed economy of the sort roundly attacked by such early liberals as Adam Smith, Bastiat, Montesquieu, and others. To say that *capitalism* is causing the sufferings that Mexicans endure at the hands of their own system seems patently absurd.

Miranda writes the passage cited in a section justifying the resort to violence in self-defense. Yet his designation of the source of the "aggression" he discerns seems to be prompted by ideological motives, not by empirical evidence or plausible assertion. Were the Mexican economy organized as, say, the Japanese economy is organized, and if the cultural habits inculcated by its systems were more like those of the Japanese, one might be sure that there would be no hunger in Mexico (or elsewhere in Latin America).

In its potential for agricultural development, Latin America is possibly the single most favored of all the world's continents. One shares with Miranda his sense of outrage and injustice. The *internal system* of most of the nations of Latin America, as he rightly declares, needs drastic change: politically, economically, and (as he emphasizes) culturally. Recognizing that for Miranda "capitalism" is a catch-all phrase for selfishness, evil, spoliation, and even "genocide," one may not even wish to quarrel with him about his usage; what he means—mistaken as he is in applying it—is clear enough. And, yes, the sufferings he points to are absurd, unnecessary, outrageous, and in need of change. The question is whether Miranda's "communism" will help—

or utterly destroy—the poor people of Mexico and the rest of a God-favored continent.

Possibly, though, what Miranda means to suggest is that it is the *United States*—and Western Europe, i.e., the capitalist nations outside Latin America—that are the chief cause of Latin America's woes. In Brazil, one professor put that charge to me this way: "São Paulo is the multinational headquarters of the world. Your banks and investments multiply here. Your capitalist companies come and suck the wealth away from us. We grow poorer while you grow richer." My reply to him was to look, rather, at Japan and the East Asian nations that, with far fewer natural resources than Brazil, have virtually eliminated poverty in their midst during the brief period of the last thirty years, and are now producing a huge proportion of the world's cumulative gross domestic product. To which he replied: "But that's not fair. After all, you have so many multinational companies and investments in those countries." Oh, I replied, I get it: you are poor because of our companies and investments here, whereas they are rich because of our companies and investments there. Sometimes Latin American intellectuals seem desirous of blaming everyone but themselves (and their own theories) for Latin America's woes.

Suppose that the United States disinvested totally in Mexico and in Latin America. Suppose that current debts owed by Latin American countries to foreign banks and investors were cancelled, and no new ones allowed. Suppose, in short, that U.S. capitalist enterprises were allowed no contact whatever with Latin America. Does anyone really imagine that conditions for the poor in Latin America would improve?

The fraction of U.S. international investment that goes to Latin America now is only about 16 percent. By contrast, about 70 percent of U.S. investment abroad goes to Western Europe, Canada, and Japan.[34] Why do these large investments not impoverish the latter, while the smaller proportion (on a much larger continent) allegedly punishes the Latin American poor?

Liberation theologians are fond of blaming the United States. They should fashion the most empirical, factual prosecution they can. Then the defense should be allowed to respond. The people of the United States would willingly pay immense sums to see the poor of Latin America prosper as, since World War II, the West Europeans, the Japanese, the East Asians, and other peoples have begun to do. The prosperity of Latin America's poor is very much in the interest of the United States. Modern economics is not a zero-sum. The more that all Latin Americans would prosper, the more North Americans would prosper. The immensely increased prosperity of Western Europe and Japan since World War II has not made the United States poorer. On the contrary, their growth has assisted ours. After World War II, the U.S. produced 53 percent of gross world product; the *proportion* is now down to about 25 percent.[35] But that has not made the U.S. poorer. In actual fact, the poverty of Latin America is a huge depressant on the wealth of the entire Western Hemisphere and the world as a whole. When Latin America finally seizes its proper role of world economic leadership, all other nations will benefit. Capitalism is like that.[36] It is not based, as traditional economies were, on Miranda's central idea, viz., that the only way to become wealthy is to take from others but, rather, on the far more radical idea: viz., that the growing prosperity of each of the world's nations feeds into, nourishes, stimulates, and enhances the prosperity of all others. Free economic activities among consenting adults have as their aim—and their proven record of accomplishment—a mutual satisfaction of interests, to the benefit of all.

"Unless a demand of buying power is foreseen which makes a profit likely," Miranda writes in the passage cited above, "there is no production."[37] This is demand-side theory. Was there demand for word processors before they came into existence? Quite often, advances on the supply-side induce the efforts which bring demand into balance. No doubt, it is crucial to expand the buying power of the destitute and the poor of Latin America. One way to do that is to increase the supply—not only the investment in production, and the employment that results from it, but also to engage those multiple millions of the unemployed and the underemployed in economic activism. Poor persons in Latin America have few places to turn to for credit. Simple institutions such as Savings and Loans, Credit Unions, the Farm Bureau Credit, and other devices that in other nations enable poor persons to borrow enough to launch enterprises of their own are scarcely to be found. No wonder so many millions of talented and able people are, economically speaking, inert. Development in Latin America must begin (as elsewhere) at the bottom. Latin American intellectuals ought to be studying the ways and means of realistic economic activism. The Spanish and Portuguese Crowns taught them, alas, to look to the state for their needs; they still do. The lure of communism for Latin American intellectuals has its roots in ancient habits of dependency. These must be broken. Only economic activism among the poor and the lower middle classes can effect the necessary transformation.

14. You neglect the terrible history of such companies as United Fruit. In fact, you neglect the whole story of the "robber barons."

The United States is a largely Protestant country, and we are prepared to feel guilty for our success even before we hear the prosecution. Thus, I am prepared to believe that some persons and some companies did in fact do evil. The extent to which they did so cannot be left to mythology; it should be accurately assessed. One should in fairness listen both to the prosecution and to the defense. Thus, I have read with some care a prosecutorial study of United Fruit, *Bitter Fruit: The Untold Story of the American Coup in Guatemala.*[38] I am prepared to believe that this company, as charged, engaged in many improper, immoral, and illegal activities. If so, that company stands condemned by its own record. Fairness makes me wish, however, that I could hear the case for the defense, as recounted from the side of the executives and others involved in that company. Perhaps they have no adequate defense; not having heard it, I cannot judge. For the sake of discussion, though, let us assume that all the charges are true.

Still, I was surprised to learn from that book the conditions prevailing in Central America when United Fruit began its operations. If immorality is to be charged against United Fruit, parallel charges must be lodged against many in Central America for behaviors and practices in existence before there was any "Yankee" presence at all. In addition, even in making its case, the prosecution acknowledges the many achievements and real contributions of United Fruit: jungles cleared for heretofore non-existent cultivation, railroads built under enormous difficulty, electric power and telephonic communications installed, roads and villages begun, schools and churches and clinics built. Not many known enterprises are purely evil. In this case, there seem to be some achievements on the good side of the ledger, as well as on the evil.

The overriding evils, however, come down to three: (1) an immense cultural arrogance, which demeaned many human beings; (2) a failure to grasp the importance of nurturing the entire surrounding culture in the habits of democracy, honest dealings, and to undertake the social transformation of destitution and poverty into a thriving and creative economy; and (3) highhanded methods of political governance, collusion and civic corruption. To the exact degree in which United Fruit is guilty of these charges, it stands seriously condemned. It should be all the more condemned, because United Fruit springs from a people and a nation whose values and principles it betrayed. It had every reason to know better. It can find no excuse.

As a matter of policy, it is important for citizens of free countries to monitor closely the behavior of such companies and, where they are wrong, to protest against their activities. A company chartered under the statutes of U.S. law, and springing from the cultural values and ideals of the U.S., must be held to the highest standards. It is chartered, in a sense, as a public trust. The public is right to condemn whatever deserves condemnation, and to seek to correct abuses. Publicly registered companies must be held to the law, to common moral principles, and to the pressures of public opinion. These are not inconsiderable.

As for "the robber barons," similar principles apply. It should be noted, however, that the left sometimes uses such phrases generically, without intending to single out any specific breach of morality except the very existence of successful builders of commercial or industrial establishments. The accusations of the left often attack the institution, not its specific behaviors. As a matter of historical inquiry, historians from many points of view need to assess the moral record of corporations, domestic and international. Ironically, the history of business corporations is little attended to by historians. One should also note that a large majority of "the captains of industry," at least in the United States, were of low birth and humble means. Many were persons of extraordinary talent. Some were inventors of a very high order. The history of labor unions—to which in *The Guns of Lattimer*,[39] concerning the United Mine workers in Pennsylvania, it has been my privilege to contribute—illustrates many ways in which the professed "good intentions" of some owners and managers needed to be corrected and enlarged by bitter struggle, by the advance of law, and by the raising of public consciousness and standards. Moral progress seldom occurs without such struggle. Traditional ways are discarded painfully. Higher standards, achieved through the culture and made routine in daily practice, come only with strenuous effort. But they do come.

15. In The Ratzinger Report, *Cardinal Ratzinger writes that in bourgeois societies, "money and wealth are the measure of all things" and "the model of the free market imposes its implacable laws on every aspect of life." The result is, he writes, that "economic liberalism creates its exact counterpart, permissiveness, on the moral plane." Do you agree?*[40]

The decay of religious faith in Europe is a matter of serious concern. But it is difficult to find a country in the world in which religion has greater vitality, and is taken with greater daily seriousness, than in the United States. The Gallup Organization charts religious conviction, belief, and practice on an international scale with some regularity.[41] Of all the developed countries, it finds, religious belief and practice in the United States are on a level closer to third world countries (and higher than most of those) than to other developed countries. Further, it is correct to note that a free market and a free society allow for a tremendously broad range of choice, including the choices of those who act in a materialistic fashion. But they also allow for free persons to act in fully religious and humanistic ways.

In this respect, free markets are no more permissive than God himself, who sends his rain on the just and the unjust alike. If a liberal culture becomes "permissive," in the sense of permitting or even encouraging moral laxity, that is because free citizens of full religious faith have not sufficiently exerted themselves to alter the cultural climate. It was in that very effort that, from the 1830s until well in this century, the great Sunday School movement, and many other movements of self-mastery, impulse-restraint, and self-improvement thrived in the United States. "Moral Awakenings" have been common in our history. The Temperance Movement, Abolition (of slavery), and even Prohibition (of alcohol) are examples from the past. Today, one sees the rise of the religious evangelicals, the charismatics, the Right-to-Life groups, the "Back-to-Basics" movement and many others. The so-called Puritan ethic in the United States is alive and well. (What else is suggested by the self-punishment of exercise classes and the pain of daily jogging?) These are not contrary to the liberal society or to the free market. Quite the opposite. The freedoms of a liberal society and a free market include the freedoms of religious activism, practice, and strict observance.

Cardinal Ratzinger, then, is not talking about a *causal* relation. He is addressing a cultural fact. In some free societies, there is a noticeable decline in religious faith and moral practice. This is deplorable. It is deplorable, particularly, as a threat to the moral foundations of free societies. Insofar as human beings become materialistic in their attitudes or practices, they abandon the living spring of free institutions. Forgetting the primacy of the spiritual, they forget the ground of all human rights, which are endowed in individuals by their Creator, and are rooted in the liberties of the human spirit and their correlative responsibilities. The quickest and shortest route toward understanding how it is that human beings have rights that transcend any state or social order is to see that these rights come directly from the Creator and reside in man's spiritual nature. Without a vivid and active faith in some such first principles as these, the very foundations of the liberal society crack.

Even in practice, a people that loses spiritual vitality and the spiritual virtues essential to democratic living undermines democracy itself. A person who cannot govern himself and his own passions is not fit to exercise that consent over the commonweal that constitutes self-government. The same is true of the free economy. The spirit of capitalism requires that persons do not consume their store today, but sacrifice present consumption for the sake of investing in the future. Research and development for the future can only be financed from such savings. A people that would give way to "instantaneous gratification" or wallow in "consumer debt" undercuts its own future. That is why a Puritan society, thrifty and simple in its tastes, supplies in many ways a better foundation for a dynamic economy than a merely consumerist society. Daniel Bell finds in this point "the cultural contradiction of capitalism," viz., that its very success engenders vices that undermine it.[42] But Bell's is after all a hopeful, not a pessimistic, prognosis. It means that the decline of a dynamic economy is neither necessary nor inevitable; much depends upon the reservoir of virtue among its citizens. One of the most hopeful developments in American public life during the last twenty years, James Q. Wilson writes in the prestigious journal *The Public Interest,* is the return of the idea of character and virtue.[43] These are the foundations of a democratic capitalist society, in both its capitalist and its democratic parts.

Four

LIBERATION THEOLOGY AND THE POPE

The Brazilian liberation theologian Hugo Assmann and I had dinner late one night in Rio de Janeiro in 1985, and at this dinner he explained to me that my critique of liberation theology was just barely coming to be known among liberation theologians. Many regard it, he said, as part of an "offensive" against liberation theology originating from both Pope John Paul II and President Reagan.[1] Liberation theologians, he explained, feel both misunderstood and under attack. The accusation seemed to me absurd; most religious writers in North America and Europe bend over backward to be sympathetic to liberation theology.

While I doubt that President Reagan has ever read a word of liberation theology, or even has a clear idea of its existence, it pleased me, to tell the truth, to think that I was perceived by liberation theologians as being on the side of the Pope. Most of my own criticisms of liberation theology antedate any declarations by the Pope. But I do think that, in many ways—particularly in the defense of human rights, and in the emphasis on liberties of conscience, association, work and political action—my own thought and that of the Pope are on the same wavelength. At least, I would wish it so.

It is clear, of course, that Pope John Paul II does not speak, as I do, in praise of the liberal society such as is found in the United States. He has uttered harsh words against capitalism. The experience of the Americas—North and South—lies outside that of most Europeans. Liberation theologians are quick to cite their own originality, claiming a measure of intellectual independence from Europe. A similar claim must also be made by North Americans. Nonetheless, out of a body of experience quite different from that of Pope John Paul II, I share many of his fears that liberation theology will not, in practice, actually liberate.

Thus, in this chapter I would like to reflect on the critique of liberation theology offered by Pope John Paul II, taking my first text from an early statement of Pope John Paul II in Latin America—at Puebla in 1979—and later texts from his later statements.

*   *   *

On his highly publicized voyage to Mexico late in January 1979, Karol Wojtyla, only recently become Pope, faced two systems of authoritarianism. He faced Latin American feudal regimes of a cruelty well known to the bishops he was about to address, some of whom had experienced prison themselves. And he faced a rising enthusiasm, particularly on the part of foreign-trained Latin American clergymen, for Marxist "liberation."

The Pope addressed the Conference of Latin American Bishops (CELAM) at Puebla on January 28. At first his 8,000-word sermon drew words of disappointment and sarcasm from many of the "liberation theologians" he was taken to be attacking.[2] Then began a process by which the Pope's straight sentences were gradually softened and transmuted until, we were told by the New York *Times* (February 18), the theologians in question celebrated the end of the conference by drinking beer, singing "folk songs from all over the continent," so that "well past midnight their songs echoed through the streets . . . sounding suspiciously like a victory celebration." What had actually happened? Had the Pope attacked "liberation theology"—or had he given it official sanction?

The meeting at Puebla was the third major meeting of CELAM in twenty-five years.[3] At the first one in Rio de Janeiro, the bishops of Latin America had established a continent-wide organization. Over the years, they formulated some fairly clear views about their own special needs and the general need for a reorganization of the international church. Thus, at the Second Vatican Council (1961–65), their regional unity was already conspicuous, and their interventions helped the "progressive" forces at the Council do much more than expected. Then in 1968—the year of vast student unrest in the United States, Mexico, France, and elsewhere—the bishops met for the second time, at Medellín, Colombia, and produced a document that addressed the public-policy needs of the continent.[4] Tinged with Marxist rhetoric, that document gave rise, two years later, to the first writings self-described as "liberation theology," that is, formal attempts to translate Christianity into Marxist categories. Works in this genre have multiplied since.

Pope John Paul II went straight to the heart of all this in the opening paragraphs of his address at Puebla.[5] He said immediately that his "point of departure" was "the conclusions of Medellín" as well as the sympathetic support of those conclusions by Pope Paul VI in *Evangelii Nuntiandi*. But he did not hesitate to qualify his praise of "all the positive elements" that the Medellín conclusions contained, with the warning that he was not about to ignore the "incorrect interpretations at times made and which call for calm discernment, opportune criticism, and clear choices of position."

The misconception that the Pope wished to sweep away was that Christianity is reducible to Marxist categories. He opposed those "re-readings" of the Gospel that "cause confusion by diverging from the central criteria of the faith of the Church." He opposed those for whom "the Kingdom of God is emptied of its full content and is understood in a rather secularist sense," as if that Kingdom were to be reached "by mere changing of structures and social and political involvement, and as being present wherever there is a certain type of involvement and activity for justice." And he particularly opposed those who "claim to show Jesus as politically committed, as one who fought against Roman oppression and the authorities, and also as one involved in the class struggle. This idea of Christ as a political figure, a revolutionary, as the subversive man from Nazareth, does not tally with the Church's catechesis."

The Pope observed that "our age is the one in which man has been most written and spoken of," yet it is also "the age of man's abasement to previously unsuspected levels, the age of human values trampled on as never before." Like Solzhenitsyn in his commencement address at Harvard the year before,[6] Pope John Paul II attributed this to "the inexorable paradox of atheistic humanism." By contrast, "the primordial affirmation of [Catholic] anthropology is that man is God's image and cannot be reduced to a mere portion of nature or a nameless element in the human city." He rejected a "strictly economic, biological, or psychological view of man," insisting instead that "the complete truth about the human being constitutes the foundation of the Church's social teaching and the basis of true liberation. In the light of this truth, man is not a being subjected to economic or political processes, these processes are instead directed to man and subjected to him." It is necessary, in short, to reject a materialist interpretation of history and to defend the primacy of the spiritual.

At this point, Pope John Paul II showed himself in consonance with the traditional political philosophies of Western civilization. Tocqueville, for example, had made a similar observation: "Every religion places the object of man's desires outside and beyond worldly

goods and naturally lifts the soul into regions far above the realm of
the senses. Every religion also imposes on each man some obligation
toward mankind, to be performed in common with the rest of mankind, and so draws him away, from time to time, from thinking about
himself."[7] Correspondingly, the Pope discerned in "human dignity a
gospel value that cannot be despised without greatly offending the
Creator," and then launched one of his two explicit condemnations of
Latin American practices:

> This dignity is infringed on the individual level when due re-
> gard is not had to values such as freedom, the right to essen-
> tial goods, to life . . . it is infringed on the social and political
> level when man cannot exercise his right of participation, or
> when he is subjected to unjust and unlawful coercion, or sub-
> mitted to physical or mental torture, etc. I am not unaware of
> how many questions are being posed in this sphere today in
> Latin America.

The Pope then turned to problems of action. The mission of the
Church, he said, "although it is religious and not social or political, cannot fail to consider man in the entirety of his being." This mission "has
as an essential part action for justice and the tasks of the advancement
of man." But the Church "does not need to have recourse to ideological systems in order to love, defend, and collaborate in the liberation
of man . . . acting in favor of brotherhood, justice, and peace, and
against all foes of domination, slavery, discrimination, violence, attacks
on religious liberty, and aggression against man, and whatever attacks
life." The Church has a commitment, like Christ's, "to the most needy.
In fidelity to this commitment, the Church wishes to stay free with regard to the competing systems, in order to opt only for man."

The Pope then went on to define liberation in a Christian way,
first positively, and then with this negative: "liberation . . . in the
framework of the Church's proper mission is not reduced to the simple and narrow economic, political, social, or cultural dimension, and
is not sacrificed to the demands of any strategy, practice, or short-term
solution." The important thing is "to safeguard the originality of
Christian liberation," and "to avoid any form of curtailment or ambiguity" which would cause the Church to "lose her fundamental meaning" and leave her open to "manipulation by ideological systems and
political parties."

In the real world, Marxism has been immobilized for decades as
the ideological internal life of totalitarian states and of parties aspiring

to that status. As an explanatory system, Marxism "explains" little. There is nothing in the Latin American system, to which the liberation theologians point, for which Marxism affords the only or the best explanation. Marxism offers no "method" either of inquiry or of action by which modern life is to be accurately understood, its future predicted, or its utopian hopes realized. Contemporary Marxist literature, as Kolakowski shows, is dogmatic, sterile, helpless, out of touch both with modern economics and with cultural life. But what Marxism does do very well today is to inspire millions with fantasies of utopian fulfillment, and blithely to identify as the roadblock to that fulfillment some malevolent other. One would wish that the works of liberation theologians were less innocent of the sophisticated criticism aimed at Marxist theory in the light of its historical praxis. Pope John Paul II has not been able to afford to be so innocent.

*   *   *

Throughout his pontificate, Pope John Paul II has elaborated on the clear-eyed account of Marxism he gave in Puebla. He has attempted to awaken theologians, to beg them to become more critical, lest they ally themselves with those bent on the creation of totalitarian processes whose consequences theologians do not allow themselves to foresee and whose dynamics they cannot control. Throughout, the Pope has insisted upon the independence and integrity of the Church. He has based himself on sound political philosophy. He has invoked a liberal conception of the transcendent status of religion with respect to politics and the state, and he has appealed to a liberal conception of the dignity of the individual person vis-à-vis such collectivist notions as class, party, and state. He speaks for the authentic interests of the poor and the oppressed, against those who would transmute their sufferings into envy, hatred, and coercion. He has refused to adopt the role of Dostoevsky's Grand Inquisitor, who offered bread in exchange for liberty. As the Pope told the bishops of southern Africa:

> The solidarity of the church with the poor, with the victims of unjust laws or unjust social and economic structures, goes without saying. But the forms in which this solidarity is realized cannot be dictated by an analysis based on class distinctions and class struggle. The church's task is to call all men and women to conversion and reconciliation, without opposing groups, without being "against" anyone. Every form of

ministry and service in the church must be an expression of
the love that is in the heart of Jesus.[8]

The Pope's aim, then, is to liberate the poor. It is worth trying to
see the difference—in the Pope's eyes—between true and false liberation in more detail. For in our bloody century, not all who have cried
"liberation! liberation!" have actually achieved it.

*   *   *

Like the liberation theologians, Pope John Paul II is opposed to
the injustices and violations of human rights *within* the traditional societies of the third world. Like them, too, he sees that the planet must
be looked at as a whole, and that its overarching *systems* must be questioned, so as to reduce injustices and inequities. Unlike them, however,
the realities of the Soviet form of Marxism remain in his mind as a
vivid warning. He is wary of "Marxist analysis." He knows two things
from personal experience. The first is that Marxist premises travel on
iron rails to Marxist conclusions. The second is that, embodied as a
system, Marxism is the very opposite of liberation.

There are reasons for this. Marxist theory is naive about the state.
Marxist theoreticians begin by "analyzing" the faults of free societies.
Their analysis prompts them to "correct" these faults by entrusting total power to the state. They do not recognize that, in practice, states
too are ruled by elites. It is precisely those new bureaucratic elites that
Pope John Paul II vividly criticizes in *Laborem Exercens* (1981), the encyclical delayed a few days before its originally scheduled release by
the assassination attempt upon his life in St. Peter's Square.[9] To say
that injustice is bred by "private ownership of the means of production" invites the illusion that injustices will cease with "state ownership
of the means of production." There is a joke in Poland about this:
"Capitalism is the exploitation of man by man; socialism is the reverse."

We have already seen (in Chapter One) that the Vatican Instruction on Liberation Theology includes a moving passage—so moving
that some, on good authority, hint that it was penned by the Pope himself—on the deceptions committed in our time in the name of liberation. Here and elsewhere, the Pope has begged liberation theologians
to become more critical—not only of capitalism, which the Pope also
criticizes—but especially of Marxism, the ways of thinking it insidi-
ously nourishes, and its historical record.

By insistently raising questions about liberation theology, the

Pope has already achieved two significant aims. First, he has alerted the faithful, inciting them not merely to accept what they hear but also to question it. Second, he has obliged liberation theologians to begin issuing clarifications. In the wake of the Vatican Instruction, most have asserted that they are *not* Marxist in the ways the Pope condemns. Some have now asserted that their fundamental purpose is not political in the ordinary sense, but *spiritual*. They are trying, they insist, to awaken the conscience of the poor, both to learn from the popular religion of the poor and to encourage the poor to *act together* in the faith: to form associations, civic groups, base communities.[10] Thus, learning to act together, the faithful can both pray together and take action to help one another in their basic needs. United, they can protest grievances, dig wells, repair local roads, improve local housing, set up clinics, and accomplish other major tasks in improving their conditions.

Indeed, in the seven years since Puebla, eleven nations of Latin America have passed from being military dictatorships to setting out upon the road to democracy. In Argentina, Brazil, Uruguay, Peru, El Salvador, Guatemala and elsewhere, liberation theologians no longer confront military rulers but elected officials, often enough of the center-left. Hugo Assmann and others assert that this new situation has forced them to shift their focus from "repression" to "oppression"— that is, from problems of political liberation to problems of economic liberation.

Democracy, of course, is no magic cure. Once the road to democracy is entered upon, there remain the same teeming millions to feed, to clothe, to teach, and to care for in illness and disease. Thus, democracy puts liberation theologians under new stress. How well do they actually speak for the poor? What role will they play under democratic institutions? To which parties will they throw their own support, and how many of the people will those parties actually represent?

For my part, I strongly welcome the new emphasis upon democracy that one begins to hear from liberation theologians. As they turn their thoughts to the hard *praxis* of making democracy work, they will have to say more and more about the institutions of democracy: the separation of powers; an independent judiciary; the roles of the loyal opposition; institutions of dissent and civil disagreement; habits of compromise and the practical adjudication of differences; freedom of the press; the separate roles of religious and civic officials; and the like. True, such questions are typically resolved in many different ways in different cultures (often even in different regions of the same country). Resolved they must be. For democracy is not an incantation. It is a *praxis*. It must be made to work.

A next step also looms. One of the conditions for the successful functioning of a new democracy is economic growth, especially for the poorest and those at the lowest rungs of the economic ladder. There are two reasons for this. Unless the large majority of the poor sees the prospect of steady improvement in its lot during its lifetime, many will become impatient with democracy. For democracy is only one part—the political part—of political economy. The economic part must also be addressed. Political liberation, while good in itself, must be completed by perceptible liberation from the onerous grinding of poverty.[11] For poverty is a kind of imprisonment. Without material goods, citizens find their liberties of action seriously constrained. Economic liberation and political liberation must proceed together.

Economic growth is necessary for a second reason. When there is economic growth, each citizen can compare where he or she is today both with improvements already experienced, and with those still hoped for. For democracy to work, perfect egalitarianism is not necessary. Most citizens know that individuals differ in talent, desire, effort, application, lifetime goals, tastes, luck, psychology and personality. Thus, Pope Leo XIII wrote in 1891:

> Let it be laid down, in the first place, that humanity must remain as it is. It is impossible to reduce human society to a level. The *Socialists* may do their utmost, but all striving against nature is vain. There naturally exists among mankind innumerable differences of the most important kind; people differ in capability, in diligence, in health, and in strength; and unequal fortune is a necessary result of inequality in condition. Such inequality is far from being disadvantageous either to individuals or to the community; social and public life can only go on by the help of various kinds of capacity and the playing of many parts, and each man, as a rule, chooses the part which peculiarly suits his case.[12]

What citizens have in common is the desire in each to achieve personal progress—to be better off today than one was yesterday, better off tomorrow than one is today. When a large majority experiences such satisfaction, a democracy attains not only a certain stability but a widespread sense of mutual cooperation and goodwill. Thus Tocqueville noted how in the infant American Republic the citizens, individually prospering in their goals, developed a visible, tangible love both for the Republic and for their fellow citizens.[13]

Where there is no improvement, however, citizens can only compare their present lot with the lot of others. Once awakened, the fierce fire of envy destroys democracies. Democratic living and civic virtue then grow faint and deathly ill. Moved by passions of envy, citizens see no alternative except to conspire to control the state as a means of aggrandizing themselves.[14] In such a case, the republic collapses into the war of all against all. The point is that a thriving democracy depends upon a cooperative way of living. One of its hidden and least understood laws is that all must find in it improvement in their own material conditions. Only when all share in the fruit of economic betterment is love for the commonweal awakened in all.

In a crucial sense, then, a democracy must base its hopes for survival upon economic growth—not just any sort of economic growth but economic growth personally experienced in the lives of the vast majority. The task for liberation theologians, therefore, is to imagine those techniques of economic growth compatible with their avowed purposes of liberating the poor from crushing poverty. How can that be done?

Obviously, I have reached my own considered views about how that might be done, at least in the context of the United States. Today, however, the world offers the panorama of some 165 different experiments in political economy. There are many models to study. One can study what has worked—and what has miserably failed. In the end, the issue is empirical. Whatever one's grandiose dreams, reality is a harsh teacher. From some experiments, results emerge that are *worse*, not better. Consider the sad man-made fates of Tanzania, Ethiopia, Uganda—indeed of most of African agriculture.[15] Yet in many countries during the same decades—India, for example—the threat of starvation has given way not only to self-sufficiency in food, but to net earnings from food exports.[16]

One need not be "ideological" about how to produce economic success. The important point is to produce it. For the safeguarding of democracy, economic growth from the bottom up is a *sine qua non*. In this sense, there is a theological imperative to imitate the Creator, in whose image we are made—to create what does not yet exist.

Here, too, Pope John Paul II has anticipated the argument. In *Laborem Exercens*, his encyclical on human work—a lively topic in debates in Poland between Catholics and Marxists—issued as part of that great line of papal encyclicals marking the anniversary of Leo XIII's *Rerum Novarum* (1891), the Pope chose as his structural metaphor the creation story of Genesis.[17] Work is a sharing in the creative activity of the Creator. It has its objective dimension insofar as it changes the world. It has its subjective dimension insofar as it springs from the creative intelligence and will of the worker. All of history is "the great work-bench," at which human beings exert their labor to imagine and to build a better world. Considering the *subject* of work, the worker, one must note that a "better" world means a world with greater room for liberty. Behind liberation theology, therefore, entwined with it, comes "creation theology." The two go hand in hand, liberty and creativity.

How to build institutions that encourage more of both is the structural, political, and economic task we all face. A few remarks on creation theology now seem apposite.

Five

CREATION THEOLOGY
IN LATIN AMERICA*

All of these [manufactured goods] are given or sold to us ready-made. Everything that we are and will be is given to us because we do not control our own lives. We move along indifferently without even a plan against the essential immorality that tolerates this paralysis of creativity.

Latin American societies do not encourage new ideas. We are unconcerned with the task of changing the world in which we live. We do not allow for our own creativity. It would be wrong to suggest that we live in backward societies that despise changes, since we are so pleased to notice them when they occur. We are simply reluctant to initiate those changes on our own.

Our poor revolutionaries have never gone more than skin-deep in their analysis of social evils. They stir up bloody revolutions in order to change unjust situations. They do not understand that in these modern times the most profound revolutions take place not in barracks or in the mountains, but in the laboratories and in the offices of the most daring intelligentsia.[1]—*Carlos Alberto Montaner*

Poor ideas, Cardinal Newman once said, can be driven out solely by the power of a stronger idea. The central idea Pope John Paul II turns to for comprehending the development of peoples is the story of cre-

---

*An earlier version of this chapter was delivered in the form of two lectures, delivered both in Brazil and in Argentina during 1985.

ation.[2] This is the appropriate story. In my own lectures in Latin America, I have found it quite powerful and intend in this and the following chapters to explore some of its implications.

All around the world today, there is a "Great Awakening." Everywhere the people cry out for two liberations: from tyranny; from poverty. Human beings rightly demand the systemic, routine fulfillment of these two desires. In effect, they are demanding "the system of natural liberty": that liberty that frees them from tyranny, and makes them participants in political activism; and that other liberty that frees them from poverty, and makes them participants in economic activism.

The dream of a *liberating, creating, inventive* political economy is now universal.

In this chapter, we concentrate our attention, not on the universality of this dream, but upon its embodiment in present-day Latin America. In natural beauty and in natural endowment this great continent came from the hand of the Creator as one of the most richly gifted in all the world. Here are great rivers, great rain forests, great seaports, great endowments of minerals and almost every sort of natural resource. Here are great farmlands and ranches. When God created Latin America, it must have given him great satisfaction. He saw it, and saw that "It was good" (Gen 1:12).

What, then, is the prognosis for the future? Only 25 years from today—in the year 2010—what shall we see in Latin America? We shall see what the generation of the now living makes of its great gifts. How creative will this generation be?

1. THE POWER OF CREATIVITY

Consider the nations of the East Asia Rim (notably South Korea, Taiwan, Singapore, Hong Kong, but also Japan and others). At the end of World War II these nations were among the poorest, most devastated and seemingly resourceless nations on the planet. Within twenty-five years, they had multiplied their national wealth many times over, raised up most of their poor, and become economic leaders of the world. By 1985, their standard of living was coming to rival that of Southern Europe. In the next fifteen years, some predict, their standard of living will be higher than that of Northern Europe.

The lessons to be learned from East Asia are two. First, rapid and broad economic development is still possible on this earth, even within a single generation. Second, the cause of the wealth of nations is not natural resources. If natural resources were the cause of the wealth of nations, Japan and the other nations of the East Asia Rim would be poor; their natural resources are few. The cause of wealth is the human wit and human discipline through which peoples organize themselves for communal, associative *creativity*.

Part of the great inheritance of Latin America is its long and profound acculturation in the traditions of Judaism and Christianity. These great world religions teach that every single human being is "made in the image of God, the Creator." Every human being is an original source of creativity. In each, there is a spark of the Creator.

This spark is the primary cause of economic and political development. From human wit and human discipline come cooperation, invention, and sustained activism. Human wit and human discipline are the primary "capital" of the human race. The cause of economic development lies coiled within the human spirit. Despite the teachings of certain philosophers of Scotland and London, despite Karl Marx, labor is not the source of economic value. The source of economic value is human intellect.

If labor were the sole source of value, why would there be unemployment? Why would companies not seek to hire more and more laborers, rather than invest in labor-saving machinery? Marx was never able to cite evidence for his theory.[3] Böhm-Bawerk demolished it nearly a century ago.[4] Most socialists today have abandoned it.[5] Human wit creates employment through inventing goods and services never seen before. The labor theory of value is a fundamental error in Marx. It is a serious economic error. Worse, it is a profound error about the human spirit.

As in the case of oil, everything we today call a "resource" was invented by human wit. Until human wit works upon them, the givens of nature have no use. Economic value comes from human creativity.

That is why I speak about "creation theology," rather than "liberation theology." It is true that the primary aim of creation theology is to liberate human beings from tyranny and from poverty. But the means for doing so is not destruction; the means is creation. First to be created are institutions that encourage human beings to act as true images of God: to become creative in a routine and regular way. For creativity is a social achievement. It must be achieved by a whole society acting together. It is not the fruit of one person alone. Without a supportive society, even the greatest genius is frustrated. A whole society must be organized to favor creativity.

Consider the transformation of material conditions on this planet since the year 1800. Almost everywhere, literacy and education are rising, the average age at death has risen to about 60 worldwide (58 in the LDCs, 63 in Brazil), and slow but steady (and in some cases rapid and spectacular) progress is being made.[6] What can we expect in another 185 years? One can anticipate, at the very least, similarly sustained progress. Even in the next 25 years—by the year 2010—one can anticipate new nations joining those of the East Asia Rim. China itself, adopting new ideas in economics, has almost doubled its food output in two short years. India, ten years ago regarded as in danger of famine in 1984, has been for three years a net exporter of food. Oppressive limits upon the human race lie less in nature than in heavy-handed institutions that repress the creativity of the human spirit. These it is in our power to change.

It is distinctive of Judaism and Christianity among the world's great religions that they teach us that each human being is a creator— and that it is the vocation of every Jew and every Christian, not merely to accept the world, but to change it: to unlock the secrets hidden by the Creator in every human breast and in every aspect of nature.

Who would have expected that in ordinary sand is hidden silicon, and that in a single chip of silicon no bigger than a fingernail, millions of bits of information could be stored, as in today's computers and electronic word processors? We are living through a revolution greater than the mechanical wizardry that lay at the heart of the Industrial Revolution. The typewriter was mechanical. The word processor is electronic. Spirit and matter ever more closely interpenetrate. The old boundaries are collapsing. The bases of production—and, above all, the bases of human communication—are being transformed before our very eyes. This earth is being re-created anew.

The political world, too, is changing, although less rapidly. Democracy seems again to be on the rise. Ninety percent of the population of Latin America now lives again under the beginnings of democratic governance.

Yet democracy itself is only half the vision of a genuinely creative and free political economy. Democracy is indispensable to a free people, governing themselves through their own consent. But democracy alone is not sufficient, if it cannot find the means whereby even the lowliest of its citizens can better his or her condition. Part of the promise of political economy is not only to liberate human beings from arbitrary tyranny, but also to liberate human beings from poverty. Political economy has two sides: democracy and economic growth.

The success of democracy, in fact, depends upon economic growth. A democracy must create new wealth that did not exist before, new wealth for all to share. Democracy must be creative, or it will come to be rejected (much to the loss of its citizens). Above all, democracy must liberate the creative energies of all its people.

In Latin America, the secrets of democracy seem to be well understood, and the ideal of democracy has flourished there much longer than in most parts of the world.[7] Through trial and error, Latin Americans keep returning to democracy. Through hard experience, Latin Americans seem to insist upon the observation of Winston Churchill: Democracy is a poor form of government, only all other forms are worse.

Still, the other half of the secret of political economy is less well assimilated. Successful in democracy, Latin Americans do not so easily organize their societies to liberate the economic creativity of their talented and enthusiastic citizens. Latin Americans are very open to change. Latin Americans respond quickly and well to new inventions, new technologies, new processes. The people of Latin America are not closed, but open. Still, on the whole, Latin Americans are content to allow *other* peoples to do the inventing, and to be the creative ones. Meanwhile, they themselves are, on the whole, content to be the recipients of the creativity of others. Carlos Alberto Montaner again:

> Latin American societies do not encourage new ideas. We are unconcerned with the task of changing the world in which we live. We do not allow for our own creativity. It would be wrong to suggest that we live in backward societies that despise changes, since we are so pleased to notice them when they occur. We are simply reluctant to initiate those changes on our own.[8]

This situation is bound to change.

If these observations are fair—not in every detail, but in the round—then the task of a theology of creation in Latin America is vast indeed—and immensely hopeful. For among the peoples of the world, Latin Americans are far from being the poorest, the least developed, the least endowed by nature. If during the next 25 years, Latin America should also liberate the creative energies of its 406 million citizens, what an extraordinary period of creativity the world will see. Millions of Latin America's brightest youngsters are now superbly educated and well-prepared for their responsibilities. Heirs of a great Jewish-Christian tradition, they already sense their profound vocation to be inventors, creators, and makers of new things in new ways.

I do not doubt that the problems are severe. Today, 37 percent of Brazil's population is under 15 years of age. The situation is comparable throughout Latin America. This means that some 70 million new jobs will have to be created between now and 1999, just to find employment for those children who have already been born. These jobs will scarcely be found in traditional agriculture. They cannot be supplied by multinational corporations. Throughout Latin America, there will have to be an explosion of entrepreneurship—the creation of ten or twenty million new small businesses, each employing 3–10 new workers. Such creativity is possible; the ways to achieve it are known, but the task is difficult.

What must be done to put a theology of creation into practice? In any one nation, it is not for outsiders to say. Every nation, every people, and even every individual becomes a creator in a unique way. The Japanese do not do so as the French, the Italians, the Germans, or the British do. The concept of the creative economy is an analogous concept, not a univocal one. Each society is creative in its own way. The ways of creativity are pluralistic; they are adapted to the ways in which one culture differs from another in our diverse human family. One of the advantages of a free economy is that it is pluralistic in its possibilities.

As the ancient philosophers saw, there are always in this world tendencies toward "the one," and other powerful tendencies toward "the many." Many elements in the contemporary world make each of us more like the others. Science, technology, communications, and many modern products exert homogenizing influences. The laws of electricity in Peking work as they do in Buenos Aires and Rio de Janeiro and St. Louis. Refrigerators, autos, toasters, and television are similar around the world. Yet this superficial homogeneity of technological culture allows ever greater room for the exploration of the differences which make each culture unique. "Human capital"—the resource of creativity within every human being—is always unique and irrepeatable. The Japanese way, brilliant for the Japanese, is not that of the United States. And each person (the point cannot be often enough stressed) is an original; no other was made by God exactly like him or her.

Any political economy which wishes to incite the creative energy of every one of its citizens must recognize that the vast majority of economic activists must of necessity start small and in their local environment. The wealth of nations does not "trickle down" from the heights. It wells up from millions of small entrepreneurs at the base—in, so to speak, base communities. Economic activities are always social, or, as I prefer to say for more exact accuracy, *associative*. Every small business is an associative activity. Even if a person works alone, it is also with suppliers and with customers. Economic activity is always associative. A nation in search of creativity must, therefore, empower millions of small associations at its base. Wealth wells up from the inventiveness, activism, and creativity of millions of small producers and entrepreneurs.

Economic talent is as valuable to any society as is talent in music, in fiction, in dancing, or in any of the other arts. The commercial arts are not inferior to the liberal arts. For the commercial arts are also liberating. They liberate many from poverty. They succeed by good service to others. The networks of commerce are social: they knit together and give substance to a necessary part of the common good.

In a practical way, therefore, every nation which wishes to meet the desires of its people for liberation from tyranny and liberation from poverty must do all it can to enable every one of its citizens to become an economic activist. It must become easy for every ordinary citizen to start a business. Incentives must favor creativity. The virtues of sound, honest work and good service must be embodied in daily practice—as a judicious system of rewards will ensure. There must be institutions of credit specializing in the small loans that ordinary citizens require to form a creative business. Bankruptcy laws must respect the fact that many small businesses fail—and those who do fail must recognize that they can learn from failures and come back to try again and again. A high failure rate is, ironically, an index of superior creativity.

Is it not true that among many persons, not least those of aristocratic culture and religious dispositions, economic activism is looked-down upon in comparison to political activism, moral activism, and artistic activism? Such an attitude, where it exists, is its own punishment. For God bestowed on millions of human beings immense economic talents. He gave such talents to many among the poorest, even more than among the children of the already rich. To allow those talents to develop to their fullest is tremendously to enrich the common good of all.

At this point, I should add a note about what my message is *not*. It is not about *laissez-faire*. It is not about free enterprise alone. On the contrary, commerce and industry can blossom only where law and a common universal morality are observed. As their source lies in the human spirit, so they must obey the laws of the human spirit, or they will perish. Democracy depends upon the rule of law. All must abide by that law. But, in addition, economic activities can prosper only under a system of reliable and well-respected law, and only where the moral law is obeyed. For economic activities in a free society are free, voluntary, mutual. They depend upon the free cooperation of many, upon trust swiftly arrived at, and upon mutual reliability. The more lawlike and moral a people, the less costly its economic life. Every human vice and failing injures sound economic activity.

In a word, liberty entails a strong sense of community. Cooperation must be freely yielded. And without free cooperation economic activism is necessarily frustrated. Liberty is a social virtue, a virtue of communities; it is not an individualistic virtue. A civilization of egotists, a "me-generation," sins against community, cooperation, and teamwork—and hence against the fabric of a creative and free political economy.

Every society which stimulates and rewards the creative spirit of all its citizens, especially among the poorest, reaps a bountiful harvest. It will become a creative society. And, in this sense, it will be a more lively and inventive society ten years from now than it is today—and yet more lively and inventive twenty-five years hence.

In *Underdevelopment Is a State of Mind*[9] Lawrence E. Harrison argues that the single most determining factor in economic development is the human factor: the factor of culture. At root, this means that the way a people thinks about itself and about the world—and the way it organizes itself—is decisive.

Suppose that a culture, tutored in its innermost heart by Judaism and Christianity, holds that every human person, made in the image of the Creator, has as his or her human vocation the call to become a co-creator with God, unlocking the secrets which God has hidden in his creation, and inventing new goods and services for the betterment of human kind. Suppose, in short, that a culture organizes itself for creativity. How will it do so?

In general, there are two ways: through institutions and through transmittable, teachable virtues.

2. THE INSTITUTIONS OF CREATIVITY

Human beings live in institutions as fish swim in the sea. Human beings are institutional animals. In fact, the metaphor must be stronger: Human beings not only live in institutions as fish swim in the sea; rather, institutions live in humans and form the human soul. Clearly, the institution of language enters into our souls, guiding the way we perceive reality itself. Each human language is different from every other. Typically, persons of one language perceive the world quite differently from those of another. Alas, my knowledge of Spanish and Portuguese is rudimentary. But my experience of Italian, French, and German teaches me that a remarkably different way of "seeing" and "thinking" is inherent in the traditions of these three languages. So also is it for English. The Italian language goes softly, often by indirection, and by remarkably frequent use of the feminine gender; French is splendid for aphorisms, for abstractions (*liberté, égalité, fraternité*), and for clear and distinct ideas. German is excellent for heaping up modifications, qualifications, distinctions, and comparisons. English tends often to be blunt, concrete, and physical (*slam, crack, bang*).

The case is much the same for other institutions. The institutions of the Roman Catholic Church seep into the soul in a way very different from the institutions of the Protestant churches—not only in rituals and liturgies and vestments, but also in the lines of authority and in the place given individual conscience.

So also with the national sports which peoples play. *Soccer* is a game of the feet, as *baseball* is a game of the hands; and the rules of the team and of the individual are quite different in those two games. Even the role of law is different in each. Baseball gives instruction in the American way of life: its checks and balances, its respect for law, its singling out of every individual and its emphasis upon the cumulative play of the entire team. Whoever would understand America must understand baseball. (And football and basketball—our other two "national" games.)

It goes without saying that political institutions—the ways in which peoples organize themselves for self-government—not only spring from differing habits and perceptions, but reinforce quite different habits and perceptions. So, also, the different ways in which different cultures organize themselves for economic activities deeply affect the psyches, habits, desires, incentives, dreams, and the morale of peoples.

All around the world today, as we have seen, the peoples of the world seem to want (1) democracy and (2) development. All the families in Latin America, especially the poor, wish to "better their condition." And yet a question remains unanswered. If the goal is democracy and development, is the gate to that goal narrow? When a culture demands democracy and development as the end, must that culture adapt itself to the necessary institutional means toward that goal? It seems unlikely that any culture can achieve a particular goal without disciplining itself to the ways of seeing and acting that make that goal realizable in fact. Democracy and development are moral goals. They impose a new morality necessary to their achievement.

On the side of democracy, it is by now universally clear that a truly democratic regime can be achieved only through the achievement of certain clearly specified institutions. There must be elections. There must be free political parties. There must be a separation of powers: executive, legislative, and judicial. There must be institutions of human rights: trial by jury, *habeas corpus*, and the rest. And there must be a separation of systems: the political system must be separated from powers over conscience, information, and ideas—that is, from the institutions of conscience (such as the churches), from the institutions of information (such as the press), and from the institutions of ideas (such as the universities, publishing houses, and free associations of poets, writers, artists, and other citizens).

Why is democracy necessary? Because every human being sometimes sins. No one person (or class) can be trusted with too much power. The various forms of human power must be divided, and held in check-and-balance. The moral root of this necessity is the fact of human sinfulness. No human being is always saintly. And even saints cannot be trusted with total power.

Behind this idea lies the insight of Montaigne: Human beings are sometimes cruel.[10] Human beings need protection from our own cruelty. Each of us has reason to fear that we cannot bear too much torture. We have reason to fear for our conscience under torture. We have reason to protect ourselves from all potential torturers. The root of the desire for liberation from tyranny lies in our justified abhorrence of power in the hands of potential torturers.

On the left, it sometimes used to be said that democracy is a "bourgeois illusion." Now, even among Marxists (outside Marxist nations, at least), this view has all but disappeared. Those who have known the yoke of tyrants and dictators cannot plausibly hold that protection against tyrants is an illusion. The cruelty of tyrants is, sadly, no illusion. In the twentieth century we have seen almost unimaginable cruelty. Thus, the intellectual foundation of democracy is quite secure. Virtually all persons everywhere seek the indispensable protection of their God-given and inalienable rights. These protections seem to be nowhere available except in the institutions of democracy.

Less secure, however, is universal recognition of which institutions actually lead to economic development. Liberty from tyranny is in some ways easier to achieve than liberation from poverty. Yet, in order to win the love of all citizens, democracies must show themselves to be capable of producing economic development. Not only that. They must produce "opportunity societies"—societies in which every family has the opportunity "to better its condition," that is, to rise out of poverty. Democracy without broad development and universal opportunity for every single family cannot endure.

The dream of a good society is not only a dream of political liberation. It is a dream of *economic* liberation, too. That is why the most significant revolution of the modern era was first described as "political *economy*." This means advancement on two fronts at once: a society must forge ahead both in politics and in economics. The single most important modern discovery is that entire peoples *can* do something about their immemorial poverty. Poverty can be eliminated. Put positively: Every people on this planet can produce new wealth in a sustained and systematic way, until a solid material base is placed under every single person. If sufficient new wealth can be created, there is no reason for poverty. Every human being can be liberated from poverty. Democracy alone is a great good. To be fully successful in the second liberation that the peoples of the world desire, however, democracy must be paired with a dynamic, creative economy.

I recognize that, in much of Latin America, the word "capitalism" is always used pejoratively. Marxists certainly describe it so. But, significantly, so also do many traditionalists, of the pre-capitalist worldview. Often, clergymen, whose traditions are pre-capitalist, are opposed to capitalism. So are most literary traditions, whose roots are pre-capitalist. Therefore, I will not insist on the word "capitalist." Some may prefer to call the economic institutions to which I am pointing "the creative, dynamic, social market economy." The *word* is not significant. What is significant is the *reality*—that is, the creative set of institutions which do, in a regular and predictable manner, produce development from the bottom of society upwards.

In Latin America today, I do not see a single capitalist economy. In virtually every state of South America and Central America, the state plays a disproportionately weighty role, much as it did in pre-capitalist Great Britain, before Adam Smith. Often, the banks are nationalized, as are many, if not most, of the major corporations. Often, half or more of all citizens receive the major part of their income directly from the state. Often, the two most powerful classes are the landholders and the military. Relatively speaking, the middle class is small. Economies seem to be organized from the top down. The small-business sector, which ought to be the largest and most dynamic sector, is relatively small and powerless.

I hope these observations are accurate and fair. I am trying to speak descriptively, avoiding judgment. Moreover, fairness requires mention of how much immense progress has been made since, say,

1945 or even 1960. Seldom in history have nations made as much progress as Latin America has during the past forty years in raising the gross national product, moving millions upward into the middle class, increasing the numbers of youths with university degrees, expanding secondary school enrollments, raising literacy levels, lengthening the average lifetimes of its citizens, bringing down infant mortality, and the like.[11] Present difficulties often blind human beings to the tremendous achievements of the generations of their parents and their grandparents. It is always wrong to be ungrateful.

Yet it is a sign of realism and of courage to face tasks still to be done. One senses this realism and this courage all over Latin America. But the overwhelming facts of poverty, unemployment, underemployment, the lack of universal education, immense housing shortages and the rest oblige realists to concentrate upon institutions of economic development. The first principle I mean to stress (through repetition) is that those who seek to generate broad dynamic growth must begin at the bottom. One must empower people, especially among the poorest.

Liberation theologians often assert that the early success of capitalist economies was based upon "exploitation." As evidence, they invoke the mythical Marxist concept of "surplus value." They entirely overlook three features of the immense transformation introduced by the new ideas of democratic capitalist liberation beginning about A.D. 1780. The first important fact is that the explosion of capitalist dynamism welled up from the bottom, in the new economic arrangements of many small farms and many small enterprises. The second is that many of the early capitalists arose from the lower classes, from among the poor. The third is that the motor force of capitalist liberation is not so much "capital" (i.e., financial resources) as the imagination and daring of a new type of economic activist: the entrepreneur. Too many economists in the West neglect this point, as Israel M. Kirzner has pointed out.[12] The spirit of capitalism is preeminently the spirit of enterprise: the imagination to conceive of new products, new services, and new methods, and the practical wisdom to achieve successfully what at first seemed impossible. The center of the capitalist spirit lies in the creative imagination. Capitalism is the mind-centered system, and its social base lies in a legal structure that liberates human imagination and human praxis in the economic sphere.

Before the birth of the capitalist spirit, nations such as the United States, Great Britain, the Netherlands, Sweden and France had social structures rather like those of Latin American nations today: a sharp division between feudal classes such as the nobility and the peasants, strict controls over virtually every aspect of economic life imposed by the state and its extensive bureaucratic apparatus, and a more or less "organic" conception of the corporate nature of social life. The role of the individual was constrained in all spheres, but perhaps more in the economic sphere than in any other. It was against such historical realities that the capitalist spirit burst into history as new, revolutionary, and threatening to established orders. Among books to consult upon this background, I have found most useful Joseph Schumpeter's *History of Economic Analysis; A History of Economic Doctrines* by Charles Gide and Charles Rist; Henry William Spiegel's *The Growth of Economic Thought;* Max Weber's *General Economic History;* and Barry W. Poulson's *Economic History of the United States.*[13] It may be useful here to recollect several examples of capitalist creativity, some from the past, some from the recent present. The Swedish economist Sven Rydenfelt contrasts these cases with fifteen stories of "socialist failure," particularly in agriculture and in the continued oppression of peasants. But here we may follow only the first side of his argument.[14]

Why were inventiveness and creativity released precisely at the end of the eighteenth century? And why first in England? The Swedish economist Eli F. Heckscher answers as follows:

> The difference was not due to the fact that England had been the industrial pioneer, since France had been more of a pioneer than England during the 17th century. Neither was it due—at least not primarily—to the fact that England had coal and iron ore, since the most fundamental revolution was in the cotton industry. Not a single pound of raw cotton was produced in England.
>
> Neither was the cause a greater interest in industrial techniques in England than in France—rather the opposite was true. In [France] a stream of State regulations with hundreds of legal paragraphs were issued to control the various branches of industry, especially the textile industry; it was a stream unequaled in England. A whole hierarchy of civil servants was created in France to supervise the observance of the regulations. The French guilds were engaged in the same task, while England scarcely had any civil servants designated for this, or, indeed, for any other duties. The printed calicoes, for instance, may have cost 16,000 lives; certainly the number that was made galley slaves for illegal importation was much greater than that.
>
> And so these very measures prevented French trade and industries from utilizing any number of possibilities that were

beginning to present themselves. In other words, government regulation [in France] froze the existing state of affairs.[15]

During the fifty years from 1781 to 1833 the use of raw cotton increased by 48 times in England. During the ninety years from 1823 to 1913, the production of pig-iron increased by 48 times, the production of coal by 77 times.[16] The British historian Paul Johnson describes this breakthrough:

Prior to the eighteenth century it was rare for even the most advanced economies, those of England and Holland, to achieve one percent growth in any year. Beginning in the 1780s, England achieved a then-unprecedented annual growth rate of two percent. By the end of the decade a rate of four percent had been attained—a rate which was to be sustained for the next 50 years.

During the nineteenth century Britain increased the size of its work force by 400 percent. Real wages doubled during the period 1800–1850, and doubled again from 1850 to 1900. This meant there was a 1600 percent increase in the production and consumption of wage goods during the century. Nothing like this had happened anywhere before in the whole of history.[17]

The capitalist transformation occurred primarily in agriculture, among peasants. In 1800, Sweden was a backward country at the far corner of Europe, ninety percent of whose workers labored in agriculture. An ancient village system, collectivist and traditional, paralyzed the Swedish countryside. Following the British idea of the freehold and peasant rights of ownership, Sweden instituted land reforms liberating individual farmers. Almost immediately, individual farmers broke free from the tyranny of conservative collectivist majorities. Creative powers were unleashed. New lands were suddenly brought under cultivation—jumping from 1.5 million hectares in 1805 to 3.2 million in 1865. New methods of cultivation and breeding came into being, and the more daring experimented with new crops and new animals. In the agricultural province of Shane, land under cultivation leapt from 15 percent to 50 percent within the century. By 1980, only 3 or 4 percent of the labor force worked in agriculture, producing far more food than Sweden needed, although Sweden's climate and soils are not by any means among the most favored by nature.[18]

"Nowhere else in history is it possible to find a period of such unlimited economic liberty and optimum entrepreneurial environment" as in the infant United States in the generations following 1783, a Swedish economist writes.[19] During the two centuries 1775–1975, the population of the U.S. increased by 68 times, a population explosion unprecedented in history, yet "enterprise, liberated from its bonds, could create jobs for all these people, jobs that paid the highest wages in the world."[20]

In Japan, following World War II, the economic situation could hardly have been more bleak, as Professor Reischauer recounts:

> The war left Japan a thoroughly devastated and demoralized land. . . . Approximately half of the urban housing of Japan had been burned to the ground by American air raids. Tokyo's population had shrunk by more than a half, Osaka's by almost two-thirds. With the destruction of the cities and the virtual disappearance of the merchant marine, which had maintained the flow of Japan's economic lifeblood, industrial production had plummeted, standing in 1946 at a mere seventh of the 1941 figure. The people were clothed in rags, ill-fed, and both physically and emotionally exhausted.[21]

Welcoming the American system of economic liberation, which had already been foreshadowed in the Meiji reforms of the 1860s—with their particular emphasis upon education as the central form of capital, *human* capital—the Japanese rose from the ashes to be ranked thirtieth among all nations in gross national product by 1955. By 1968, the Japanese, possessing virtually no natural resources and representing one of the most densely populated living spaces on the planet, had climbed to second.

In war-ravaged Germany, overwhelmed with eight million homeless refugees, German factories had been stripped of machinery by their conquerors. Thus, manufacturing production in 1948 measured 50 percent of its volume in 1939. Nonetheless, beginning with antiquated machinery, but led by the creative enterprise unleashed by Minister of Finance Ludwig Erhard, manufacturing production soared in three years to 130 percent of what had been produced in 1939. By 1960, unemployment had been reduced to 1 percent, while the number of employed workers rose from 14 million in 1950 to 21 million. Soon 4.5 million foreign workers had to be imported to fill the jobs created by entrepreneurial energy. Total American aid between

1945–1953 amounted to $3.5 billion, only a tiny fraction of the new capital created and reinvested.[22]

Marx had written that capitalists "steal" wealth from laborers. Yet in capitalist countries not only did the wages of workers rise to historically unprecedented heights, but many who began as workers launched enterprises of their own. Marx had predicted that the processes of capitalist production—which he failed to understand—would inexorably "immiserate" the workers. Quite the opposite happened. The myths that Marx purveyed as "science" were one by one refuted by history.[23] Marx had overlooked the role of enterprise and the powers of creativity. Missing those, he missed the essential point.

The heart of the capitalist idea is to begin *at the bottom,* by releasing the economic creativity of the poor. Several nations of the East Asian rim—Hong Kong, Singapore, Taiwan, and South Korea—observed the lessons to be learned from the Fabian socialism of India and from Communist socialism in China and North Korea. They also observed Japan. Like Japan, they had suffered in the war. They had extremely low standards of living. They had virtually no natural resources. Their populations, already large, were growing rapidly. Per capita income in Taiwan in 1945 was an incredibly low $70.[24] By 1980, it had reached $2,280. The real GNP of Taiwan doubled every seven years—in 1980, it was *eleven* times greater than in 1952. Destitution is gone, and Taiwan's income distribution is among the most equal in the world. The case is similar in South Korea, racked not only by severe Japanese repression during World War II but suffering horribly during the long Korean war of 1949–53. In 1962, per capita income was $87. Twenty years later, it was $1,600. The average increase in real wages exceeded 7 percent per year during the same twenty years.[25]

*   *   *

It is a curious fact that liberation theologians should speak often of freedom—but not of economic freedom. Yet for most peasants and most poor persons the major part of their human activities consists of economic activities. Is this portion of their lives not also worthy of freedom? This fact is even more curious, when one sees that the essential requirement for liberation from poverty is the liberation of economic activism, economic imagination, and economic inventiveness. If one wishes to double the income of the poor, then double it again, and again, and again, the path of doing so has by now become well-traveled.

Economic creativity, like every other form of creativity, is nourished by conditions of liberty. Governments that try to control every aspect of economic activities end by paralyzing them. The suppression of the economic liberties of poor persons prolongs their poverty, offends their dignity, and suffocates their creativity. In this respect, creation theology speaks for the liberation of the poor in a way liberation theology does not.

I speak here as a theologian who tries to study the needs of peoples for economic development; I do not speak as an economist. Still, in the rising wealth of the United States after 1776, as in the capital creation of Great Britain after the advent of capitalism (which for convenience may be dated with the appearance of Adam Smith's book, *An Inquiry Into the Nature and Causes of the Wealth of Nations* in 1776), the facts oblige one to note the crucial importance of the multiplicity of small farms and small businesses at the base of society, generations before the appearance of the large corporations.

Today, too, small business is crucial in the United States. From 1970, when the number of employed persons stood at 79 million, to the end of 1985, the U.S. created 29 million new jobs for a total of 108 million. During this period, employment in the large corporations and in government at all levels (local, state, and federal) was nearly static. About eighty percent of these 29 million new jobs were created by small businesses. One cannot emphasize too much the importance of creating millions of new small businesses. Each small business raises up not only one family, but typically one or more other employees as well. Any people seeking to create new jobs must establish as creative an environment as possible for the launching of thousands upon thousands of small businesses.

The second principle I wish to stress, therefore, is the need to support the small business sector, the local entrepreneur. This support must first be moral. A society must honor its entrepreneurs as it honors all its creative people—in the arts, in diplomacy, in journalism, in the law, or in any other profession. Entrepreneurs are creative. They know the existentialist's anguish in decision, risk, liberty, possible failure, and creative success. They, too, practice a high human art. A society which seeks to employ many millions of the unemployed and the underemployed ought to encourage many such artists of the economy.

But such persons need more than cultural acclaim and moral support. They are the builders of the future. In order to build, they need access to credit. The banking industry must favor people at the bottom, even from among the poorest, in order to help them to get started. A peasant in a remote village needs credit in order to purchase a truck, so that he may bring his neighbors' produce to market. Those active in establishing markets need credits to finance their civilizing, peaceful, lawlike and productive activities, without which no economy can function. Business must be regarded as a high human vocation, the vocation of co-creators who help to build an associative, free, voluntary society.

In addition, small business needs relief from punitive taxation. On one island in the Caribbean, a tax rate of 60 percent begins at under $2,000 of earned income. At such rates, who has any incentive to extend his activities? The extension of economic activism at those rates is punitively expensive. Moreover, there is a sharp distinction, terribly real, between high tax *rates* and high tax *revenues* actually obtained by governments. When tax *rates* are too high, actual *revenue* declines. A government can *lower* tax rates in order to receive *higher* actual revenues. The incentive effects of taxes must always be carefully studied, in any society which attempts to promote creative economic activists. Economic activists are not irrational. When they are punished for success, they avoid success. When they are rewarded for success, they act more creatively. The principle, then, is to maximize economic activity by adjusting tax rates so as to favor it, not so as to punish it. What a society rewards, it obtains in abundance. What it punishes, it discourages.

Latin Americans, perhaps, would benefit by studying the schemes of reward and punishment—through credits and through taxes—used in Japan, Taiwan, South Korea, Singapore, and other states. In fact, wherever nations have succeeded in making their societies more economically creative, their example is worth studying. Economics is a science and an art concerned with reality, not with words or promises. One must always study what works, rather than utopian schemes which raise no grain and feed no hungry ones.

Why does a theologian speak of tax policy? Because tax policy extends the reach of the state into every family and into the creative activities of every human person. Next to the military power and the police power, the greatest power granted to limited governments is the power to tax. This power must be used creatively and to promote creativity, not punitively and to repress creativity, if any society is to fulfill the mandate of building a people made in the image of the Creator.

So much for a few considerations about the *institutions* required for a creative political economy. Let us turn now to the *virtues* required.

3. THE VIRTUES OF A CREATIVE SOCIETY

Most philosophers and theologians ignore the high virtues required by a political economy aimed at liberating its people both from tyranny and from poverty. This is a great mistake. The liberation of peoples from tyranny and from poverty is primarily a moral task. As the French poet Charles Peguy once wrote upon a sign hung on his doorway: "The revolution is moral or not at all."

The virtues required for a creative political economy, however, are not the virtues required by a traditionalist society.[26] The great discovery of the modern era is that human beings are not merely helpless and passive in the face of politics and economics. On the contrary, they can shape the polity and the economy under which they will live. They can make their own political economy. In a sense, this is their greatest work of art: the construction of the system of polity and economy under which they will live.

In traditionalist societies, the highest virtue was, in effect, resignation. When Dante wrote: *"Nella sua volontá è nostra pace,"* he could in the medieval era have been understood as teaching people patience and acceptance. Those words cannot be so understood under modern circumstances. Today "social ethics" means that every people is responsible for its own system. Government is just only if it is by the consent of the governed. An economy is just only if it is the economy freely formed by its own participants. Persons must choose. They must accept responsibility. They must become creative of their own destiny.

Obviously, they do so, in the first instance, chiefly through the institutions they choose to live under. That is why we first considered institutions. A poorly designed political economy frustrates even a virtuous people. Consider Poland. How is a system just if a steelworker labors hard for hours to produce steel, which then rusts in the lot because the state planners failed to find a market in which it can be sold at a cost commensurate with the cost of producing it?[27] No matter how virtuous the steelworker, his work goes for naught if the system does not function. Contrariwise, even when a people is not particularly virtuous, a creative system of political economy has the characteristic of making the fruit of their work abundant. A good system rewards even people of lesser virtue, as a poor system punishes people even of high virtue. Thus, *system* and *virtue* are not the same.

Nonetheless, no system can long survive if the virtues of its people fail. Human beings are human beings, not parts of a machine. Whatever their role in the system—and every complex modern society depends upon a differentiation of roles—the way in which they perform that role has vast human effects. If they are honest and conscientious, persons of good and accurate workmanship, imaginative, creative, always thinking about new and better ways of doing things—then the system of which they are a part benefits by their good work. If not, at their station, then the system fails. And everybody else suffers because of their failures. In this sense, no system is better than the cumulative virtues of those who occupy its positions of responsibility.

Economic tasks, as we have said, are essentially associative. That is why modern peoples so enjoy team sports. These sports offer a metaphor for their own daily lives. No team is better than its individual players and their capacity for playing together, picking up for one another's weaknesses or miscues, and reinforcing one another's strengths. Too much of the literature of modern capitalistic economies emphasizes the individual. Individual creativity is uniquely important. But the most important factor in a modern free economy is teamwork, together with all the virtues required for voluntary, cooperative association.[28]

A modern business enterprise is an associative enterprise. It requires the high practice of every social virtue: courtesy, civility, frankness, cooperation, mutual regard and respect, the sort of moral competition that inspires each person to be as good as each can be. It requires—as shown in the book *In Search of Excellence*,[29] a study of several conspicuously successful business enterprises—the striving on the part of all for excellence. This excellence is, first of all, moral. It has tremendous economic effects.

Think of what happens in any business enterprise when typical, common vices replace the virtues: when dishonesty, careless work, laziness, an incapacity for working with others, bad temper, surliness, thievery, and lying replace their moral opposites. Can any moral person long work for such a firm? Can the goods or services produced by such a firm be of any reputable quality?

In addition to the common, ordinary virtues of daily life, a creative political economy makes special demands. It demands imagination. The cause of the wealth of nations is human wit. Human wit is ever fecund in discovering new ways of doing things, new services to supply for the human community, new goods to enhance its way of living. Perhaps too obviously, the primary virtue of a creative society is human creativity.

Why, for example, do we not each have personal telephones, which each of us can carry with us, enabling us to communicate instantly, even at great distances, with those with whom we wish to be in contact? Why cannot such telephones also supply us, as with television, with visual images of those with whom we speak, as we speak to them? Such instruments are bound to be invented soon. They are bound to be part of daily life in the near future. Where will they first be invented? In Japan? In the United States? In West Germany? Why not in Brazil? No matter, they will come. And so also with many other new instruments rendering the human world more human, the human will more able to act, the human community closer in its capacities for communication.

Institutions of learning that favor the virtue of creativity will benefit by it. Families that instruct their children in creativity will take joy in the achievements of their children. Nations which reward creativity will reap its benefits.

4. CONCLUSION

Perhaps I have said enough to suggest that modern circumstances lay upon the human race new moral possibilities—and thus new moral responsibilities. To be a citizen in a modern society is to bear a new moral destiny. Yet such a destiny is at one with the destiny established for us in the Book of Genesis, in which we read that men and women were made in the image of God, the Creator of the Latin American continent, the Creator of all things, the Creator of us all. It is a good creation. Our vocation as Christians and Jews is to seize the clues left by our Creator, in order to bring his work to the beauty he has hidden within it. Our vocation is to do so free from tyranny and free from poverty. Our vocation is to do so both in liberation and in that humane creativity which is the goal of any genuine liberation.

This is the vision, in any case, of creation theology.

LATIN AMERICA:
A SAMPLING OF STATISTICAL PROFILES

Much of the dialogue among North Americans and Latin Americans proceeds without due reference to empirical realities, even while rather extreme empirical claims are being made. In order to help ground the ongoing discussion of factual matters, the following sample of statistical profiles is here presented.

Table 1 reveals the remarkable record of average annual growth rates in most countries of Latin America between 1965–1973, as contrasted with the period from 1973–1983.

Table 2 reports the structure of production in Latin America in 1963 and in 1983.

Table 3 reports average annual growth rates in public consumption, private consumption, and gross domestic investment during 1965–1973, as compared with 1973–1983.

Table 4 reports the percentage of the population of working age (suggesting the vast reservoir of youths under age 15).

Table 5 reports the proportions of the labor force engaged in agriculture, industry, and services in 1965 as compared with 1981.

Table 6 reports the amount and percentage of U.S. direct investment abroad for the years 1972–1982.

Table 7 reports the contribution of the 10 primary exports of Latin American countries to the total value of all exports, averages for 1972–76, 1978–83, and 1984.

Tables 8 and 9 report some of the more common quality of life indicators for Latin America, such as infant mortality rates, life expectancy, caloric intake, and so forth.

These tables suggest clear trends away from agriculture, looming problems of unemployment (as youths already born but now under 15 enter the work force between now and the end of the century), and sharp variations in the crucial factor—the average annual percentage of gross domestic investment.

Differences between countries are often quite striking.

Table 1:
GROWTH OF PRODUCTION IN LATIN AMERICA

Average annual growth rate (percent)

Country	GDP		Agriculture		Industry		Manufacturing*		Services	
	'65–73	'73–83	'65–73	'73–83	'65–73	'73–83	'65–73	'73–83	'65–73	'73–83
Haiti	1.7	3.0	-0.3	0.7	4.8	5.3	3.0	6.1	2.5	3.8
Bolivia	4.4	1.5	3.5	1.5	5.1	-0.6	4.2	1.7	4.3	2.6
Honduras	4.4	4.0	2.4	3.3	5.8	5.1	6.5	5.5	5.5	4.0
El Salvador	4.4	-0.1	3.6	0.7	5.2	-1.4	5.1	-2.4	4.4	0.0
Nicaragua	3.9	-1.3	2.8	1.4	5.5	-0.9	7.2	0.8	3.6	-2.9
Costa Rica	7.1	2.7	7.0	1.7	9.3	3.0	..	..	6.1	2.9
Peru	3.5	1.8	2.0	0.9	4.1	1.6	4.4	0.4	3.6	2.2
Guatemala	6.0	3.7	5.8	2.3	7.2	5.1	7.4	4.0	5.8	3.8
Jamaica	5.4	-1.7	0.6	-0.2	4.5	-4.3	4.0	-3.6	6.8	-0.3
Dominican Rep.	8.5	4.4	5.9	3.2	14.4	3.9	12.0	4.4	6.9	5.2
Paraguay	5.1	8.2	2.7	6.0	6.8	10.6	6.1	7.4	6.5	8.5
Ecuador	7.2	5.2	3.9	1.9	13.9	5.0	11.4	8.9	5.1	6.5
Colombia	6.4	3.9	4.0	3.7	8.2	2.2	8.8	1.9	6.9	4.8
Cuba	..	..	..	..	..	..	..	..	..	..
Chile	3.4	2.9	-1.1	3.7	3.0	1.7	4.1	0.5	4.4	3.6
Brazil	9.8	4.8	3.8	4.2	11.0	4.7	11.2	4.2	10.5	5.0
Argentina	4.3	0.4	-0.1	1.5	5.1	-0.7	4.6	-1.8	5.5	1.1
Panama	7.4	5.3	3.4	1.4	9.3	4.2	..	..	7.8	6.4
Mexico	7.9	5.6	5.4	3.5	8.6	6.2	9.9	5.5	8.0	5.7
Uruguay	1.3	2.5	0.4	1.5	2.0	2.4	..	..	1.1	2.7
Venezuela	5.1	2.5	4.5	2.6	4.1	1.5	5.7	3.7	6.0	3.1
Trinidad and Tobago	3.5	5.2	1.6	..	2.3	..	..	..	4.5	..

*Manufacturing is a part of the industrial sector, but its share of GDP is shown separately because it typically is the most dynamic part of the industrial sector.

Source: World Development Report 1985 (World Bank, Washington, D.C.) Table 2, pp. 176–77.

Table 2:
STRUCTURE OF PRODUCTION IN LATIN AMERICA

| Country | GDP (millions of $) | | Distribution of gross domestic product (percent) | | | | | | | |
| | | | Agriculture | | Industry | | Manufacturing* | | Services | |
	1965	1983	'65	'83	'65	'83	'65	'83	'65	'83
Haiti	350	1,630	..	..	..	..	..	..	..	..
Bolivia	920	3,340	21	23	30	26	16	16	49	52
Honduras	460	2,640	40	27	19	26	12	15	41	47
El Salvador	800	3,700	29	20	22	21	18	15	49	59
Nicaragua	710	2,700	25	22	24	32	18	26	51	47
Costa Rica	590	3,060	24	23	23	27	..	..	53	50
Peru	4,900	17,630	15	8	30	41	20	26	55	51
Guatemala	1,330	9,030	..	..	..	..	..	..	..	..
Jamaica	870	3,140	10	7	37	34	17	19	53	60
Dominican Republic	960	8,530	26	17	20	29	14	18	53	55
Paraguay	550	4,610	37	26	19	26	16	16	45	48
Ecuador	1,150	10,700	27	14	22	40	18	18	50	46
Colombia	5,570	35,310	30	20	25	28	18	17	46	51
Cuba	..	..	..	..	..	..	..	..	..	..
Chile	5,940	19,290	9	10	40	36	24	20	52	55
Brazil	19,260	254,660	19	12	33	35	26	27	48	53
Argentina	14,430	71,550	17	12	42	39	33	28	42	49
Panama	660	4,370	18	..	19	40	12	..	63	..
Mexico	20,160	145,130	14	8	31	40	21	22	54	52
Uruguay	930	4,750	15	12	32	28	..	..	53	60
Venezuela	8,290	8,170	7	7	23	40	..	17	71	53
Trinidad and Tobago	660	8,620	5	..	38	..	19	..	57	..

*Manufacturing is a part of the industrial sector, but its share of GDP is shown separately because it typically is the most dynamic part of the industrial sector.

Source: World Development Report 1985 (World Bank, Washington, D.C.), Table 3, pp. 178–89.

Table 3:
CONSUMPTION AND INVESTMENT IN LATIN AMERICA

	Average Annual Growth Rate (percent)					
	Public Consumption		Private Consumption		Gross Domestic Invest.	
Country	1965–73	1973–83	1965–73	1973–83	1965–73	1973–83
Haiti	3.1	5.1	0.8	2.9	14.4	8.4
Bolivia	8.4	2.3	3.1	2.9	6.9	−11.4
Honduras	7.0	6.3	3.8	4.3	4.3	0.7
El Salvador	8.3	3.3	3.0	0.6	3.7	−5.7
Nicaragua	3.2	13.4	2.7	−4.3	3.3	−2.7
Costa Rica	6.8	3.7	5.1	1.9	9.3	−3.4
Peru	5.4	3.2	5.6	1.9	−2.6	−2.7
Guatemala	5.7	6.7	5.4	3.7	5.3	1.2
Jamaica	13.6	2.6	4.5	−2.0	7.5	−6.5
Dominican Rep.	−3.6	6.5	8.6	4.5	19.2	2.5
Paraguay	6.2	10.3	5.0	7.0	8.4	14.0
Ecuador	7.0	8.5	5.2	6.4	6.0	3.2
Colombia	8.8	6.5	6.5	4.5	6.7	6.0
Cuba	..	..	..	..	..	..
Chile	6.3	0.4	4.8	2.6	..	−0.3
Brazil	7.3	4.4	10.2	6.0	11.3	2.5
Argentina	2.4	2.9	4.3	0.3	6.7	−2.0
Panama	9.7	..	5.2	..	15.4	..
Mexico	8.7	6.9	7.7	5.4	8.4	4.5
Uruguay	2.1	3.7	4.1	1.1	3.9	7.0
Venezuela	6.8	5.2	5.5	7.1	9.0	2.5
Trinidad and Tobago	*	*	4.9	7.7	2.4	13.0

*Public consumption figures are included in private consumption.

Source: World Development Report 1985 (World Bank, Washington, D.C.), Table 4, pp. 180–1.

Table 4:
LABOR FORCE OF LATIN AMERICA

Country	% of pop. of working age (15–64)		Average annual growth of labor force (percent)		
	1965	1983	'65–73	'73–83	'80–2000
Haiti	54	55	0.7	1.5	2.0
Bolivia	54	53	1.8	2.5	2.8
Honduras	51	50	2.4	3.3	3.5
El Salvador	51	52	3.2	2.8	3.4
Nicaragua	49	51	2.8	4.0	3.8
Costa Rica	49	59	3.6	3.6	2.8
Peru	52	56	2.4	2.9	3.0
Guatemala	51	54	2.9	3.0	2.9
Jamaica	51	56	0.7	2.6	2.6
Dominican Rep.	48	55	2.7	3.2	2.8
Paraguay	50	55	2.6	3.3	3.0
Ecuador	51	53	2.6	2.6	3.3
Colombia	50	59	3.1	2.8	2.6
Cuba	59	64	1.0	2.1	1.7
Chile	56	63	1.3	2.6	2.0
Brazil	54	59	2.5	3.1	2.4
Argentina	64	61	1.4	1.0	1.4
Panama	52	57	3.1	2.6	2.4
Mexico	50	53	3.1	3.1	3.2
Uruguay	63	63	0.3	0.5	0.9
Venezuela	50	56	3.7	4.1	3.4
Trinidad and Tobago	54	61	1.8	1.2	2.3

Source: World Development Report 1985 (World Bank, Washington, D.C.), Table 21, pp. 214–15.

Table 5:
DISTRIBUTION OF LABOR FORCE IN LATIN AMERICA

	Percentage of labor force in:					
	Agriculture		Industry		Services	
Country	1965	1981	1965	1981	1965	1981
Haiti	77	74	7	7	16	19
Bolivia	58	50	20	24	22	26
Honduras	68	63	12	20	20	17
El Salvador	59	50	18	22	23	28
Nicaragua	57	39	16	14	27	47
Costa Rica	47	29	20	23	33	48
Peru	50	40	19	19	31	41
Guatemala	64	55	16	21	20	24
Jamaica	34	35	25	18	41	47
Dominican Rep.	64	49	13	18	23	33
Paraguay	55	49	19	19	26	32
Ecuador	54	52	21	17	25	31
Colombia	45	26	20	21	35	53
Cuba	35	23	24	31	41	46
Chile	26	19	21	19	53	62
Brazil	49	30	17	24	34	46
Argentina	18	13	34	28	48	59
Panama	46	33	15	18	39	49
Mexico	50	36	21	26	29	38
Uruguay	18	11	30	32	52	57
Venezuela	30	18	24	27	46	55
Trinidad and Tobago	23	10	35	39	42	51

Source: World Development Report 1985 (World Bank, Washington, D.C.), Table 21, pp. 214–15.

Table 6:
U.S. DIRECT INVESTMENT ABROAD AT YEAR-END 1972–1982 BY RECIPIENT REGION (IN MILLION U.S. DOLLARS)

	1972	1973	1974	1975	1976	1977	1978	1979	1980	1981	1982
Canada	25,771 (27.3%)	25,541 (24.6%)	28,404 (23.9%)	31,038 (24.9%)	33,932 (24.9%)	35,200 (23.5%)	37,071 (22.1%)	40,243 (21.4%)	44,978 (20.9%)	45,129 (19.9%)	44,509 (20.1%)
Europe	30,817 (32.7%)	38,225 (36.9%)	44,782 (37.7%)	49,533 (39.9%)	55,139 (40.4%)	60,930 (40.7%)	69,553 (41.4%)	82,622 (44.0%)	96,539 (44.8%)	101,514 (44.8%)	99,877 (45.1%)
Japan	2,375 (2.5%)	2,671 (2.6%)	3,319 (2.8%)	3,339 (2.7%)	3,797 (2.9%)	4,143 (2.8%)	4,972 (3.0%)	6,208 (3.3%)	6,243 (2.9%)	6,755 (3.0%)	6,872 (3.1%)
Other Developed Countries[1]	5,395 (5.7%)	5,746 (5.5%)	6,520 (5.5%)	7,013 (5.6%)	7,530 (5.5%)	7,952 (5.3%)	8,876 (5.3%)	9,595 (5.1%)	10,590 (4.9%)	11,998 (5.3%)	11,818 (5.3%)
Latin America	16,796 (17.8%)	16,484 (15.9%)	19,491 (16.4%)	22,101 (17.8%)	23,934 (17.5%)	28,110 (18.8%)	32,662 (19.5%)	35,056 (18.7%)	38,882 (18.0%)	38,864 (17.2%)	33,039 (14.9%)
Africa	3,091 (3.3%)	2,376 (2.3%)	2,233 (1.9%)	2,414 (1.9%)	2,775 (2.0%)	2,802 (1.9%)	3,175 (1.9%)	3,028 (1.6%)	3,778 (1.8%)	4,228 (1.9%)	5,069 (2.3%)
Middle East	1,992 (2.1%)	2,588 (2.5%)	2,215 (1.9%)	-4,040 (-3.3%)	-3,730 (-2.7%)	-2,667 (-1.8%)	-2,194 (-1.3%)	-999 (-0.5%)	2,113 (1.0%)	1,992 (0.9%)	2,703 (1.2%)
Asia and Pacific	3,354 (3.6%)	3,818 (3.7%)	4,519 (3.8%)	5,747 (4.6%)	5,904 (4.3%)	6,217 (4.1%)	6,757 (4.0%)	7,440 (4.0%)	8,505 (3.9%)	11,099 (4.9%)	12,347 (5.6%)
International	4,743 (5.0%)	6,196 (6.0%)	7,335 (6.2%)	7,067 (5.7%)	7,114 (5.2%)	7,160 (4.8%)	6,934 (4.1%)	3,567 (1.9%)	3,951 (1.8%)	4,780 (2.1%)	5,110 (2.3%)
Total	94,337 (100%)	103,676 (100%)	118,819 (100%)	124,212 (100%)	136,396 (100%)	149,848 (100%)	167,804 (100%)	186,760 (100%)	215,578 (100%)	226,359 (100%)	221,343 (100%)

Note: (1) Includes Australia, New Zealand and South Africa.
Source: U.S. Department of Commerce, *Survey of Current Business*.

Table 7:
CONTRIBUTION OF THE 10 MAIN
LATIN AMERICAN PRIMARY EXPORT PRODUCTS*
TO EACH COUNTRY'S TOTAL
VALUE OF MERCHANDISE EXPORTS,
AVERAGES FOR 1972–76, 1978–83, AND 1984

Country	1972–76	1978–83	1984
Argentina	25.9	16.2	11.6
Bahamas	–	–	–
Barbados	37.8	13.4	5.9
Bolivia	29.6	–	–
Brazil	54.9	31.4	28.3
Chile	71.4	47.5	43.9
Colombia	62.9	54.1	59.4
Costa Rica	65.3	60.9	61.3
Dominican Republic	62.7	49.9	38.1
Ecuador	68.9	17.3	12.7
El Salvador	61.9	66.3	62.2
Guatemala	59.3	46.7	46.9
Guyana	38.8	32.0	30.5
Haiti	40.5	32.5	24.7
Honduras	53.6	34.1	27.4
Jamaica	16.6	6.3	4.9
Mexico	23.7	4.2	2.8
Nicaragua	61.4	60.3	53.7
Panama	44.5	32.4	35.1
Paraguay	31.4	54.2	72.7
Peru	44.2	17.9	16.2
Trinidad and Tobago	33.3	–	–
Uruguay	29.1	16.7	20.0
Venezuela	65.0	–	–
LATIN AMERICA	49.7	19.7	17.2

*Beef, Maize, Bananas, Sugar, Coffee, Cocoa, Soybeans, Cotton, Iron Ore, and Copper

– = less than 5% of total merchandise exports

Source: Inter-American Development Bank, Economic and Social Progress in Latin America, Table 64.

Table 8:
QUALITY OF LIFE INDICATORS FOR LATIN AMERICA

Country	GNP per capita (US$) 1983	infant mortality (under 1 yr.) 1960	infant mortality (under 1 yr.) 1983	life expectancy at birth (years) 1983	Daily calorie supply per capita total 1982	Daily calorie supply per capita as % of requirement 1982
Haiti	300	205	130	53	1,903	84
Bolivia	510	170	125	51	2,158	90
El Salvador	710	155	70	65	2,060	101
Nicaragua	880	150	75	60	2,268	113
Costa Rica	1,020	85	19	73	2,635	118
Peru	1,040	150	100	59	2,114	90
Guatemala	1,120	130	70	61	2,115	97
Jamaica	1,300	70	21	70	2,489	111
Dominican Republic	1,370	130	75	63	2,179	96
Paraguay	1,410	90	45	65	2,820	122
Ecuador	1,420	130	70	63	2,062	91
Colombia	1,430	100	50	64	2,551	110
Cuba	1,410	70	17	73	2,997	130
Chile	1,870	115	23	67	2,669	109
Brazil	1,880	120	70	63	2,623	110
Argentina	2,070	60	36	70	3,363	127
Panama	2,120	75	26	71	2,498	108
Mexico	2,240	100	55	66	2,976	128
Uruguay	2,490	55	30	70	2,754	103
Venezuela	3,840	90	39	68	2,557	104
Trinidad & Tobago	6,850	65	24	70	3,083	127
LATIN AMERICA	1,890	na	na	65	na	na

(na = not available)

Sources: UNICEF, State of the World's Children, 1986; World Bank, World Development Report 1985, Table 24; Population Reference Bureau, 1985 World Population Data Sheet.

Table 9:
LITERACY AND EDUCATION IN LATIN AMERICA

Country	% of adults literate male/female 1983	% enrolled in primary school as % of age group*		% enrolled in secondary school as % of age group		% enrolled in higher ed. as % of age group	
		1965	1982	1965	1982	1965	1982
Haiti	37/33	50	69	5	13	na	1
Bolivia	76/51	73	86	18	34	5	16
Honduras	73/67	80	99	10	32	1	10
El Salvador	na	82	61	17	20	2	6
Nicaragua	89/88	69	104	14	41	2	13
Costa Rica	90/75	106	106	24	48	6	27
Peru	54/39	99	114	25	59	8	21
Guatemala	na	50	73	8	16	2	7
Jamaica	na	109	99	51	58	3	6
Dominican Republic	90/85	87	103	12	41	2	10
Paraguay	84/76	102	103	13	36	4	7
Ecuador	86/84	91	114	17	56	3	35
Colombia	96/96	84	125	17	46	3	12
Cuba	94/91	121	109	23	72	3	19
Chile	76/73	124	112	34	59	7	10
Brazil	94/94	108	96	16	32	2	12
Argentina	86/85	101	119	28	59	14	25
Panama	86/80	102	110	34	63	7	23
Mexico	93/94	92	121	17	54	4	15
Uruguay	87/83	106	122	44	63	4	20
Venezuela	96/93	94	105	27	40	8	22
Trinidad & Tobago	96/93	93	99	36	61	7	5

*Primary-school age is generally defined as 6–11 years. For some countries with universal education, the gross enrollment ratios may exceed 100% because some pupils are below or above the country's standard primary-school age.

(na = not available)

Sources: Unicef, State of the World's Children, 1986, pp. 84–85; World Bank, 1985 World Development Report, Table 25.

Six

BASIC CONCEPTS
OF LIBERATION THEOLOGY

As one can see with special vividness in the works of Enrique Dussel, liberation theology is a way of looking at world history in the light of its own *mythos* (or sense of reality), its own *story* (or imaginal narrative line), and its own *horizon* (or range of vision).[1] It begins from within a distinctive standpoint, and projects upon other cultures the positions it imagines they hold, looked at from this point of view.

Until recently, liberation theologians have been more preoccupied in establishing the distinctiveness of their point of view than in showing that this point of view is valid and true. In this sense, liberation theology is still in the form of an hypothesis. "Look at the world this way," it says, "from this point of view. Stand over here with us." All this is a useful exercise. But at some point there must also come the question: Is the point of view *true?* Can it be sustained? Is it too narrow? Is its fulcrum set down at the wrong point, so that everything else is distorted?

Whatever its truth, the point of view of liberation theology is interesting. It repays the effort made by outsiders to suspend judgment for a while, and sympathetically to "pass over" into it. In this chapter, I would like to "walk in the moccasins" of liberation theologians for a while by reviewing some of their basic concepts. I am particularly interested in their fundamental concepts, the ones that establish their sense of reality, story, and horizon. Concerning each of these, I pose certain questions.

As my guide, I choose Enrique Dussel, the Argentine philosopher now writing from Mexico. This is because Dussel is a philosopher who has set himself the task of articulating the basic concepts of liberation in a clear, coherent, and highly systematic fashion, and in a prose designed to speak to outsiders who are beginners in liberation theology. The advantage of following Dussel is that he uses a clear unvarnished language. Many of the theologians, by contrast, express themselves in terms familiar to all Christians everywhere, while using these terms in new ways. This "bending" of language introduces many ambiguities and uncertainties. By contrast, Dussel uses the language of philosophy and common sense. To be sure, he is a *Christian* philosopher, often using themes or terms taken directly from the Christian faith, in a way that would hardly occur to a non-Christian philosopher. Nonetheless, his language has a useful neutrality. And he is trying to summarize the views of his colleagues.

The basic text I will follow is *History and the Theology of Liberation* (1972),[2] along with *Philosophy of Liberation* (1980).[3] The first situates liberation theology in time, by a narration beginning from the origins of humankind and the neolithic era. The second situates liberation theology by means of a spatial metaphor: a circle within a circle.[4] The small inner circle is called "CENTER," and includes Japan, the U.S., and Western Europe on the capitalist side, with the U.S.S.R. and part of Eastern Europe on the socialist side. The much larger, surrounding outer circle is called "PERIPHERY." This circle shows five arcs including (1) Latin America, (2) the Arab world, (3) black Africa, (4) India and Southeast Asia, and (5) China. This spatial metaphor expresses a particular vision of "geopolitics." Similarly, Dussel's historical panorama calls the era from 1808–1962 "The Era of Neo-Colonialism," and asserts that "The Church Starts a New Era (1962–   )," beginning from Vatican Council II. These two visions of history and geography are not bereft of ideology.

No one can think without at least an implicit picture both of the historical chain of which we are a part and of our relation in space with other cultures. Thus, to assert that Dussel's pictures of reality are ideological is not to attribute a fault. On the contrary, it is to call attention to two points. First, Dussel's readers need to think carefully about their *own* historical and spatial metaphors, often buried in unconscious habit. Second, every human being needs to doubt whether his own historical and spatial metaphors are true.

I call such systematic doubt "the experience of nothingness."[5] On the one hand, human beings necessarily think in fundamental historical and spatial metaphors. On the other hand, our unrestricted drive to ask questions often shatters the fundamental metaphors to which we have become accustomed, because they are no longer adequate. Suddenly, in such a case, we seem to be falling through emptiness. As we fall, we find no firm structures of imagination to grasp. We fall into the nothingness that reflects our own infinite capacity to question any structure. All imaginative or ideological structures are designed to cover over our elemental nothingness. They do so, not so much in order to deceive us (although they may do that) as to enable us—embodied as we are—to take hold in manageable order of what William James called the "blooming, buzzing" confusion of reality.

The experience of nothingness, left to itself, reduces human beings to inertia. We cannot see how to act; indeed, to act at all seems pointless. In order to act, we must conceive of a story to act within. We must impose upon the infinite possibilities of reality an order. That is why concepts of order—of *ordo,* of system—are fundamental to any active society.

The human problem, in a nutshell, is to find a social order suited to our unrestricted drive to raise questions, an order that allows us to act without covering over, or disguising, our unrestricted drive to raise questions, that unlimited *why?* within us. As wonder is the beginning of wisdom, so fidelity to the source of wonder, to the *why?* within us, drives us to question what is, and to imagine new possibilities. The unrestricted drive to raise questions is the fundamental source of human dynamism in history. It is also the source of our hunger for God: "Our hearts are restless, Lord, until they rest in thee" (St. Augustine). Nothing finite—certainly not politics or social action or ideologies of history—escapes our questioning.

Given the images of history and space that give liberation theology its distinctive shape, what may we say?

Initially, it is instructive to note that liberation theologians first of all conceive of themselves as *oppressed.* They imagine themselves as victims, dependent, outside the "CENTER," dominated by others. Such concepts are the foundation of their basic vocabulary. Everything else is seen in relation to these.

Thus, the large first step Enrique Dussel takes in describing the point of view of liberation theology is to write: ". . . we must do our thinking within a basic context of oppression itself."[6] This is a grave step. Taking it, liberation theologians commit themselves to a powerful *mythos:* We are the oppressed, others are the oppressors. This fundamental vision is radically divisive. Is this step necessary? Is it supported by the facts of everyday experience? Is it true? Clearly, the liberation theologians, who ground themselves here, believe that this vision is true. Otherwise they would not embrace it.

Yet not so fast. Suppose that it is *not* true. What other purposes might such a step serve besides fidelity to truth? One must question every ideology. One must question radical first steps most radically of all. This first step serves one clear purpose. It shifts responsibility. If I am oppressed, then I am not responsible for my condition; the oppressor is. Furthermore, if I am oppressed, then my primary duty is to fight against the oppressor. This first step, then, has three consequences. First, it shifts responsibility for my condition from myself to others. This is already a great relief. Second, it forces me to imagine my life as primarily constituted by war, division, and struggle: the oppressed versus the oppressor. Third, this step places me within a vision of history at least analogous to that of Marx and Lenin: struggle between oppressed classes and oppressor classes is the fundamental interpretive key to history itself. History is combat, of one class against another. History is class struggle. The basic ethical question is: "Whose side are you on, oppressor or oppressed?" Taking sides becomes the first ethical choice.

Yet this vision cannot be metaphysically true. It carries within it a self-contradictory principle. On the one hand, it says that history is class struggle. On the other hand, it says that justice ought to prevail. But if the last is true, then the main interpretive key to history is not oppression but justice, not struggle but reconciliation. Which is it? Are oppression and conflict the fundamental law of history? Or is the fundamental law justice?

At war here are the Marxist and the Christian philosophies of history. Liberation theologians have flirted with combining both. That is incoherent. The problem begins in their very first step. Once their first self-defining act is to declare themselves "oppressed," they have sided with Marx and Lenin. Their hope, then, is to "humanize" Marx and Lenin, to "Christianize" them, at later stages in their argument. "We will begin with the category of oppression," they say, "and with the category of class struggle. But later we will show that this does not necessarily lead in the direction of atheism, materialism, and brute power."

However, if they will wish to make moral claims later, they need a moral conception as their very first principle. If the chief interpretive key to history is liberty and justice for all, the description of the early stages of history is not precisely expressed as "oppression." One of the favorite prayers of St. Gregory the Great (A.D. 540–604), which I keep displayed before me on my desk, is "*Ut possit florere cum libertate justitia*"—"That justice with liberty may flower." This prayer suggests that justice and liberty are seeds, like the mustard seed of faith, destined to flourish and to flower. Inserted into the dark soil of history, their growth is natural and, if not quite inevitable, nonetheless alive with potency straining toward fruition. The historical narrative of liberty with justice, of justice with liberty, has its spirals of rise and decline, its imperatives of struggle, of effort, and even of revolt. But these poten-

cies within the human mind and heart, and within the social texture
of every part of human life (even within the bosom of the darkest of
totalitarian oppressions), belong to human nature in its every part.
The first step of Christian self-identification, therefore, is not solely,
"I am oppressed," but, rather, "I am also essentially (never completely)
free and in love with justice." Inherently free and in love with justice,
I need bend my knee to no one, may stand erect and proud. I am not
merely a victim. I am not merely oppressed. Within me I carry the
seeds of liberty and justice, and the vision of a world that mirrors these
in all its institutions, a world (eventually) of reconciliation in mutual
liberty and mutual justice.

In short, liberation theology makes its very first step too hastily. It
concedes too much to powers of darkness, division, and brute power.
If the fundamental law of creation is oppression, then the most cynical
will conclude that history entails the necessity of further oppression.
In the name of the vision emanating from their own egos, the oppressed will struggle against their oppressors (with whom they have
nothing in common) until they, the oppressed, gain the upper hand
and become themselves the oppressors. This is the logical—and also
the concrete, historical—outcome of Marxism. Societies like the
U.S.S.R. do not "abandon" Marx. On the contrary, as Leszek Kolakowski shows (and more importantly history shows), everything they
do can be justified from important texts in Marx.[7] To his credit, Enrique Dussel also sees that Marxism is flawed in its very ontology.[8] He
proclaims himself a socialist, but not a Marxist. Just the same, alas, his
own very first ontological step is Marxist.

It is easy to understand why liberation theologians take this step.
As Dussel says, many were educated in Europe and, on their return,
found that they had been educated away from the common world of
the poor of Latin America,[9] and the condition of the Latin American
poor shocked them. In addition, mental habits of dependency have
prevailed in Latin America; for generations, decisions crucial to daily
life in Latin America were made in Spain and Portugal. Meanwhile,
Great Britain capitalized on the productivity of its farms, as did the
United States; Latin America did not. Thus, while the Industrial Revolution occurred in Western Europe and the United States, Latin
America fell once again into dependence upon other cultures for the
leadership that would bring it into the modern world. Well into the
twentieth century, Latin America did not produce for itself many of
the new industrial goods and modern services of fully developed societies. For most of its manufactures, and for a good deal of the capital
necessary for catching up, Latin America came to depend upon in-

fusions from abroad. The feeling of despair about the condition of the poor awakened traditional mental habits of dependency. Others in other cultures—at the "center"—acted. Latin America was relatively passive.

In addition, the folk culture of Latin America is family-centered, not civic-minded. Social organization, civic participation, and associations outside the family are not common. Relatively few Latin Americans participate in organized political, economic, and social activities. Sector after sector is unorganized, voiceless, "marginalized." Only small bodies of elites—lawyers, government officials, church hierarchies, educated professionals, and soldiers—are organized. For vast majorities in the social pyramid, the social texture of life is thin, hardly more than family-centered, and bereft of social power. A few activist elites—often locked in bitter rivalries—represent almost the entire substance of social potency. The masses slumber.

In such a context, each one of us might be tempted to proceed exactly as the liberation theologians have proceeded. Announcing our independence of our "European educations," we each might be tempted to insist upon our own originality: we each might declare our own "intellectual and cultural independence."[10] Like others, we might breathe the modern air of *neodoxy* (judging the truth by what is new, loving the new even more than the true).[11] In addition, we might each feel a certain envy regarding societies that succeeded better than we. We, too, would feel what Carlos Rangel describes as the Latin American "love-hate" relation with the U.S.[12] Thus, we might be tempted to stick a thumb in Uncle Sam's eye. What would be more satisfying than to suggest that we are Marxists, without committing ourselves to Marxism. *That* would throw the U.S. into an equivalent of apoplexy!

But is it true that the situation of Latin America, vis-à-vis the U.S., Japan, and Western Europe, is accurately described as "oppressive"? Suppose that Latin America after 1945 had had no trade with such outside cultures, no contacts, no outside investment, no foreign aid. Would conditions in Latin America today be more favorable than they are? Put this another way. Granted that the United States has made many foolish foreign policy and even military interventions in some nations of Latin America, and that in virtually all cases it has conducted itself with a painful measure of superiority and arrogance: there are many reasons for resentment. But can it really be said that *every* act of the United States regarding Latin America during the twentieth century has been harmful, damaging, and oppressive? Is there nothing at all on the good side of the ledger? How would a prudent, realistic judge, intent upon strict justice by a Christian standard, discern the exact balance sheet of U.S. influences upon Latin America? Perhaps, on balance, the sum is negative. That seems to many observers, even to many Latin American intellectuals, doubtful. But that it constitutes "oppression" is wildly wide of the mark.

Latin American liberation theologians say that "we must do our thinking in the context of oppression." Yet among the citizens of this earth, Latin American societies are far freer and more dynamic than most. Their situation is hardly to be compared with that of black Africa; or with that of Saudi Arabia, Syria, Libya, Iran, Iraq; or with that of China. As for Asia, several nations of the East Asian rim do less well than Latin America along the axis of democracy, but far better along the axis of economic development and the emancipation of the poor. Further, if one discusses Eastern Europe—Hungary, Bulgaria, Czechoslovakia, Poland, and the others—with liberation theologians, some admit that they would not like Latin American nations to become as "joyless" as Eastern European cultures. But some are silent about the degree of oppression suffered there. And some volunteer that they wish that the poor in Latin America would be on at least as high a level as the poor of Eastern Europe. Such comments sicken Eastern Europeans I have known, who think that such Latin Americans are naively romantic about degrees of oppression. One Eastern European writes,

> After the Second World War . . . the Socialist states nationalized not only the factories, not only the schools (the future), but also the peoples themselves. Their language, their imagination and even their past. Even the snowflake falling on lovers' hands.[13]

Oppression in Latin America? The word is broad. In this sad world, one must compare oppression with oppression.

Enrique Dussel writes, however:

> . . . we must also ponder this very situation of oppression itself. We are forced to look at the overall situation from the bottom of the heap, as it were, and hence our way of liberating ourselves from the present situation will differ from the approach of people in the dominant countries. The affluent societies have one road to take, we have another to take. And only people within our concrete situation can truly describe the process involved.[14]

That last sentence is partly true. Each people must discern its own situation and choose its own course of action. In an interdependent world, however, when Christians elsewhere are summoned into dialogue with Latin American theologians, they have an intellectual obligation to respond freely, critically, with civility and with respect, that Latin Americans are *not,* as this world goes, on "the bottom of the heap." In this world of many continents, degrees of liberty, degrees of justice, degrees of intellectual and economic and social vitality clearly exist. Pluralism is the rule, not the exception. As we have seen, the Japanese way is not that of Great Britain, nor the way of Spain that of West Germany, nor Singapore that of Jamaica.

Yet one of the disappointing features of liberation theology is its abstractness and generality. Far from being descriptive, concrete, and practical, it is intricately speculative, ideological, and academic. Words like *praxis, action* and *revolution* convey intellectual excitement. But one can read volume after volume of liberation theology without learning much about the economics, politics, or histories of the specific countries in which they are written. One learns from them almost nothing about the differences between Costa Rica and Nicaragua, or between Peru and Argentina. The teeming variety of the thirteen remarkably different nations of South America—so different again from the nations of Central America—is nowhere reflected. How can such abstruse books be credited with leading to *praxis?* Liberation theology to date is theoretical, not down-to-earth.

Noting this pervasive vagueness of thought, Dussel wrote skeptically in 1972 of the future of the Christian Democratic parties in Latin America: "Today it seems unlikely that such parties will exert the same influence they once did, for many people now feel that they have failed to effect the social revolution they proclaimed." He then describes a trend that troubles him:

> Many Christians are moving towards Marxism as a purely political and economic interpretation of reality. Following the line of thinking espoused by people like Louis Althusser, they feel that they can dissociate Marx's thinking as an economist and social observer from his anthropological and ontological underpinnings. In other words, they feel they can be Marxists in economics and Christians in their faith.
> This feeling is open to serious question. . . .[15]

He argues against Marxism, while holding that "some forms of socialism are compatible with Christianity." He adds: "We seem to be moving towards more serious consideration of socialism."[16]

For reasons sketched earlier, it does seem likely that the statist traditions of Latin America will lead at first toward a socialist organization of the economy. But, while this trend is probable, it will run into harsh realities. Socialism is not a system designed to create a dynamic, growing economy from the bottom up. Socialism is designed to produce a redistributive, relatively static and gray society. One must consult socialist experiments in North Korea, North Vietnam, Tanzania, Ethiopia, Hungary, Romania, and elsewhere. For Latin America, socialism may be a likely path. But it exacts its price and imposes serious penalties. These ought, at least, to be considered.

Many who claim to desire socialism actually desire not a particular set of economic institutions, but "a new man." They want a society characterized by caring, generosity, compassion and unselfishness. To some extent, they naively combine the picture of a society in which citizens are saintly Christians with a picture of socialist economic institutions. Their claim is that institutions "condition" humans. Thus, if one can somehow construct the "right" sort of institutions, humans will be conditioned to walk in the paths of Christian righteousness. About this claim, there are two questions, one theological, one pragmatic. The first is: Is it theologically orthodox? Christian theology does not hold that the establishment of an order congruent with Christian principles will "condition" citizens to act as virtuous Christians. The Christian doctrine of sin is far more realistic than that. There are *no* institutions in history that human beings have not corrupted by the deadly vices to which the human heart is prey. The ravages of human sinfulness cannot be stayed by external arrangements. Existing socialist institutions offer no grounds for believing that they produce a new, uncorrupted, caring man. "Realism" means particularly one thing, Reinhold Niebuhr said in 1969, "that you establish the common good not purely by unselfishness but by the restraint of selfishness. That's realism."[17] The trouble with socialism is that it lacks checks and balances. It does not restrain selfishness. It channels selfishness into the quest for military and bureaucratic power.

If the theological objection is severe, the pragmatic question is even more telling. In practice, socialism creates centers of unchecked political power. Political power is morally far more dangerous than economic power. The latter is checked not only by political power, by law, and by moral traditions. It is also checked by internal necessities of many kinds, including competition among regions, entire industries, and individual firms. In addition, the social function of markets is to prevent economic agents from working their naked will; the market forces them to satisfy customers. Markets force behavior to be other-regarding, not solely because of a natural sense of mutuality and cooperation but also for reasons of survival. If American customers prefer Japanese autos, even great firms like Chrysler can be brought to the edge of collapse—unless and until they can win back their customers in the marketplace. Under socialism, there is little if any competition in the marketplace, and customers have virtually no choices. There are few if any restraints upon government firms. In the last analysis, all power in socialist systems is political. It is supported by police, informers, and the military. There are no checks upon socialist elites. Criticism and dissent are regarded as treason. There is a reason for this. Socialists regard their system as the embodiment of a moral vision. To criticize it is deemed immoral.

This confusion between socialism as a *moral ideal* and socialism as an *economic institution* causes much vague and fuzzy idealism, until the ship of state is actually launched. Then it will shatter on the rocks of reality. The record of the voyages of socialist experiments is full of shipwrecks. Most failed for want of checks and balances. All were at first utopian about institutional power, until the cynics seized its levers. In socialist dictatorships, savage human passions have no check. Latin Americans who choose socialism, therefore, will have to be extremely clear about the checks and balances they will introduce into it, so that Latin American experiments in socialism do not end as have socialist experiments elsewhere.

Thus, for example, many persons inspired by liberation theology have diagnosed the abuses of tyrants (such as Somoza) and have heroically given their lives in overturning them. Liberation theology has its martyrs. But not all the martyrs, even in the revolt against Somoza, were inspired by liberation theology. Furthermore, several of the most vocal leaders among the liberation theologians in Nicaragua—Ernesto Cardenal, Miguel d'Escoto, and others—have been accused of betraying Nicaragua to a new oppression, that of a Marxist-Leninist clique held in power, and ideologically held in line, by Cuban and Soviet financing, military power, and secret police. The outcome is still doubtful. What cannot be denied is that the cause of liberation theology has already been wounded, perhaps mortally, by the *praxis* of liberation theologians among the Sandinista ruling class. The moral correctness of that *praxis* is not indisputable.

In this context, liberation theologians may wish to reconsider their opposition to private property. Many link private property to selfishness. They think of it as the fundamental institution conditioning citizens to self-interest, self-enclosure, and separation from the community.[18] Yet the main reasons for the institution of private property are quite different. The first is that private property is to human liberty as incarnation is to the spirit. It is the bodily means by which human beings express their liberty to act in the world. Without material instruments, spiritual liberty is deprived of a capacity for autonomous action in history. The second is that private property is, effectively, a limit against the power of the state. If the state owns everything, citizens have no place on which to stand over or against it. Against literature, e.g., the state can decide not to make newsprint or presses available.

The third reason is a lesson from human experience, already apparent to the Fathers of the Church and embodied often in Catholic social teaching, viz., that human nature is such that humans work more diligently at what is their own, attached as it were to their own dignity as human subjects, than (except rarely) at tasks performed in common. The fourth reason is that private property gives incentives to families and their heirs to improve upon family endowments across the generations and even the centuries. Thus private property is an institution encouraging social dynamism and social satisfaction. These reasons do not suggest that the institution of property is without problems. But the chief problem with the institution of private property lies not in that institution itself; it lies in the fact that in most societies too many remain propertyless. It is the universal expansion of private property, not its abolition, that is the chief moral imperative to be derived from reflection upon social history.

Thus, although liberation theologians may contrive for a time to call for the abolition of private property, they will need to study closely the results of such experiments. Human nature is such that, almost certainly, they will want to change their judgment about the social losses certain to follow. Man's embodied nature is highly likely to assert itself again and again.

*   *   *

Another absolutely central term in liberation theology is *capitalism*. Dennis Goulet writes that liberation theologians "reject capitalism—even a capitalism which is rectified or attenuated by welfare policies—as radically immoral and structurally incompatible with social justice."[19] José Míguez Bonino writes: "For us Latin Americans today socialism, as a socio-economic structure and a historical project . . . represents our obedience in faith and it is the matrix of our theological reflection."[20] Alfredo Fierro holds: "Political theology is the specific and proper form of theology in an epoch dominated by Marx."[21] And again: "Political theology is a theology operating under the sign of Marx, just as truly as scholasticism was a theology operating under the sign of Aristotle and liberal Protestant theology was operating under the sign of Kant."[22] And yet again: "Many of today's theologians, and almost all those who have concerned themselves with political theology, seem to admit unreservedly the validity of the Marxist analysis insofar as socioeconomic realities are concerned."[23]

It may well be, as some assert, that not all the liberation theologians are Marxist. Certainly, some are socialists, who reject important elements of Marxism. It is impossible to discover any, however, who are in *favor* of capitalism or a free economy. I have not found any who, in naming the "enemy" and the "oppressor" from whom they seek liberation, are not anti-capitalist. Capitalism, in the eyes of liberation theology, is the enemy. Concretely, this means that the economic system of the United States is their primary target. They think of it in terms not far different from those of the Ayatollah Khomeini, who calls the United States "the Great Satan." Enrique Dussel calls the U.S. economy "Mammon,"[24] and places the C.I.A. "in the tradition of" Hitler's S.S.[25]

Most elites of the United States who are well-educated in the humanities and social sciences have also been taught to be anti-capitalist. The humanists of Great Britain and the U.S. have long denigrated "the dark satanic mills" (William Blake), the "philistine" (Matthew Arnold), "babbittry" (Sinclair Lewis), the "booboisie" (H. L. Mencken), "robber barons," and the rest. Even many conservatives are anti-capitalist, for aristocratic reasons. The ideal class romanticized by many is the aristocracy. Upon the bourgeoisie, the businessman, and the *nouveaux riches* ("fat cats"), ridicule is heaped. Anti-capitalist sentiments are part of a capitalist education.[26]

What do liberation theologians mean when they attack capitalism? I have never yet found one who means by that term the reality known to us in the United States. Thus, Enrique Dussel, the most theoretical and exact of the liberationists, writes: "In this manner the capitalist system is adequately defined by the fact that division of labor crystalizes in capital that absorbs the surplus value achieved by the industrial laborer, whether of the center or of the periphery."[27] And again: "The being of the capitalist economy is merchandise, the product that bears an exchange value. . . . In capitalism, however, products are produced not primarily to fulfill necessities but to be a mediation of profit; merchandise, not need."[28] He cites as his authority the Marxist historian Emmanuel Wallerstein.[29]

Three notions are crucial to the concept of capitalism shared by most liberation theologians: (1) the labor theory of value; (2) the theory of surplus value; and (3) the primacy of the exchange function or merchandising. None of these is unique to capitalism. All three are found in pre-capitalist systems. In fact, the origin of capitalism lies in the insight that all three of these principles are false.

(1) *The labor theory of value.* For Dussel, as for Marx, "The ultimate foundation, the Being of all economic systems, is human labor not yet differentiated; *laboriousness,* work as work. . . ."[30] This, Dussel says, is characteristic of all economic systems. For Marx, labor means physical exertion, sweat, effort. Quoting Aristotle, Marx holds that "money is sterile and produces no offspring." Money (capital) by itself yields no profit. Mere money mouldering in a vault for centuries might increase in value by not one cent. How, then, can anyone produce a profit except through labor? Thus, for Marx, all value to be found in any product inheres in the labor invested in its making (or in the making of the machines that are used in its production). Labor of the head and labor of the hand or back are, for Marx, of equal worth. Labor is the source of all economic value. This is true in all systems, according to most liberation theologians, following Marx. This is the theory.

But consider the actual situation. Two farmers working equally hard side by side are not of equal intelligence. One finds a system for organizing his activities that allows him—even, perhaps, with inferior tools and inferior land—to produce a higher yield. Such is the characteristic case in human life. Of forty students in a classroom, all do not work with equal seriousness. Yet even among those who do, and even among those of equal raw intelligence, some work more *intelligently* than others. Their systems of studying are superior, perhaps even to the point of allowing them to study more materials with an equal output of *laboriousness.* For myself, I call this the "creativity theory of value." It is not laboriousness that adds value. It is wit, attention to detail, penetration, organization, inventiveness.

In biblical times, Jerusalem was a trading capital. There were private property, markets, exchanges, incentives, and profits—but there was no capitalism. One can think of the ancient Mediterranean order as mercantilist; merchants there were aplenty, and much buying and selling. But no "inquiry into the nature and causes of the wealth of nations" had yet been launched; that was to await Adam Smith's revolutionary classic in 1776. Even Adam Smith, however, was a traditionalist in his understanding of labor. Not quite like Marx, but not entirely unlike Marx, he too held to an ancient error, the labor theory of value.[31] Nonetheless, Smith set in motion the insight that was to lead, in the United States in the Constitution of 1787, to the recognition of the crucial role of invention. In the body of the Constitution of the United States, before the justly famous Bill of Rights, the term "rights" is invoked only once: to protect the rights of "writers and inventors" to the fruits of their own discoveries. This insight is crucial to capitalist development. This insight led as well to the Merrill Act of 1862, through which Abraham Lincoln stressed the importance of building the American West around centers of discovery and invention, the land-grant colleges.

> . . . the chief use of agricultural Fairs is to aid in improving the great calling of *Agriculture,* in all its departments and minute divisions; to make mutual exchange of agricultural discovery, information and knowledge, so that, at the end, *all* may know everything which may have been known to but *one* or to but *few,* at the beginning—to bring together especially all which is supposed to not be generally known, because of recent discovery or invention.
>
> And not only to bring together, and to impart, all that has been accidentally discovered or invented upon ordinary motive; but by exciting emulation, for premiums, and for the pride and honor of success—of triumph, in some sort—to stimulate discovery and invention into extraordinary activity. In this, these fairs are kindred to the patent clause in the Constitution of the United States; and to the department and practical system based upon that clause.[32]

From farm to farm, what makes the difference for economic dynamism is not *laboriousness,* but *intellect.* Capitalism begins in the human spirit. Wit, invention, and discovery are the sources of wealth, far beyond money or labor or rents or land. Institutionally, this insight led to the primary institution of a capitalist society: the Office of Trademarks and Patents. Social incentives were established for citizens with practical ideas. An immense tide of inventiveness and "know-how" was thereby unleashed.[33] There followed new industries based upon these inventions. On invention more than on any other factor, the wealth of the United States was based. Indeed, for many generations, the wealth of the United States rested hardly at all upon trade or foreign investment. Even there, the first of the U.S. multinational corporations (circa 1870) was the Singer Sewing Machine Company[34]—building abroad, and selling, a useful invention not to be found elsewhere.

Marx, a materialist, failed to understand the role of the human spirit in the invention of new economic value. His vision of economics left out the single most dynamic factor.

(2) *Surplus value.* "These two great discoveries," Friedrich Engels writes, "the materialist conception of history and the revelation of the secret of capitalist production through surplus value, we owe to Marx. With these discoveries socialism became a science."[35] A bogus science, as we shall see. According to Marx, since money in his view is sterile, the only way a capitalist can realize a profit on his investment is by paying labor only a fraction of the gains labor produces. Since he held that *all* value belongs to labor, Marx called the share of the capitalist "theft." This is the crux of socialist science. And it is flatly wrong.

As the Soviet mathematician Igor Shafarevich points out, Marx did not approach *Capital* in a scientific spirit; his was not a scientific search for truth.[36]

> The unquestionably immense *success* of Marxism in the nineteenth and the beginning of the twentieth centuries by no means proves its correctness as a scientific theory. Other movements, Islam, for instance, have enjoyed no less success without ever having laid claim to being "scientific."
>
> The direct impression left by the works of the founders of Marxism leads to the same conclusion—they lack the climate characteristic of scientific inquiry. For the authors, the world of science is divided into two unequal parts. One part consists of a narrow circle of followers, another of enemies, plotting against them and ready for any crime against the truth for the sake of attaining their goals.[37]

Marx was expressing a passionate hostility against his own culture. He did not inquire into its characteristics, good and bad, in a scientific spirit; he set himself the *task* of destroying it. To this task he bent his argument. At one crucial point in that argument, for example, he needed the concept of "surplus value," rooted in the "labor theory of value." So he implanted that concept in his argument, even though it was neither logically self-evident nor supported by empirical evidence. On the contrary, as even friendly readers soon noted, common experience told against it. In introducing the second volume of *Capital*, Engels commented on this crucial gap in the argument, and promised that Marx would redress the glaring fault in Volume III. Marx never did, neither in Volume II nor elsewhere.[38] Indeed, before the end of the nineteenth century, Böhm-Bawerk so thoroughly exposed the glaring fallacy in Marx's argument that serious socialists have avoided resting their case upon this untenable position.[39]

In simple terms, if labor is the sole source of value, owners and managers would always choose to employ larger numbers of laborers since this strategy, according to Marx, is the sole source of profit. Instead, owners and managers know that increments of capital, not least in labor-saving machinery, can vastly increase their productivity and their profits. Marx, of course, could not admit the role of invention, for to do so he would have to admit that capital, too, is a source of profit. So it is—not only in the sense of inanimate factors such as labor-saving machinery, but also in the sense of creative intelligence perceiving new opportunities, recognizing needs not yet satisfied in existing markets, and organizing untapped efficiencies in distribution and marketing. As Israel M. Kirzner points out, discovery is the key to the capitalist process.[40] Inquiring intellect keeps searching for a better grasp of rapidly shifting reality, trying to invent new processes, products, and applications that had heretofore eluded human notice. By launching a system of sustained discovery, the capitalist era laid the groundwork for the creation of immense wealth never possible by the exertion of pure labor alone.

Before the capitalist era (which became self-conscious only in 1776), wealth was based primarily upon land. The wealthy were large landholders (as in Latin America until quite recently). The vast majority of laborers were agricultural workers. What did the large landholders of the feudal era—clergy and aristocrats, mostly—do with their surplus? They held large entertainments, built great buildings, sponsored festivals, raised armies. They *consumed* their surpluses. Only with the invention of joint stock companies, techniques of bookkeeping, the building of roads, the safety of the countryside, and the insight that intelligence and invention could be applied to the production of new, better, and different goods than the world had ever seen before were the possessors and the consumers of wealth led to a new moral possibility.

It was at this point that Adam Smith's insight into the role of invention and intellect could come to fruition. Under the new conditions, instead of consuming their wealth, the wealthy were induced to *invest* it. This entailed new initial costs and substantial risk. Before they could sell the new goods they intended to produce, they had to produce them. For a considerable period of time, they would have to pay for laborers, for materials, and for the construction of (initially quite small) factories and plants, without having yet sold any products by which to recoup these costs. They had to persuade agricultural work-

ers accustomed to long periods of idleness and seasonal employment
to take up the burdens of daily labor, while they themselves took up
the burdens of conception, organization, construction, and the invig-
oration of heretofore non-existent markets.

As John Stuart Mill put it in the *Principles of Political Economy*, for
both laborers and for investors the incentive lay in the prospect of
greater rewards for both.[41] Thus was born the *idea* of meeting old
needs in new ways, and of meeting new needs not before known. This
idea opened up the prospect of "progress"—the bettering of the living
conditions of all, and of the nation as a whole. This vision was *social*.
And the gains, if they materialized, would be socially shared. For em-
bracing harder and more systematic labor than formerly, the laborer
would be rewarded with higher wages, paid more regularly than formerly. For investing in the future, rather than for consuming his surplus in the present, the investor would be rewarded with a percentage
of the expected gain. The success of the enterprise depended upon
both. Both would benefit.

Historically, this new conception might not have worked. A given
enterprise might produce products, which no one would buy, or products of such design that not enough of them would be bought to pay
the costs of producing them. The new idea, like all expressions of human liberty and creativity, required a spirit of venturesomeness and
risk. The inventor saw himself to be an artist of the practical order.
His product might be aesthetic—a better wine, a finer lace, a cheaper
and better bread, chocolates, silk stockings, fine cutlery or glass. Or it
might be aimed at the humbler, daily needs of all: safety pins; cheaper,
machine-sewn clothing; a sewing machine; eating utensils; plates and
cups; ordinary table cloths; packaged cereals or biscuits; tea for common use (not solely for the nobility), salt, etc. In either case, human
imagination had to seize upon the potential market for the product.
And practical wisdom (always in short supply) had to solve problems
of production, packaging, transport, and marketing. There were an
infinite number of ways to fail. Countless enterprises do fail. Still, a
profit of only two or three percent a year would indicate that the enterprise was not merely spinning its wheels, but creating new wealth.
Cumulatively, when thousands of enterprises were creating new
wealth, the national wealth would also rise. "Progress" would become
a tangible, historical fact. From 1780 to 1930, Great Britain averaged
an annual growth rate of at least three percent per year.[42]

Is it immoral for persons of imagination and enterprise to be offered social incentives for abstaining from consumption, for venturing
what they have, and for putting the underemployed to gainful and

productive work? On the contrary, a society that does not arrange such incentives permits the creative economic imagination of its citizenry to lie fallow. Thus, from an economic point of view, have many societies in history stagnated. The standards set by the feudal aristocracy might be (almost certainly were) aesthetically superior to those of the new, vulgar, low-born persons of economic activism. In almost all cultures, the *nouveaux riches* among industrialists and entrepreneurs were mocked for their low birth and humble manners. Adam Smith himself had harsh words for them.[43] Many of them, after all, came from the ranks of the former serfs, the landless, the poor. They lacked aristocratic birth. But they had God-given talents of economic imagination. Any society that wishes to nourish economic activism does well to offer such persons incentives and institutions appropriate to unleashing that imagination.

The inventors of new goods and new services do not take wealth from others. They create new wealth, which without them their people and the world at large would never have seen. In their hands, money is not sterile. Wed to creative intellect, it adds new wealth to the common store. It opens up manifold new opportunities to all: to laborers in the form of steady (and typically growing) wages, to the talented among laborers who break away with their savings to launch new enterprises of their own, to transporters who carry their goods to market, to merchants who offer them to the public, and to the national treasury in otherwise non-existent taxes. This is how the *idea* behind capitalism, like a rock thrown in the placid water of tradition, generated ripples of benefit to the multitudes.

Here lies the secret of "development." Nations that learn it reap its benefits and mightily diminish destitution and poverty in their midst, raising the standards of living of all. Indeed, a cycling of economic elites soon follows, as new inventions render the old obsolete, and old fortunes fall as new fortunes arise. The Lord has shed economic talents very broadly, more profusely among the poor than among the children of the already rich, so that tomorrow's economic inventors typically arise from among today's poor.

Marx was mesmerized by the static traditionalist society of his youth. He thought "classes" were fixed. He underestimated the role of the human spirit in economic dynamism. He was blind to the individual talent and individual genius lavished so abundantly by the Creator among his people, above all among the multitudes of the poor. Marx imagined that human society is directed from the top down, as if the poor lacked all intelligence and creativity. He did not understand the dynamics of institutions of liberty. That is why all who follow him

end up creating gray, static, lifeless, and bureaucratic-military societies, whose fundamental dynamic is hatred, suspicion, conflict, and
war.

The labor theory of value and the concept of surplus value are
intellectual errors of mammoth proportions.

(3) *Exchange and merchandising.* Were exchange and merchandising the central elements of capitalism, we would still be exchanging,
buying and selling the same goods as in the days of the *Manifesto* of
1848. What is original about capitalism, as Max Weber saw, is its *spirit*—
although even Max Weber misidentified that spirit.[44] And what is original about the capitalist spirit is its emphasis upon creativity, invention,
and discovery. Therein lies the economic dynamism of the United
States, Western Europe, Australia, Canada, Japan, the "four little
dragons" of the East Asian Rim, and the others among the relatively
few capitalist countries on earth. Today, the forefront of inventiveness
lies in communications: in satellites, computers, word processors, and
electronics. It lies, too, in genetic research, aquaculture, lasers, and fiber optics. Soon enough, it will lie in the replacement of oil and natural
gas by sources of energy now imperfectly understood in methanol, hy-
drogen, and other substances.

Merchandising is the *last* step of capitalism, not its first and defining difference. I do not mean to be dismissive about the skills of American inventors in bringing their products speedily into common use.
But merchandising is an art as ancient as the bazaars of biblical Jerusalem. *Invention* is the distinctive activity of capitalist societies. Under
capitalism, the primary form of capital is the human mind.[45]

Capitalism is also and above all a *social* system. Among its *institutional* presuppositions, three deserve to be singled out. First, a stable
legal structure defending the rights of private property against the
depredations of the military and the state is indispensable, if individuals are to feel safe to devote their energies toward projects whose ultimate fruition lies in the distant future. Economic tasks are inherently
of immense difficulty; there are an infinite number of ways in which
they can fail. To commit oneself to capitalist acts is to commit oneself
to making many sacrifices in the present in order to construct a new
future. Unless, in the meantime, one can count upon a stable pattern
of law and morality to protect one's private efforts, that risk is insur-
mountable. Without a stable order of private property, the incentive
of the rich and the talented is to live for the present—*Carpe diem!*—
and to let the future bury the dead. By contrast, private property is the
institutional expression of human liberty oriented into the future.

Second, economic imagination and new inventions must be institutionally and legally respected as primary forms of private property. The reason why this is so is entirely social. A society that stifles the inventiveness of its dreamers, inventors, and persons of economic imagination strangles in their cribs infants of thought. One must respect the rights of the inventors and authors in embodied ways. Patents and copyrights are indispensable institutions of dynamic societies.

Third, access to credit must be universally available. The poor are a nation's chief carrier of the ideas of the future. Because they are poor, many persons of inventiveness and imagination lack funds of their own; their only capital lies in their minds and imaginations. They must have access to venture capital. Local, accessible institutions of capital are as necessary to them as air to the wings of eagles.

Since Marx failed so completely to understand the dynamics of modern economies, it is sad to see theologians, who purport to speak in the sacred name of "liberation," claim that they rely upon "Marxist analysis." It cannot be easy for those who have experienced Marxist societies to respect them for that. Instead of stones, theology in Latin America should give the poor bread: not only the bread that one breaks with one's hands and eats, but the bread of creativity, imagination and inventiveness.

It is not those who say "The poor! The poor!" who will enter the Kingdom of Heaven, but those who actually put in place an economic system that helps the poor no longer to be poor.

Theologians have an obligation to think ahead for the Church, experimenting with new ideas and institutions, which may one day form the basis for Catholic social thought, as it develops in the future. Liberation theologians deserve credit for challenging us to think more seriously about the problems of such nations as those of Latin America. But it is necessary to examine further whether their own option for the future—they call it "socialism"—is sufficiently different from what Latin America already has. In the past, liberation theologians say, the Catholic Church was at fault for too easily baptizing the existing order. There remains the danger that one day a future generation will blame the liberation theologians for too easily baptizing the existing revolutionary project of the left. In that charge, there would be an especially poignant cutting edge, precisely because the practical results achieved by socialist revolutions in the twentieth century are dreary and oppressive.

Thus, it is important to know what liberation theologians mean when they use the symbol "socialism." In order to grasp that meaning, it is necessary first to examine two concepts fundamental to liberation theology, "dependency" and "the poor."

Seven

WHAT IS DEPENDENCY?
WHO ARE THE POOR?

Latin Americans and their leaders have not considered that the idea of progress and the desire for innovation have determined the course of recent history. We belong to another tradition, the Hispanic or Hispanic-Roman, which thinks of society as immutable. It has a slow vegetable growth which unfolds in a fixed pattern and relegates creativity to an ornamental level.

Living in a static society, we have developed a restricted social outlook. On the periphery of the world it is not necessary to be disciplined, methodical, curious, or constant. If the objectives of our lives were to transform substance or ideas, to question the world in which we live, and to deny it by acts of intellectual rebellion, we would have no choice but to alter our temperaments and to transform our social values. It is a dangerous blunder to keep repeating that the success of countries such as the United States is due to the exploitation of the Third World countries or to good fortune in the distribution of natural resources. Each day more experts are convinced that the key element in the development of wealth is "human capital." In 1945, Japan was destroyed, and its people were hungry. Forty years later, it is one of the most prosperous, productive centers of the world. Japan has thoroughly used its immense human capital. What is behind the Japanese—or Swiss, Swedish, German, Korean, English, Singaporean, American, Dutch, or Norwegian—miracle? What is behind the miracle of each society that has risen spectacularly in the last few centuries? It is simple: a temperament adapted to pursued objectives and the use of valuable human capital. If we cannot change our objectives because they have been determined outside of our borders, then we must change our idiosyncrasies in order to substantially improve our human capital.—*Carlos Alberto Montaner*[1]

When liberation theologians speak of the poor, do they really mean all the poor, or only those who are already engaged in the *praxis* of socialist revolution? And when they speak of "dependency," two questions arise. What do they mean? And are they correct? To these questions we now turn.

1. DEPENDENCY THEORY

Gustavo Gutierrez, like other liberation theologians, is fond of saying that his analysis of the Latin American socioeconomic situation is based upon "studies of the most rigorous scientific exactitude."[2] In the social sciences, alas, such exactitude is unattainable. Points of view are many, variables are too numerous to control, definitions are in dispute, and methods are at best probabilistic. Liberation theologians have an old-fashioned dogmatic faith in social science, rather than in theology. Thus, from the beginning their argument has depended on a theory of Latin American development first presented by some social scientists rather simplistically. In recent years, the latter have modified their views.

During two summers, 1984 and 1985, two U.S. scholars sympathetic to liberation theology prepared successive papers assessing the status of dependency theory today and its exact role in liberation theology. Michael J. Francis of the University of Notre Dame isolated two "easily defensible" theses of dependency theory, and three "controversial propositions," for which there is less evidence and the issue is hotly disputed.[3] Arthur F. McGovern, S.J., of the University of Detroit, recounted the history of dependency theory in its several different reformulations, distilling from it the irreducible points that continue to serve the purposes of liberation theologians.[4] Both scholars concentrated on the situation of Latin America.

Dependency theory arose during the late 1960s as a way of explaining what was going *wrong* in Latin American development. Although national economic growth rates were often high—in historical terms spectacular—there was widespread dissatisfaction. Populations were growing rapidly. Immense internal migrations toward the cities

created vast tracts of slums. Although mortality figures kept rising (sig-
nifying better health), the condition of the poor seemed otherwise to
worsen, both absolutely and relatively. Absolutely, many of the poor
had been uprooted from their native villages and now lived in sprawl-
ing, often violent shanty towns with far too little work, income, or
means of social organization. Relatively, the income of the poorest
quintile seemed static or declining (much depends in this dispute upon
the years chosen for analysis), while unparalleled prosperity seemed
confined to the highest quintile. Great new superhighways and city
freeways were built, and magnificent new highrises gleamed in the urban sun. Among the poor, one's eyes could see the terrible and tangible differences between the orderly if sleepy villages of 1945 and the
teeming, unsightly *favelas* of recent years. One's eyes saw—and one's
ear heard—an unfolding story of desperation. Far away, in Hong
Kong, Singapore, Taiwan, South Korea, and Japan, populations that
entered the period after 1945 in even more desperate poverty than
that of Latin America had by 1970 experienced an almost miraculous
uplifting of the poor.[5] Not so in Latin America. Dependency theory
attempted to explain what was going wrong.

Here are the two solid theses of dependency theory set forth by
Professor Francis:

> *Proposition 1: Because of their dependence on the developed
> "core" countries, the peripheral countries are experiencing a growing
> loss of national control over their economic, political, social, and cul-
> tural life.*
>
> *Proposition 2: The current economic growth in the less-devel-
> oped countries is unevenly distributed among sectors of the society.
> Because income distribution is so badly skewed, the poorest half of
> most societies is left relatively untouched by economic growth.*[6]

In a strict sense, both these propositions are falsified by the record of achievement of the countries of the East Asian Rim mentioned above. Even more rigorously than the developed capitalist
nations, the latter have followed a liberal theory of capitalist development, low taxes, and free trade. In the terms of propositions 1
and 2, they have succeeded spectacularly, where Latin American
countries have failed. Indeed, so great has been their success that it
has put great pressure upon China under Zeng-zhao Ping and India
under Rajiv to adopt similar methods, also with striking success.
Nonetheless, if we accept propositions 1 and 2 as aimed precisely at
Latin America, they do have a certain plausibility. For one thing,

they are in line with Latin American tradition. "Latin America was born dependent," Gutierrez writes.[7] For another, they suit the Latin American habit of looking elsewhere for economic, political, and cultural leadership. Latin American thought has never defined itself as a world pioneer. On the contrary, it has always followed the paths of others, often with less success than those it imitated from afar. It is not easy to think of areas of life in which Latin America has taken the lead. Until recently, at least, Latin America has been a continent with a *dependent frame of mind*.

Professor Francis next lists three "controversial" propositions of dependency theory.

> *Proposition 1: The condition of dependency makes economic growth more difficult for countries on the international periphery.*
>
> *Proposition 2: The "trickle down" process is not going to occur in the third world countries or will take such a long time to happen as to doom many future generations to poverty.*
>
> *Proposition 3: The condition of being dependent is correlated with being undemocratic.*[8]

These propositions are deservedly called "controversial." The first two run afoul of the stunning successes of Japan and the "four little dragons." Professor Francis mentions other difficulties: "The countries most integrated into the world economy have tended to grow more quickly over a longer period than those that are not."[9] In addition, regions least touched by the West seem the most retarded of all; and those most touched seem to be the most advanced.[10] But Francis prefers those studies that show that reliance on *foreign investment* in the long run slows development. He also cites Eastern European countries as models for less developed countries, since their socialism has the "ability to generate capital investment and to impose tight limitations on foreign investment."[11] (Such "capital investment" is made possible by low wages and rigid political controls.)

In proposition 2, Francis mentions the "trickle down" process. This is not the only alternative. What is most striking about the countries of the East Asian Rim is their choice of a process through which wealth "wells up" from the bottom. In Hong Kong, e.g., wealth wells up from the multitude of small businesses. At the end of 1980, 20,000 factories employed fewer than 10 persons; 8,000 employed between 10–49; 1,500 employed between 100–999; and only 40 employed more than 1000. Incorporation fees are a mere HK$300 plus $4 per

$1000 of authorized capital. Legal formalities required to set up a small business are few and inexpensive; for about US$30, one can lawfully open a small business in Hong Kong.[12]

In order to construct a capitalist development model, then, it is essential to build from the "bottom up," not from the "top down." Secondly, it is not necessary to rely on foreign investment. Latin America is a continent with huge internal capital. At present, however, domestic investment faces enormous risks of confiscation by government, spiralling inflation, and unpredictable government policies. It is protected by few incentives. In a real sense, dependency on foreign investment follows from government policy. Finally, the effect of foreign investment cannot be measured solely by its amount; a very great deal depends on *how* it is invested and by whom. Much foreign investment in Latin America is directed by government agencies and government-owned corporations. State control, not free private decision-making, dominates the major portion of most Latin American economies.

As for proposition 3, Francis underestimates the desire of Latin American peoples for democracy, a theme much underlined by Octavio Paz:

> Our peoples chose democracy because it appeared to them to be the highroad to modernity. The truth is precisely the opposite: democracy is the result of modernity, not the path to it. The difficulties we have experienced in instituting democratic rule are one of the effects—the most serious one, perhaps—of our incomplete and defective modernization. But we were not wrong to choose this system of government: even with its many tremendous shortcomings, it is the best of all that humanity has invented. We have been mistaken, it is true, about the method for attaining it, since we have limited ourselves to imitating foreign models. The task awaiting Latin Americans, one requiring efforts of imagination at once bold and realistic, is to rediscover in our own traditions those seeds and roots—they are there—that will enable us to implant firmly and nourish a genuine democracy. It is an urgent task, and there is almost no time left.[13]

Since 1979, some eleven Latin American nations have moved in the direction of democracy: Argentina, Brazil, Uruguay, Bolivia, Peru, Colombia, Panama, Honduras, El Salvador, Guatemala, and Haiti.

They join Mexico, Venezuela, Costa Rica, and others. The major recalcitrant dictatorships are Chile, Paraguay, and Cuba.

Another point should be made. Latin American theologians often seem to assume that North American corporations are not only inherently rapacious but clamoring to enter Latin American markets. During recent decades, however, the process has been exactly in the opposite direction. Even regional giants like the United Fruit Company have been discouraged in Latin American markets, and have retrenched and diversified elsewhere. No U.S. firm, for example, now maintains more than ten percent of its gross investments in the Central America-Caribbean region.

In 1983, U.S. citizens had a total of $883 billion invested overseas. (Foreign citizens had investments totalling $663 billion in the U.S.)[14] Three-quarters of this overseas investment was placed in Europe, Japan, Canada, and Mexico. Of the remainder, a larger part (about 16 percent of the total) is in Latin America, the rest in Asia and Africa. Each year, the American economy has a gross national product of more than $3 trillion. One can see instantly that the size of total U.S. investment in Latin America is less than one percent of annual U.S. G.N.P. Were all of Latin America closed to U.S. investment, or even trade, the adjustment in the U.S. would be significant but hardly major.

*   *   *

For his part, Arthur J. McGovern, S.J., sketches the history of dependency theory from Raul Prebisch in the early 1960s, through Fernando Enrique Cardoso and Andre Gunder Frank. McGovern judges that the more moderate Cardoso is the most significant dependency theorist for liberation theology, but that Frank, who takes a Marxist point of view, is more influential among North American social scientists. Frank links dependency theory to the Leninist theory of imperialism. By contrast, Cardoso sharply disagrees: "We do *not* see dependency and imperialism as external and internal sides of a single coin."[15] McGovern is the first scholar to study the precise use of dependency theory by liberation theologians, especially Gustavo Gutierrez and Leonardo Boff.

McGovern begins with Gutierrez: "Dependence and liberation are correlative terms. An analysis of the situation of dependence leads one to escape from it."[16] For Hugo Assmann in *Theology for a Nomad Church,* the whole enterprise of liberation theology makes little sense apart from the factual judgment that the poor of Latin America suffer not from simple poverty but from oppressive structures, linked to external forces of domination.[17] Assmann's view is closer to that of Marx and Lenin, as updated by Frank. In *A Theology of Liberation* (1971), by contrast, Gutierrez sides with Cardoso, calling attention to the importance of external domination but insisting that external factors—contrary to the Leninist theory of imperialism—are not the only factors. Gutierrez approvingly quotes Cardoso's warning against having "recourse to the idea of dependence as a way of 'explaining' internal processes of the dependent societies by a purely 'external' variable . . . which is regarded as the real cause."[18] The main importance of dependency theory for Gutierrez, at this stage, is that mere reformism, mere modernization, is not enough, and that revolution is necessary. Gutierrez further believes that such a revolution cannot be a liberal, capitalist revolution, but must be socialist.

It is important to see that Gutierrez never fully justifies his embrace of socialism; as we shall see in the next chapter, what he means by the term is not clear. From Cardoso's moderate view of dependency theory, it is quite possible to conclude that Latin America would achieve greater economic and cultural independence through democratic capitalism. It could pursue its own distinctive experiment in free economic development from the bottom up. It could encourage greater self-reliance on locally generated capital. Like Cardoso, who favors a moderate socialist course, Gutierrez does not take that route.

Nine years later, in a collection of essays written over several years, *The Power of the Poor in History*, Gutierrez again says that "External dependency and internal domination are the marks of the social structures of Latin America."[19] He treats the earlier dependency theories as by and large a boon, but holds that they focused too much attention on the conflict between nations (center versus the periphery) and not enough on the worldwide class struggle. In a sense, Gutierrez has gradually adopted a more empirical attitude toward dependency theory, calling attention to its many variations and the many sound objections marshalled against them. These qualifications become especially apparent in his essay on theology and the social sciences (1984), presumably in response to the Vatican's criticism of liberation theology.[20] Here Gutierrez treats dependency as a fact—parts of which are illuminated by various dependency theories—and calls for greater care in criticizing such theories and in incorporating other theories. This open-mindedness is admirable.

Leonardo Boff, McGovern continues, writes that "Latin America stands on the periphery of the big-power centers and is dominated by them."[21] And, "Development and underdevelopment are two sides of the same coin."[22] But Boff is both skeptical about dependency theory and reluctant to believe that Andre Gunder Frank's call for revolution is wise. Dependency theory "is only a theory, not an established truth. It is one stage in an ongoing investigation and has its own intrinsic limitations. It offers a good diagnosis of the structure of underdevelopment, but it does not do much to offer any viable way out."[23] Boff sees Canada as a model for Brazil—it, too, has a kind of dependency, but also a pattern of economic growth.[24] No one can simply opt out of the interdependent modern world.

McGovern also rejects Andre Gunder Frank's formulation of dependency theory: "Latin America is underdeveloped *because* it has supported the development of Western Europe and the United States."[25] Indeed, McGovern prefers to speak of dependency "analysis" rather than dependency "theory," for its intention, he believes, is not to explain but to call attention to various factors peculiar to Latin America. In culture and ethos, Latin Americans are unlike the Japanese, the North Americans, and even the Western (or Southern) Europeans. Culture matters. So do the traditional institutions of Latin America— the large estates, the many peons. So also do Latin American patterns of production. Adam Smith's outline of a "natural path of growth," McGovern writes, is that a nation ought, first, to develop its agriculture (through relatively egalitarian free enterprise in rural areas, as in the U.S. Middle West); second, to produce for its own urban markets; and third, to produce for international trade.[26]

Alas, Latin American patterns of land ownership follow those of the feudal era (and the plantation system of the U.S. South). Too often, the landholders produce food, not for their own peoples, but for foreign export. Even in the manufacturing sector, Latin America produces too little for its own internal basic needs. Scores of millions lack electricity, electric lights, refrigerators, cheap packaged foods, and other basic products.

Thus, Hugo Assmann, at the same conference addressed by McGovern, speaks bitingly of Brazil as "a land where cows never see people and people never eat meat."[27] Given the immense tracts of uninhabited land in Brazil, whose population is only half that of the United States, it is difficult for Americans to understand such failures of Brazilian agriculture. In the U.S., only two percent of the population is engaged in farming, and yet produces food in unimaginable abundance. In this sense, *system* does matter. And the Latin American system is already in need of a fundamental reordering, from the bottom up.

Latin America, further, has allowed itself to become unusually dependent upon foreign capital: foreign aid, foreign investment, foreign financial services, and foreign technological know-how. The result is that all crucial economic moves in Latin America depend disproportionately upon decisions made elsewhere—by the International Monetary Fund, for example. Both Francis and McGovern supply considerable detail upon this point.

On the other hand, Francis and McGovern fail to note that Latin America does have immense reservoirs of internal capital. Alas, domestic systems are so little ordered toward stable and fruitful domestic investment that vast proportions of that internal capital are invested in safer havens outside Latin America—in the U.S. and Europe, in particular. Indeed, by some accountings, Latin Americans own foreign assets abroad amounting to very large proportions of the total Latin American borrowings of foreign capital (the debt).[28] The internal wealth of Latin America is not well attracted to local investment. Such local investment is absolutely crucial to internal development and self-reliance. By discouraging it, Latin American nations insure a dependency they could tremendously reduce through their own efforts. They have the resources—natural, financial and human. Nicholas Eberstadt writes in *This World* 14 (1986):

> Not all Third World nations with substantial international financial obligations now find themselves in financial difficulty. . . . South Korea's foreign debt today approaches $50 billion; yet it seems to meet its payments of interest and principal on time and has not found it necessary to enter into "rescheduling" negotiations. Why is this? The answer is that, to date, the government has managed to earn a higher rate of return on the foreign money it is putting to use than it is obliged to pay back in interest. . . . [A]ny discussion of a debt crisis in Latin America raises the question of how those funds were spent. What is the cause of what must obviously have been low rates of return? . . . . Faced with easy access to credit from Western banks in the wake of the OPEC oil price increases, many governments seem to have adjusted their policies toward less, rather than more, productive uses of capital. . . . In many nations much of the borrowed money appears to have been used to maintain unsustainably high levels of consumption for the general population through a complex and ambitious array of subsidies. Common rhetoric notwithstanding, these subsidies

conferred immediate benefit on very broad portions of the populations in question. Indeed their broad incidence was precisely the reason for their widespread popularity.

*   *   *

Returning now to McGovern's argument, a comment may be helpful. From the situation as McGovern describes it, two paths diverge. Gutierrez, Dussel, and others speak of the sources of the aid, investments, loans, and technologies that Latin America has made itself dependent upon as "dominators." They use these facts to claim "oppression." This is one path. The other path is to suggest that Latin Americans need not have made such choices. They might have closed the door against foreigners, as China did. Mahatma Gandhi in India also rebelled against "modernity," foreign industry, and foreign investment, while insisting upon indigenous development. The closing of Latin American markets against foreign investment would not have had much significance prior to 1941, since at that point both trade between Latin America and North America and foreign investment in Latin America were relatively minor. The sea lanes of the Atlantic were much more traveled between both continents and Europe than between North and South America. During World War II (when the Atlantic sea lanes were closed), and particularly after 1960, trade and investment between North and South America multiplied. The liberation theologians seem now to regard this as a great error. Perhaps it was.

The major conventional criticism of this post-war era of trade and development is that the bottom 50 percent of the Latin American population has benefited little from it, except in terms of better health and longevity. "Peripheral capitalism, particularly in Latin America," Raul Prebisch has written, "is characterized by a dynamic which excludes the great masses of the people. It is a dynamic process oriented towards the privileged consumer society. . . ."[29] Production is too heavily oriented toward sale in foreign markets and to the affluent elites of Latin America. Income distributions in Latin America, it is alleged, remain among the most unequal in the world. And the exclusion of so many Latin Americans from political, social, and economic activism has negative effects upon the emergence of the vital, stable middle class that is necessary for democracy.

Regarding income distributions, it should be noted that Latin American industrial workers—the proper "proletarians" in orthodox

Marxist analysis—rank in the top twenty-five percent of income earners. They are among the relatively affluent. It is the scores of millions of Latin Americans in the non-modern sectors of the economy who are the poorest. Again, were the system of law in Latin American nations favorable to domestic investment, there would be much greater incentives for Latin American capital to stay at home, thus creating new goods, services, and employment throughout the Continent. The failure of Latin America to reach its own immense economic potential must be attributed to its anti-capitalist, anti-creative institutions, laws, regulations, and hereditary elites.

McGovern argues that liberation theologians approach the dilemmas specified in this analysis with three major values.[30] First, they insist upon autonomy, self-respect and a sense of worth among the "non-persons" of history, the marginalized ethnic groups and scorned cultures. Second, they desire liberation from material poverty, from political tyranny and torture and repression of every kind, and from repression of conscience, thought, and speech. (This is, as we have seen, the classic liberal agenda.) Third, they insist that basic needs for the sustenance of life and the basic decencies of daily living must be met for all. With these aims, I believe, liberals as well as liberation theologians are in agreement. (The "basic needs" approach, however, is consistent with life in a well-kept prison; unless matched to civil and economic liberties, it tends to too materialistic a view.)

The question comes down, McGovern writes, to which "specific structures, institutions, and policies" will best realize these values.[31] On political matters, liberation theologians have recently begun to support the institutions of democracy. Well they should, since Octavio Paz identifies democratic institutions as the only political institutions that enjoy legitimacy in Latin American consciousness.[32] The major remaining dispute concerns the form of the *economic* institutions best suited to attain the goals mentioned by McGovern. Such economic institutions must meet two criteria: (1) they must be suited to Latin American habits, aspirations, abilities, and values; and (2) they must be likely at least to diminish dependency and to raise up the poor of Latin America from the prison of material poverty.

With McGovern, I am prepared to believe that sentiment in Latin America, while favoring a "mixed" system of private and "socialized" sectors, may come down somewhat more on the socialist (or statist) side of political economy than does the United States. I would wish, however, that the East Asian pattern had more appeal to Latin Americans than socialism appears to have. I would wish that liberation theologians thought more critically about what has gone wrong in so many socialist experiments during the past century. I would wish that they were not so dangerously vague about what they mean by socialism ("a system that truly represents the vast majority of the people"; "a socialism without the deficiencies of existing socialist countries"[33]). In the end, though, Latin Americans will make such decisions on their own—and reap the appropriate fruits, bitter or sweet, as the case may be. The issue, in the end, is *practical:* how to get from the bitter present to a better economic future.

When Latin Americans hear the word *capitalism,* McGovern writes, they do not mean what we mean.

> Capitalism, as Latin Americans have experienced it, has not brought a high standard of living or even significant progress toward such a standard to the vast majority. It has not opened up widespread opportunities for individual free enterprise; instead, concentration of ownership and wealth prevails. State power has been used more often to protect this system and its privileged elites than to safeguard human rights and include the majority. Foreign ownership in industries, whatever benefits it may confer, diminishes autonomy and national pride; hence many do not see capitalism as *their* system at all. In the Latin American church, even the staunchest critics of liberation theology do not attempt to defend Latin American capitalism. Bishop Alfonso Lopez Trujillo affirms: "We are convinced that capitalism is a human failure." Roger Vekemans, S.J., calls for a "Christian socialism" to avoid the evils of capitalism and Marxist socialism.[34]

All this makes one sad. It might be entirely possible for Latin Americans to fashion a new form of liberal capitalism unlike those of Japan, Canada, Australia, the United States, and the other existing exemplars. That there may be a pluralism of such forms is inherent in the idea of democratic capitalism. Eventually, in fact, some of the following institutions of liberal capitalist societies, if not all, may come to seem practical to liberation theologians: widespread private home ownership; ease in launching small businesses; access to credit for all; a spirit of enterprise, pioneering, and invention; habits of civic, social, and economic association and cooperation; a tradition (marred by human weakness) of honesty in dealings, punctuality, and an internalized respect for law; and emphasis upon dissent, questioning, and new ideas. (In this short list, I emphasize values of most significance to economic activism.)

In short, debate about the "specific structures, institutions, and policies" that might realize the dream of liberation theology has hardly begun. Still, it is already clear that dependency theory, as modified by Professors Francis and McGovern, does not absolve Latin Americans of responsibility for their own economic choices.

Carlos Alberto Montaner concurs with this judgment:

> We Latin Americans, with more inhabitants than the United States, possess as much or more potential wealth. Spawned by Europe—just as the United States—we have universities that are more than four hundred years old. We have urban centers that were already established when Chicago was a prairie overrun by buffalo. Unconsciously, we have renounced our contribution to shaping our own destiny.
>
> We are accustomed to passing the guilt and responsibility on to others. We do not realize that in almost five centuries at a university such as San Marcos, hardly a discovery of scientific importance was made, and not one original idea was advanced in the humanities. . . .[35]

Latin Americans have *chosen* to depend upon the more developed capitalist countries. Too many among Latin American business elites do not pursue discoveries and innovations of their own but prefer the relative safety and low investment inherent in relying upon technologies, goods and services already developed elsewhere. There has been a widespread failure to incarnate the spirit of discovery in a distinctive Latin American fashion.

*   *   *

If Latin Americans wish to close Latin America to multinational corporations, foreign investments, and foreign loans, they may do so. But that may be more costly to them than to the U.S. Strictly, the U.S. is not very dependent upon its economic activities in Latin America. Whether with the help of capital investment from foreign firms or without such help, the real problem Latin America must solve is how to promote economic activism among its impoverished millions. A capitalist revolution at the *bottom* of Latin American society would bear rapid fruit. The poor need access to credit, easy entrance into presently closed markets, ease in incorporating their own small businesses, and tax relief for capital formation and capital investment at home.

Once this process began, the internal market of Latin America would rapidly expand—as it has in Hong Kong and elsewhere. Moreover, once it became safe and profitable to invest at home, "capital flight" by Latin American citizens would cease. If all the available capital of Latin America were invested at home, instead of abroad, new industries and commercial ventures would multiply. Unemployment would be diminished. The circle of prosperity would widen from the bottom up. Since God bestows economic talent even more lavishly among the poor than among the children of the already rich (who are tempted to be less venturesome), social mobility would increase rapidly and great new enterprises would be born.

An empirical study of dependency, in short, does *not* show that the destiny of Latin America depends more upon external factors than upon internal changes in Latin American law and practice. On the contrary, Latin American institutions and practices discriminate against capitalist activities among the poor, and discourage internal investment and internal invention even among the affluent. It is obvious that liberation theologians grasp neither the metaphysic of liberalism nor the social role of markets. Their own accounts of liberalism are sketchy and ill-informed. In Latin America, they face pre-capitalist, mercantilistic, and patrimonial institutions that they mistakenly label "capitalist." They suffer under a social order very like the one Adam Smith opposed in Britain in 1776: a social order dominated by a land-holding class and a mercantile elite committed neither to a mind-centered economic dynamism nor to markets open to every class of the citizenry. We should join them in opposing the existing order.

In Peru, the liberal activist Hernando de Soto has pointed out that state regulation almost totally strangles the economic liberties of the lower classes. Some 2.5 million street vendors, artisans, and manufacturers work without legal protection because they cannot cut through governmental red tape.[36] Ninety-five percent of Lima's public transportation (buses and taxis) are run by this illegal "informal sector." Forty-three percent of all Peruvian housing built during the past 30 years has been built informally. Sixty percent of Lima's food is distributed informally. To build homes requires 7 to 14 years to receive government authorization. It can take 289 days to form a legal corporation, and the cost in bribes, government fees, and foregone income is five times the average worker's annual earnings, some $8,700. Hernando de Soto writes:

> This disorder in our affairs is the result of a cultural lag—our institutions are simply no longer suitable to the new reality.

As long as there is conflict between the legal order and the
way the majority of the people must earn their living, build
their homes, obtain transport, food and credit, the country
will remain in a critical situation.[37]

De Soto explains that "Western Europe emerged from mercantilism centuries ago, but the Spanish colonies did not. Because of the
legal system, the real power—both economic and political—remains
with an elite. What we are now seeing in Latin America is a sponta-
neous challenge of this power. The Informals are making the formal
law irrelevant."[38] The poor needed to be liberated from the power of
elites.

Instead of encouraging economic activism, Latin American law
and practice punish it. Despite such adversities, the magnitude and the
ingenuity of the vast "informal sector" in Latin American economies
show that the Latin American population as a whole has an abundance
of economic talent which is now being systematically repressed. In
Latin America, the law excludes the vast majority from free capitalist
activities. Latin America continues in ancient habits of dependency because self-reliance and personal dynamism are shackled. Breaking
these bonds would liberate the economic talents of the poor. Given its
abundance of natural resources, Latin America would then become
one of the most prosperous continents on earth.

*   *   *

One cannot close this discussion without speaking, at least briefly,
of Latin American debt. Fifteen years ago, the Latin American left severely criticized foreign investment by multinational corporations and
spoke in favor of borrowing. The idea was to break dependency, so
that Latin Americans could be masters of their own development.

Who incurred these debts? Mostly, the borrowers were Latin
American governments and large (often state-controlled) firms. Studies of this debt show that in some countries (Argentina, e.g.) as much
as seventy-five percent or more of these loans, once received, were not
invested in Latin America, but in the United States and Europe.[39] This
use of borrowed money was gravely injurious to Latin American economic progress. In addition, many other loans were squandered in activities not productive enough to create new wealth—in fact, not
productive enough even to repay capital and interest. Such vast sums
ought to have been used creatively. They weren't. A large amount was
lost through corruption and personal self-aggrandizement on the part

of government officials and others. The record of what was done with immense amounts of money, borrowed in effect from the savings of citizens in other lands, is not a pretty one. Such massive corruption is rooted, here as elsewhere, in excessive state control over Latin American economies.

Without entering further into a clarifying discussion of who is at fault, it is significant to note that once borrowers receive borrowed money, power passes into the hands of the borrowers. They have the money. If they choose to default, the lenders lose everything they loaned. Of course, such defaults have consequences for the borrowers, too. Further international credit can scarcely be extended to them.

In 1980, the prime rate for interest in the United States was 22 percent. It has now fallen to less than half that, not far above where it was when the loans were first executed. Nonetheless, it appears that immense hardships have now descended upon Latin American governments that can scarcely carry the burden. What ought to be done?

Certainly, it is in the interest of all parties to renegotiate the debts so that all parties can survive the crisis intact. In particular, the new democracies of Latin America are threatened by the economic austerities now made necessary. Latin American governments tried to help the poor, not by generating economic dynamism, but by borrowing. The bubble of illusion generated by living on borrowed money has popped. The defense of democracy depends upon a negotiated resolution.

Yet, in fact, the debt issue runs deeper than the mere fact of indebtedness. A crisis may always be viewed as an opportunity for radical restructuring. If Latin American governments do not unleash vigorous economic activism, the mere cancellation of the debt will solve no fundamental problem. Those who opt for socialism or for expanded state control over the economy want merely to repress wealth-generating activism. That would mean retrogression, not advance. It would represent more statism, not less.

Perhaps the cancellation of these enormous debts is inevitable; in short, massive defaults. But it would be immoral merely to cancel these debts without exacting as a price the end of economic repression in Latin America. The source of economic dynamism lies in the inventive minds of millions of economic activists, succeeding in their own local economic projects. Until Latin America halts the repression of economic activists, particularly among the 200 million of Latin America's poorest citizens, the cancellation of the current debt would leave a broken cistern, still running dry.

If hundreds of billions of dollars of borrowed money can be lost without visibly creating new wealth in Latin America, so could hundreds of billion dollars of foreign aid or capital transfers. Money does not create wealth. Only the creative use of money does, and that depends upon institutions and habits that reward, rather than punish, creativity.

2. WHO ARE THE POOR?

In *The Power of the Poor in History,* Gutierrez distinguishes the "progressive theology" of Europe and the United States from "liberation theology." Following great Protestant thinkers, "progressive theology" addresses itself to the educated elites of modern capitalist societies, as secular unbelievers.[40] By contrast, liberation theology addresses Latin Americans who are neither secular nor unbelievers but divided into oppressors and oppressed. "Here the oppressors and the oppressed share, superficially at any rate, the same faith."[41] In Latin America, some of the educated elites are progressive, some traditionalist. Liberation theology does not stand either with the progressive elite or with the traditionalist elite—but with the poor.[42]

Liberation theology is highly suspicious of the claims of liberalism, capitalism, and modernity. "Theologically, modernity has been rather unfruitful in Latin America."[43] In addition, liberation theology stands especially with the non-Western population of Latin America, with the Indians, *mestizos,* and blacks. For Gutierrez, "class struggle" means essentially the struggle of these *"non-persons,"* these non-Western, non-modern populations. It is time for them, he holds, to become agents of their own destiny. Liberation theology roots itself among such persons, shares their pains and struggles, tries to hear *their* voice, and then tries to amplify this voice to the world.[44] When Gutierrez writes of "the oppressed" in Latin America, therefore, he does not exactly mean (as most North Americans might expect) *all* Latin Americans. He has special concern for "marginalized ethnic groups" and "scorned cultures," whom he links to the more generic "exploited classes."[45]

Liberation theology, he says, has two fundamental insights. The first insight is that theology is *reflection,* and thus a second-order activity. Prior to it must come involvement in the *experience* and *activity* of the liberation it stands for. The second insight is that such involvement, in Latin American certainly, must spring from a "decision to work from the viewpoint of the poor"—the marginalized ethnic groups and scorned classes.[46] History must be *"reread from the side of the poor*. The history of humanity has been written 'with a white hand,' from the side of the dominators. History's losers have another outlook."[47] When Gutierrez speaks of "class struggle," he appears to mean a rather more racial and ethnic conception of "class" than most students have noticed.

Gustavo Gutierrez is short and olive-skinned; when he studied in Europe, he must have seen in the eyes of others that he was from "the other side," from a poor family in faraway Peru. Orbis Books says of him:

> After a first-rate theological education in Europe, he returned to minister to working-class people in Lima and found that the first-rate education did not fit the situation. As a result, he had to start learning all over again, in the midst of his involvement with the people in Lima, a slum area of Lima in which he still lives and works.[48]

This is the context in which liberation theology began.

When Gutierrez speaks of "the poorest" he means (and often says explicitly), the "Indians, blacks, and *mestizos*" of Latin America.[49] He criticized the preparatory document of Puebla for praising Western culture without hearing the indigenous voices of the continent that have always been *oppressed* by Western culture, a Western culture that is not theirs.[50] "Oppression and marginalization of the poor—of the Indians, originally—is an old Latin American tradition. It goes all the way back to colonial times."[51] He speaks of the native peoples of Latin America as "underdogs." "From the very beginning of the *Conquista* the native American peoples rebelled against their dominators."[52] One of the great influences upon Gutierrez is José Carlos Mariátegui, who "sought to think through the reality of Latin America in creative Marxist terms. A native of Peru," Gutierrez continues with justifiable pride, Mariategui "sees the Indian question as a demanding and permanent theme for reflection."[53] For Gutierrez, three terms are linked: (1) the poorest; (2) the Indians, blacks, mestizos and other non-Westerners, the "non-persons," those who have not yet "acted" in history; and (3) a Marxist interpretation of capitalism.

Gutierrez offers the following capsule history:

> The bourgeoisie is the social class that arose in the cities of a dying feudal world. Little by little this class established itself as the dominant one, and henceforward it would constitute the driving force of the economic system we know under the

name of capitalism. Reaching the peak of its power in the industrial revolution, the bourgeoisie would now be in control of an economy based on private enterprise—and on the vicious exploitation of workers (in Europe) and the poor (in colonial and neocolonial lands). Shortly the bourgeois class would become the driving force in politics, too.[54]

The footnote to this passage refers the reader to Chapter 25 of Karl Marx's *Capital*. According to Gutierrez at another place, liberals hold that "all human beings are equal."[55] But he again adds a footnote from Marx: "Marx will severely criticize this. For him there is real inequality between the buyer and the seller, from the moment the majority of the population must sell their physical labor in exchange for a wage."[56]

For Gutierrez, the name for what oppresses Latin America is capitalism. He seldom uses the term without an adjective such as vicious, savage, cruel, exploitative, oppressive, or dominating. He links capitalism to what preceded it. "Latin America was born dependent," he writes:

> . . . any changes taking place in Europe wrought changes in Latin America. The eighteenth century was the beginning of the end for Spanish power, both economically and politically. England was becoming a match for Spain . . . on the high seas, and this meant international trade. . . . The old colonies had come unequivocally within the capitalist system.[57]

A white liberal elite in Latin America then flew flags of "liberty," "democracy," and "modernity," while serving commercial and financial interests abroad. Traditionalists served the older colonial order rooted in the remains of the old bureaucracy. The Catholic Church sided with the traditionalists against the liberals. The United States replaced Britain as the chief capitalist power. During "the liberal era in Latin America," liberals "strove to overcome the remaining traces of barbarism among the poor of Latin America." This era of cultural arrogance "turned out to be only a cheap imitation of what was happening in the North Atlantic world."[58] Despite beautiful words, the United States "only instituted a more refined exploitation of the Latin America masses," who slowly broke through "the lie."

> What had been a movement for modern freedoms, democracy, and rational, universal thought in Europe and the United States, in Latin America only meant new oppression,

and even more ruthless forms of spoliation of the populous classes. The exploitation carried on among us by the modern nations—those shining knights of "liberty"—occasioned a traumatic experience not easy to forget about when we hear of "freedom and democracy."[59]

The poorest, Gutierrez says, are awakening. No longer passive and asleep, they are becoming agents of their own history. Hating the system they find themselves in, they are "forgers of a radically different society."[60] "The socialist revolution in Cuba—whatever analysis some observers may make today—opened up new outlooks."[61] Camilo Torres and "Che" Guevara exerted "definitive influence in Christian circles." And so Gutierrez sums up the cycles of Latin American history: "Latin America has always been a land of oppression and repression."[62] What is different today is a broad popular resistance. "This is the context in which the liberation of theology was born and grew. It could not have come to be before the popular movement itself. . . ." The poor "are calling into question" the political economy that "oppresses and marginalizes them. . . . This is why they take the road of social revolution and not the reformist palliatives. This is why they go in search of liberation, not developmentalism; they call for socialism."[63]

Not only is Gutierrez' interpretation of capitalism Marxist, so is his interpretation of how an intellectual vanguard (liberation theologians) ought to root itself in popular movements, and so also is his interpretation of what the poor of Latin America desire: socialism. Indeed, to understand Gutierrez fully, one needs to grasp the Marxist view of truth.

According to Marx, history embodies a pre-determined outcome, which it is folly to resist, even though its narrative line is not straight. History is "dialectical." It moves forward by contradiction and struggle. The important point is to understand the struggle of history "scientifically"—and to opt for the right side. The right side, the inevitably victorious side, the side with ultimate power, is the proletariat. Marx reaches this interpretation by a "scientific" study of economic reality, which he holds to be more fundamental than political, moral, or cultural power. (It goes without saying that he disdains "bourgeois religion"—and "Christian socialism"—most of all.[64]) Decisive in economic power, he thinks, is "ownership of the means of production." The owners are the bourgeoisie. Those who work but do not own are the proletariat. Of course, in order to have a proletariat, one must first have a bourgeoisie; in order to have socialism, one must first have capitalism. Marx centered all of history upon the axis of the proletariat. In the name of the proletariat, Marx despised peasants and *campesinos,* and mocked their "rural idiocy." In the name of the proletariat, Marx wrote in the *Communist Manifesto:*

> The lower middle class, the small manufacturer, the shop-keeper, the artisan, the peasant . . . they are all not revolutionary but conservative. Nay, more, they are reactionary, for they try to roll back the wheel of history.[65]

Lassalle underlined the same principle in his Gotha program: "In relation to the proletariat, all other groups constitute a single reactionary mass."[66]

But Marx didn't have much respect for the proletariat either. Marx, Lenin, and Engels spoke often of the "stupidity" of the proletariat, called them an "ignorant rabble," and despised their corrupt willingness to evade their historical task. What was this merciless task? Marx wanted them to "survive fifteen, twenty, fifty years of civil war and international strife." Instead, the ungrateful proletariat earned his contempt, by seeking incremental improvements in their living conditions.[67] Thus, the Russian socialist Nechayev wrote in cynicism and despair:

> The government itself might at any moment come upon the idea of reducing taxes or instituting similar benefits. That would be a real misfortune, because even under the present terrible conditions the folk are slow to rise. But give them a little more pocket change, set things up even one cow better, and everything will be delayed another ten years. And all our work will be lost. On the contrary, you should use any opportunity to oppress the people. . . .[68]

Thus Bakunin, too, wrote with disdain of the moral weakness of French workers regarding true socialism:

> Frenchmen themselves, even the workers, were not inspired by it; the doctrine seemed too frightening. It was, in fact, too weak. They should have suffered greater misery and disturbances. Circumstances are coming together in such a way that there will be no shortage of that. Perhaps then the Devil will awaken.[69]

Four points require comment. First, for Marx, truth means siding with the weak-willed proletariat, helping it to grasp its "scientific" mission to seize political supremacy. To be faithful to truth means siding with the oppressed, the carriers of truth. Second, truth means understanding revolutionary *praxis*. What matters is the triumph of the proletariat in history. Everything else is false and immoral. Third, not all who are poor are true carriers of revolutionary *praxis*. Many are called, but only the proletariat is chosen. And even among the proletariat there are dupes and deceivers. Some are reactionary. Some are easily bought off by social improvements. The worst of all are those socialists and other "progressives" who would sell out for something less than the full dictatorship of the proletariat. Some who are "tactical" allies must be recognized as "strategic" traitors.[70] Finally, in the words of the *Communist Manifesto:* "The theory of Communism may be summed up in a single sentence: 'Abolition of private property.' "[71]

In *The Power of the Poor in History*—whose very title captures the mythic vision of Marx—Gustavo Gutierrez outlines how liberation theology proceeded "insight" by "insight" to reach a program analogous to that of Marx. Permit me to stress the word *analogy*. There are essential differences between the final vision of Gutierrez and that of Marx. Gutierrez, for example, wishes to construct a religious socialism, not a materialistic one; Marx despised the former. But the *formal* similarity between the vision of truth enunciated for liberation theology and that of Marx is plain. (Gregory Baum has given a particularly clear statement of this formal similarity.[72]) In Chapter 3 of *The Power of the Poor in History,* Gutierrez recounts the history of how this happened.

The first insight came from the "political theology" of Germany in the 1960s. Political theology taught Latin Americans that the fundamental problem for theology today is not the relation of faith to reason, but the relation of faith to *social practice*. Until then, theology had been too rationalistic and too individualistic. Now it was called to be political. One cannot change hearts without changing systems of political economy.[73]

The second insight arose from the Bandung Conference of 1955, which focused the attention of third world theologians on the problems of *development*.[74] That emphasis shifted after the discovery of "dependency theory," a major school of which argued "scientifically" (as we have seen) that the underdevelopment of some was *caused* by the development of others. The "true causes of the misery and the injustice" suffered by the poor of the third world had at first been seen as a mere lack of development. But later these causes came to be seen as deliberate oppression by the developed world.

The third insight arose from the German "theology of revolution" and "theology of violence" that arose after 1966. Having been educated under the influence of German theology, most liberation theologians learned three lessons from the theology of revolution. First, the existing social order is unjust and must be overturned. Second, the existing social order is best understood in terms of class struggle on an international basis. Faith becomes a "motive and justification for the involvement of Christians in a revolutionary process." Third, three faults appeared in the structure of the theology of revolution: (1) it attempted to "baptize the revolution," which is wrong; (2) it gave a "somewhat fundamentalist interpretation to biblical texts"; and (3) it still remained a bourgeois reflection, forming theological premises and then "applying" them to reality "from above." It was still "not a critical reflection *from within* the liberation process."[75]

This is the point at which liberation theology proper was born. Now at last it "could take the one last step, and now gradually enter into a new world: the world of the other."[76] Following every formal step of "Marxist analysis" liberation theology identified truth with "opting for the poor." (In Latin America, this notion was necessarily somewhat larger than "the proletariat," given a setting in which vast majorities are peasants, not industrial workers.) Second, liberation theology, like Marxism, identified truth with a "popular movement" of "revolutionary praxis." It saw history as a "dialectical struggle between classes." And it chose sides, in order to be on the side of truth, justice, and historical vindication. Here, as we have seen, Gutierrez does not go all the way with Marx. He wishes to maintain *some* "critical distance" for theology. Theology must grow out of the revolutionary praxis of a popular movement (in this it differs from European political theology and the theology of revolution). But it does not wish merely to "baptize the revolution," and does not wish to declare any "given social order" to be identical with the Kingdom of God. *How* it will stay within the popular movement of revolution and still not lose critical distance is left quite unclear. But Gutierrez is well aware of the need to do so.

In the third and fourth formal steps, Gutierrez also agrees with Marx. By "poor," he does not mean all the poor, only those already involved in revolutionary *praxis*. Theology must stay inside this practice, not stand "above" it or "before" it.

Finally, Gutierrez interprets history as Marx does in four concrete ways: (1) He calls for a radical change in private ownership of the means of production.[77] (2) He declares that there is an international, universal class struggle.[78] This is an undeniable fact.[79] (3) He believes that "rigorous scientific analysis" shows that the poor are not simply poor, in a neutral or innocent way, but *oppressed:* caused to be poor, kept poor. (4) He holds that socialist economic institutions, not capitalist economic institutions, are best designed to liberate the poor.

Here is how his analysis is summarized in *The Power of the Poor in History:*

> [T]he poor person does not exist as an inescapable fact of destiny. His or her existence is not politically neutral, and it is not ethically innocent. The poor are a by-product of the system in which we live and for which we are responsible.[80]

There is a democratic capitalist interpretation of this fact. It is that the poor of most third world countries are prevented from acting with due economic liberties. They have no access to ownership, credit, ease of incorporation, legal economic enterprise, or the exercise of invention and other economic talents. And this is unjust. Now that the secrets of how all persons can "better their condition" are well known, it is immoral to repress economic activism.

Gutierrez does not take this route. Instead, he takes a socialist turn: "The oppressed cannot be considered apart from the social class to which they belong. . . . The poor . . . are members of one social class that is being subtly (or not so subtly) exploited by another social class."[81] Gutierrez accuses the developed classes and nations of exploiting the poor, of *making* the poor poor. This cannot be a universal explanation. Many of the very poorest persons on earth, in the most remote areas, have virtually no contact whatever with developed nations. Far from being exploited, they live in isolation. Not all poverty can be due to exploitation.

Oddly, in Gutierrez's economics of "liberation," individuals drop from sight. Gutierrez prefers to speak of a vast abstract collective: class. And it is not at all clear what he means by "class." The difficulties inherent in the term are well known to social scientists. Contrary to Marx, for example, nationalism seems even now to be a stronger bond among workers than economic class. In the World Wars of our time, proletarians rallied to their respective nations. Even Stalin had to drop his appeals to communism, asking sacrifices instead for "Mother Russia." In addition, certain forms of ethno-religious struggle are far more bitter than, and cannot be explained solely as examples of, class struggle. Shocking social struggles are to be seen in Iran-Iraq; in Lebanon; in Northern Ireland; among Hindus, Muslims, and Sikhs in

India. Again, socialist nations have engaged in bitter nationalistic warfare: Vietnam and China; Vietnam in Cambodia; the U.S.S.R. in Hungary, Czechoslovakia, and Poland. Finally, in free economies, there is widespread social mobility, upward and downward. Class is nowise fixed at birth. "Class" is not a sufficient key for interpreting the world. Since the term is so central to his work, Gutierrez owes us a clearer explanation of his meaning. (In spirituality he stresses the person.)

He singles out, for example, among the poor their "most clear-sighted segment, the proletariat."[82] Is it the case in Latin America that industrial workers (the proletariat) are more involved in revolutionary *praxis* than *campesinos*, and more "clear-sighted" than the intellectuals, professionals, teachers, and clergy of the left? Gutierrez uses "class" far more loosely than Marx—not to mention writers such as Djilas, Rizzi, Burnham and others who have observed the crucial significance of a "new class" in socialist movements and societies.[83] Nonetheless, Gutierrez concludes the above analysis: "Hence, an option for the poor means a new awareness of class confrontation. It means taking sides with the dispossessed."[84]

There is a crucial assumption, yet unproven, in this analysis. Do all the poor see reality in terms of class confrontation? Do they all wish to side with the extreme right or the extreme left? Do they see only *two* alternatives? It seems, rather, that substantial majorities of the poor in Latin America are more moderate than Gutierrez posits. Most support Christian Democratic parties and other parties of the center. Most resist being drawn into "confrontation" and "class war," for gains they judge to be dubious. When Gutierrez says "poor," whom does he really mean? All the poor, or only the poor who share his own preferences?

To think of the poor as a class is to ignore the individual dignity of each person among them. There is at least as much complexity, subtlety, and differentiation in the individual personalities of the poor as among any other social class. In economics, Gutierrez speaks of human beings in a merely collectivist language, as if they were bees in a hive or cattle in a herd. He does not speak so in spirituality.

Moreover, even years after the fact he cites with some approval the movement "Christians for Socialism" in Chile, condemned by the bishops of Chile in 1972. We shall consider that movement more fully in the next chapter, but two features of its thinking are here apropos. First, the preparatory document for that group (which Gutierrez helped to write) was intentionally divisive: "The class struggle seems to be a new dividing line between Christians."[85] Christian is to be separated from Christian, in line with the perspectives "opened up a decade ago by the Cuban revolution."[86] Second, this divisiveness was intended to be rigorous. It extended to "the elimination of any and every kind of idealism in visualizing the 'Christian element.' "[87] And it aimed particularly at isolating "tactical allies" who might refuse to go the final Marxist mile and might thus turn out to be "strategic enemies."[88]

Again, as I asked in *Freedom With Justice*,[89] have the opinions of the poor special epistemological status? What sort of intellectual warrant should be given to public opinion, even if it is the public opinion of "the poor" and "the oppressed"? Even supposing that that public opinion has been rigorously gathered—a supposition nowhere verified in the literature of liberation theology—what reason is there for believing that it is not ideologically tainted? Extensive survey data are available for Latin America. Such surveys show that public opinion in various Latin American nations, especially among the peasants and the workers, is quite complex and seldom that of the liberation theologians. Who, then, are "the poor" for whom they speak?

It is one thing to claim that the poor ought to be heard. Of course, they should. "The cry of the poor" may, further, even be said to be *relatively* privileged as a theological source, as compared with the testimony of the few wealthy or the fledgling middle class, not so much on the basis of truth or accuracy (which remain to be assessed) as on two other bases. First, one may suppose (although it is by no means certain) that theologians and other intellectuals who read books, give lectures, and appear on radio and television are more likely to be sympathetic to the rich and to the bourgeoisie, and, therefore, need to encourage one another incessantly to compensate by paying more attention to the poor. In fact, this supposition is doubtful. In our generation, the "war on poverty" is major news everywhere, and few targets are easier to attack in print than "the rich" and "the middle class." Still, for argument's sake, let us grant the supposition.

Second, one may suppose that the poor, who suffer various painful disabilities just because they are poor, are likely to voice their real grievances. I agree. Further, their suffering should be eased. And their legitimate grievances should be rectified.

But it is sometimes also claimed, at least implicitly, that what the poor say is *ipso facto* true, and that the "analysis" of the situation given by the poor is *ipso facto* a true analysis. For this claim there is not the slightest shred of evidence.

What the poor cry out deserves to be sympathetically heard. It does not, however, suffice to still critical and practical inquiry. The poor may have things wrong. Their opinions are not necessarily God's, nor do they necessarily carry ontological warrant. Three points need to be made.

For one thing, no more than others do the poor speak with one voice. Not all are Catholics. Not all are democrats. Not all are Marxists. The opinions of the poor are complex, multiple, various. The opinions of the poor deserve the same weight as those of any other social class and must, like them, meet tests independent of subjective desire. If the poor, for example, overwhelmingly supported Hitler, that would not make them—or Hitler—correct. If the Islamic poor overwhelmingly endorsed the annihilation of the Israeli people, that would not make them correct. If the Hindu and Islamic poor engaged in fratricidal blood-letting, that would not endow their activities with binding moral imperatives. If the poor of Latin America were to be entranced by a contemporary equivalent of Mussolini—another Peron, e.g.—that would not justify their every opinion and action.

Second, *comunidades de base* may be seen as a contemporary parallel to the voluntary associations in every social class which Tocqueville discerned in North America.[90] North Americans typically form small local communities, committees, study groups, and action groups in profusion. Each such small community has some wisdom to contribute to the common good. None has intellectual warrant to dominate all others, not even if it were a majority formed around moral principles: a "moral majority."

Third, in capitalist societies (ironically) those who claim to speak for the poor acquire instant intellectual prestige. Liberation theology certainly acquires such prestige by claiming to represent the voice of the poor.

Whether liberation theologians actually do speak for a majority of the poor, however, is far from certain. The truthfulness of liberation theology is not, and cannot be, established by basking in the prestige conferred upon the poor by Jewish-Christian culture. An "option for the poor" is entirely admirable; but the U.S. Statue of Liberty expresses it, too. There remain many conflicting social philosophies which claim to lift up the "huddled masses, yearning to breathe free." The issue as to which does the better job of lifting up the poor is not settled by the claim to be speaking for the poor. It is settled by actual achievement.

We can conclude. When liberation theologians speak of the "poor," it does not seem that they mean all the poor, but only those who both share their own revolutionary consciousness and are now active in revolutionary praxis. The attempt to simplify human reality by speaking solely in terms of "class" does violence to the individuality of each human person. When Father Gutierrez speaks of the poor, he seems especially to have in mind the non-Western Indians, blacks, and *mestizos,* most of whom are by no means industrial workers or prole-tarians.

Finally, it is not clear what liberation theologians mean, in practice, by socialism, or through which structures they expect it to liberate the economic activism of the poor. What is the concrete, institutional meaning of the term socialism in the thought of liberation theologians?

Eight

WHAT DO THEY MEAN BY SOCIALISM?

If one looks through the indices of books of liberation theology under the heading of "socialism," one will come to see that what liberation theologians mean by the term is shrouded in ambiguity. Some plainly do not *wish* to be too clear, in order perhaps to frustrate their critics. Some are ambiguous as a matter of principle, not wishing to pre-judge future developments. Nonetheless, one can distinguish four types of socialism active in Latin America: the Cuban model; the traditional socialism of the intellectuals; the socialism of such liberation theologians as Juan Luis Segundo and Gustavo Gutierrez; and the "democratic socialism" of such North American observers of Latin America as Arthur F. McGovern, S.J. We shall examine each in turn.

1. THE CUBAN MODEL

It is clearly possible that Latin American liberation theologians might choose the path of Cuba. Some would probably demand modifications in the direction of democracy and pluralism. Others might demand those personal liberties and incentives that allow for a more joyful life than may be observed in Cuba at the moment. Actually, though, few liberation theologians ever criticize Cuba. Some hint that they wish they could go down the Cuban path. Most certainly speak well of Che Guevara, Cuba, and Castro. One cannot flatly, then, eliminate the Cuban possibility.

Besides, it is characteristic of Marxists to mask their true aims, disguising their true purposes by speaking the language of bourgeois ideals and maintaining silent cover within a "popular front," until they are in a position fully to declare themselves. Mendacity of this sort is a classic tactic.

Genuine idealists in such popular fronts are seldom cynical

154

enough to concentrate upon seizing firm control of the military, the police, and the intelligence services. The role assigned them is to provide for the outside world the patina of bourgeois idealism. Meanwhile the Marxists seize strategic positions, in control of every instrument of force. No liberation theologian has issued warnings about this possibility, or prepared citizens to be on guard against it. Again, most liberation theologians not only use Marxist analysis in an unguarded way; they also indulge in an idealistic reading of the "humanistic" side of Marx.[1] Arthur F. McGovern, S.J., himself leans very far in this direction. He is far less discerning of the dangers—precisely to humanism—in Marxist thought than is Leszek Kolakowski.[2] These two forms of innocence are deadly. Historically, when the crunch has come, hard utopians such as Lenin and Stalin disposed ruthlessly of soft utopians such as Trotsky. This was Castro's pattern in betraying Hubert Matos and many others among his colleagues.

The great Mexican writer Octavio Paz is a vigorous critic of the United States, and he blames the introduction of Soviet power into the Western hemisphere very largely upon the arrogance and ignorance of the United States. He recalls how "Fidel Castro's movement stirred the imagination of many Latin Americans, particularly students and intellectuals." Castro seemed to be "the heir to the great traditions" of Latin America. He symbolized "independence and unity . . . anti-imperialism, [and] a program of radical and necessary social reform." Still,

> . . . the failure of the Castro regime is evident and undeniable. It is notable in three cardinal areas. The international: Cuba continues to be a dependent country, though it is now the Soviet Union that holds sway over it. The political: the Cubans are less free than they were before. The economic and social: its population is experiencing worse shortages and undergoing more hardships than twenty-five years ago. The accomplishments of a revolution are measured by the transformations it brings about; among them, the change in economic structures is of prime importance. Cuba was a country characterized by the monoculture of sugar, the essential cause of its dependency on the outside world and of its economic and political vulnerability. Cuba today is still dependent on sugar.
>
> For years and years, Latin American and many European intellectuals refused to listen to the Cuban exiles, dissidents, and victims of persecution. But it is impossible to hide

the truth. Just a few years ago, the whole world was stupefied
by the flight of more than a hundred thousand people, an
enormous figure if we consider the total population of the island. We were even more amazed when we saw the refugees
on movie and television screens: they were neither bourgeois
partisans of the old regime nor political dissidents, but humble folk, men and women of the people, starved and desperate.[3]

Although Mario Vargas Llosa, Octavio Paz, Carlos Rangel, and
others who began on the Latin American left have seen through the
illusions both of Cuba and of Marxism, there are many Christian intellectuals of the left who have not. One major international group,
called "Christians for Socialism," was formed in Chile in 1971. The
patterns of its thinking are self-evidently and expressly Marxist. Its desired model is plainly Cuba or something rather like Cuba. Indeed,
Fidel Castro was present at the creation of Christians for Socialism. At
a meeting in Santiago with "about 120 leftist priests and religious" (as
their own account puts it), Castro announced a new Marxist tactic. He
asserted that Christians are "not merely tactical but also strategic allies"
of Latin American revolution.[4] Unlike Eastern Europe, where Marxists attacked the Church as a strategic enemy, in Latin America Marxists have embraced Christianity as a "strategic ally."

Christians for Socialism was organized accordingly—Hugo Assmann and Gustavo Gutierrez helped draft its early documents—to
bring together Christian leaders "actively engaged in the struggle that
the people of Latin America are waging to free themselves from capitalist imperialism." Their first convention in Santiago in 1972 aimed
"to probe more deeply into the concrete experiences of Christians who
are actively involved in the revolution to liberate Latin America."[5]

Strategically, for the Marxists, the purpose was to bring "the option for revolution" to an operational area "as broad as Latin America
itself." Strategically, for the liberation theologians—at that time few
and without a leading literature—the purpose was to establish a new
and obligatory frame of reference. The revolutionary moment in
Latin America "is to be the *frame of reference* in our work of study and
reflection."[6] "The *criterion of selection* in sending out invitations" limited
the invitees to self-declared revolutionaries.[7] The point of view of the
convention was deliberately restricted. It aimed to look at the world
"primarily in terms of *the emergence of the proletariat and the mobilization
of the people.*" It established a principle of censorship. Its own framework must serve henceforth as the "framework for all subsequent re-

flection." The convention intended to place all of Christian life under judgment in this framework. Christians had a choice. Either they could be *"impediments to, or mainsprings of, the progress of the revolutionary struggle."*[8]

> Right at the start we must make explicit our revolutionary option in favor of implementing socialism through the rise of the proletariat to power. Once this has been done clearly and unmistakably, then we have a set of basic criteria for judging and evaluating the role that the "Christian element" is actually playing or can play in our countries. That role may be a positive one of stimulation or a negative one of obstruction. Here is an example of what we mean. Insofar as operational politics is concerned, the very notion of "revolutionary consciousness" will include as an intrinsic component the notion of power being held by the people—the latter being led by the proletariat—and of effectiveness as an indispensable element in the gradual attainment of power. This entails the elimination of any and every kind of idealism in visualizing the "Christian element," because our focus is concentrated on the historical terrain of the actual revolutionary struggle. We are speaking of course of a directly political focus, since it is revolutionary. On this historical plane idealistic questions—e.g., Should the Christian take a political stance or not?—become totally meaningless. The option for revolution is our point of reference at all times. As an option already made, it is also the source of governing criteria.[9]

The preparatory draft is candid. "We cannot prescind from the posture of historical materialism. That is, we must situate ourselves on the material and this-worldly terrain of history and have recourse to Marxism as an analytical tool . . . the emergence of the struggling people must serve as the key to any ultimate interpretation."[10]

> If we are looking for keys to a deeper interpretation of the role that the "Christian element" has played in history, we will not find them within theology—insofar as the latter is taken as an ideological realm that can be set off in isolation. We may indeed find related elements of much importance in theology taken as such. But it is *the structural functions that the "Christian element" actually performs in socio-economic formations* that will best enable us to unmask the various crypto-theologies and

then move on to read the "expressed theologies." ... The ideological character of Christianity in its sociological mani-festations—and we mean this in the pejorative sense of the word "ideological"—can only be unveiled through *an analysis of the functions it performs within the framework of the modes of production and other socio-economic formations.*[11]

The draft insists that the *"basic option on our part"* is "strategic rather than merely tactical participation" in the revolution. It warns that "a tactical ally can turn into a strategic enemy." Some progressive or even leftist allies, for example, go only so far in the revolutionary process, then serve to block its final aims. "It is along these lines, per-haps, that we must analyze postconciliar progressivism (Medellín in particular), the positions and accommodations of certain agents of the hierarchy, and the position of certain 'leftist' Christians."[12]

The more serious revolutionaries, long-term and strategic, will emphasize *"the emergence of the proletariat and the growing mobilization of the people,"* since the roots of the Latin American struggle "are to be found in the *mode of production* that typifies most of Latin America, a mode of production based on *dependent capitalism.*"[13] The perspectives of the revolutionaries "were opened up a decade ago by the Cuban revolution," and these ideas are spreading in "reaction to the economic domination of the United States and to its unsound foreign policy," with the result that "a new anti-capitalist and anti-imperialist con-sciousness is on the rise."[14] The growing commitment of certain Cath-olics to the revolution "is not solely generated *internally* by its own process of updating and *aggiornamento* (Vatican II, and Medellín which has given rise to a new theology of liberation)," but "is rather *conditioned by the economic and political happenings* mentioned briefly above." The crisis engendered in the Church "divides Christians with opposing political stances." Indeed, "the class struggle seems to be a new dividing line between Christians."[15]

To these extraordinary claims, the Cardinal of Santiago and the bishops of Chile gave charitable, painstaking but firm reply. These may, perhaps, be summarized in a sentence of the Declaration of the Chilean Bishops (April 1973): "It is not difficult to surmise the un-derlying inspiration for these judgments: It is the Marxist-Leninist method of interpreting history in economic terms."[16] The bishops pro-hibited priests and religious from participating further in "Christians for Socialism."

This condemnation of Christians for Socialism did not, of course, interrupt the spread of its ideas. As for Christians for Socialism, so for

liberation theologians generally, the first step is to fashion an exquis-
itely simple analysis of the political-economic situation of Latin America. A simple template is designed according to the primitive socialist
understanding of economic activities. Like two red-hot branding irons
applied to human flesh, this template has only two markings: "oppressed" and "dependent capitalism." The second step is to brand oneself "oppressed," in order to launch a struggle against one's clear class
enemy. The third step is to make theological reflection subservient to
the "experience" of that struggle. Its point of view is not intended to
be transcendent. It is a point of view from *within* a movement, intended
to *serve* that movement, and *under judgment by* that movement. It speaks
of an "option for the poor," but it does not actually wait for a majority
vote among the poor.

Whatever the size of the "popular movement" liberation theologians claim to speak for, such a movement has no *a priori* epistemological or theological status. Popular movements often act as mobs;
they are not necessarily democratic or humane. Nazism, too, claimed
to be (and was, alas) a popular movement, as was Mussolini's Fascism—
and the Peronism that Juan Peron fashioned from the Fascist template. Is a movement of the people a legitimate theological starting
point? Everything depends on the spirit that animates such a movement, and the principles expressed in its conduct. Cardinal Ratzinger
has caught this point exactly:

> . . . we find that in the moral convictions of many liberation
> theologies, a "proportionalist" morality also often stands in
> the background. The "absolute good" (and this means the
> building of a just socialist society) becomes the moral norm
> that justifies everything else, including—if necessary—vio-
> lence, homicide, mendacity. It is one of the many aspects that
> show how mankind, when it loses its mooring in God, falls
> prey to the most arbitrary consequences. The "reason" of the
> individual, in fact, can from case to case propose the most dif-
> ferent, the most unforeseeable and the most dangerous ends.
> And what looks like "liberation" turns into its opposite and
> shows its diabolic visage in deeds.[17]

Many observers believe that this is precisely what has happened
in Nicaragua. The most popular figure in Nicaragua, by far, is Cardinal Obando y Bravo, to whom the poor of Nicaragua have flocked
in crowds of 250,000 or more—until in 1985 the government disal-
lowed him to speak to open-air meetings and began an ominous cam-

paign to crush the popular resistance to tyranny represented by the Church in Nicaragua.[18] Nicaragua is clearly following the Cuban model, more slowly than Castro in the process of economic collectivization, but just as efficiently in organizing the secret police, neighborhood committees, and military power. Like Castro, it has been constricting like a boa the unions, press, and other private organizations. There are, alas, Christians in favor of the Cuban model.

2. THE TRADITIONAL SOCIALISM OF THE INTELLECTUALS

The sad story of socialist revolutions in our century has obliged many socialists in Europe, North America, and Latin America to distinguish socialism sharply from Communism. (This is why Christians for Socialism warned against "tactical allies" but "strategic enemies.") Many socialists loathe the societies of the U.S.S.R., North Korea, Vietnam, Cuba, and—increasingly—Nicaragua. Thus, the great Mexican writer Octavio Paz describes himself as a socialist and a democrat but rejects membership in the movement (very strong in Europe) of Social Democrats. He criticizes the left in Latin America "from the standpoint of the suffocating power of the state," not only in Communist countries but in Western countries. He calls the state *The Philanthropic Ogre*,[19] in the spirit of Hilaire Belloc's *The Servile State*[20] and Alexis de Tocqueville's "new soft despotism."[21] "The state has been and is the dominating personality of our century," he writes. "Its reality is so enormous that it seems unreal: it is everywhere yet it has no face. We don't know what it is or who it is."[22]

As Thomas Wilson puts it, the state is far more an "invisible hand" than the market is.[23] Scholars have hardly begun to study its income and expenditures, and to assess how much it detracts from or contributes to the well-being of peoples. Economists shed great light on the private sector, but the doings of the public sector are left invisible in darkness.

For Paz, the true tragedy of our era is not the failure of capitalism but the failure of socialism. "I believe," he says, "that the answer for the United States and Western Europe is socialism. And the fact that there isn't socialism there is one of the saddest and most disappointing things in the world for me."[24] Yet he also believes that the emphasis on a socialist option for developing countries is wrong. "Socialism was conceived for industrialized nations." It is not designed to help poor nations move to economic dynamism.

Look at Cuba. A revolution can be gauged by its ability to transform an economy. Under Batista, Cuba was a monoculture of sugar. Under Castro, Cuba is still a monoculture of sugar. Cuba has changed its dependence, but not its economy. It was sort of an American brothel and now it is a Soviet barracks, a bureaucratic colony.[25]

Paz remains a socialist. But he has broken definitively from the Marxists.

If there is one profoundly reactionary sector in Latin America, it is the leftist intellectual. They are people without memory. I have never heard any one of them admit he made a mistake. Marxism has become an intellectual vice. It is the superstition of the 20th century.[26]

The American Catholic writer John C. Cort also draws a sharp distinction between Marxism and socialism. He much admires the work of liberation theologians, of Gustavo Gutierrez in particular. But he thinks that many of them, Gutierrez included, make a tragic mistake in interpreting socialism in a Marxist way. This interpretation comes out clearly, he argues, in the language of "class struggle" used by Gutierrez. Cort praises Gutierrez profusely, but faults him for saying without qualification that all around the world members of "the affluent owners of the means of production are engaged in a 'struggle' with members of another class, the workers who work for them or who cannot find work." Cort qualifies: "Not all the owners, not all the workers. In many places just and harmonious relations exist between members of these two classes."[27] Gutierrez and the others, he writes, are wrong to think that this struggle goes on between *all* owners and *all* workers and must continue until the workers "dispossess the owners" and concentrate all productive power in the hands of the state. This is Marxism, not socialism. Cort holds that such passages as the following from *A Theology of Liberation* are careless and unnecessary:

There is one characteristic in particular which holds a central place: the division of humanity into oppressors and oppressed, into owners of the means of production and those dispossessed of the fruit of their work, into antagonistic social classes.[28]

Worse, in a nearby note Gutierrez quotes with approval Marx's statement that "the class struggle necessarily leads to the dictatorship of the proletariat," as "a transition to the abolition of all classes and a classless society."[29] Cort writes:

> Such statements, together with repeated calls for "the collective ownership of the means of production," indicate that Gutierrez is not talking about the democratic and pluralist variety of socialism envisioned in the Frankfurt Manifesto of the Socialist International, which is a dominant force in Western European countries today. No, he is talking about Marxist-Leninist Communism as practiced in Cuba, in particular, and, though he does not concede this, in the Soviet Union and China.[30]

Cort is also dismayed that in 1972 Hugo Assmann, Galileo Girardi, and Gutierrez wrote "the final document" of the convention of Christians for Socialism. In that document, Lenin is quoted twice: "Marxism *learns* from the concrete practice of the masses. Nothing could be further from its mind than the notion that it is to *teach* the masses certain forms of struggle. . . ."[31] Cort finds such lack of transcendence very dangerous. But what troubles him most is that Gutierrez much too carelessly accepts the central Communist principle of the abolition of private property. When Gutierrez wrongly insists that the employment of one person by another is by its nature alienating, enslaving, and exploitative, Cort argues, the only way out is state ownership and a dictatorship of the proletariat in a classless society. And these are horrible blind alleys.

"Father Gutierrez is a great, good man to whom we owe a profound debt for his passionate and scholarly insistence on the implications of the Gospel for *some* sort of socialist restructuring of our capitalist economies," Cort writes.[32] "The question is *what* sort?" Pius XI in *Quadragesimo Anno* explicitly denied that the wage contract is essentially unjust. So does the 1951 Frankfurt Manifesto of the Socialist International. In short, Gutierrez and those liberation theologians who agree with him are still thinking as Marxists, not as socialists.[33]

Enrique Dussel also holds the wage contract to be inherently unjust.[34] This position defies not only *Quadragesimo Anno* but experience and common sense. In Marxist-Leninist regimes, the wage-relation is not abolished. Neither is the class structure. The Soviet nomenklatura is far more removed from the people than are owners and proprietors in capitalist countries.[35] The state is the sole owner and employer, and a single class controls every lever of power. This may be Communist; it is not socialist.

As Octavio Paz writes:

No serious author today, in 1980, maintains that the Soviet Union is a socialist country, nor that it is, as Lenin and Trotsky believed, a workers' state deformed by a bureaucratic excrescence. If we think of it in terms of institutions and political realities, it is a totalitarian despotism; if we take a look at its economic structures, it is a vast State monopoly with peculiar forms of transmission of the use, the enjoyment, and the benefits of wealth and the products of labor (not the ownership of property, but what is equivalent to holding stock in a capitalist society—namely, being listed as belonging to the *nomenklatura* or being a card-holding member of the Russian Communist Party); if we take note of its social division, it is a hierarchical society with very little mobility, in which classes tend to become petrified as castes, dominated at the top by a new category at once ideological and military: an ideocracy and a stratocracy. This last description is particularly apt: the Soviet Union is a society fashioned in the image and likeness of the Communist Party. And the models for this party were the Church and the army; thus its members are clerics and soldiers, its ideal of community the cloister and the barracks. The cement binding together the religious and the military order is ideology.[36]

As most non-Marxist intellectuals use the word, socialism is consistent with the principle of private property, the ownership by peasants of their own land, and the ownership by small businessmen and small industrialists of their own enterprises. Socialism is consistent with economic creativity and inventiveness. It is consistent with relatively free markets. Socialism is not communism. From their writings, liberation theologians seem to go beyond socialism. How much beyond is not quite clear. Intellectual and moral resistance to communism—in Cuba, in Nicaragua, and elsewhere—is poorly defined.

3. JUAN LUIS SEGUNDO

Of the many forms of liberation theology in Latin America, Juan Luis Segundo writes: "There is something common and basic for all of them—the view that men, on a political as well as an individual basis, construct the Kingdom of God within history now."[37] Unlike Europeans, some liberation theologians allow for no critical distance between theology and politics. But this is an old tradition in Latin cultures. In Spanish and Portuguese, such words as *compromise, dissent, civil disagreement,* and *loyal opposition* have no exact equivalents. Liberation theology is Either/Or. *Either* you are for the revolution *Or* you are an enemy. Few liberation theologians concede that their own economic views may contain large portions of error or that their opponents may in some measure be correct. Father Segundo, for example, is very modest about the content of the socialist model for which he demands absolute commitment; he refuses to "give a more detailed account" of it. But he is absolute about the commitment Christians must make to it.

What does Father Segundo mean by socialism? "We give the name of socialism to a political regime in which the ownership of the means of production is removed from individuals and handed over to higher institutions whose concern is the higher good."[38] For Segundo, the choice for socialism is the crux of theological discourse today. Socialism is the way to the Kingdom of God on earth. But this is to place an old-fashioned faith in government officials. How does Segundo know that "higher institutions" will automatically practice "concern for the higher good"? Will politicians become by some magic sin-proof? In addition, as Arthur F. McGovern, S.J., points out,[39] Segundo has illicitly declared socialism successful in advance by adding into it *by definition* "concern for the higher good." This tactic unfairly stacks the deck. And it displaces the "option for socialism" from the realm of practical reason to the realm of pure definitional logic.

Segundo's definition of capitalism is not much better. "By capitalism we understand the political regime in which the ownership of the goods of production is open to economic competition."[40] Actually, that is not quite the way Adam Smith put the argument. In Smith's day, the state controlled and regulated most economic activities, including where individuals should invest their savings. That way of proceeding, Smith observed, was of little benefit to the common good. Economic progress was blocked. Economic activism was paralyzed. By contrast, Smith proposed a different experiment, based upon empirical observation. Allow individuals to make economic decisions as freely and intelligently as they can in the affairs they know best—their own—and each will be more likely to prosper. The butcher will do better, the baker will do better, the farmer will do better. From the bottom up, most will learn by trial and error how to improve their condition. The personal success of each will, cumulatively, add up to national success. This social vision, aimed at the common good, is the fundamental option of the capitalist experiment. (Incidentally, capitalism is not accurately called a "political" regime; it is the system of *economic* liberation most appropriately *matched* to a political regime committed to democracy and human rights.)

It is not easy to understand why Father Segundo would wish to deprive peasants of ownership of their own homes and lands, or why he would deprive the poor of their right to launch businesses, small factories, and service establishments of their own. Nor is it clear what he means by "ownership of the means of production." If he means large factories, or large industries, he appears to be talking about a relatively small proportion of current Latin American production. In Latin America today, most large enterprises are already owned by the state. It is not evident that still more state ownership—in Latin America or elsewhere—would produce greater "concern for the higher good." Those nations that permit private ownership, as Smith predicted, do seem to be more inventive, more dynamic, and driven to produce goods of higher quality and greater attractiveness.

In the judgment of Arthur F. McGovern, S.J., Segundo's definition of socialism "would rule out a land reform movement in which every family might own and be able to cultivate its own farm. Handing over ownership to higher authorities, on the other hand, could mean exclusive control and major profits going to a small government elite."[41] By adding into the definition of socialism the phrase "whose main concern is the common good" Segundo absolutizes socialism. On the contrary, McGovern argues, "The Church, and every moral agent, should exercise a 'reserve' in deciding whether a concrete, actualized system does or does not serve the common good."[42] Thus, for his own part, McGovern means by socialism that the Church should call for "an end to the *monopolization* of land and commercial enterprises by a small wealthy elite." It should call for "a type of democratic, mixed-economy socialism consistent with human dignity and freedom."[43] While rejecting Segundo's absolutism, McGovern praises Gustavo Gutierrez for urging cautious language and careful distinctions in speaking of socialism, and for insisting that the message of liberation "is not identified with any social form, however just it may appear to us at the time."[44]

4. GUSTAVO GUTIERREZ

We have already noted that what Gustavo Gutierrez means by "class" and by "the poor" is intellectually unsatisfying. There are also many questions to raise about what he means by "socialism." Here again is a *locus classicus:*

> The first and main question here is a radical one. It is a question of the prevailing social order. Latin American misery and injustice go too deep to be responsive to palliatives. Hence we speak of social revolution, not reform; of liberation, not development; of socialism, not modernization of the prevailing system.[45]

The main content of "socialism" here seems to be the destruction of the existing order. No information is conveyed about the order that will replace it.

Gutierrez seems to sense this, for he next writes: " 'Realists' call these statements romantic and utopian. And they should, for the rationality of these statements is of a kind quite unfamiliar to them."[46] Since scientific rationality is quite familiar to us, it follows that these statements are not intended scientifically. How are they intended then? "It is the rationality of a concrete, historical undertaking that heralds a different society, one built in function of the poor and the oppressed, and that denounces a society built for the benefit of a few." But what "concrete, historical" shape will such a society have? Silence. How do we know "a different society" will be a better society, especially for peasants, who have been even more oppressed under existing socialist societies than under previous feudal regimes? Gutierrez exaggerates some: "It is an undertaking 'in progress,' based on studies of the most rigorous scientific exactitude. . . ." No studies of society ever attain to the "most rigorous scientific exactitude" of mathematics and physics. All are highly debatable. Indeed, in order to approach toward even a measure of scientific rigor, every proposition in the social realm must be stated in the form of a testable hypothesis. What are the testable hypotheses of Gutierrez's socialism?

Gutierrez takes his first "point of departure in the exploitation of Latin America's great majorities by the dominant classes." But as we have seen, the vast majority of Latin American workers are agricultural workers. The proportion working in manufacturing or industry is small, and that proportion ranks in the highest quarter of income earners. Thus, the rebellion of "Latin America's great majorities," if there is such, must necessarily be mainly against the quasi-feudal, precapitalist class of landholders. Secondly, the point of departure of Gutierrez lies in "the perception that we live on a continent that is economically, socially, politically, and culturally dependent on power centers outside it, in the affluent countries." But, even in the hands of Gutierrez, dependency theory has been modified until very little is left of it. And even what remains appears to be falsified by the success of several nations in achieving spectacular development, from initial conditions considerably worse than those of any nation in Latin America. Dependency theory alone does not explain why Latin America is poorer than East Asia or North America, but wealthier than Africa.

Even in the context of dependency theory, Gutierrez feels constrained to modify social science by a patently ideological claim: "The theory of dependency would be mistaking its way, and betraying the truth, if it did not situate its analysis in the framework of a class struggle taking shape all over the world."[47] Where is there such a "class struggle"? The oppressed of the U.S.S.R. do not seem to be part of it. The peasants of China, oppressed by Mao Zedong, are now being liberated in some slight degree by incremental steps in the direction of private property, entrepreneurship, and incentives. Are the oppressed of Iran and Iraq engaged in "class struggle"? The bitter war between Vietnam and Cambodia, already so rich in savagery, does not seem to be a matter of class struggle. The forced displacement and starvation of hundreds of thousands of helpless Ethiopians does not seem to spring from class struggle.

Finally, though, Gutierrez does state the shape of the future he has in mind. It is the clearest statement of his I have been able to find:

> Only by overcoming a society divided into classes, only by installing a political power at the service of the great popular majorities, only by eliminating the private appropriation of the wealth created by human toil, can we build the foundation of a more just society. This is why the development of the concrete historical march forward of a new society is heading more and more in the direction of socialism in Latin America. But it is a socialism that is well aware of the deficiencies of many of its own concrete forms in the world today. It endeavors to break free of categories and clichés and creatively seek its own paths.[48]

This vision has three parts, each of them highly problematic. First comes the establishment of a classless society, or at least "overcoming a society divided into classes." Gutierrez has given no empirically testable definition of class. How will one recognize a classless society? Perhaps he means one in which all persons wear the same clothes, all have relatively similar incomes, and no one is permitted either to excel or to be rewarded for excelling. It is not clear. Will there be clergy? Teachers? Bureaucrats with power? Soldiers with guns? Police with the apparatus of torture? On what basis there will be no classes is not plain.

The second claim is that "political power" will be "installed" in order to serve "the great popular majorities." Presumably, this means the consent of the governed, who express their will through popularly elected representatives. History shows that popular majorities are typically conservative, much more so than intellectuals. Moreover, popular majorities tend to desire private property and the right to make their own economic decisions. In particular, the peasant class is naturally capitalist. For peasants, owning one's own property means an end to peonage and serfdom. Peasants resent price controls imposed by socialist bureaucrats as much as they resent feudal lords; the one set of lords is as bad as the other.[49] Insofar as Gutierrez desires a truly democratic order, he need not call it "socialism." Some forms of socialism do *not* install "political power" that serves "great popular majorities."

The third claim of Gutierrez is that socialism will eliminate the private appropriation of the wealth created by human toil. Does he mean that the bread earned by the toil of the worker will be taken from him? Does he mean that all wealth created by labor will be appropriated by the state? He may mean that workers will organize themselves into communes, in which wealth will be appropriated by the community. There have been many such experiments in history. Characteristically, they have failed in three crucial respects. First, individual excellence is not rewarded; hence, individual effort tends to fall to the level of the least productive. Second, invention ceases. There are no rewards, only social punishments, for proposing better methods, goods, or services. Communal societies stagnate. Third, communal societies have been obliged to repress entrepreneurial talent, because it inevitably leads to differentiation and to inequalities. They have had to suppress even tiny shoots of individuality, in the name of conformity.[50] By contrast, popular economic dynamism arises from creative ideas among those of the poor who have entrepreneurial talent. In short, this claim by Gutierrez is, and has been, subject to historical testing. The results of these tests are not favorable to his project.

One may doubt, therefore, whether the true force of what Gutierrez means by socialism is a testable hypothesis about material improvement in the lives of peasants and the other poor. Gutierrez shows himself remarkably indifferent to inquiry into socialist economic methods. His passion lies elsewhere. Earlier he wrote that liberation

theology does not "baptize the revolution." But it does baptize whatever the oppressed, and those who act in their name, wish to do.
"Hence the whole project must start out with their values. For it is
among the masses that this radical questioning of the prevailing order,
this abolition of the culture of the oppressor, is arising. Only thus can a true
social and cultural revolution be carried out."[51] Here three further
questions arise.

The first question is one of fact. Is it the case that "the masses,"
the vast majority of Latin Americans, desire socialism? To be sure,
Latin America has experienced neither the Industrial Revolution, nor
the Protestant Reformation, nor the *embourgeoisement* of the poor. The
masses may well desire to be free from torture and from poverty. They
may well desire to listen to rock and roll, to wear jeans and Western
T-shirts, and to share in the affluence of Japan, Southern Europe, and
other regions. It is a factual question whether they want what Gutierrez asserts they want.

The second question is also one of fact. If the whole project of
liberation theology must start out with "their values," i.e., the values of
the people of Latin America, what, in fact, are those values? Are liberation theologians permitted to question those values, or to channel
them into new directions? It is not clear why the values of the masses
ought, just as they are, to be baptized. An epistemological claim for
those values is being inappropriately smuggled into the argument,
without any clear statement about what those values are and why they
ought to be accepted as normative.

The third question is whether Gutierrez actually means "the abolition of the culture of the oppressors." If so, the claim is totalitarian.
It demands annihilation of the soul, the heart, the mind, and the imagination of those of us with whose views of how to raise up the poor he
disagrees. No doubt, Gutierrez wrote this phrase carelessly. But it is
worrisome precisely because of what comes before it, where he writes:
"This effort to create a different society also includes the creation of
a new human person."[52] Gutierrez explains this as a new type of politics. "But today, those who have made the option for commitment to
liberation look upon the political as a dimension that embraces, and
demandingly conditions, the entirety of human endeavors."[53] Such a
politics consumes the whole of life. It seems to regard its political opponents, not as independent persons whose reasoning ought to be
heard in civil argument, but as persons whose entire culture is to be
abolished.[54]

In existing socialist societies, politics is no longer regarded as an
empirical, prudential argument concerning mean and ends, in which

every person sees at least a portion of the truth. It is regarded as a field within which one side must prevail and the other be destroyed. This is ideology at high pitch. It is all the more dangerous because no one is ever told what the "new society" is that he must support, or what the "new man" is like that he must become. Presumably, once the old order is destroyed, those who retain control over the new army, the new police, and the new media of communications will explain the new rules. Those who cannot be re-educated will be discarded. This has been the normal pattern of socialism in our time. Against it, Gutierrez has not yet offered checks and balances.

More striking still, Gutierrez has not for fifteen years devoted attention to the ways in which historical socialism has led to the oppression of the poorest and the weakest members of society, especially the peasants.

In brief, it is impossible to believe that Gutierrez has thought through the new society he means to create. He asks us simply to assume—despite massive twentieth century evidence to the contrary—that his socialism will be better than the others. It is, therefore, impossible to argue that the main interest Gutierrez takes in socialism lies in testable hypotheses about some future set of socio-economic institutions. The main content he gives to that word is the radical abolition of the prevailing order and of the culture of the oppressors. The structures and institutions of the future do not seem to interest him.

5. DEMOCRATIC SOCIALISM

There is always the possibility, though, that liberation theologians have had so many enemies on the right that they have not yet fixed in their sights their enemies on the left. This, some may say, is the reason for the serious ambiguities in their position. One North American student of liberation theology, Arthur F. McGovern, S.J., who is heroically sympathetic to its work, tries to chart a course through these ambiguities. McGovern concludes that liberation theologians would support a Nicaragua reformed in the following way: (1) clear support for democracy in the political system; (2) clear support for pluralism in the religious, moral and cultural system; (3) support for the private ownership of homes, land, and small businesses ("enterprise" as distinct from the capitalism of the large corporations); (4) some skepticism about the practical utility of the nationalization of industry and the collectivization of farms; (5) the institution of free markets, at least on some significant scale and at least for small operators and individuals; (6) and some respect for incentives and income inequality based upon merit, so long as income differences are neither pre-determined nor excessive.[55]

McGovern's reading of liberation theology is consistent with his own defense of a democratic socialist alternative in the United States, in whose articulation he takes Michael Harrington as his model.[56] To what extent Latin American liberation theologians would agree with him is for them to say. McGovern certainly distinguishes his views on these matters from those of such liberation theologians as Juan Luis Segundo and José Miranda, which are more radically socialist or Marxist than his.[57] McGovern's vision of "economic democracy" may properly be described as an affirmation of very large portions of the democratic capitalist agenda, totally so in points (1) and (2) above. Even in points (3) to (6), McGovern comes down *in principle* on the democratic capitalist side, although he favors some high degree of control by the political system over the economic system. About the *degree* of such control, there are sound arguments on both sides. Partisans of one side or the other will certainly differ on a case-by-case basis. Yet in crucial respects McGovern is, in principle, a democratic capitalist: he rejects the abolition of private property; absolute principles of nationalization and collectivization; the abolition of markets; and radical egalitarianism.

If McGovern's interpretation of what the liberation theologians mean by socialism should come to be accepted by liberation theologians, that would be a helpful development. But one cannot read what liberation theologians say about socialism, text by text, without gaining the clear impression that they intend to be considerably more radical than McGovern. At the very least, their *emotions* seem more radical. One discerns in their writings a surging passion against private property, markets, and incentives that contrasts quite vividly with the balanced and reasonable tone advanced by McGovern. As the latter notes, liberation theologians are much clearer about their desire to overturn the existing system in Latin America, than about what they intend to put in its place.[58]

Typically, nonetheless, liberation theologians insist that, for them, socialism is not only a theory about economic institutions but also—and even more—a theory about human values. And when they list the values inherent in socialism, they most often mention respect for human dignity; a spirit of sharing; cooperation; and concern for the less fortunate. Two questions arise.

First, is it the claim of liberation theologians that such values follow from the *idea* of socialism or, rather, that these values are empirically found only in, or more frequently in, socialist societies? If they intend to speak in the mode of *praxis* rather than in the mode of abstract idealism (as they normally do), they cannot intend the first claim. And, empirically, the second appears to be false.

Second, do they mean to say that such values are contrary to the constitutive ideas of democratic capitalist societies? They can scarcely mean that such values are never empirically found in such societies since, on the contrary, such values appear—in abundance—in democratic capitalist practice. Indeed, as John Stuart Mill makes plain in *The Principles of Political Economy,* the political economy of democratic capitalism is constitutively dependent upon exactly such values as cooperation and respect for individual dignity. Further, the express intention of democratic capitalist societies is to raise up the poor, to raise the standard of living of all, to afford equal opportunity, and to respect the human rights endowed by the Creator in every person.

In short, liberation theologians exhibit a tendency to *define* socialism so as to include within the concept their highest ideals, and to *define* capitalism as the absence of all such ideals. This is a form of definitional imperialism. It is, further, a form of abstract idealism, remote from the careful assessment of historical practice.

At this point, of course, the liberation theologians charge that they have learned by experience that the "capitalist" elites of Latin America have no intention of opening their closed system so as to allow participation in it to the poor. That is why they came to reject capitalism, developmentalism, and the existing system in the first place. At first, they, too, believed in reform. Bitter experience forced them to conclude that only revolution will do.[59]

With the liberation theologians, we may all agree that the social system of Latin America requires fundamental reordering, not simply reform. The questions in dispute are how to analyze the present situation and what to recommend for the future. About *political* democracy and cultural *pluralism,* liberation theologians and those who cherish the liberal society seem to be in agreement.

Concerning how to analyze the existing defects in the Latin American *economic* system, liberation theologians call the existing economic order in Latin America capitalist. That is a serious error. Those who cherish the liberal society reject the current Latin American economic order. But why do liberation theologians (using the symbolic word *socialism*) propose changes in the direction of a still greater statism and a still greater politicization of Latin American life? That is a cure that would only deepen the current disease. Indeed, a reasonable hypothesis is that the option for socialism will lead Latin America to dictatorships (of the left, rather than the right), to the immiseration of the peasants, to the suppression of economic activism, and to increased ec-

onomic dependency upon the Soviet Union and its allies. Such trage-
dies have already befallen Nicaragua and Cuba.

At this stage in the late twentieth century, socialism is no longer
an innocent idea. There have been scores of socialist experiments. On
the whole, these experiments have been discouraging, most of all to
socialists.

Nonetheless, if McGovern is correct, and liberation theologians
mean by socialism the six propositions he sets forth, that would be a
very hopeful development, indeed. If they clarify whether they are
democratic socialists or Communists—*for* the Cuban model or *against*
the Cuban model—all will know better how to judge their intentions
for the future.

6. THE ISSUE BETWEEN CAPITALISM AND SOCIALISM

There is a widespread opinion that liberalism is distinguished
from other political movements by the fact that it places the
interests of a part of society—the propertied classes, the
capitalists, the entrepreneurs—above the interests of the
other classes. This assertion is completely mistaken.
Liberalism has always had in view the good of the whole, not
that of any special group. . . . Historically, liberalism was the
first political movement that aimed at promoting the welfare
of all, not that of any special group. Liberalism is
distinguished from socialism, which likewise professes to
strive for the good of all, not by the goal at which it aims, but
by the means that it chooses to attain that goal.—*Ludwig von
Mises*, Liberalism in the Classical Tradition[60]

In 1922, the Austrian economist Ludwig von Mises pointed out
that socialist ideas were well-formed by the middle of the nineteenth
century. Socialism, he wrote, was designed as an attack upon the liberal
society. The liberal society held that the material position of the wage-
earning classes can only be permanently raised by an increase in capital, and this none but a capitalist economy based upon private ownership of the means of production can guarantee to create.[61] Against
this, socialism held that the socialization of the means of production is
a system that will bring wealth to all.

Since 1922, history has shown that liberal societies have, as promised, raised the standard of living of ordinary people to levels our
ancestors could never have imagined.[62] Meanwhile, not having the in-

formation provided by markets, socialist systems have never been able to learn the needs and desires of purchasers, the costs of production, or the appropriate prices for goods and services. Socialist economies have necessarily been blind, inefficient, constantly in excess or in shortage, and discouraging to invention. In daily life, they have been gray and coercive. Since the reasons why this must be so follow from socialist principles, von Mises was able to predict the judgment of history with considerable prescience.

No known system of socialism has ever "liberated" its peasants. The Swedish economist Sven Rydenfelt describes fourteen modern socialist experiments in *A Pattern for Failure: Socialist Economies in Crisis*. One generalization holds true in all cases:

> The prophets of the socialist gospel have always promised to redeem the world from oppression and exploitation and to celebrate the weakest and poorest members of society. In all socialist countries the peasants constitute the poorest and weakest group. . . . Socialists in power have systematically favored the strong, well-situated urban groups—industrial workers, police, soldiers, and bureaucrats, the political supporters of the regime—while, just as systematically, they have oppressed and plundered the peasants.[63]

Until 1982, peasants in the U.S.S.R. were not permitted to travel from their places of residence, even internally, and still today their mobility is strictly limited. Like blacks in South Africa, they must carry internal passports, and their other rights are fewer than those both of South African blacks and of their own great-grandparents who were serfs.

Notwithstanding the demolition of Marxist principles by many scholars in the nineteenth century, von Mises says, Marx saved socialist ideas by four shrewd steps. First, Marx denied that human reason could properly criticize a social system, since all thinking is determined by one's social class. Thus, "bourgeois" criticism of socialism is invalid. Second, Marx held that history will necessarily bring about the abolition of private property and the socialization of the means of production, through expropriating the expropriators. True science consists in being in tune with this necessity. Third, no one is to be allowed to put forward any concrete proposals for the construction of the socialist Promised Land. Socialism is not allowed to be identified with any concrete program. Since socialism will inevitably come, reason should not try to imagine it in advance, but docilely yield to its immediate imperatives. Fourth, anyone who is in tune with historical necessity is to be defined as good, noble, and moral. Anyone who attempts to criticize the socialist project is to be defined as serving the egotistical interests of a doomed class, lacking in intellectual credibility, and exemplifying selfishness. Socialists, therefore, need never to meet the arguments of their critics but only to attack their persons (and their class).[64]

In these four steps, Marx sought to make socialism impregnable. No socialist can criticize historical necessity, socialist actions or achievements, or the concrete shape of the socialist future. No socialist needs to heed criticism from non-socialists. Socialists need only to be committed to action, to follow the dictates of the Party, and to make relentless war upon private property and markets by every means available. In other words, socialist intellect must be ceaselessly critical of liberal societies, but never critical of socialist societies. Gertrude Himmelfarb, reviewing the history of British historians who have been members of the Communist Party during the period 1920–1985, shows from their own writings how they deliberately ruled out of bounds any criticism of socialist experiments—even during the Ukrainian famine, the Stalinist purges, and right up until today.[65]

Von Mises posits the issue sharply. Liberals hold that the poor will more systematically, more quickly, and more thoroughly advance out of poverty through private ownership of the means of production, through owning their own property, through markets, and through institutions that favor liberty and creativity than through any other known system. Socialists attack these principles. What they will put in their place they *purposefully* leave unclear, awaiting the necessities of history, dictated by the socialist elite then in power.

What, then, of socialists such as John C. Cort, and—he claims—those of the 1951 Frankfurt Manifesto of the Socialist International? Many who call themselves socialist today *defend* the principles of private property, private (although they prefer cooperative) ownership of the means of production, markets (although they prefer considerable state regulation), and institutions of liberty and creativity—in the political, economic, and moral-cultural spheres. To which one finds an anticipatory reply in von Mises: "If anyone likes to call a social idea which retains private ownership of the means of production socialistic, why, let him! A man may call a cat a dog and the sun the moon if it pleases him."[66]

One reason Cort wishes to defend the principle of private property is to prevent "the dictatorship of the proletariat" or any other sort of dictatorship. Such persons as he speak confidently of *democratic* socialism because they wish to preserve political, civil, and religious liberties. And, although Cort desires cooperative forms of ownership,

these too are forms of *private ownership*. The state as owner of everything is, as Octavio Paz says, an ogre.

There is good reason to hold, then, that most democratic socialists
are, in principle, democratic capitalists.[67] They are critical of certain
practices in contemporary liberal societies. They desire more caring
and compassion, more cooperativeness and practices of brotherhood.
They desire more governmental control over economic acts by consenting adults. They come down more strongly on the side of the *political* in political economy, less strongly on the *economy*. For example,
often they propose that workers should have a greater say in what they
produce; there should be more democratic procedures within the life
of firms. To this, von Mises replies that they ignore the votes of consumers in the market. Their proposal to allow only workers and management to vote on economic matters is as if they entitled only
government officials and government workers to vote on political matters. They ignore the market to their peril and to the detriment of society as a whole.[68] This seems to be the result of experiments in worker
democracy in Yugoslavia.[69]

But these disagreements about how private property, markets,
and institutions of economic creativity can best be brought to serve the
people are not disagreements of principle. They are disagreements
concerning how best to serve the common good. To a very large extent, the issues may be decided by empirical observation of what works.
For example, the failure of the socialist experiment in France under
François Mitterand, contrasted with the simultaneous dynamism of
the liberal idea under President Reagan in the United States, has recently changed the burden of debate in France in precisely this way.
Not for a hundred years has the liberal idea gained such new power
in the younger generation.[70] As von Mises wrote in 1922, speaking
from bitter experience:

> I know only too well how hopeless it seems to convince im-
> passioned supporters of the Socialist Idea by logical demon-
> stration that their views are preposterous and absurd. I know
> too well that they do not want to hear, to see, or above all to
> think, and that they are open to no argument. But new gen-
> erations grow up with clear eyes and open minds. And they
> will approach things from a disinterested, unprejudiced
> standpoint, they will weigh and examine, will think and act
> with forethought. It is for them that this book is written.[71]

The same point may be made with references to the final chapter
of Arthur F. McGovern's *Marxism: An American Christian Perspective*.[72]

McGovern is honest enough to try to project the society of the future as he imagines it will be under "economic democracy." He wishes to retain political, civil and religious liberties. He does not wish to abolish private property, markets, incentives, institutions of economic creativity, or entrepreneurship. He values highly the dynamism of the U.S. economy as he has known it. But he would like to impose certain controls upon the large corporations. He would like more experiments in ownership by workers and in worker-management. He would like to introduce new forms of cooperation and participation in decision-making. Indeed, many firms already have launched experiments in some of these directions. Thus, his suggestions are neither anti-capitalist nor contrary to capitalist principles. The question is, to what extent will they work? To what extent will they prove to be counterproductive? And will the domain of economic liberty remain intact, so that a great range of different types of organization may compete with one another and so that methods most helpful to the common good may be found?

Just as *democratic socialists* argue for more substantive *political* controls upon economic activities, whether on the part of the central state or in the form of decentralized, private worker-participation, so *libertarians,* on the other side, argue for the maximum possible economic liberty for owners, entrepreneurs, workers and consumers. Libertarians believe that the market is the best, most reliable, and most creative servant of the common good. Democratic socialists believe that forms of political control, external or internal, better serve the common good. As for myself, while personally resisting both democratic socialism and libertarianism, I hold that the principle of political economy legitimates arguments from both those extremes. Every disputed question should be decided in context and in terms of its fruits. It is not inconsistent to lean in one case toward the "political" side, and in another to the "economic" side of political economy. Each of the two systems, political and economic, requires correction by the other.

Experience has taught me to put less faith in political activism, and more faith in economic activism. But both are necessary. We must look to the results, and be prepared to make corrections accordingly. In the long run, however, the greatest danger to appear in the twentieth century, to cite again the image of Octavio Paz, is the well-meaning *ogre.* The problem with tilting too far in the democratic socialist direction is that the state, once it aggrandizes power to itself, can scarcely be persuaded to relinquish it. This fear of the state places me on the "neoconservative" side of the debate—neither libertarian nor democratic socialist, but a person of the left who has grown to be critical of the left because of its excessive reliance on politics and the state, to the neglect of economic activism.

To ask liberation theologians to be neoconservatives is, no doubt, to ask too much. They are, for the time being, moved by a quite different will. For the socialist temptation is of ancient and sturdy root. It has a will of its own. The nature of that will must now be explored.

Nine

WHAT IS THE
INNER WILL OF SOCIALISM?

In all poor countries, peasants constitute up to 90 percent of
the population. . . . With few exceptions the regimes in these
poor countries pursue socialist policies. . . . In all socialist
countries the peasantry, a remnant of capitalism, is treated as
an outgroup, whose sole task is to produce cheap food for the
ingroups in the cities. The status of the farmer in socialist
states, in fact, corresponds to that of the serfs under feudalism.—*Sven Rydenfelt*, A Pattern for Failure[1]

Bertrand Russell admitted that Marx more desired the destruction of
the bourgeoisie than the improvement of the lives of the proletariat.[2]
About the latter, in any case, Marx wrote scarcely a practical word. The
greatest of all Marxist theoreticians of the twentieth century, Leszek
Kolakowski, has concluded that, in essence, Marxism is neither a practical nor a scientific theory but an expression of mystical will.

The influence that Marxism has achieved, far from being the
result or proof of its scientific character, is almost entirely due
to its prophetic, fantastic, and irrational elements. Marxism
is a doctrine of blind confidence that a paradise of universal
satisfaction is awaiting us just round the corner. Almost all the
prophecies of Marx and his followers have already proved to
be false, but this does not disturb the spiritual certainty of the
faithful, any more than it did in the case of chiliastic sects: for
it is a certainty not based on any empirical premises or supposed 'historical laws', but simply on the psychological need
for certainty. In this sense Marxism performs the character
of a religion, and its efficacy is of a religious character. But it

179

is a caricature and a bogus form of religion, since it presents
its temporal eschatology as a scientific system, which religious
mythologies do not purport to be.[3]

There is a vivid way to see this. Most of the world's poor are not
proletarians; they are peasants. The lot of peasants in Communist
Ethiopia, Vietnam, Tanzania, Cuba, the U.S.S.R., and other Marxist
nations of the world has been marked by famine, shortages, restriction
of movement, and local domination unparalleled even during the feudal era. To confuse existing Marxist societies with the socialist dream
is most deeply to offend democratic socialists.

But even the latter need to examine their consciences. What do
they actually want? What's left of the will of the left? Answering that
question, George Bernard Shaw once wrote:

> I also made it quite clear that Socialism means equality of in-
> come or nothing, and that under Socialism you would not be
> allowed to be poor. You would be forcibly fed, clothed,
> lodged, taught, and employed whether you liked it or not. If
> it were discovered that you had not character and industry
> enough to be worth all this trouble, you might possibly be ex-
> ecuted in a kindly manner; but whilst you were permitted to
> live you would have to live well. Also you would not be al-
> lowed to have half a crown an hour when other women had
> only two shillings, or to be content with two shillings when
> they had half a crown. As far as I know I was the first Socialist
> writer to whom it occurred to state this explicitly as a neces-
> sary postulate of permanent civilization; but as nothing that
> is true is ever new I daresay it had been said again and again
> before I was born.[4]

What is the meaning of this Shavian drive toward "equality of income"? The phrase is not to be taken literally. I have never met an
intellectual or a literary socialist who actually cuts his income to the
national median (let alone to the level of the poorest), in order to live
according to his own beliefs. Moreover, sophisticated socialists will tell
you that they do not mean *literal* equality. They intend, they say, to
limit *excessive* inequalities of wealth.

Some assert that this means something on the order of 9:1 or 10:1,
as between the best paid and the least. (Socialist intellectuals think intellect and education should receive the higher level.) As I have shown
elsewhere, not quite one percent of households in the United States

earns more than ten times the poverty level ($100,000 or above).[5] Thus, socialist hatred for the rich is directed at a very narrow target.

Surely, socialism entails more than resentment against a top one percent. Even within a capitalist system, one could attain 10:1 equality by the simple expedient of limiting the income of the top one percent or by confiscating it. Of course, this would have its costs. In 1983, the last year for which official figures are available, the top one percent paid forty percent of their adjusted gross income in federal income taxes, or twenty percent of all income taxes paid.[6] Eliminating the top one percent would be eliminating a lot of revenue. But it could be done. Certainly, though, socialism entails more than a small technical adjustment of that sort.

Liberation theologians use the symbol "socialism" to name the future society of which they dream. They show surprisingly little interest in discerning or describing the actual institutions in which they intend to embody that dream in history. They do not point to any existing historical models, and they do not describe even in large brush strokes any hypothetical future model. It is hard to be convinced that they actually give the word *socialism* any socioeconomic content whatever. To believe that they do, one must also believe that they are holding that content secret; that they know it, but do not want to reveal it.

No, the only hypothesis that fits the way liberation theologians actually use the word *socialism* is that, in the socioeconomic order, it stands for something "new," "radical," and "revolutionary," and that it will usher in an era (miraculously) of the "new man." But what this order *is,* institutionally, they do not care enough to inquire. Therefore, one is forced to seek out the psychological satisfactions that using the word *socialism* affords them. Using that word certainly gives them no guidance about the shape of the non-capitalist institutions of their desire.

Just the same, socialism is an ancient idea. It is at least as old as Plato. Thus one can use the word to name an invariant inner will, expressed in analogous institutions in various strata of history. This inner will of socialism is not best characterized as the pursuit of science. On the contrary, writing of this inner will in his introduction to a study of socialism by the Soviet mathematician Igor Shafarevich, Aleksandr I. Solzhenitsyn notes "the mist of irrationality that surrounds socialism" and its "instinctive" aversion to scientific analysis.[7] Socialism has always been a kind of mysticism. In some ways its passion is directed more toward religious or moral values than toward economic institutions. Socialism rejects the world that is; what a socialist world will be it has always protected in obscurity. In this sense, as an ancient mys-

ticism its appearance long antedates Marx. Indeed, Marxist literary efforts have produced scores of books about the *Forerunners of Socialism,*
going back many centuries.[8]

1. THE SOCIALISM OF THE INCAS AND THE JESUITS

Gustavo Gutierrez writes: "We must recover the memory of the
'scourged Christs of the Indies' and, in them, the memory of all the
poor, the victims of the lords of this world." And he adds:

> The great milestones on this long journey have to be stud-
> ied—the primitive Christian community, the great pastors
> and theologians of the first centuries, the Franciscan move-
> ment and Joachim da Fiore in the Middle Ages, the Hussite
> movement in the fifteenth century, the peasant wars in Ger-
> many and Thomas Münzer in the sixteenth, the defense of
> the Indian and Bartolome de Las Casas, Bishop Juan del
> Valle, and so many others of the same era in Latin America,
> Juan Sanotos Atahualpa in the eighteenth century in Peru,
> and the peasant struggles and popular piety in more recent
> times in Latin America.[9]

Gutierrez is correct. Long before Adam Smith composed his *Inquiry into the Nature and Causes of the Wealth of Nations* (1776), or Max
Weber first published *The Protestant Ethic and the Spirit of Capitalism*
(1904), recording the birth of a truly new idea in world history, the
idea of socialism had already had a long career. Solzhenitsyn writes:

> If one considers human history in its entirety, socialism can
> boast of a longevity and durability, of wider diffusion and of
> control over larger masses of people, than can contemporary
> Western civilization. . . . It could probably be said that the
> majority of states in the history of mankind have been "so-
> cialist." But it is also true that these were in no sense periods
> or places of human happiness or creativity.[10]

As in the case of Gutierrez, so with Plato and the Gnostics, socialist
doctrines are always *reactions:* Plato as a reaction to Greek culture, the
Gnostics as a reaction to Judaism and Christianity, Gutierrez as a reaction to the present order. But these reactions always have a consistent direction. Their invariant features are two: first, to destroy the

present order; second, to enforce equality of a certain type. Solzhenitsyn again:

> Socialism seeks to reduce human personality to its most prim-
> itive levels and to extinguish the highest, most complex, and
> "God-like" aspects of human individuality. And even *equality*
> itself, that powerful appeal and great promise of socialists
> throughout the ages, turns out to signify not equality of
> rights, of opportunities, and of external conditions, but
> equality *qua* identity, equality seen as the movement of variety
> toward uniformity.[11]

When liberation theologians speak of "socialism," they draw upon
(as Gutierrez does) an ancient vein of thought. For this reason, it is
highly illuminating that Shafarevich in his study of the socialist idea in
history includes chapters or passages on many of the very forerunners
Gutierrez alludes to: the socialism of antiquity; the chiliastic socialism
of the middle ages; the great utopias of Enlightenment philosophy;
the socialism indigenous to Latin America; the socialist novel; the
meaning of "social justice." In addition, Shafarevich looks carefully at
the "Asiatic formation" that Marx nervously took note of, that is, at the
socialisms of ancient Mesopotamia, ancient Egypt, and ancient China.
In order to have state socialism, it was not necessary to await "the abolition of private ownership of the means of production" and "the
triumph of the proletariat." Socialist states already existed in the ancient world of Asia "before which contemporary Marxist thought
stands baffled, having discerned its own hideous countenance in the
mirror of the millennia" (Solzhenitsyn).

Shafarevich devotes chapters to each of the invariant features of
the socialist idea. He surveys eight different interpretations of its motive force and analyzes its historical institutionalizations in the economy, the organization of labor, the family, and religion. He discerns
the invariant war of socialism upon individuality in the name of a peculiar understanding of equality (the equality of *uniformity* mentioned
above by Solzhenitsyn). And he isolates the actual psychological goal
of socialism, as it is invariantly stated in the writings of socialists. Gutierrez and his colleagues have no excuse for not differentiating what
they mean by socialism from its other historical embodiments.

Gutierrez, for example, often mentions the history of Peru. It was
precisely in Peru in 1531 that one of the great socialist experiments of
all time was first encountered by a small expedition of 200 Spaniards:
the Empire of the Incas. This empire was a forerunner to the socialist

state constructed by the Jesuits some 100 years later in Paraguay (1609–1767). These Latin American socialist experiments deeply impressed the European imagination.[12] Many of the details of later socialist utopias and communes derive from them. Through them modern socialism has a Latin American lineage. This Latin American socialism is at least as old as the chiliastic socialism of Central Europe (Joachim of Flora and Thomas Münzer, e.g.) on which Marx drew so heavily. Shafarevich devotes twenty pages to these Latin American models, citing extensively from L. Baudin, *Les Incas du Perou;* R. Karsten, *Das Altperuanische Inkareich;* and Garcilaso de la Vega, *Commentarios reales di los Incas,* and citing parallel volumes about Paraguay. It is worth summarizing his account.[13]

By 1531, the Inca Empire had thrived for 200 years, encompassing the territory of contemporary Peru, Ecuador, Bolivia, and large upper portions of Chile and Argentina. Its population was 12 million. Its capital Cuzco had a population of 200,000, and its magnificent palaces and temples, decorated with finely polished and exactly fitted façades two hundred meters long, shone in the sun. The streets of Cuzco were paved, and a complex system of aqueducts brought water from afar. The stones of a nearby fortress weighed twelve tons; the Spaniards could not believe it had been constructed by men. The road system was superior to that of Spain, and state storehouses were full of produce, utensils, and military equipment.

The capacities of the Incas for organization were stupendous. They had to be. Among the Incas, the Iron Age had not arrived. As the Spaniards found, their technology was unbelievably primitive. The land was tilled with wooden hoes. All travel was by foot. All labor was by hand. Although the Incas had devised no writing system, a complex system of knotted strings was used for an exact accounting of minutest activities.

Liberation theologians are fond of citing instances of exploitation by outsiders: by multinational corporations today, and before that by Spanish conquerors. Thus, Enrique Dussel told the Religious News Service in December 1985:

In Latin America we have supported the world's economy with our lives. After the conquest (in the 1500's), Indians in Bolivia would be lined up by the Spanish soldiers. Every seventh man would be picked out to work on the silver mines of Potosi. The chosen were allotted a week-long drunken orgy before descending into the pits. But they went into the mines understanding that they would work until they dropped dead, sacrificed to the god, money. Working conditions may have changed but the god remains the same. We insist on worshipping Jehovah, the god of life. The god of death, call it wealth or international capital or Mammon, must be named and challenged and defeated in our time.[14]

But Dussel could well go back earlier, to the socialist labor of the Incas. The Incan Empire achieved great glory through a perfect bureaucratic organization of 12 million persons, in which every aspect of individuality was subordinated to the purposes of the state. The population was divided into three classes: the hereditary ruling Incan elite; the masses of the population conscripted for labor and military service; and the state slaves, the conquered peoples who worked the state land and served as house servants to the Incas.

Every aspect of every Incan life was controlled from the top. Everyone reported to someone. Privacy was forbidden. To facilitate supervision, doors of peasant cottages had to be kept open even during the eating of meals. All land and utensils belonged to the state. Private property was forbidden. Each person received two cloaks, of a color identical for all within the same region. Neither money nor trade was permitted. Private initiative was wholly eliminated and private life was regulated in minutest detail. Marriage was by official decree, on scheduled occasions, between spouses chosen by the ruling Incas. The state distributed concubines. Each year, young girls of eight or nine from throughout the empire were selected for four years of special education as "the elect." At the age of thirteen, these girls were divided by the Incas into three categories: some for services of worship to the sun, moon, and stars; some as wives or concubines awarded to members of the ruling class as signs of favor; some as human sacrifices to be offered to the cosmos. The parents of "the elect" were forbidden by law, under threat of punishment, from showing any sign of regret. All other unmarried women were also allotted as state property by the Incas. (The status of women in neighboring tribes was far higher.)

The cardinal principle of daily life was uniformity. Citizens lived in identical houses on identical blocks, wore identical clothing, used identical utensils, walked identical roads, and worked in identical public buildings. The impression was of an awesome prison. Anything that offended the spirit of standardization was looked upon as dangerous and hostile. The birth of twins and a strangely shaped rock were alike thought to be threatening. Difference was thought to manifest the power of evil.

Since state law governed all activities, all crimes were crimes against the state and understood as serious threats to total social control. Stealing fruit from a state farm was a capital offense. Capital punishment was frequent and imaginative. Offenders were hanged by the feet; stoned to death; thrown into a gorge; hanged by the hair over a cliff; thrown into a pit with jaguars or poisonous snakes. For the most serious offenses, all relatives of the accused were also executed. Torture before death was often prescribed. In certain cases (such as mutiny) burial of the executed was prohibited. Disgrace was total. Incarceration in underground jails—inhabited by bears, jaguars, snakes, and scorpions—could also be tantamount to a death sentence. Forced labor in gold and silver mines was routine. Banishment to labor in difficult tropical climes was used as a threat, carried out often enough to be more than credible.

How did 200 armed Spaniards overcome a superbly armed Empire of 12 million? In Africa, the Zulus—facing armed Englishmen—mounted long and successful resistance. Perhaps, Shafarevich hypothesizes, an ingrained fear of unplanned events eroded Inca will. Throughout the Inca Empire, scholars today discern the atrophy of individual initiative, the coerced habit of acting only under command, a pervasive apathy. The removal of all personal stimuli had led to massive indifference, indifference even of children to the fate of their parents, indifference to the fate of the state. There was no distinction between "mine" and "thine," no allowance for personal assertion of any kind. The roots of personal action had been cut.

Ironically, Thomas More's *Utopia,* written in 1516, contained many details of the way of life first discovered among the Incas in 1531. He had called his imagined state "No Place," but there *was* such a place. As stories of the Incas spread after 1531, this coincidence excited Western imagination.

*   *   *

A hundred years later, not far away, the Jesuits raised an army among the Guarani Indians of Paraguay to defend the latter against slave traders from São Paulo. The Jesuits achieved this aim by resettling the Indians, nearly 200,000 strong, into communal "reductions," on the pattern of the ancient Inca settlements of which they had heard. Between 150 and 300 Jesuits, assigned by twos to command the "childlike" Indians in each reduction, made every decision of daily life. One Jesuit seldom appeared except at religious services. The other was in charge of secular life. Each day the latter communicated through a list of daily orders given to *corregidors* or *alcaldes* elected to convey orders to the multitudes. Each day the Indians lined up to receive their orders. One Jesuit preached a sermon, then all able-bodied persons were marched off to their assignments. They were obliged to do so singing.

The principle of ownership was communal. Trading and selling were strictly forbidden. Land, utensils, tools, clothing, and supplies were expressly *lent* to the Indians. Nothing could be owned.

The Jesuits constantly complained in correspondence of the indifference of the Indians to working their own fields. They could not understand how some preferred to be punished for poor work, rather than to work diligently as instructed. Father Cardiel wrote in 1758: "For 140 years we have been fighting this, but there has hardly been any improvement. And as long as they have but a child's intelligence, things will not get better."[15]

The Indians made shoes for export, but were not allowed to wear them. They were not allowed to learn Spanish. No Indian (except soldiers or herdsmen) had a right to ride horseback. Identical clothing was mandatory for all. Chimney-less cabins housed all; smoke had to escape through the door. According to the Austrian Jesuit Sepp, who arrived in 1691,[16] the Indians slept on the floor or in hammocks, crowded among dogs, cats, mice, rats, and cockroaches, in windowless, one-room huts which exuded a smoky and unbearable stench. Contact between persons in different reductions was not permitted.

Twice each year during official ceremonies, the Fathers assigned spouses among single men and women. Worried about the apathetic birth rate, the Fathers even rang a bell each night to summon couples to "their marital duty." The Fathers did everything possible to stifle individual initiative. They expressly prevented their charges from developing a sense of interest that might make them independent-minded. They did not blame the social system they had imposed for stifling the development of personality. On the contrary, they blamed the Indians. Father Escadon wrote in a letter: "In truth and without the slightest exaggeration, none of them has greater faculty, intelligence and capacity of common sense than as we observe in Europe in children who can read, write and learn but who are nevertheless in no condition to decide for themselves."[17]

Sad portraits by the Jesuits—enthusiastically reported in Europe—did not prevent European intellectuals, reading of this fantastically organized community faraway, in which the Jesuits kept the poor from hunger, gave them rest on Sunday, and guaranteed each shelter and a cloak, from rising to a certain admiration. Thus Montesquieu in *The Spirit of the Laws:*

> The Society of Jesus had the honor . . . of proclaiming for the
> first time ever the idea of religion in combination with the
> idea of humanity. . . . The society attracted tribes scattered in
> villages, provided them with secure livelihood and clothed
> them. It will always be admirable to govern people so as to
> make them happy.[18]

Voltaire called such socialism "a triumph of humanity."[19]

And yet this reduction of the lives of human beings to the level of
life lived in an anthill, solely to meet their bodily "basic needs," seems
to Shafarevich grotesquely inhuman.[20]

The picture Shafarevich gleans from examples of "Asiatic socialism" in Mesopotamia and Egypt is scarcely more attractive.[21] From
such examples as these, numbing in the roll-call of human suffering,
we learn that the mere abolition of private property is no guarantee of
human felicity.

2. THE INNER WILL OF SOCIALISM

Even in its most enlightened and democratic forms, socialism is
affronted by economic liberties rooted in individual will. The force of
the word *socialism* is that such liberties must be placed under social control. But what are the reasons why this must be so? The reason usually
given is that liberty inevitably leads to inequality. Equality in this context is not taken to mean equality under the law, equality of opportunity, or equality in the freedom to choose among one's own
economic possibilities—the forms of equality essential to the democratic capitalist vision. Socialists tend to despise such equalities as these,
desiring in their place some form of economic equality or equality of
income. That this is an odd desire is evident from the observable fact
that human beings are by nature unequal in size, shape, stature, looks,
talents, heart, mind, and will. How could such inequalities of nature
not lead to economic inequalities? And why should all these inequalities of nature be legitimate, while legitimacy is denied to economic inequalities? (Of course, some socialists have not shrunken from the
harsh logic that all human differences be narrowed: of sex, physical
looks, dress, taste, and choice.)[22]

Further, the dream of equality is necessarily coercive. By nature
and by nurture, human beings are each unique. Each personality is
different from any other. Indeed, such individual uniqueness is one
ground of human dignity. Each unique person is made in the image

of God; and personal differences, infinite in their variety, are a mirror of the infinity of God, each individual reflecting an aspect of God's own rich and immeasurable life. Individuation is a principal refractor of godliness.

Shafarevich argues that, in principle, socialism is hostile to religion, precisely for reasons such as these. In being affronted by the inequality inherent in individual uniqueness, socialism is pulled over toward being hostile to the principle of individual rights. These rights are endowed in each person directly by the Creator, through the intermediary of no social organization whatever. By this path, God is the ground of individual dignity. Attempting to "socialize" this individuality, socialism empowers political forces to suppress it. It does so chiefly in the economic sphere (but, in practice, in a much larger sphere as well).

Since it is not natural for human beings blindly to accept economic uniformity, socialism must contrive by all available means to suppress an innate hunger for individualization. This necessity accounts for the drabness, grayness, and uniformity in every known socialist regime—and even within socialist movements. *Pas d'ennemis à gauche.* The power of the principle of uniformity within radical or socialist movements has often been observed. Revolutionary socialist leaders (Castro, Ortega) often prefer to appear on the international stage in uniform. They want to show solidarity, militance, disciplined order. To show individuality is regarded as "bourgeois." A desire to be like others is deeply rooted in all human behavior; but in socialist groups, in particular, this tendency is erected into principle. The particular structure that socialism gives to equality, in short, is uniformity.

Under socialism, the favorite term of address is "comrades," as if individual differences do not matter and should not be voiced. A favorite symbol is "solidarity," a word whose meaning in democratic societies, as Romano Guardini once put it, is "acting together" in voluntary association, but whose meaning in socialist contexts suggests marching in ranks. Socialists love mass movements and phrases like "mobilization of the masses."

The traditional color of liberal flags is the *tricouleur,* suggesting pluralism and a division of power. The traditional color of the socialist flag is a monochromatic red. The red symbolizes uniformity. Yet even from the first historical appearance of the red flag of socialism, in France in 1832, the solid red flag was also meant to suggest fire, danger, struggle, and blood.[23] In all known human societies, there are obvious differences and multiform differentiations between person and person. The socialist impulse is to look past these, in order to see persons as expressions of a collective, significant solely in their collective roles, not in their individuality.

In all societies, even in socialist societies, there are manifest inequalities and injustices. Nowhere does there exist heaven on earth. Against the "old order" of capitalism, the socialist reaction is outrage, protest, revolution, and destruction. The old order must be destroyed. That much is clear. But what sort of society will replace the old? How will Christian socialism, in particular, defend the principle of individuation? How this can be done through the enforcement of economic uniformity is unclear.

Human individualization is not fully given at birth. Only slowly does the maturing human person come to self-appropriation, acquiring exact self-knowledge (and that only painfully) and self-invention (choosing what sort of person each uniquely chooses to become). In socialist societies, initiative and self-interests (however noble) are systematically repressed. Unexercised, how is self-appropriation ever to be achieved?

Here lies the reason for the apathy and indifference so widespread in existing socialist societies, against which socialist leaders must always try to rally their people by evoking mass enthusiasm. For socialists, the spirit of enterprise must be confined within mass-controlled channels.

Democratic socialists, even the most humane among them, do not sufficiently reflect upon the importance for moral growth of a system of private economic initiative. Socialists have a tendency to imagine that economic growth simply happens. They have no positive view of enterprise, initiative, invention, and self-exertion. They disparage the creative imagination of the individual person. They wish all motivations to be socialized, not indirectly and from the bottom through the voluntarism inherent in markets, but directly through political mobilization from above. Socialists see social dimensions first, individual human persons second (if at all). The liberal society begins with the unique person, engaged in the universal work of liberation by choice and in free cooperation.

In human beings, of course, both dimensions—personal and social—are essential. A human being is both a unique person, able to act autonomously and in individual ways for individual motives, but also a brother or sister to every other human being. Socialists overlook the *social* dimensions of the economic activities of individuals, even when the latter act freely and in ways unfettered by the state. Human beings voluntarily associate themselves; Lone Rangers are exceedingly rare.

Here, in particular, liberation theologians seem to embrace images of human life that emphasize organic connectedness: the oneness of a folk in kinship, a common memory, a common social location ("class"), and a common religion. They write very little about pluralism. Occasionally, they speak with disdain of "contract theories." Do they really imagine that if human beings voluntarily associate themselves, by implicit or express agreement, such association is thin, merely legal, less than humane? In economic life, they seem to regard distinctive individual achievement as a threat, which they mean to curb by every barrier possible.

Biblically, both Judaism and Christianity are religions of covenants, rooted in contracts freely entered into (and daily renewed) both by God and by human beings. It is not counter to human nature to enter into voluntary contracts. On the contrary, to do so is the highest expression of personal liberty and human association. This is why the marriage contract has for centuries been regarded as a reflection of the covenant between God and humankind. At this institution at the origin of every human life is a covenant freely entered into.

*   *   *

Systematically, there is an asymmetry between socialist societies and democratic capitalist societies. Socialism is holistic. It is an overriding moral system governing both economics and politics. The moral system of socialism is remarkably trusting about political power. It employs the latter to coerce economic behavior. The structure of socialism is like a pyramid. Moral (ideological) power is concentrated at the peak, suffuses political power at the next level down, and constrains every economic activity at the bottom.

That is why dissent from the decisions of a socialist form of organization cannot be understood merely as an expression of deviant individual will. Obdurately maintained, they can only be regarded as willful heresy. Robert Heilbroner has frankly acknowledged socialism's need to maintain its own orthodoxy: Socialists must not assert, he writes, that

> among its moral commitments, socialism will choose to include the rights of individuals to their Millian liberties. For that celebration of individualism is directly opposed to the basic socialist commitment to a deliberately embraced collective moral goal. . . . Because socialist society aspires to be a good society, all its decisions and opinions are inescapably invested with moral import. Every disagreement with them,

every argument for alternative policies, every nay-saying
voice therefore raises into question the moral validity of
the existing government. . . . Dissents and disagreements
thereby smack of heresy in a manner lacking from societies
in which expediency and not morality rules the roost.[24]

Socialism assigns the solidarity of the group priority over individual
dissent. For a socialist, it is impermissible to embrace liberty of
thought *as a matter of principle.* In socialism, there can be no principle
justifying the validity of individual dissent, its social necessity, and its
moral integrity. To insert such a principle into socialist thought would
render the latter indistinguishable from "bourgeois individualism."
In principle, no socialist can promote the autonomy of the individual
person. In principle, no one who gives priority to the autonomy of
the individual person in key areas of life can be socialist.

This is why socialist movements always engender powerful sec-
tarian currents. Deviants have no choice but to break away and start
again. This is also why socialist speech employs so many quasi-reli-
gious terms.

At bottom, socialism is a *moral* vision, imposing itself upon every
conscience, even to the extent that dissent and deviation are sponta-
neously regarded as self-centered and immoral. There is no principle
in socialism defending the autonomy of the individual. Once such a
principle enters socialist thought, socialism becomes a type of democratic capitalism. Otherwise, its suppression of personal economic activities by consenting adults becomes incoherent.

By contrast, the inherent design of democratic capitalist systems
is intended to favor simultaneously both the expression of a rich and
thick voluntary social life and as much room as good order permits
for individual initiative. Since the world of economic activities consumes more hours of the day than any other, liberty for individuals
in the economic sphere is in practice the major sphere of human liberty. Moreover, economic activities are inherently social. No one can
be an economic activist in total isolation. Economic activism is necessarily expressed through activities in association with others. Thus,
liberty for the individual is consistent with powerful social virtues of
teamwork, cooperation, and civic responsibility. While democratic
capitalist societies are necessarily rooted in moral principles and
moral practices, without which they cannot function, they do not impose one single vision of social morality upon all, as socialism must
do. Democratic capitalist societies tend, in principle, to strengthen the
roots of pluralism and diversity. Socialist societies tend, in principle,

to strengthen the unified collectivity and to impose upon it a single morality.

Thus it is that any admirable socialism, thoroughly democratized, must introduce the principle of personal autonomy. It must stimulate responsibility and voluntary participation by every individual. Once it does so, however, it must learn to accept private property, markets, incentives, enterprise, invention and a broad sphere of autonomous economic activity. For individuals, once they begin to act, become self-motivated and capable of initiative. At that point, democratic socialism becomes indistinguishable in principle from democratic capitalism.

In short, the inner will of socialism properly so-called heads toward equality-as-uniformity. Its aim is to repress the individual creator, especially in economic life. It directly opposes the economic liberation of the human person. One of its social consequences is public grayness, monotony, and stagnation, such as one sees in every socialist nation. By dint of massive efforts at social control, it is true, the Incas, the Guarani Indians of Paraguay, the Egyptians who built the pyramids, the immemorial collectivist labors of the Chinese, and the nations of the Soviet empire today are capable of impressive economic achievements. But it cannot be said that such societies are lively and diverse expressions of human liberty, respectful of the rights of individual persons. Scientific, bureaucratic, total socialism does not stop at the level of public grayness. The total social control it requires must reach into the human spirit. Its aim is to create a "new man." Its ambition is total.

What socialism regards as evil in the "old man" is ownership, initiative, ambition, achievement, and individual success. For the socialist, no one ought to stand out. All should be equal. What must be eradicated is the bourgeois sense of self, the desire to be regarded as an individual, any expression of selfishness or private gain. At the extreme, even a demand for privacy raises suspicions. Everything the self has should belong to all. What is there to keep private, to hide, or to squirrel away? The ideal of the socialist society is identical conditions for everyone.

In the human spirit, this means identical thoughts. Movements of the left always exert great peer pressure as a form of censorship. Dissenters learn to keep silence. Individuals learn to go with the group. Leaders assassinate the reputations of rivals by showing how their thinking has become deviant. At the extreme, so powerful is the socialist sense of moral correctness that dissent is regarded as a loss of grip on socialist reality. The social model for the socialist vision is the orderliness of the hive and the contentedness of the herd. A believer in socialism is expected to believe with his whole mind, heart, and soul—and thus to extinguish in the self every scintilla of individual will, thought, or affection. How this works in practice is unforgettably described by a believing socialist:

> We are a party of men who make the impossible possible. Steeped in the idea of violence, we direct it against ourselves, and if the party demands it and if it is necessary and important for the party, we can by an act of will put out of our heads in twenty-four hours ideas that we have cherished for years. In suppressing one's convictions or tossing them aside, it is necessary to reorient oneself in the shortest possible time in such a way as to agree, inwardly, with one's whole mind. . . . Is it easy to put out of mind things that only yesterday you considered to be right and which today you must consider false in order to be in full accord with the party? Of course not. Nevertheless, through violence directed against oneself, the necessary result is achieved. Giving up life, shooting oneself through the head, are mere trifles compared with this other manifestation of will. . . . This sort of violence against the self is acutely painful, but such violence with the aim of breaking oneself so as to be in full accord with the party constitutes the essence of a truly principled Bolshevik Communist. I am familiar with objections of the following kind. The party may be absolutely mistaken, it is said, it might call black something that is clearly and indisputably white. To all those who try to foist this example on me, I say: *Yes, I shall consider black something that I felt and considered to be white, since outside the party, outside accord with it, there is no life for me.*[25]

This war upon the principle of individuality, therefore, aims at the extinction of the self. Such extinction is not an expression of selflessness. It is a form of self-immolation. It runs so counter to nature that it is like rushing willingly into death. The privileged heroes of the socialist imagination are martyrs who die for the revolution. Not their success, but their self-immolation, is held in highest honor. For no one dares to say in what socialist success consists. What matters most for socialists is revolution. The destruction of the old order has far more vividness than do imperfect programs for the improvement of the life of the poor. (Secretly, the people are regarded as stupid.)

In this respect, the inner will of socialism is analogous to the inner will of romantic love. In the myth of romantic love, hero or heroine can live "happily ever after" only in death. Thence the sweet sadness of Romeo and Juliet, Tristan and Isolde, Anna Karenina, and so many others. At death love is most self-immolative and at its "purest." After death, the lover will never have to live with the beloved, never have to bear the constant pointing out of personal faults, never grow weary of the grinding faults of the other. In romantic love, the other is not the object of one's love. The proper object is love itself, for which death is the sole certification.[26] In death, such love is purest.

Similarly, in the arena of political economy, the romantic revolutionary will never have to endure the small losses and small gains of the intractable problems of dismal economies, the ingratitude and indifference of a sullen populace, the plots and intrigues and jealousies of political rivals. Building sewer mains and issuing licenses are crashing bores. Managing a socialist state is even drearier than being bourgeois. The romantic revolutionary can live "happily ever after" only in a revolutionary death.

Thus, the theme of death, dying, bloodshed, violence, suicide and self-immolation are constants of socialist literature. Often, even the dead are mummified as in ancient Egypt: the "comrade" in death resembles every other. As the inner will of socialism is for equality as uniformity, so it seeks the extinction of personality. As its inner will is the wish for self-immolation, so it longs for death, in which every human being is uniform.

Shafarevich collects many texts of personal witness to this inner will. Human beings are never pure enough for true socialism. Many deserve to be punished for willful deviance. One reads terrible pages of how the unfit—those who refuse the romantic dream of becoming "the new man" or "the new woman"—may be, for their own good, consigned to annihilation, in order to cleanse the earth. This is the place, perhaps, for one or two of the most poignant testimonies. The first comes from a medieval Taborite tract, the second from Bakunin's "The Principles of Revolution":

Let each gird himself with the sword and let brother not spare brother; father, son; son, father; neighbor, neighbor. Kill all one after the other so that German heretics should flee in mobs, and we destroy in this world the gain and the greediness of the clergy. So we fulfill God's seventh Commandment, for according to the Apostle Paul, greed is idolatry, and idols and idolators should be killed, so we can wash our hands in their accursed blood, as Moses taught through example and in his writing, for what is written there is written for our edification.[27]

*   *   *

Therefore, in accordance with strict necessity and justice we must devote ourselves wholly and completely to unrestrained and relentless destruction, which must grow in a crescendo until there is nothing left of the existing social forms. . . . We say: the most complete destruction is incompatible with creation, therefore destruction must be absolute and exclusive. The present generation must begin with real revolutions. It must begin with a complete change of all social living conditions; this means that the present generation must blindly raze everything to the ground with only one thought: As fast and as much as possible. . . .

Though we do not recognize any other activity besides the task of destruction, we hold to the opinion that the form in which this activity manifests itself may be quite varied: poison, dagger, noose, and so forth. The revolution blesses everything in equal measure in this struggle.[28]

It is essential for liberation theologians to distinguish what they mean by socialism from the ancient, gray and dreary saga, splashed by red, of the socialist inner will to uniformity in death.

For the rest of us, the constitution of liberty establishes happier horizons.

Ten

THE CONSTITUTION OF LIBERTY

In *The Philosophy of Liberation*, the Argentine historian and philosopher Enrique Dussel composes a metaphysics of the world as he sees it. I admire his ambition. But it is not only socialism that has an implicit metaphysics; so also does liberty.

In general, the philosophers of the liberal society have been better at making the institutions of liberty work in practice, than at making explicit their own philosophic presuppositions. In this chapter, at least a skeleton of those presuppositions should be attempted.

Dussel thinks he is rejecting all of Western philosophy, which he refers to as the ideology of the center and the ideology of cruel oppression. In fact, as his name might suggest, he borrows profusely from German philosophy (including Marx). His vision is romantic and erotic. His cardinal image—from which he derives the utopia that drives his thought—is that of the infant suckling at his mother's nipple.[1]

Equally fundamental is the image of the father, against whom he is in hostile and unrelenting rebellion.[2] Dussel's poetic discussions of eros and festival do not really mask the aggressive hatred that infuses his every line. His manicheism is intense. He writes of the war of Life against Death, periphery against center, the maternal God against the patriarchal Mammon.

Nietzsche taught us to read philosophy for its *will*. Repetitively, Dussel uses Hitler and the S.S. as basic metaphors for Western civilization. "God is dead"—"that is to say, Europe is dead because it deified itself. At least the fetish has died for us and with it the United States."[3] By "fetish," he means an idol in the place of God. He intends to be an "atheist" against the center, which has "deified" itself. This idol must be broken into little pieces.

There are, nonetheless, many Latin Americans who are noble champions of liberty. They see clearly enough that much is wrong with

197

Europe and the United States. Yet they support the project of human
liberation first launched in human history through Christian civilization, particularly in Northern Europe and the United States. They use
the transcendental ideals of that project to criticize the grievous fail-
ings of Northern Europe and the United States. I am thinking of such
brilliant writers as Octavio Paz, whose *One Earth, Three or Four Worlds*
opens with scorching critiques of Western Europe, the United States
("The Imperial Democracy"), and the U.S.S.R., but whose final pages
appeal luminously to the long task of democratizing Latin America.[4]
I am thinking, as well, of Carlos Rangel[5] and Mario Vargas Llosa,[6] and
a small band of others for whom "liberty" has an institutional, constitutional meaning.

In writing of liberty, then, in the tradition of the three fundamental liberations proposed by the liberal tradition—liberation from
torture; liberation from poverty; and liberation from the censorship
of conscience, ideas, and information—one is writing, not about one
small part of the world, but about the whole human species. One is
aiming at "the system of natural liberty," the liberty natural to every
human being. One is writing about the institutions that make liberty
real in routine and regular fashion. One is writing about liberty not
solely as an intellectual ideal, but as it is incarnated in human habits,
institutions, and free associations. Liberty has a constitution.

Underlying this constitution of liberty, moreover, there is a metaphysic. This metaphysic is not solely an anthropology. It is a vision of
the universe seen from the point of view of humankind, but without
implying that man is at the center of the universe. On the contrary,
this metaphysic holds that the human being, qua human, is under
judgment. This judgment is rendered by three agents: first, by oneself,
in one's own unrestricted capacity to question oneself; second, by that
in oneself which manifestly comes from beyond oneself, the light in
which the self questions every aspect of its own being and its own actions; and, finally, by the Light whose presence one perceives as the
power suffusing one's own inner light. Man is the animal whose nature
is to be under unrestricted questioning, the animal that transcends
himself, the animal that is open to his Creator.

All philosophers speak from within traditions that give the terms
they use concrete meanings. Philosophers must use a social, historical
language; there is no other. I write as a Christian philosopher, recognizing that other philosophers will describe what they discern
through terms outside those of the Christian tradition. Dussel points
out that his own philosophical framework "sets out, of course, from
the periphery but, for the most part, it uses the language of the center.

I could not do otherwise."[7] Yet Dussel, too, uses the language, not solely of secular philosophy, but also of Christianity.

In this sense, each of us, each human being, is embodied and historical. If we communicate across the concrete contexts and the histories that separate us, it is by way of analogy. Each points to human experiences that we share as human beings (of being born, being nursed, becoming independent, being in love, inquiring, choosing courses of action, approaching death). Using such analogies, we attempt through civil conversation to come to fuller knowledge of where each stands; how each interprets human life beneath these stars, with the wind upon our faces; and how we imagine the human project in which all are ultimately engaged. Such conversation constitutes civilization. Through it, we question one another.

I begin, then, with the following propositions.

1. THE LIBERAL ETHIC

1. Every human being sometimes raises questions, sometimes merely by a look or by a gesture, sometimes in words. The capacity of the human being to raise questions is the fundamental drive both of the liberal society and of human progress. Whether one speaks of the internal voyage of the human soul, or of the progress or decline of the social order, the human drive to raise questions is fundamental. Until they question tyranny, citizens slumber. They will not yet have felt the stirrings of liberty.

2. This drive to raise questions is unrestricted, restless, infinite. Everything human may be questioned: a person's own state of soul, motives, ends; the structure of a social order; a received sense of reality. There is an infinity of new ways to look at things; of new potential standpoints; and of new directions for action.

3. Without a sense of reality (by which they select what is relevant from what is irrelevant, what is illusory from what seems solid); without a sense of the local scene and the larger drama within which their action "makes sense"; without a narrative purpose, human beings cannot act. For action is concrete, relational, purposive, and successive (one act follows another). Action must have "a point."

Humans gain this "point" from the narrative of which they are a part. In this respect, human action presumes prior choices: a vision of reality; an interpretation of the historical drama; one's own chosen role; images by which to define others and one's relations to them; a predilected future. All these choices must be fixed in mind, at least in a pre-conscious way, before action makes sense.

4. The unrestricted drive to raise questions can call each or all of these prior choices into question. When it does, the actor is momentarily disoriented. At such times, conversions or changes of direction, whether superficial or radical, may more easily take place.

5. When the process of raising questions disrupts one's sense of reality and assumed story radically, however, and when it calls into question even the alternatives one is tempted to put in its place, a human being begins to experience a certain dizziness, an emptiness, a loss of form and purpose. Action becomes, at least temporarily, impossible. This experience I call "the experience of nothingness,"[8] because it breaks down the forms through which we have habitually perceived, imagined, and acted. As Nietzsche put it: The "why" that we had put into reality we suddenly pull out.[9] Then we are enveloped in the blooming, buzzing confusion (and the darkness) of raw experience.

6. The experience of nothingness has for humans a primordial character. It takes us back, first, to the primal chaos. Second, it brings us face-to-face with the profound unrestrictedness of our own drive to ask questions. *All* questions may be asked. When too many are asked at once, perplexity overwhelms us, we feel "at sea," vertigo seizes us, nausea arises. This experience is a crucial revelation of our own fundamental nature. We are *inquiring spirits*, embodied to be sure, but liable to question everything that formerly seemed solid. The experience of nothingness is, in the extreme, the ground of "brainwashing"—when everything formerly believed in, perceived, and imagined is broken down. Torture, intent upon "dehumanizing" us, "breaking" our spirits, and totally disorienting us, may reduce us to nothingness. As it were, it returns us to the *tabula raza* at which we began.

The experience of nothingness is frightening. In a pluralistic age of rapid change and intense external (and internal) stimulation, however, it is far from rare. Even the young, perhaps especially the young, may often walk along its edges.

7. In an important way, this experience of nothingness lies at the heart of the liberal vision. We sense that under torture it might at any time be imposed upon us. In at least petty ways we ourselves, in our daily lives, are often cruel to others. But some persons—the torturers—make cruelty their profession. Given total and unchecked power, the number of torturers in any society may multiply. This has happened often in our own era and in every era. Even philosopher kings, given total power, may sooner or later be tempted to torture others—

for their own good, for state security, for the common good. Some pretext is always at hand.

8. Therefore, those who are called liberals cannot allow there to be a social system in which torture is permissible. For they are called liberals precisely because they desire a social order in which the only legitimate human relation is one of civil conversation, a mutually respectful questioning that preserves the dignity of each. They cannot allow there to be a social system in which torture is permissible, because they know that, under torture, they might not act as the self-determining and responsible agents they choose to be. For this reason, liberalism is properly said to begin in fear of torture.[10] Liberalism is a movement of *political* liberation because it seeks to construct institutions that delegitimate torture—that hold torture to be a crime, punishable by law. Liberals desire a state which is limited, one of whose primary limitations is that it may not torture, under any circumstances whatever.

9. This primal fear of torture moves liberals in two directions at once. In the depths of human experience, liberals perceive the indestructible light of human conscience, understanding, and responsibility. This light is "indestructible," not in the sense that no one can destroy it (for every person may be destroyed), but in the sense that this light belongs inalienably to the self. It may not lawfully be taken away by any other. So long as a person resists, that resistance is inalienable. When a person is "broken," self has been seized by another. No self remains.

10. What is the source, then, of this "light," this "inalienable self"? It comes not from other humans or the state. Dimly, one sees that it does not come solely from the self. It is experienced as "given." It is there. Yet it also holds everything about the self in question. It is, therefore, larger and deeper than the self. It holds the self under judgment. Persons become "religious" when they interpret this light as the presence of God—when they address it in personal terms, as if in conversation: "Our hearts are restless, Lord, until they rest in thee" (St. Augustine). Or as Jesus did in his "dark night": "Father, into thy hands I commend my spirit."

Perhaps no culture has explored the "dark night" more deeply than the Hispanic, especially through St. John of the Cross, who was himself submitted to dungeon and torture by the Inquisition. My own little volume, *The Experience of Nothingness,* is written as a commentary on the most famous of St. John's poems about *nada.*[11]

11. The first direction of liberal thought, therefore, is inward, toward the inalienable rights endowed in each human person by the

Creator—the mark of the Creator in his creature, that creature made in his own image. The possession of such rights is the mark of self, of personhood, of self-determination, and transcendent restlessness.

2. THE LIBERAL METAPHYSIC IN POLITICS

12. The second direction of liberal thought is outward, toward institutions. Of all political philosophies, liberalism is the most practical. Its foundational choice is to construct institutions that respect the image of the Creator in human beings. (I use Christian language, canonized for secular use in the U.S. Declaration of Independence.) The aim of liberalism is to construct institutions that respect such rights in a routine, regular, reliable way.

Many political philosophers of the past worried rather more about principles and concepts. Liberal political philosophy was the first to concentrate its attention upon *institutions*. For liberalism began with a concrete problem: How to construct a republic within which torture would no longer be legitimate? It set out—it was the first such philosophy—to build institutions of human rights, by design and in considerable detail. Liberalism thinks *institutionally*, not because it abandons "substantive" issues in order to deal with "procedural" issues, but because it recognizes the incarnate nature of human beings. Human beings are embodied persons. Therefore, one must take care to protect their bodies, which otherwise torturers will abuse in order to break their spirits. Earlier philosophies, intent on protecting principles, doctrines, and the spirit, had too often left the body vulnerable to Inquisitors.

Liberal philosophy, then, begins with the unrestricted drive to raise questions, with the experience of nothingness, with fear of torture. Therefore, liberals think institutionally. But there is another reason for liberals to think institutionally.

13. If the human spirit is to be free to inquire, then there are likely to be many provisional answers, many creeds, plural persuasions. Those who would think "substantively"—to decide what the shape of "the new man" ought to be, *for all the others*—will be tempted to apply torture to the recalcitrant whom they may "substantively" define as defective. Those who proceed by way of "substance" put themselves in the place of God. They alone, they think, possess the correct eschatology, envisage the appropriate utopia, are the intellectual vanguard of the true human destiny. Their "radical" criticism of others is with due probability likely to be murderous. They are much too likely not to "dialogue" with their critics, but to annihilate them.

14. When human inquiry is unrestricted, according to its inmost nature, pluralism will with virtual certainty result. Through which *procedures* then, in which *institutions*, according to which sets of *checks and balances*, will reasoned dialogue and civil disagreement be guaranteed? Liberal logic leads directly to the institutions of democracy, created for such purposes. Its direction is not to enforce one metaphysical vision upon all, but to set up checks and balances so that no one metaphysic may be obligatory for all.

15. It is important to note how anti-gnostic, how anti-platonic, liberal realism is. The liberal realist recognizes the weakness of humankind, the frailty even of the philosopher-king, the fallibility of every "intellectual vanguard." It entrusts no one with political orthodoxy. The liberal trusts no one but God, lets God be God, puts no political apparatus in the place of God. The liberal society is prohibited from conferring transcendence upon itself. It is "under God."

16. The liberal ordinance, therefore, dictates a government that is self-denying. Thus, not even secular atheistic liberals may rightfully impose their unbelief upon the others; nor can believing liberals impose belief upon atheists. The liberal view does not require every person to be theologically or ideologically neutered. It requires only that the institutions and procedures of the public square allow each person (or group) to state his case as cogently, reasonably and civilly as each can.[12]

17. In this respect, two forms of liberalism must be distinguished. In the beginning, some liberals held a highly optimistic vision of humans as perfectible, reasonable, moral animals, guided by reason and high ideals. This was liberal utopianism. To some extent, such utopianism had a good practical effect. When a society expects much of its citizens, particularly in their public roles, it is likely to elicit from them higher performance. The reverse is also likely.

But liberal *institutions* are not designed upon this utopian basis. On the contrary, checks and balances are established against every form of human power, precisely upon the ground that every human being sometimes sins. As individuals, in their own intimate behavior, human beings sometimes injure those they love; each sometimes sins. In *group* behavior, however, these human weaknesses are magnified. In *Moral Man and Immoral Society*, Reinhold Niebuhr discussed nearly a dozen reasons why this is so. Speaking of those who do not recognize this difference he wrote:

> What is lacking among all these moralists, whether religious
> or rational, is an understanding of the brutal character of the

behavior of all human collectives, and the power of self-interest and collective egoism in all intergroup relations. Failure to recognize the stubborn resistance of group egoism to all moral and inclusive social objectives inevitably involves them in unrealistic and confused political thought. They regard social conflict either as an impossible method of achieving morally approved ends or as a momentary expedient which a more perfect education or a purer religion will make unnecessary. They do not see that the limitations of the human imagination, the easy subservience of reason to prejudice and passion, and the consequent persistence of irrational egoism, particularly in group behavior, make social conflict an inevitability in human history, probably to its very end.[13]

This view is that of the liberal realists.

18. Thus, a biblical theme extremely important to the metaphysic of liberalism is that of human earthiness, contingency, sin: the "modesty," the "lowliness," of the biblical view of man. *One ought not to expect humans to behave as if they are gods, angels, heroes, or saints.* One must understand, as God does, "what is in man."

The liberal metaphysic is opposed to utopianism of every sort. While it is future-oriented, open, and hopeful, liberal realism is also modest. In politics, Aristotle said, one must be satisfied with a "tincture of virtue": even in nature itself, natural laws only "work for the most part." One must expect from each field of study only the degree of certainty proper to it—and, in human affairs, that means: very little.[14] The famous painting of Raphael, which shows Plato pointing to the heaven of ideas, and Aristotle pointing to the imperfect earth, captures liberal realism quite nicely. It does so in secular terms, quite compatible with the instruction given Jews and Christians in the Bible.

3. IN ECONOMICS

19. As for politics, so for economics: the fundamental liberal principle in economics is that the drive to raise questions is and must be unrestricted. Herein lies the dynamism of the free economy. The future is as open as the mind of man. One must create an economic system worthy of the openness of human intellect: open to the radical criticism of the present, to invention, and to discovery.

Only after some years did the liberal economy come to be known as "capitalist." Insofar as *capital* was imagined to be inanimate—either as money or as machines—this name was chosen in error. For the free economy places money at risk through investing it in the uncertain future, and it places every generation of machinery upon the path of obsolescence. But insofar as *capital* designates the human mind (L., *caput*) the first of all economic resources, the name is aptly chosen.

20. It is absurd, then, to call capitalism a "conservative" idea.[15] On the contrary, in the structure of daily life a capitalist economy precipitates one revolution after another. The discoverers of the steam engine, the locomotive, the automobile, and the airplane did not revolutionize transport alone but an entire way of life. Today's revolutions in electronics and computers are more profoundly altering the conditions of life than did the Industrial Revolution. Those who are in favor of human inventiveness—and, therefore, of the free mind-centered economy—are *inherently* "progressive."

The latter term, alas, has been inappropriately captured by socialists, nostalgic for the pre-human uniformity of nature. The central thrust of a capitalist economy is toward the future, is dynamic, is open-ended, and is characterized by rapid change. Alvin Toffler in his eccentricities was correct to describe the effect as *Future Shock.*[16]

21. Institutionally, four fundamental changes have been introduced into the social order by the free or mind-centered economy: (1) the corporation; (2) elaborate techniques of budgeting and accounting that impose close disciplines over small losses and small gains; (3) the accessibility of credit and insurance; and (4) the legal protection of inventions, discoveries, new processes, and trademarks. In earlier chapters, perhaps enough has been said about these. But it is crucial to point out that all of these advances are both social and institutional. To define capitalism in terms of the individual alone is a serious error. Moreover, each of these institutions requires for its proper functioning a certain integrity of character and an appropriate range of human virtues. Such institutions cannot function if the moral ethos necessary to make them work either perishes or is not yet in place in the habits of a people. Systematic dishonesty, corruption, favoritism, failure to keep one's word or to honor contracts, and other such vices vitiate such institutions at their source. Their source lies in human character.

22. In addition, the mind-centered economy rests upon a particular conception of economic intelligence. The first problem to be met is how to achieve an economic *order*. Intuitively, common sense imagines that if there is to be an order, someone must impose it. *Dirigisme* has always shaped the traditional economic order, and is today the order most often exemplified in the nations of the world. The capitalist insight, by contrast, is counterintuitive. It holds that the source of a

maximally intelligent social order lies, not in the minds of directors or planners or other imposers of order, but rather in the concrete decisions of multitudes of individual economic agents using their own intelligence to the fullest.[17]

23. Here the capitalist metaphysic begins with an empirical observation. As usual, this observation is modest, anti-utopian, realistic. When each economic agent makes the most intelligent decisions he or she can, taking into account all contingencies, those decisions are more likely than not to be economically fruitful; otherwise, intelligent economic agents would alter their behavior. Moreover, human agents are "mixed" creatures; they are not *purely* economic agents. They seek to follow their own life plans, to seek their own comforts, to accept civil and political responsibilities, to live as ethical, religious, and aesthetic beings. Thus, when they make economic decisions, they take into account their other life-purposes as well, and their own positions in their own life-cycles.

Furthermore, one may observe that when many economic agents are successful within the scope of their local decisions, cumulatively these successes add up to increases in national success. The individual agents may or may not *intend* such national success. Nonetheless, cumulatively, the *effect* of their personal successes adds up to national success. This difference between intention and effect is an important theoretical distinction; and it has important practical consequences.

24. Two metaphysical assumptions in market theory need to be mentioned. The first concerns world process, the second human knowing. (Together, these two are isomorphic.) Concerning world process, liberalism holds that history is dynamic, contingent, and open. History is ruled neither by random chance nor by determinism. Human will can affect it. Events happen according to schemes of probabilities, not according to necessity.

Concerning human knowing, liberalism holds that the realm of the unknown (and of the future) is immense, so that compared to it human minds seeking understanding are like tiny flashlights in immense darkness.

The openness of history—the range of immense possibility just beyond us—is the premise of all theories of liberation, including some versions of liberation theology.[18] (Others are based on determinism.) The openness of human inquiry is a companion premise crucial to the liberal society. Only liberalism puts both together.

Since human action is itself dynamic, contingent, and open, human agents must act within a vast and dark horizon. Their actions occur within a rapidly shifting, dynamic context, in which other agents unknown to them are also acting, in ways unknown to them. Such actions have many unforeseeable consequences. Thus, human knowing penetrates the future weakly, if at all. Even the most carefully studied, monitored, and regulated actions often have unforeseen (and tragic) consequences.

On January 28, 1986, for example, after twenty-four successful and virtually routine space flights, the twenty-fifth, the space shuttle U.S. Challenger, carrying six crew members and a woman teacher, exploded in a ball of flame after just 74 seconds of ascent, its debris then falling in gentle tracers to the ocean far below. No one clearly anticipated—although some did fear—such consequences.

25. From these premises, two problems arise for economic order. How can a dynamic order become a coherent order? And how can that order realize values compatible with humanistic, Jewish and Christian values? Intuitively, to meet the first problem, most persons seem to believe that any coherent order must have a rational planner. Order, they hold, must be *ordered*.[19] Intuitively, to meet the second problem, such persons would seem to want a rational planner to impose upon economic activity the desired values. The difficulty with these intuitive hypotheses is that, empirically, they do not seem to work. State-directed economies seem to suffer from incoherences and breakdowns far more pervasive than those of non-directed economies.

In addition, the assumption that private citizens cannot in their own economic actions embody humanistic, Jewish and Christian values, and that such values need to be imposed by *public officials,* leaves two facts out of consideration. First, what is to guarantee that public officials will act virtuously? The record of public officials in displaying personal virtue is not a happy one. *Quis custodes custodiet?* Second, why must it be supposed that private citizens will be moral only if coerced by political elites? State-directed economies seem to breed not personal virtue but personal cynicism. They do so by unchecked corruption, by selfish political motivations, and by economic incompetence.[20]

This last point may be strengthened: Economic activities necessarily involve every citizen, every product, every service, and every exchange within the nation. Billions of transactions occur every day. It is strictly impossible for any group of planners to have sufficient information about such transactions, not only in advance but even after the fact. On this impossibility, statist regimes routinely falter. It is "not merely difficult but quite impossible even in the age of the computer, to collect, process, and assess all the immensely detailed information that would be required if no use were to be made of the market. The Communist countries did not find it possible to do so."[21] Thus, even socialist theoreticians have had to reconsider their antipathy to markets.[22]

26. By contrast, the metaphysic of liberalism proceeds by a counterintuitive but empirically confirmed observation. Even when no economic agent intends, or even foresees, the order that will emerge from the accumulated sum of individual economic decisions, nonetheless, when free markets of a certain character are functioning, the unintended (and unforeseen) result of individual activities is a surprisingly coherent order. It may seem to intuition that this is impossible. To empirical observation, however, it is a fact. In free economies, schedules are met, things work, the economy as a system functions dynamically, shortages are quickly repaired, excessive production is quickly checked, etc. A coherent order emerges, apart from anyone's intention.

> Many things, having full reference
> To one consent, may work contrariously;
> As many arrows, loosed several ways,
> Fly to one mark; as many ways meet in one town;
> As many fresh streams meet in one salt sea;
> As many lines close in the dial's center;
> So may a thousand actions, once afoot,
> End in one purpose, and be all well borne
> Without defeat.[23]

There is, then, a crucial difference between the *ends* of economic agents and the common *result* of their activities. Free markets convey instantaneous information about transactions, desires, shortages, and overly optimistic forecasts. Markets are a social device for acquiring massive amounts of social information without massive information costs. The market system is designed to produce social order, counterintuitively. It does so by focusing upon results rather than upon intentions.

27. In a sense, Adam Smith misstated his initial formulation of this insight. When a person employs his own capital, Smith wrote, he is led "to promote an end which was no part of his intention. . . . By pursuing his own *interest*, he frequently promotes that of the society more effectively than when he really intends to promote it."[24] The mistake here was to say "interest." Smith's true point is that in a market system, it is quite unnecessary for anyone to *know* everything. Such complete knowledge is impossible to achieve, and the belief that it can be achieved is doubly dangerous: "The statesman, who should attempt

to direct private people in what manner they ought to employ their capitals, would not only load himself with a most unnecessary attention, but assume an authority which could safely be trusted, not only to no single person, but to no council or senate whatever, and which would nowhere be so dangerous as in the hands of a man who had folly and presumption enough to fancy himself fit to exercise it."[25]

Intuitively, as we have seen, persons suppose that a coherent outcome requires a coherent plan. Not so, Smith. From observation, he saw in market *results* surprising coherence planned by no one, but suffused with considerable intelligence. We should accordingly reformulate Smith's observation in this way: "A very large number of actions taken by many people, often people removed from each other in time and place, can have *unforeseen results that nevertheless form a coherent pattern.*"[26]

Smith's error was to say by pursuing his own "interest," where he should have said "by pursuing his own most intelligent judgment." The larger idea can be put this way: "When an economic activist follows his own most intelligent judgment in order to accomplish a fruitful economic outcome at his own station in the economic order, even without trying to imagine the finished whole of all similar acts by others, such an activist more effectively promotes the welfare of society than when he tries to think for, and to plan for, the whole society." A slightly different way of putting this point is as follows. When each person applies the maximal economic intelligence of which he is capable, at his own station and in matters for which he is responsible, the entire economic order is more suffused with accumulated acts of intelligence than if some one public official (or team of public officials) attempted to impose a coherent order.

It was on this principle that Abraham Lincoln supported the Homestead Act of 1862. Instead of opening the American West to a board of government planners, and instead of imitating the plantation and slave system of the American South (or of the *latifundia* and large estates of much of Latin America), Lincoln chose the path of multiplying the number of small owners, thus multiplying the number of individual economic decisionmakers. In a sense, this legislation anticipates the famous Catholic "principle of subsidiarity," enunciated in 1931 by Pius XI.[27] It ensured that economic decisions would be made as close as possible to the concrete texture of immediate events. (One ought to note, though, that the Homestead Act—a fundamental *systematic* decision—was made at the national level, as a political decision. The "political" in political economy is often crucial.)

28. Economics is the study of human action concerned with ma-

terial scarcity and the creation of wealth, in the light both of social systems and of the actions of individuals. The field of such actions is
governed neither by pure randomness nor by necessity; human actions can make a systematic difference in historical outcomes. Thus,
Adam Smith's *Inquiry Into the Nature and Causes of the Wealth of Nations*
suggests in its very title that human inquiry is crucial to economics, that
a systematic knowledge of causes is possible, and that action informed
by such knowledge can result at least in the diminishment of the poverty of all nations and, at its term, in the elimination of such poverty.
In short, through human inquiry and action, a sound material base can
be put in place under every single person on this planet. Put otherwise,
the existing wealth of nations is neither random nor pre-determined
by natural necessity but open to sustained and systematic development. Economics is the field of human action in which human beings
achieve self-mastery over their own material conditions of scarcity and
wealth.

29. Among the assumptions of this viewpoint are the following:
(1) the *future* of human economic development is *open* to human action; (2) a decisive role in human development is to be played by *human
judgment* separating illusions from realities, false perceptions from
true, conventional understandings of the causes of wealth from more
accurate and discerning understandings; (3) the critical factor in economic development is that form of human action described as *enterprise,* i.e., sustained alertness in detecting current errors of judgment
and practice and an alertness to heretofore undetected ways to reduce
current scarcities or to create new wealth.[28] Enterprise is a habit of
mind oriented to action, a specific human virtue either innate or acquired (or some combination of both) and natural to all human beings,
although (as is the case in all the virtues) more highly developed in
some cultures and in some persons than in others.

30. To understand *enterprise* more exactly, it is useful to distinguish among three forms of rationality. (1) *Calculative rationality* is the
form of human reason whose perfection lies in deducing correct solutions (arriving at correct calculations), once ends, means, boundary
conditions, basic operations, and existing states of affairs have been
defined. This form of rationality is most useful to economics considered as a science, under conditions of equilibrium. Once all the relevant materials have been defined, correct actions consist in "summing"
correctly the relevant factors and pursuing the course of action so defined.

(2) *Dialectical rationality* is that form of human reason whose perfection consists in rejecting false or inadequate *ultimate ends* in the de-

finition of purposes for human action, and in arriving at appropriate or adequate ultimate ends.

Existentially, human beings disagree about ultimate ends. Some define the point of living in one way, some in another. Much depends upon the story each human being chooses as best descriptive of the narrative line he or she chooses to pursue in sequences of human action. Those who disagree may point out disadvantages in the definitions of ends given by others, while pointing out advantages in their own definition. Dialectical reasoning is highly useful to all individuals, since through it—especially in spirited dialogue with others—matters heretofore unnoticed are often brought to light, errors of perception or oversights or mistaken lines of reasoning may emerge, and possibilities heretofore unconsidered come into view.

If self-knowledge were ever instantaneous, complete, and entirely luminous, dialectical reasoning would not be necessary. But human beings are always ignorant, partially blind, or mistaken even in their knowledge of themselves, their own purposes, and the story they are currently pursuing. The Socratic injunction, "Know thyself," is intended to suggest the considerable darkness about themselves in which human beings always dwell. Self-knowledge is never complete. Therefore, dialectic reasoning is always necessary for personal progress in self-appropriation.

The same necessity is experienced by societies and cultures, as they learn from experience. From such considerations arise the possibilities of human moral progress. From them, as well, arise the utility—even the necessity—of the open society, through whose pluralistic and unfettered institutions dialectical reasoning is free to bring ever fresh criticism to bear. Societies, like persons, often do learn from history (its lessons articulated by dialectical reasoning) and often do change direction accordingly, choosing to pursue new ends or, at least, to proceed through new ways.

(3) *Prudential reasoning* is that form of human reasoning whose perfection consists in the wisest possible choice of proximate ends and means in the light of ultimate ends. There is no simple *definition* (that can be stated abstractly) concerning "the wisest possible choice." This is because human individuals are unique and human circumstances are unique. What works for one person (a batter in baseball, for example) may not work for another. Each must choose the disposition of personal forces best suited both to the self at that moment and to the situation at hand. Since some persons do so characteristically and by habit—and since the fruits of their so doing usually become apparent to others—such persons become known as "wise." Others like to seek

their advice. Such persons become the *criterion* for sound prudential reasoning. To act wisely in practice is to act *as such persons would act* (due account being taken of the differences between such persons in their own situations and oneself).

Such a definition of practical wisdom (or prudential reasoning) escapes circularity because not *all* persons are appropriate models; persons of practical wisdom are relatively rare and usually stand out among their peers, especially over time. While no one is perfect, such persons more often than not achieve their own ultimate ends through felicitous choices of proximate ends and means. They seem to have a facility for discerning quite early the errors into which others often fall and for discerning, as well, and with seeming ease, the most expeditious and fruitful choices amid the labyrinth of possibilities. Just as some persons may quickly solve a crossword puzzle, pass easily an academic test, solve a mathematical problem—and come thus to be distinguished as "bright" rather than "dull"—so also some persons show extraordinary discernment amid practical perplexities. They show "brightness" in practical discernment. Where others see difficulties, they discern opportunities. Experience shows that they are often correct. When they are not, they also have an extraordinary facility for seeing *why* not, and for correcting future judgments accordingly. Such persons are vital assets in any community.

31. Enterprise is, therefore, to be understood as a form of prudential reasoning as applied especially to reducing material scarcities and creating new material wealth. Israel Kirzner defines enterprise as "alertness," a term not distant from the classical term "discernment" of which I have been availing myself. One will note the alertness of the family cat when, at the end of a long afternoon, the refrigerator door is opened. Such alertness may be merely a form of instinct, hunger, and association. In human beings, alertness or discernment operates over fields far larger and often far more remote and abstract. In economic life, in particular, alertness or discernment comes clearly into evidence when a person of enterprise becomes aware of errors in the way current markets are functioning, aware of oversights and misperceptions and opportunities lost. Such a person may see earlier than others possibilities for new services or new goods not heretofore available, or new methods for doing more cheaply or better things already done.

32. In this sense, the person of enterprise is an agent of disequilibrium. He or she brings into economic activities something new and destabilizing. In the past, no funds whatever may have been expended for the matter of his or her invention. Once the enterpriser has inter-

vened, however, others in the market must adjust to new competition. Since new inventions create jobs never before available, and since the new invention provides either a new good or service or a cheaper, better way of providing older goods or services, new wealth is created. Older inefficiencies are overcome. New possibilities are launched. Typically, one achieved possibility opens the way to others, heretofore impossible.

In short, the distinctive factor in economic development—in creativity and progress—is the human action of enterprise, a form of practical wisdom applied to reducing scarcity or creating new wealth. In enterprise we see the dynamic factor in economic progress. Without enterprise, there is repetition, stagnation, equilibrium.

33. Since scientific reasoning is designed for situations of equilibrium, in which terms and operations have a certain definable stability, economic science *qua* science has had little to say about the vital factor of enterprise.[29] Von Mises and Hayek, proceeding upon the rather more ethical and humanistic plane of human action, have not failed to notice its decisive importance.

34. It is enterprise, indeed, that lies at the heart, not only of the capitalist spirit, but also of capitalism as a system. What is distinctive about capitalism as a novel form of economic activity is not markets, private property, exchange or profit, since all these existed under mercantilism, feudalism, and other pre-capitalist forms of economic activity. Nor is its distinctive factor "private ownership of the means of production," for such forms of ownership are by no means new to the capitalist era. In addition, mere private ownership of the means of production, without enterprise, would by no means yield the dynamic of capitalist discovery, invention, and creativity. What is precisely new in capitalism is the factor of enterprise. More exactly, it is the invention of *institutions* to encourage the virtue of enterprise among the widest possible range of citizens. As Servan-Schreiber observed in *The American Challenge,* the distinctive character of American institutions—the institutions *par excellence* of capitalism—is that they are designed to promote, to elicit, and to reward the habit of enterprise throughout the population.[30] Capitalism is not simply the *sum* of private practices of the virtue of enterprise; it is a *social system* designed to encourage the broadest and most daring exercise of this habit.

35. Capitalism, therefore, as its name suggests, is best defined as *the mind-centered system:* a system designed to encourage the development of prudential reasoning applied to the reduction of scarcity and the creation of new wealth. Historians such as Daniel Boorstin in *The Discoverers* and Page Smith in *The Rise of Industrial America* have de-

tailed how this characteristic design blazed an historical path.[31] Israel Kirzner, as we have seen, has articulated the process in the terms of economic philosophy.

36. There are, then, two paths to enhancing the degree of intelligence and coherence in the economic order. The first is to hold that coherent intentions require a coherent plan, imposed from above. The second is to hold that coherent outcomes spring from maximizing the number of intelligent decisionmakers as close as possible to concrete transactions. The liberal metaphysic holds, on empirical grounds, that the second achieves a more intelligent and coherent result than the first. This hypothesis is subject to disconfirmation.

37. The free market, therefore, is a social institution, designed to effect the achievable maximum of social intelligence and social coherence. The market is not so much designed to enhance the individual responsibilities of economic decisionmakers, although it certainly does that, as to enhance the degree of social intelligence and social coherence. It is an achievement of social ethics, not of individual ethics.

38. This line of thought raises anew the second question mentioned above. How can a liberal social order realize values compatible with humanistic, Jewish, and Christian ethics? No one claims that any social order, short of the Kingdom of Heaven, will assure perfect human, Jewish, or Christian virtue. No earthly order guarantees that. The claim, rather, can only be comparative. It, too, is subject to empirical falsification. *Compared to any other economic order,* a liberal order will achieve a higher practice of humanistic, Jewish, and Christian values.

39. It does so in two ways. First, it maximizes the opportunity for every decisionmaker to act in the most humanistic, Jewish, and Christian way open to that individual. Strictly economic outcomes are almost never a person's sole interest. Second, it maximizes the reliance of each person upon the integrity and cooperation of others. Thus, Adam Smith writes: "In civilized society [any person] stands at all times in need of the co-operation and assistance of great multitudes, while his whole life is scarce sufficient to gain the friendship of a few."[32]

A market system depends upon habits of cooperation and trust in others. When others must systematically be distrusted, costs of transactions are exorbitant; sclerosis sets in.

40. Moreover, the market obliges each of its participants to be other-regarding, not from motives of charity (although these are not excluded), but in order to win acceptance from others. In order to be successful over time, each economic agent must win a reputation for integrity, reliability, and service. Whatever the motives of individuals,

the result is that each member of society is taught by markets to pay due regard to the wants and needs of others. That sellers sometimes take advantage of purchasers is reflected in the ancient saying *caveat emptor*. But those who depend upon broad markets and consistent loyalty down the years must prove worthy of trust.

41. The reason for this is that market transactions are voluntary. They consist essentially in free acts between consenting adults. Of course, no human beings enjoy pure, angelic liberty. Each is constrained by concrete realities. Without markets, however, individual liberties are far more constrained than they are with markets. If the state is the only effective payer of wages and purchaser of goods and services, citizens have only those choices permitted by the state. By contrast, as payers of wages and purchasers of goods and services are multiplied, freedom of choice expands. The larger the number of payers and purchasers, the freer the scope of economic choice. This is a sound economic, as well as a sound moral, principle.

42. Not all human goods and services are appropriately assigned to markets. The education of the young is so crucial to the conduct both of a democratic polity and of a mind-centered economy that the state may be assigned some responsibility for universal education. (Adam Smith so assigned it.[33]) It does not follow that the state ought to be the *only* supplier of educational opportunity. In education, as in other fields, competition is the best ethical corrective for human laxity, incompetence, and tyranny. The case is similar with welfare provisions for those too young, too old, disabled, afflicted with illness or nervous disorder, etc., and unable to be self-reliant. A good society is properly judged by how well it cares for those unable to care for themselves.[34] The state may play an important role in welfare policy as in education and other fields. But the state is not wisely allowed to be the *only* provider of care.

43. A similar logic applies to those other portions of social life that are not entirely amenable to the methods of the market. Markets are not a universal device for every purpose.

Questions of public goods and externalities, for example, may require attention from the political side of political economy more than from the strictly economic side. The practical question is: *What works best, with fewest evil consequences?* One may need to imagine special forms of markets, under special regulation by the state, to deal with complex matters. For example, the state may assume responsibilities for the supply of drinking water and sanitation, while "contracting out" portions of these responsibilities to privately owned and competitive services designed to meet them in regulated ways.

44. To sum up: the liberal society has a preference for an economic order based upon the social institution of markets because such an order is empirically best matched to a dynamic, contingent, open universe. In their very design, markets meet the demands of human action in a dynamic, contingent and open world. Markets liberate a maximal number of intelligent, responsible, individual economic actors, while binding each of them to habits of integrity, reliability, trust, cooperation, and other-regardingness. Such habits fall far short of saintliness. But they represent a basic moral minimum for civic virtue. Given this minimum, human beings may use their liberty to flower forth in generosity and saintliness—or, alas, in such mediocrity or wasted liberty as is our common lot. The call of sanctity may be heard.

45. These brief notes toward an appropriation of the basic presuppositions of the liberal society within the classic Catholic tradition of Aristotle and Aquinas illustrate the work yet to be done in Catholic social thought. Catholic thinkers have paid for too little attention to the great classics of economic thought: to Ludwig von Mises' *Human Action;* Friedrich von Hayek's *The Constitution of Liberty;* Wilhelm Roepke's *The Humane Economy;* Joseph Schumpeter's *The History of Economic Analysis; The Federalist;* and many other essential books concerning the foundations of the liberal society. An immense task of appropriation lies ahead of us. In my opinion, many of these classics cry out for critical inclusion within the tradition laid out by St. Augustine and that "first Whig," St. Thomas Aquinas. Rethinking the liberal classics in the context of the metaphysics of Bernard Lonergan and Karl Rahner would go far toward reconstructing both the intellectual and the social order of Western thought. In this task Lord Acton, too, has much to teach. And John Courtney Murray, S.J., in *We Hold These Truths,* has here as elsewhere anticipated us.

*　　　*　　　*

In these brief and fragmentary comments I have lingered longest upon the ideas of economic liberty, rather than political and civil liberty, and moral-cultural liberty. I have done so for two reasons. The constitution of economic liberty is less well known among intellectuals even in the West. And economic liberties deploy the instruments through which political and moral-cultural liberties are active in the world of time and matter. Private property, as Chesterton remarked, is the canvas and the paint by which Everyman exercises artistic creation.[35] Economic liberties give material substance to political and civil liberties, and to intellectual and artistic liberties. To own printing

presses—in general, to have autonomy over economic instruments—
is an indispensable condition for other liberties, among incarnate creatures such as we.

In the United States in 1983, only one percent of income tax returns reflected an adjusted gross income of $100,000 or more, not
quite ten times the official poverty rate of $10,280. It is socially im-
portant to encourage this top one percent to invest their wealth creatively. For the poor and the middle class, that is, for the other ninety-
nine percent, economic liberty is also a necessary condition for economic creativity. Their autonomy over their own economic activities—
where they will work, how they will improve their properties and their
conditions, whether they will start enterprises of their own, how they
will choose to spend or to save or to invest their incomes—grounds
their freedom of action in this world. Maximizing the efficacy of that
liberty is essential to human liberation. It is also the secret to economic
creativity. Made in the image of the Creator, every human person
bears the risk of using economic liberty in failure and in success, and
the responsibility to create for posterity during his or her life more
wealth than he or she consumes. Only so does human economic progress proceed.

In these intellectual struggles, much is at stake for the poor of the
world. Ideas have consequences, especially for the poor. These days,
the consequences of bad ideas are slowly leading more and more in-
quirers toward the rediscovery of the constitution of liberty: political
liberty from torture, economic liberty from poverty, and liberty of conscience, information, and ideas. The best years of the liberal society are
yet to come.

Slowly, God willing, liberal institutions will by trial and error be
constructed around the world. It is a noble task to further them. The
heart of Judaism and Christianity—their convictions about freedom
and responsibility—is liberal.

Nothing so lifts up the poor as the liberation of their own creative
economic activities.

"The God who gave us life gave us liberty."

Eleven

EPILOGUE: THE SECOND VATICAN INSTRUCTION ON LIBERATION

The supreme commandment of love leads to the full recognition of the dignity of each individual, created in God's image. From this dignity flow natural rights and duties. In the light of the image of God, freedom, which is the essential prerogative of the human person, is manifested in all its depth. Persons are the active and responsible subjects of social life.

Intimately linked to the *foundation*, which is man's dignity, are the *principle of solidarity* and the *principle of subsidiarity*.

By virtue of the first, man with his brothers is obliged to contribute to the common good of society at all its levels. Hence the Church's doctrine is opposed to all the forms of social or political individualism.

By virtue of the second, neither the State nor any society must ever substitute itself for the initiative and responsibility of individuals and of intermediate communities at the level on which they can function, nor must they take away the room necessary for their freedom. Hence the Church's social doctrine is opposed to all forms of collectivism.

—"Christian Freedom and Liberation"[1]

On April 5, 1986, Joseph Cardinal Ratzinger, with the express approval of Pope John Paul II, issued a second instruction on liberation theology, called "Christian Freedom and Liberation." In an important way, the three great liberations of the liberal society—(1) from torture and tyranny; (2) from grinding material poverty and economic powerlessness; and (3) from the many oppressions of conscience, information, and ideas—here enter Catholic social teaching in a more

218

explicit and systematic way than in the past. The Vatican takes care at every point to distinguish genuine Christian ideas of freedom from Marxist ideas. The latter are well known to students of Marxist societies—and to Pope John Paul II, from his years of ideological debate with Marxists in Poland.

The initial reaction of liberation theologians in Latin America was positive. Many claimed to see the instruction as legitimating the themes of liberation theology. Gustavo Gutierrez said it acknowledges that "liberation theology is a sign of the times in Latin America." He also said that it marks the end of a chapter in debate within the Church.[2] Leonardo Boff told the Milan daily Corriere della Sera: "After this document, liberation theology will gain a new dimension." He added: "The Vatican has given universal significance to those values that initially were only those of the third world."[3] This last point is not quite true. In the Church itself, "The Reconstruction of the Social Order" has been a major theme of Catholic social thought for nearly a hundred years. The ideal of the three liberations, introduced into history by Jewish-Christian conceptions of the dignity of the human person, took flesh in history through the development of liberal institutions. Among these are the institutions that protect human rights, but also those that empower individuals in free and dynamic economic activities, including free labor unions.

Although liberation theologians decided to welcome the new Vatican instruction, not to oppose it, an aide to Cardinal Ratzinger told The New York Times "that he did not see how liberation theologians could actually support the new document. 'I'm not sure Father Boff could have read the document,' the aide said, 'because I don't see how it can be used to validate the position of liberation theologians.' "[4]

Recall, however, that liberation theologians have been rethinking their positions regarding democratic freedoms, now that so many Latin American nations have moved toward democracy since 1979. For Christian theology, the institutions of democracy are certainly better than army-led dictatorships. Now, moreover, liberation theologians will have to show in democratic contests that they do, in fact (and not simply in claim), speak for majorities of the people. Furthermore, discussion of such practical matters as massive corruption by state officials, capital flight, the debt crisis, the rise of Latin American manufactures, commodity prices, and other complex economic developments require increasing sophistication and precision of expression. As liberation theologians attempt economic analysis in this new climate, their views become subject to extensive empirical testing. Such developments are bound to draw liberation theologians into more concrete and more exact dialogue with liberal thinkers who favor the open society.

On a deeper level, one of the signal achievements of the new instruction is to distinguish clearly between the two decisive terms that appear in its title: *freedom* and *liberation*. The instruction patiently deploys a long and precise delineation of freedom in its Christian sense.

In Catholic writings, papal and otherwise, the word *liberal* is often used pejoratively, especially in German Catholic writings. Thus, Joseph Cardinal Hoffner, in an address to the German bishops' conference (September 23, 1985), pointed out how Catholic ethicists of the fifteenth and sixteenth centuries, especially in Italy and Spain, had early recognized the importance of free markets. Luis Molina, he notes, pointed out that "all strata of society have the right to climb to a higher level if that proves to be their fate. No one is entitled to a certain position in life, and everyone can ascend or descend in society." But then Cardinal Hoffner goes on:

> However, it would be erroneous to regard the Catholic economic ethicists of the 15th and 16th centuries as the forefathers of economic liberalism. These theologians were concerned about the liberty and dignity of individuals, whose decisions in the marketplace must be oriented to socially determined assessment, and not to their egotistical use.[1]

Cardinal Hoffner asserts that Catholic writers were concerned about "the liberty and dignity of individuals," implying that liberal writers, by contrast, were interested in "egotistical use." Historically, this interpretation of the classics of the liberal tradition may be disputed.[8] For example, a young Argentine Catholic writer has recently shown how influential the Catholic Salamanca School in Spain was upon the teachers of Adam Smith and Smith himself.[9] In historical fact, early liberal thinkers were deeply concerned about the common good and questions concerning the social system as a whole. The basic concept they invented, "political economy," is a concept of system far larger than the classical concept of "politics" alone.

The cardinal discusses Adam Smith, for example, but misses several important points that would link Adam Smith, a moral philosopher, more closely to Catholic thought. The question Adam Smith was raising is, in the large sense, an empirical one. If you wish to further the common good and to promote the commonweal, will you do better to encourage individuals to make the most intelligent, practical judgments they can in their own sphere of action, *or* to encourage them to think about the interests of the whole society? Smith's observation is that, on the whole, individuals will promote the commonweal more effectively through the former course than through the latter. In a sense, this view is close to the Catholic view of subsidiarity. For one thing, those activists who know best the concrete texture of contingencies directly in front of them are in the best position to make sound prudential judgments. For another, cumulatively, such small acts of prudent intelligence are likely to add up to an impressive social wisdom suffused throughout every muscle and tegument of the social body. Finally, Smith is quite aware from shrewd commonsense observation that there is commonly a broad gap between those who *intend* to achieve the common good and those who *actually* do so. Merely to claim to be intending the common good is not necessarily to achieve it in fact. These views are not contrary to classical Catholic thought concerning prudential judgments.

Clearly, some liberal thinkers worked from theories and presuppositions that are both different from Catholic views and now historically dated. Still, one of the important intellectual traditions, not least in economic matters, seriously neglected by Catholic writers is the liberal tradition. Let me be more specific. Among the writers seldom treated by Catholic theologians, and then only in stereotypes, are Montesquieu, Bastiat, Locke, Smith, Jefferson, Madison, Hamilton, John Stuart Mill, Tocqueville, Lincoln, and Lord Acton. (In more recent times, one should add Ludwig von Mises and F. A. Hayek, whose work was deeply influential upon Wilhelm Roepke, Chancellor Ludwig Erhard, and other founders of the "social market economy" praised by Cardinal Hoffner.) Surely, Catholic writers interested in profound reflection upon human freedom cannot much longer afford to neglect so significant a body of work. The long study by Ludwig von Mises, *Human Action*,[10] and F. A. Hayek's *The Constitution of Liberty*,[11] carry much ore Catholic thinkers need to mine concerning the economic workings of political and social freedom. Certainly, Catholic writers would begin from within a different horizon, and proceed from a different point of view, but profound intellectual interchange is indispensable to the progress of Catholic social thought.

In my own researches, I have found superior illumination in the classic Catholic teaching on prudence; subsidiarity; the social nature of human life; the concept of the *person* (as distinguished from the concept of the *individual*); the Aristotelian-Thomistic conceptions of virtue and habit; Christian teaching about the family; and the Catholic synthesis of the elements of moral judgment (experience, the sentiments, the passions, imagination, memory, tradition, moral logic, practical wisdom or prudence, and judgment). The traditions of Catholic social thought help mightily in clarifying certain perplexities in secular liberal thought. Tocqueville and Lord Acton used them most astutely. Catholic social teaching can help secular liberal thinking to achieve a sounder intellectual framework.

As Cardinal Hoffner himself notes: "The proponents of Catholic doctrine deem the market economy to be the right basic form for the economic system. However, they are convinced of the need to give it a humane ideal."[12] (He is, perhaps, alluding here to the brilliant German Christian economist Wilhelm Roepke, and his fertile book *The Humane Economy*.[13]) The cardinal then lists twelve "preconditions" to be met by any economy judged in the light of this ideal. To repeat all twelve here would take us too far afield. Each of the twelve represents a criticism nowadays launched against any economy, in the light of observed human problematics. The cardinal's check-list is a useful one, for which one can find corresponding treatments in contemporary liberal literature.[14]

Just the same, due credit must be given where credit is due. In 1976, to mark the two hundredth anniversary of Adam Smith's classic *Inquiry into the Nature and the Causes of the Wealth of Nations*, Sir Alexander Cairncross, Master of St. Peter's College, Oxford, wrote as follows:

Modern economics can be said to have begun with the discovery of the market. Although the term 'market economy' had yet to be invented its essential features were outlined in the *Wealth of Nations* which provided us with the first coherent model of an economic system and analysed the role of the market within such a system. Since the days of Adam Smith economists have debated the strength and limitations of market forces and have rejoiced in their superior understanding of these forces.

The state, by contrast, needed no such discovery. Its operations were only too visible and were the subject of constant political debate. It was never argued that the state could be wholly replaced by the market and Adam Smith himself laid stress on the positive functions of the state, e.g. in maintaining order, dispensing justice, providing free compulsory education, and abolishing positions of privilege and monopoly. The criteria he suggested for state activity could be used to justify an extensive programme under modern conditions, however slight the programme he approved in his own time.

What he reacted against were the ideas he dismissed as 'mercantilist' which took for granted the need to make use of political power in order to achieve economic ends.[15]

When Cardinal Hoffner writes confidently that "The proponents
of Catholic doctrine regard the market economy to be the right basic
form for the economic system," he is, in effect, absorbing the great
achievement of Adam Smith into the common treasury of Catholic wisdom. In similar fashion, many other *institutional* discoveries of liberal
thinkers have down the years come to be appropriated by "proponents
of Catholic social doctrine." Among the most signal of these is the appropriation by Pope John XXIII of the Bill of Rights of the American
Constitution, and the later Universal Declaration of Human Rights
modeled upon them, in his justly praised encyclical *Pacem in Terris*.
There are many other examples. Lord Acton was fond of recalling that
the liberal concept of the limited state has its roots in a Catholic understanding of the state.[16] Tocqueville's recognition that the "principle of association," which he observed so widely practiced in America,
is the new first principle of the New Science of Politics, has more and
more frequently been accepted (without citing Tocqueville) into Catholic social thought.[17] In *Freedom With Justice*, I showed how surprisingly
close John Stuart Mill's concept of the limited and conditional right of
private property actually is to Catholic social thought.[18] The "unalien-
able rights" of individuals, endowed in them by their creator, has become a commonplace in Catholic writings. A new and lately learned
respect for the institutions of democratic governance, such as the separation of powers, an independent judiciary, due process, universal
suffrage and civic participation, independent political parties and the
like, have more and more entered the mainstream of Catholic social
thought, despite the early fears about democracy expressed as recently
as the pontificates of Pius X and Benedict XV.
   I stress the difference between liberal *theory* and liberal *institutions*.
Most (but not all) liberal thinkers have theories about human nature
and destiny that fall short of Catholic convictions about such matters.
Some liberals were anti-Catholic; some, especially in Germany, France
and Italy, were anti-religious (sometimes merely anti-establishment) or
agnostic. Perhaps the memory of such differences in theory is still too
strong for a dispassionate assessment of true achievements and short-
comings. But in their practicality, in their concern about institution-
building, the thinkers called by friend and foe "liberal" thinkers were
both passionately and effectively much concerned about practical wis-

dom—about what would actually work for the betterment of human-kind.

Thus, even in disputing their larger theories, Catholic proponents of social doctrine (among them, Luigi Sturzo, Jacques Maritain, John Courtney Murray, S.J., Thomas Masaryk, and others) have learned much from liberal innovators concerning how to design institutions that actually enlarge the scope of human freedom in this poor world. The liberal concern for checks and balances, for countervailing powers, for practical effectiveness, for a spirit of practical compromise and the adjustment of differences, for a loyal opposition, for rights of dissent and free assembly and redress of grievances, made space also for the Church, even in societies very largely non-Catholic. The liberal invention of institutions of religious liberty had an undeniably great effect upon the rethinking of this issue brought to fruition in the Second Vatican Council.

There is one more point worth stressing. In *Laborem Exercens,* Pope John Paul II used the memorable phrase, "The priority of labor over capital," which is duly recalled in the second instruction on liberation theology.[19] Yet even this phrase has a liberal antecedent. Abraham Lincoln, a strong advocate of the independent farmer and independent craftsman, whose administration supported the Merrill Act establishing land-grant colleges in each new territory of the United States (on Adam Smith's theory that the cause of the wealth of nations is intellect, broadly diffused), had earlier employed that very phrase, in arguing in favor of free labor and in opposition to slave labor. Lincoln voiced this view twice, once at the Wisconsin State Fair in 1859, and again in his Annual Message to Congress (1861). His words are as follows:

> Labor is prior to, and independent of, capital. Capital is only the fruit of labor, and could never have existed if labor had not first existed. Labor is the superior of capital, and deserves much the higher consideration. Capital has its rights, which are as worthy of protection as any other rights. Nor is it denied that there is, and probably always will be, a relation between labor and capital, producing mutual benefits. The error is in assuming that the whole labor of the community exists within that relation.[20]

All this forms the background of the striking emphasis that the second instruction on liberation theology places upon freedom.

Indeed, after "Christian Freedom and Liberation," Catholic social thought can no longer be accurately described solely in terms of "Justice and Peace." A third term has now explicitly been added: *Freedom*, Justice and Peace. Human dignity requires respect for individual freedom—freedom ordered to justice, to the common good, and to the moral law, to be sure. But, unarguably, freedom.[21]

Even if the Vatican does not formally reconstitute the current *Institutio Justitia et Pax*, the Institution Justice and Peace, founded subsequent to Vatican II to promote the action of the Church in the modern world, the word *freedom* must after this instruction always be thought of in connection with justice and peace. It is impossible to imagine a social order that represses Christian freedom—or, indeed, the freedom of conscience of any human being—as a just society, even if a thoroughly oppressive government should succeed in damping rebellion and maintaining "peace." Justice and peace without freedom can never represent either true justice or true peace.

This addition to the basic terms of Catholic social thought is of incalculable importance.

* * *

In such ways, "Christian Freedom and Liberation" ushers the Catholic Church into a new era, intellectually and institutionally. If one compares "Christian Freedom and Liberation" to Pius IX's *Syllabus of Errors* (1864), the intellectual and institutional sweep of this achievement is undeniable. Pius IX warned the Church against the misuses of liberal conceptions of freedom. He was deeply suspicious of the free press, democracy, and the undifferentiated, almost arrogant modern concept of progress. His dire warnings have come to be echoed by many contemporary "prophets of doom," and not always without point. Nonetheless, history since Pius IX—during some one hundred and twenty bloody years—has also taught the Church bitter lessons about illiberal regimes. In the political, economic, and moral-cultural spheres, illiberal institutions have assaulted the dignity of persons.

Meanwhile, especially since the First World War, great transformations have been wrought within the liberal societies of the West, through profound institutional reform. In the late twentieth century, the liberal idea and liberal institutions have both advanced beyond nineteenth-century conceptions and practice. After sketching many of these advances in West Germany in particular, Cardinal Hoffner concludes: "We are miles away from the paleo-liberal economic system of 'laissez-faire.' "[22]

Simultaneously, a clearer distinction has become possible between the liberal society and the socialist society. To be sure, there is a middle ground, described by some (emphasizing political activism) as democratic socialism and by others (emphasizing economic activism) as democratic capitalism. In politics and in culture, and to a remarkable degree also in economics, both are variants of the liberal idea. Cardinal Hoffner describes the situation in the Federal Republic of Germany:

> Even though free democratic socialism in the West also derives from Karl Marx, it differs from Marxism in some significant respects, not least in the doctrine on social and economic processes of development. It supports a free-market system and explicitly stresses that it does not aspire to collectivism nor to a controlled economy. Instead, it wishes to promote the ownership of property among those sections of the population for whom this has hitherto been rendered virtually impossible by the prevailing social system. A characteristic feature of free democratic socialism is that it backs state interference in the economy more than other democratic parties do. Its weakness lies in its approach to society, based on a liberalist philosophy, which repeatedly manifests itself in its policies on culture, education, and schooling.[23]

Against socialism of the Marxist-Leninist type, both democratic capitalism and democratic socialism are united in radical opposition. Here, too, Cardinal Hoffner observes:

> For a number of years now, the West has experienced an astonishing relapse into the salvation promised by utopian communism. The New Left, a very heterogeneous group, probably only agrees in its negation of the existing social fabric. But just how the new social and economic order would redeem future mankind from any alienation remains a sealed book. Eurocommunism, whose ideology rests on an atheistic and anti-religious philosophy of a Marxist character such as that developed by Antonio Gramsci for Italian communism, does not cease to be a form of communism. As long as the Eurocommunists are not in power, they behave in a social and democratic manner. Only when they have seized power do they show their true face.[24]

Between democratic socialism and democratic capitalism, however, recent social experience is also obliging us to observe an increasingly widening difference. The weight of current experience—it may change again, as experience dictates—seems to be shifting in favor of democratic capitalism. Without the provision of a more abundant liberty for economic activism among all sectors of society, especially the poorest, the economic base for democratic living suffers atrophy and decline. It is possible, of course, to see democratic capitalism and democratic socialism as mutually balancing tendencies, useful and fruitful each to the other. The Church makes room for both. At the present moment of history, however, even in social democratic societies such as several in Western Europe, experience is leading both intellectuals and the public to confront economic decline and (relative) economic stagnation.

Compared to the dynamism of the U.S. and East Asian economies, "there has been no corresponding upsurge of entrepreneurship in Europe," writes Arthur F. Burns, former Chairman of the Federal Reserve System and former U.S. Ambassador to West Germany.

> There are many reasons why the entrepreneurial spirit is less firmly implanted in Europe. I have already alluded to some of them—the high level of taxation, the regulatory burdens, the immense power of trade unions, and the increasing share of labor in national income. There are also other inhibiting factors in Europe. Venture capital firms are few in number and very limited in their resources. Capital formation by way of offerings is practically unknown. . . . The institutional limitations on entrepreneurship in Europe are further inhibited by psychological attitudes. Investors are more fearful of failure and therefore are less inclined to take risks, and this is a major reason why Western Europe has been so deficient during the past ten to fifteen years in creating new jobs. . . . If the people of Western Europe cling stubbornly in the years ahead to their security blankets, the malaise of their national economies will not be cured and may in fact deepen. In my judgment this will not happen, because Europeans have become increasingly aware of the connection between the excesses of the welfare state and the inadequate performance of their economies. The startling contrast between their circumstances and those of the more dynamic economies of the United States and Eastern Asia has led to agonized introspection and a flood of studies and fresh proposals.[25]

About the institutions proper to economic liberation "Christian Freedom and Liberation" remains largely silent. This is an area for

pioneering theological inquiry. *How* to liberate the poor for increased
economic activism is an urgent subject.

*   *   *

The fundamental question raised by "Christian Freedom and Liberation" is the question raised at the beginning of this book.

> Enlightened by the Lord's Spirit, Christ's Church can discern
> in the signs of the times the ones which advance liberation
> and those that are deceptive and illusory.[26]

Of any existing theory of liberation, it is necessary for the Christian to ask: Does it liberate? Not all who speak of liberation bring actual
liberation. "The revolution," Charles Peguy wrote, "is moral or not at
all." To this may now be added: The revolution is institutional or not
at all. The fundamental test lies in institutional practice.

> Awareness of man's freedom and dignity, together with the
> affirmation of the inalienable rights of individuals and peo-
> ples, is one of the major characteristics of our time. But free-
> dom demands conditions of an economic, social, political and
> cultural kind which make possible its full exercise.[27]

Experience reveals which institutions liberate best in practice.
None does so perfectly. We shall never succeed in building paradise
here on earth. What Christians can aim at, though, is the building of
such institutions as do achieve the three fundamental liberations: freedom in the political order, freedom from poverty, and freedom of
conscience, information, and ideas. Further, Christians may aim at institutions reformable from within, by regular and routine institutional
means, through the civil discourse that constitutes the progress of civilization in history. There is no paradise on earth—but there must be
constant progress toward closer approximations of transcendent ideals.

> Situations of grave injustice require the courage to make far-
> reaching reforms and to suppress unjustifiable privileges.
> But those who discredit the path of reform and favour the
> myth of revolution not only foster the illusion that the aboli-
> tion of an evil situation is in itself sufficient to create a more
> humane society; they also encourage the setting up of totali-
> tarian regimes. The fight against injustice is meaningless un-
> less it is waged with a view to establishing a new social and
> political order in conformity with the demands of justice. Jus-
> tice must already mark each stage of the establishment of this
> new order. There is a morality of means.[28]

In this world, the purpose of such flawed institutional liberations as human beings may in fact achieve, as they strive ceaselessly to "reconstruct the social order," is to liberate the human person for the fundamental drama of human life: to become holy, to become a saint, to become an image on earth of the Creator who chose us to love, to honor, and to praise him forever, through our care for one another.

In any truly free society, alas, many will refuse this vocation. All sometimes refuse it. The free society can no more guarantee that all its citizens will fulfill their full vocation than the Church can guarantee that all its Popes, bishops, clergy, religious, and lay persons will become saints. It is for that reason that the second encyclical of Pope John Paul II concentrated upon the need humans have of mercy toward each other, and upon that most beautiful of the names of God: "He who gives his heart to those in need," *Miseri-cordia* (mercy).[29]

Philosophically, the root of civilization is the rule of law, reason, and civility; theologically, its root is mercy: "Forgive us our trespasses as we forgive those who trespass against us."

Such is the Jewish-Christian idea of freedom. Intellectually, the Jewish-Christian idea is deeper than that achieved by most secular liberal thinkers. In institutional inventiveness, however, Catholic social thought today owes very much indeed to secular innovators, whom at first it often opposed. An intellectual and institutional synthesis between the two traditions has long been overdue.

Through such a synthesis, peoples of American Jewish and Christian heritage can reappropriate the foundations both of their faith and of the inspirations of their culture. And they can begin the hard work of helping to build everywhere institutions worthy of the freedom with which every human person has been inalienably endowed by our Creator. For persons, freedom is the key. In the words of the second instruction:

> Basic principles and criteria for judgment inspire *guidelines for action*. Since the common good of human society is at the service of people, the means of action must be in conformity with human dignity and facilitate education for freedom. A safe criterion for judgment and action is this: there can be no true liberation if from very beginning the rights of freedom are not respected.[30]

Again, Thomas Jefferson: "The God who gave us life gave us liberty."

APPENDIX

VIGNETTES FROM LATIN AMERICA

It has been my privilege in recent years to travel in Latin America, to receive letters and communications from friends there, and to take part in various symposia concerned with democracy and economic development. Latin America is an unusually beautiful part of the world. It is engaged in an intellectual struggle to imagine a New Hemisphere, within which all the peoples of the Americas will be bound in the observance of the human dignity of every single person and in the creative bettering of the material condition of all. In this appendix, I collect some observations gleaned from my travels, to lend the more abstract chapters of this book immediacy.

1. CHILE WANTS DEMOCRACY!

On May 11, 1983 civil disturbances all over Chile evoked "the worst crisis atmosphere in ten years." A full-fledged general strike did not materialize, but work stoppages, school absences, tooting horns, and a sustained clanging of pots and pans in many streets awakened ominous memories of the Allende years. At least two persons died at police hands.

Six days earlier I had spent a week in Chile, sufficient to gain a strong sense that an almost universal pressure for democracy is welling up within that long, slim nation of 11 million. From the right and from the left, few hesitate to voice dissatisfaction with the current pace of the announced "transition to democracy"—and with the silent, steady abuses of human rights which continue.

Those in the U.S. government who are being torn by arguments whether or not to certify Chile for military and other aid must recognize that the forces of democracy in Chile are broad and deep. Unlike some other Latin American nations, Chile has a long and established culture of democracy. The hunger for its steady, step-by-step return is palpable.

Chile, indeed, may be an early test case of various U.S. programs on democracy. There is an urgent need to keep a steady flow of labor leaders, jurists, journalists, scholars, and other Americans coming to Chile during the next crucial months and years—each trying to shed light on how, in practice, democracy may be rebuilt and a wounded economy brought back to growth and opportunity.

By all accounts, the prosperity of Santiago and other cities during the past ten years has visibly grown by long strides—until recently. The 2.5 million households now own 800,000 autos; television sets and refrigerators have multiplied by several times. The subway in Santiago is one of the cleanest, quietest and handsomest in the world.

Yet the government's stubborn insistence on fixed exchange rates and low single-standard tariffs—which flooded Chile with unprecedentedly cheap foreign imports, encouraged huge flights of domestic capital for investment abroad, and prompted unrestrained private borrowing—has led to a sudden and ominously serious economic collapse. Unemployment of various sorts totals more than a third of the work force. A great many small businesses have gone bankrupt. Huge pyramided conglomerates in banking and industry—which should never have been permitted to develop—have come apart at the seams.

Chile has known even harsher economic times, so the crisis seems to be less economic than political. The infamous "Article 24" of the new Constitution, which gives the President totally arbitrary, unlimited, and irresponsible power, is deeply resented even on the right.

Many who are passionately anti-Marxist and contemptuous of socialism in economics are highly critical of General Pinochet for not moving the country back more swiftly into genuinely constitutional, regular, stable government. All eyes focus on this transition. Most doubt that it can wait until the scheduled election of 1989.

General Augusto Pinochet is variously described, on right and left alike, as a "rational dictator," as "the Western world's most convinced anti-democrat," and as "determined to hold onto absolute power as long as life lasts." Those who stress his "rational" side stress that he is often moved by "political facts," and argue that his "stubborn bravery," which bristles at any direct threat to his power, can nevertheless lead him to bow to the virtually universal will of all factions. To others, this seems utopian.

A certain broad area of consensus does seem to be emerging from Chilean experience during the past fifteen years. The horrible inflation, shortages, long lines, and immense discontent of the Allende years have turned many on the left away from extremes in that direction. Human rights abuses and "Article 24" have turned many on the right away from confidence in authoritarian rule. Between these extremes, there is a groping, uncertain consensus.

All sides seem to be searching (a) for a workable, stable, reliable system of democratic governance and (b) for a set of economic policies, suited to Chilean circumstances, which promise a renewal of local commercial and industrial growth.

The Catholic Church in Chile, led until May 7 by Cardinal Raul Enrique Silva, now retired and shortly to be replaced by Archbishop Fresno, has become a major force for democracy. On the left, measured against the authoritarian abuses of Pinochet, old Marxist taunts about democracy as a merely "bourgeois formality" seem empty. Those "bourgeois formalities," it turns out, mean a great deal. Many on the right agree.

Chileans of all persuasions express weariness at being experimented upon by a succession of powerful twentieth century ideologies—from the Alliance for Progress through Allende's Marxism to Pinochet's authoritarian rule. Many mock Pinochet's "Chilean way to socialism"—over fifty percent of economic activity is now in the state sector—as bitterly as they mocked Allende's "Chilean way to socialism."

Finally, doctrines being taught in the War Colleges of Argentina—just across a rugged border more than 4,000 kilometers long—about "Argentina's new destiny in the sun" also make Chileans uneasy. If Argentina, more than twice Chile's size in population, does intend to gain hegemony over the southern passage around the Cape, and over access to Antarctica, then the threats to Chile from internal political and economic turmoil are matched by a triple threat: potential war.

The population of Chile is 97 percent European. More than most, it is predominantly middle class, although the rural poor combined with the urban unemployed are generating a vast body of newly disappointed poor, their relatively recent expectations dashed.

Chile is farther away from Central America than Washington is. It is, however, in the same time zone as Washington. In May, it is autumn in Santiago; the leaves are falling. Soon it will be winter. Chile needs and deserves democracy. It is the season to care enough to help democracy—urgently.

1983

2. NOTES ON DINNER WITH ASSMANN

May 23, 1985
8:00 P.M. to 11:30 P.M. [Dictated immediately afterward]
Rio de Janeiro
Le Streghe Restaurant

For three and a half hours, Assmann did most of the talking. He is fifty-one years old, from a family five generations in southern Brazil. He has a friendly, warm, German manner. He has light-colored hair and a thick light-colored mustache. He was wearing a khaki jungle suit (four pockets on the front) and heavy sandals.

His manner was pious and spiritual, at least for the first two of three hours. I asked him to say grace, and he was pleased. He invoked a fraternal spirit.

His main point for the first hour seemed to be to persuade me that the chief purpose of the liberation theologians is spiritual renewal. He told me of the fifteen different *comunidades de base* that he himself supervises, trying to attend one meeting of each at least once a month. They meet weekly. They are creating marvelous prayers and new ideas. They are very biblical. He stressed the Bible.

He said that his own head was too European and too intellectual, and that certain things bothered him. One is that the people are often very traditionalist. Even when they encounter social or political problems, they say simply, "It's the will of God," and *"Pazienza."* He doesn't like it, but it's a mix of the old traditionalism with the new reflection on the Bible. Never have Catholics reflected on the Bible like this, he says. He asks which theologians in the world have done so much organizing on the local level.

He tells me of a network of two hundred liberation theologians in Brazil—in fact he is to meet with them the week of May 26 somewhere to the south of São Paulo. He and his German friend from Costa Rica—the same man, a Marxist, I debated in Panama City last year—are writing a book on "theology and economics." He expresses a little irritation that in 1982 I called for a theology of economics, as if it did

236

not already exist, whereas he and his friend had already started publishing titles in this area in Costa Rica in 1978. One of the titles is something about necrophilia. It does not sound too much like theology of
economics.

He recommends to me a new book by a Dutch thinker, who has
written a history of world Christianity, van Leuven, which argues that
Adam Smith ushered in an Age of Death. He says he dedicated two or
three weeks to reading it in Dutch, although that is difficult for him.
He said I must read it.

He minimizes his own role in the movement of liberation theology. He is a little irritated that I mentioned him in my book at all.

He becomes more passionate as he comes closer to the present. He
speaks of Pope John Paul II with a passionate ferocity of hatred and
opposition. It erupts from nowhere. The Pope is destroying the
Church. Assmann says that it is clear that the "attack" upon Boff is an
attack upon the Brazilian church. He boasts of his own relationship
with the Brazilian church, even though he has quit the priesthood and
is married. He is active in rewriting the new catechetics. And in the new
encyclopaedia project. And in many meetings on pastoral care. And
in the series of books on economics and theology which he keeps ed-
iting.

He speaks with detestation of Ratzinger.

He says Boff was foolish to keep about five of the most controversial pages in his new book on the Church. Assmann had advised
him not to keep them. It would be better to proceed slowly and patiently, building for ten or fifteen years from now. He suggests that
one day there will be a new Pope. This Pope, he thinks, is a reactionary.

He describes how nice it is to have a wife, how tender, how for-
giving. He insists on the deep Christian spirituality of the base communities. Clearly, that is his main theme.

But then he begins to attack me. He asks me if I know the books
by Ana Maria Ezcurra in Mexico, on "the ideological offensive," and
on "Reagan and Pope John Paul II." The point of them is to attack
the Institute on Religion and Democracy and other similar forces unleashed by the Pope and Reagan. He says he has help from the
United States and received xeroxed copies of articles from *This World*
and the publications of IRD. I asked him why he simply didn't re-
quest them, since I would be glad to send them. He repeats that he
has a pile about eight inches high, and it is clear that he disapproves.
He tells me how he attacked Peter Berger in Geneva (or somewhere)
for supporting IRD.

He tells me there is opposition to my coming to São Paulo, and many people will not appear with me. Some of his friends don't want him to come to AEI this summer. They fear he is being co-opted to legitimate something which they think is evil. He suggests that my visit to Brazil is timed to carry out Reagan's attack on liberation theology as well as the Pope's. I express astonishment at such conspiracy theories. He says he doesn't believe in conspiracy theories, but "this is how power operates."

He stresses the theme of power several times. You, he tells me, are among the powerful, we are among the weak; remember that. You don't understand anything about power, he says; there is nothing in it in your books. He shows great pleasure in drawing lines of connection between AEI, IRD, *This World,* Nicaragua, the Pope, Boff. It is as if everything that appears on the surface has a hidden, inner explanation, and that it is being manipulated from elsewhere. This is the way his mind works. It is perhaps also the way the groups in which he acts work. He points out that on the jacket of my book in Portuguese it says that I was appointed by the President to the Board of Radio Free Europe and Radio Liberty—and he adds, and probably of Vatican Radio, some say. I tell him that is a lie. But the first part is not, he says, it's here on the book.

It is clear that he hates Reagan and everything he stands for. Assmann has been to Nicaragua at least fourteen times. He has some criticism of the Sandinistas, but he praises immensely their literacy program.

He tells me that he has been in Budapest and several other cities of Eastern Europe. He does not like them. They lack liberty and, he uses his hands expressively, "the joy of life." But on a strictly material basis, he says, he would be glad to have in Brazil what they have: no unemployment, free education, free medical care, none of the poor you see in Brazil. He says that he does not want to create another Eastern Europe, and he even has some criticism of Cuba, which he does not specify.

Interestingly, his passion is aroused when the subject is political. Otherwise piety and the evocation of deep spirituality preoccupy him. When I was with him, I thought it was genuine. And I still think it may be.

The first time I broke in to argue against him was when he criticized Lonergan for lacking an eschatology. "Too much emergent probability." He said we must believe in the new man, the new brotherhood, the new justice, and that this is part of the faith. I denied that. I said that seemed to me like heresy, a kind of earthly utopianism. We moved to another subject.

A little later, he attacked me for the name "This World," which we have given our journal. A friend of his said that we don't even know how we have condemned ourselves, since in St. John's Gospel the expression "this world" always means the world of sin and oppression. I know, I said, and the task is to build a decent political economy in such a world.

He said he was reading *Freedom With Justice* on the airplane and had a chance to look through *The Spirit of Democratic Capitalism* for a few minutes while waiting for me. He said I thoroughly misunderstood the liberation theologians. I must be living on a different planet than they are, he said. I asked him how. He said I didn't talk about Gutierrez' long chapter on spirituality. I said the theme of *The Spirit of Democratic Capitalism* was political economy, and I had fewer problems with Gutierrez on spirituality, although I had some (as on the question of utopianism). He seemed deeply offended that I had singled out the Gutierrez attack on private property. That really troubled him. He disliked my use of Ramos in criticizing Gutierrez. He disliked the way I replied to the quotation from Dom Helder Camara.

He said that 500,000 children die in Brazil every year before the age of (I think he said) one. He said the Pope was guilty for every one of these deaths for preaching the way he does. This was in the car. I said that of course these deaths are unnecessary, Brazil is rich in resources, and I think the way Assmann is thinking will help it to continue.

He said that in one year (1983) Citibank had 5% of its investments in Brazil, but earned 25% of its profits in Brazil. This, he said, is the new speculative finance. He said that I did not understand international capital. He explained that every time interest rates rose, Brazil had to pay so much more money. I said he should be glad that interest rates have come down from 22% to 10% in Reagan's five years. I said that Brazil was free *not* to have borrowed that money. The choice was partly ideological since some said it was better for Brazil to be independent and borrow the money, rather than to invite foreign investment. He scoffed at the idea of Brazil's freedom, and said I didn't understand international finance.

He argued that Brazil is not only failing to develop but is being prevented from developing, in fact being deliberately *un*developed. I tried to point out facts (development in East Asia, e.g.) to show that this could not be true. He is in the grip of whole sets of facts fed him by others. He has some passionate necessity to believe in dependency theory.

About coming to AEI, he said he was undecided. He said he had discussed it with his friends and especially his wife, and he was free to go or not go. I wondered if he was under some kind of discipline. He said the format and subject had changed since the first letter he received. I tried to show him that this was not so, except that some persons had rejected our invitations. He did not know Arthur McGovern, S.J., or his book on Christianity and Marxism. McGovern is coming to our conference.

At one point I asked him if the Brazilian church was heading for another Reformation, breaking free from Rome. The biblical spirit, the popular church, piety from below—all these signs. He said he had not thought of that, and hesitated. He did not really answer. It was a new thought to him. I think it was on target.

It is clear that he and his group are working for the long-run, trying to build up cadres that will become so powerful that Rome cannot rebuke them. They are waiting for a new Pope. They are proud of the support they have from a number of the bishops. They think they are growing within the Brazilian church.

Interestingly enough, many of the points made by Assmann came up the next day when I lectured at the Pontifical Catholic University in Belo Horizonte. The same suspicions about the timing of my trip, the same defense of the spirituality of liberation theology, the same anti-capitalism and anti-Americanism. I did not have much chance to give answers to Assmann, so I enjoyed being able to answer with these others. They seemed very warm, receptive, and thankful after our two and a half hours of debate and discussion. From hostility, they went to considerable warmth. I was grateful for the preparation Assmann gave me.

Saturday, May 25: 10 P.M. Today Ambassador Meira Penna drove me to Petropolis, about forty kilometers to the north and high in the mountains. We stopped by the Franciscan monastery where Boff lives. He was not available, as we had known in advance, but I left a copy of my book. I signed it "With esteem, with fraternal affection— and with fraternal argument, too!"

Afterward, we attended a baptism about another half hour out in the country. It was in a magnificent country home in a valley. About forty persons were there. The discussions were informative and helpful. The building with the dining room, sitting room, and kitchen— far from the main house—had fireplaces and bookcases. The meat was roasted on spits over open fires outside in a kind of huge fireplace cut into the kitchen wall. A former Air Force general (the name I did not catch), now an old man, was with Vernon Walters in North Africa in

1943. He expressed pride in the two new Brazilian planes, the one for civil aviation and the trainer which the RAF has adopted.

In the evening, a journalist guest of Ambassador Meira Penna, at a cocktail reception, tells me the trainer is mostly an Italian invention; the Brazilians just went along with it. He says the problem with Brazilian businessmen is that they don't want to take the risk of invention. They find it cheaper to borrow technology by investing in European or American firms and bringing them to Brazil. There are young Brazilians waiting to create and to invent but no one has asked them. He attributes this to the colonial experience of three hundred years of being dependent on Portugal. The *psychology* of the country, he said, is dependency.

He said, in his opinion, the Church was losing ground and had turned to "liberation theology" in desperation. This did not seem correct to me. He said he thought the liberation theologians are pre-modern men, with pre-modern attitudes. They are romantic. They want a simple society. This did seem to fit what I had seen and heard.

(One of the young people at the Pontifical Catholic University yesterday told me three different times that the United States was trying to keep Brazil dependent, that we were trying to control their way of thinking, and that we were responsible for Brazil's underdevelopment. I told him that such comments made Americans feel omnipotent: guilty for *everything!* I told him we are a chiefly Protestant nation, and so like to feel guilty even before we learn the facts. But the facts don't seem to support his view. How can we control his thoughts? And why would Japan grow prosperous from U.S. aid and investment, while Brazil by the same methods had worse results?)

The journalist mentioned above felt Assmann was more powerful than most thought, although he kept in the background. The journalist was quite sympathetic to the liberation theologians, and thought the Pope and Ratzinger had erred by making a hero of Boff among young people. He thought Boff and the others are pre-modern men, who think in the old traditional way, almost like Rousseau, and without any chance of success in the real world. He linked their pre-modern sensibility to the anti-liberalism of Brazil in the 1930s, when sympathy for Germany ran high, as well as to "integralism" among the Catholics at that time.

Author's note: These notes are printed with the permission of Hugo Assmann. The author notes, however, that it reflects an informal conversation from one side only. The reader might consult the paper that

Dr. Assmann presented shortly afterwards at the American Enterprise Institute, "Democracy and the Debt Crisis," *This World*, Spring/Summer 1986.

3. BRAZIL—CATHOLICISM IN CRISIS

In Sao Paulo, Brazil, late in May 1985, scheduled to present a lecture on "Creation Theology in Latin America" in the ninth-floor auditorium of the city's major paper, *Folha do Sao Paulo,* I was subjected to my first international demonstration.

Earlier, some editors had opposed giving a democratic capitalist such as myself any hearing at all. Since democracy is only now reappearing in Brazil after twenty-one years of deeply resented military rule, the publisher wanted to signify a new era of open debate; and he prevailed.

More than an hour before the scheduled time, however, an organized group of religious-based and university leftists took over the hall, and began singing the Sandinista anthem, declaiming revolutionary poetry, and otherwise building up passion. None of the newspaper's two hundred invited guests could get in. Even the aisles were filled.

After much hesitation, the publisher of *Folha* finally decided to give me the word to go up front—alone. I walked slowly down the crowded aisle, offering to shake hands. No one accepted. As I reached the microphone, on signal, all stood and sang the Sandinista marching song, stomping their feet in rhythm, and waving their well-prepared signs and banners.

"Nicaragua libre" predominated, but so did (in English) "Novak, go home," "How many Vietnams will it take?" and, most touchingly (in Portuguese) "Liberation theology is ours." I saw at least two nuns in the crowd.

After three or four minutes of singing and yelling, they let me read my rather academic text. Later, after allowing me to answer calmly two (as the speaker seemed to think) unanswerable questions, someone signaled for the crowd to leave. As they did so, I loved best the nun in the back of the room, with clenched fist leading a chant of "Sohn-ofa-beetch! Sohn-ofa-beetch!" and "Yanqui-sheet! Yanqui-sheet!"

A few came forward to apologize and to express shame. One of

243

the nuns, who had twice been shouted down for urging the crowd to let me speak, came forward to plead the Sandinista case with civility.

After an intense week of lecturing, debating, giving interviews, and sharing lunches and dinners with various followers of liberation theology, I left Brazil with two conclusions.

First, the theme of "liberation theology is ours" has for many a deeply spiritual ring. It means finding a new way to leave behind a merely privatized religion, in order to organize the poor, in what we in the U.S. have long known as "social action." The Brazilians do so in their own Latin idiom and style. Their sincerity is impressive.

Second, as the hostile demonstration dramatized, the passion of some is intensely political. Ignorance of Anglo-American political and economic thought seems almost bottomless. The natural form of thought for some is "Marxist analysis." That is their vulgate, their daily idiom. For some, democracy is a sham. (Brazilians have never known a day of true self-government, one distinguished editor explained.) And capitalism is in some minds pure evil, with no redeeming qualities whatever.

About their own dream for the future, some say only that they want a "fraternal society," as in the gospels. If they have given any thought at all to the political, economic, and cultural institutions through which they will organize a complex society, none would artic- ulate for me even a sentence.

Most do not wish to be thought of as choosing a Soviet model (here a few became indirect and coy). Admiration for Cuba and for the San- dinistas is not quite total, but it is deep and broad.

Hatred for Pope John Paul II is in at least a few quarters intense.

The church of liberation theology, however, is still a minority even within the Brazilian church. I asked my theological friend whether he could foresee a repetition of the Protestant Reformation in Brazil—a huge split from Rome, on the part of biblically-centered, highly spir- itualized, dissenting base communities, no longer willing to follow the Pope. He was hoping, he said, for the next Pope. He had not thought about what will happen if a new Pope continues, like Pope John Paul II, to raise serious questions about liberation theology.

Catholicism is in even deeper crisis in Brazil than I had imagined. Ironically, the most passionate split concerns, not theology and faith, but political economy. Some of those I met feel deep and intense hatred, not for the American people, but for the American "system." Such persons do not like being questioned about their positive future plans. They seem most comfortable blaming the Yanquis.

One must remember, however, that these are the first months of free discussion in Brazil, after twenty-one long years of military rule. There is still much resentment, and some uncertainty about how freedom ought to be used. I am extremely grateful for having been given so many stimulating audiences and conversations in this new atmosphere. Almost continental in size, Brazil plays a critical role in the future of liberty.

1985

4. LIBERATION THEOLOGY BEGINS TO HEAR ITS CRITICS

At the beginning of August, at an AEI conference on "Liberation Theology and the Liberal Society," an unexpected new dialogue opened up. For Hugo Assmann, a former priest still in good ecclesiastical standing with Cardinal Arns and other bishops in Brazil, and one of the founding fathers of liberation theology, the latter has entered a new phase.

Dr. Assmann mainly emphasized the urgent need to negotiate the debt crisis. (Tom Bethell [*National Review* 8/23] anticipated him.) His many empirical assertions invite rational debate, and this was already an advance. But the biggest advance lay in his embrace of democracy.

Liberation theologians made some mistakes in the past, Dr. Assmann said; one was to ignore democracy. For twenty years, he said, we faced dictatorships and tyrannies, whereas now most of us live in democracies. Our early concern was internal "repression"; today, our concern is to make democracy work to alleviate the "oppression" of the poor.

In the past, Assmann said, another "original sin" of the Latin American Left was a certain elitism. The new democratic moment will require respect for popular consent and grassroots organizing. In addition, he said, liberation theologians once spoke perhaps too loosely of socialism, Marxist analysis, dependency theory, and other bits of theory borrowed from social scientists in Latin America.

In his early days, Assmann was regarded as one of the most Marxist of liberation theologians. He took care to point out in August that his early books on Marxism had been roundly criticized by serious Marxists in the international world. Even then what liberation theologians had in view was clearly *not* Soviet-style Marxism, he said. Assmann remained rather vague about the practical model he and his colleagues have in mind. It is ridiculous, he said, to imagine that Latin America will become "socialist" in the next decade or so.

In describing democracy, Assmann did not specify the *institutional* forms he intended. He was challenged on some of his phrases, e.g., "the logic of the majority" (i.e., the poor). Some of his hearers shared James Madison's concerns about the "tyranny of the majority," and recalled the misuse of such "logic" by several totalitarian regimes in this century. Nor did Assmann address the division of powers, checks and balances, and individual rights. He was not drawn out, either, on the crucial importance of property rights.

Assmann stressed that liberation theologians are neither social scientists nor political economists. Their analysis in such matters, he implied, is tentative.

While Assmann's views are his own and not to be attributed to his colleagues, his position—with Gustavo Gutierrez—as one of the two or three "fathers" of liberation theology in the late 60s and early 70s makes his testimony important. If liberation theologians are newly serious about the idea of democracy, they and those who believe in the liberal society now have common ground earlier lacking. If liberation theologians are willing to submit their claims about economic realities to empirical testing, and to follow the evidence where it leads, that, too, affords new common ground.

One should not, of course, underestimate Dr. Assmann's anger toward the U.S.; it flashed forth from time to time. But he tried very hard to avoid polemics; and he suggested that liberation theologians should not err now by excessively flaying Americans and other developed peoples with unhelpful guilt.

It is too early to say that liberation theology is willing to explore the liberal tradition fairly, or to give it credit for the two "liberations" from which the name "liberal" is derived: liberation from poverty and liberation from tyranny. Assmann did concede that liberation theologians, preoccupied with redistribution, had only begun to pay sufficient attention to the creation of wealth.

Dr. Assmann teasingly voiced anxiety. Why, he asked aloud, is liberation theology thought by so many to be so dangerous? (In his written remarks, he expressed pride about this.) Why are Pope John Paul II, President Reagan, and a host of powerful institutes and journals conspiring to "assault" poor, humble, and weak liberation theologians?

To the contrary, while hardly any major U.S. theologians fully support liberation theology, few ever criticize it openly; it is more often patronized than engaged with serious criticism. The Vatican's Instruction on Liberation Theology has obliged liberation theologians to respond, "That is not what we meant," and "Here are the ways in which we are not Marxists." A serious dialogue has at last begun.

Moreover, if the aims of liberation theology are primarily religious and spiritual, as Dr. Assmann stresses, and rather tentative about political economy, then most of the excitement about it is misplaced. Controversy has arisen precisely because of its claims about politics and economics, hardly at all about its religious qualities. Its frequent invocations of "Marxist analysis" have raised the same penetrating objections raised in the past (e.g., in Ludwig von Mises' powerful *Socialism* in 1922)—and new ones, too. Sophistication about the errors of Marxism is far more advanced than liberation theologians once recognized.

Still, what if liberation theology *is* compatible with the liberal society? With democracy, which secures human rights? And with such capitalism as stirs economic activism from the bottom up, and speedily raises the poor to middle class standards of health, education, well-being, and choice (as it has in Japan, South Korea, Taiwan and elsewhere)? Then, indeed, a "new moment" has arrived.

Premature to expect, such a transformation has more promise than any other for lifting up the tired, the poor, the huddled masses yearning to breathe free.

1985

5. THE U.S., ARGENTINA, AND THE BISHOPS

While the U.S. Catholic bishops were discussing the second draft of their pastoral letter on the U.S. economy in Minnesota June 14–18, 1985, I was being questioned sharply about their letter in Argentina. The population of Argentina is about 90 percent Catholic, composed mainly of immigrants from Spain and Italy. And Argentina was experiencing that week two new economic shocks.

On June 11, the Argentine peso was devalued (again), by 18 percent. Then, on June 14, President Alfonsin declared a "bank holiday"—i.e., closed the banks—and announced the replacement of the peso by a new currency, the "austral." Newspapers in Buenos Aires said that some Argentines will lose in that single stroke some 30 percent of income and worth.

Inflation in Argentina has been running about 100 percent *a month,* more than 1000 percent a year! I brought home for my children a one million peso note of only a few years ago, which was worth 100 pesos (about ten U.S. cents) before the banks closed.

While I was in Argentina for that week of lectures, several Slovak immigrants sought me out; all four of my grandparents came to the U.S. from Slovakia beginning about 1885. We were able to compare notes quickly on the quite different experience of immigration to Argentina and the U.S. during this century.

Argentina is a Latin Catholic nation. I met highly civilized, well-educated, well-read persons, and came quickly to admire the courtesy, kindness, and personal virtues of all those I encountered. Compared to Rio de Janeiro, Brazil, where two weeks earlier I was warned again and again against muggers and robbers in the streets, walking about in Buenos Aires (I was accurately told) is quite safe.

Argentina, of course, experienced horrible systemic violence during the counter-guerrilla warfare of 1976–1980, in which thousands of citizens "disappeared." For these gruesome abuses, military rulers of the past are now on trial. It was a horrible period. Argentina has

249

suffered much from systemic political flaws, as well as systemic economic flaws.

The Argentines I talked to—and the press and television (four out of five stations government-owned)—took the latest monetary shocks with amazing equanimity and wry jokes. I contrasted this with the deep fears I remember in the U.S. when inflation hit 13 percent per year, back in 1980, which to Argentines would now seem like very heaven.

In natural resources, Argentina is a rich country. In 1940, Argentina ranked third in the world in per capita income, and almost as high on other indices of prosperity. For over a hundred years, a liberal approach to political economy had produced steady progress. As President Alfonsin put it in his televised address June 14, the ancestors of today's Argentines had transformed "an almost deserted land" into a world leader in prosperity.

Then a tide of statist ideas, under the Peronists often masquerading as the embodiment of "Catholic social justice," began to sow misery. Today, counting only the federal government and the city of Buenos Aires—that is, *not* counting the expenditures of the other states or municipalities—government now absorbs 55 percent of Argentine gross domestic product. When revenues fail, governments have simply printed money. Thence, incredible inflation.

That is how the vast majority of Argentines have now come to be, in effect, wards of the state, in the name of "justice." Piety about "justice" seems only to breathe hotter as the currency inflates. The political economy of Argentina is today pre-capitalist, largely state-run and state-directed. The space for enterprise and private decisionmaking is very small.

As the U.S. bishops bravely invite criticism of the first draft of their pastoral, and begin the long process of revision, I hope they will help explain the advantages of the U.S. system over the Argentine system. And also why the concept of "Catholic social justice" is so easy to misuse.

In discussing political economy, questions of "system" are crucial. The founders of the U.S.—such thinkers as Madison, Jefferson, Hamilton and Franklin—knew well that they were creating "a new order." What is the nature of that "order"? What was "new" about it? How does it differ from the old "order" typical of Catholic nations such as Argentina?

These are crucial questions, not only for the United States, but also for Argentina and other predominantly Catholic nations, which today suffer under so much needless poverty, chiefly because of deeply flawed conceptions of social system.

If you were a virtuous citizen in Argentina who had set aside the equivalent of $15,000 for the education of your children, would you invest it in Argentina? Current inflation would devastate your savings. Yet if its own citizens do not invest in Argentina, how can the economy grow? A poor system frustrates even virtuous citizens.

One thing is clear as the sky over Buenos Aires: System matters. I am glad that the U.S. bishops have already decided that in their second draft, due in November, they will express more gratitude for the American system, in order to place their particular criticisms of its many faults in perspective.

1985

6. THE LIBERAL REVOLUTION

SAN JOSE, COSTA RICA: After dark, three hours before our Eastern Airlines flight from Miami flew over the east coast of Costa Rica, a squad of twenty Sandinista commandos landed by boat just below our flight path. It took six hours for the small 5000-man police force of Costa Rica to respond.

Tiny Costa Rica has no army. Moreover, with every change of government, it changes the entire personnel of the police force, so that no professional armed class can develop.

Such attacks by Nicaraguan armed forces on Costa Rican soil occur virtually weekly. The 100,000-man Nicaraguan military—in a nation whose population (2.9 million) is only slightly larger than Costa Rica's (2.3 million)—outnumbers the Costa Rican police force 20 to 1. The difference in heavy armaments is far larger than that.

Some estimate there are 500,000 Nicaraguan refugees in Costa Rica. (Marxist regimes produce refugees in abundance.) Among them are known to be a great many trained Nicaraguan infiltrators, agents, and potential saboteurs. Sandinista intelligence reaches into every sector of Costa Rican life.

A question often asked in a rather worried Costa Rica is: If the Nicaraguans invade Costa Rica, will the U.S. send help?

There is a psychological battle, too. Some Costa Ricans already believe that the Communists will win Central America; with caution, they are positioning themselves accordingly.

Others believe that, at least in Nicaragua, Communist rule (as in Cuba) is now a fait accompli. They believe the contras cannot win, and they believe the U.S. will do too little. Communist rule can be contained within Nicaragua—they hope.

Still others hold that a liberal revolution is gathering steam all over Latin America. Here, "liberal" has its nineteenth century revolutionary meaning: a democratic revolution, a revolution against state domination over the economy, a revolution of pluralism—in short, a combination of a free polity and a free economy.

The liberal theoreticians in Latin America are a small band, but a very intelligent one. They argue much better than their chief rivals, the socialists and the Marxists. Their arguments have the appeal of freshness and common sense. Young people, everywhere subjected to leftist, state-oriented orthodoxy, find excitement in liberal ideas. Latin Americans have had ample experience of the failure of statist ideas.

The leftists say the problem of Latin America is capitalism. The liberals point out that even traditionalist, right-wing regimes control most of the economy. Often they have nationalized the banks and all basic industries. Often traditionalists control education totally. There is almost no free space in Latin American economies. Insofar as it exists, the private economy is always weak, vulnerable, and heavily controlled. In many nations, credit is restricted, prices are controlled, and most wage-earners are on the payroll of the state.

At best, most Latin societies are pre-capitalist. More exactly, they are an almost feudal, mercantilist type, neither capitalist nor socialist. They are almost as thoroughly controlled by the state as are socialist economies, but according to a traditionalist ideology. (If and when socialists take over, there will be little in the economy left to nationalize. Of course, socialists of the Cuban or Nicaraguan sort would suppress the other liberties of personal life more efficiently than traditionalist regimes have done.)

The traditional ideology for the state-dominated economy in Latin America is based on the distributive idea rather than the productive idea. Civilian governments concentrate on distributing benefits to the population. Inflation skyrockets. The military then forms a government—and does the same. Inflation skyrockets. Then the military turns in despair back to civilians. The cycle continues.

The Latin American liberals want to break the cycle. They favor the intelligence, drive and motivation of ordinary people to better their own condition. They see the great progress of East Asians and argue that Latin America was once, can be again, and should be far more economically successful than Japan, South Korea, Taiwan, Hong Kong, Singapore, etc.

No doubt, many Latin Americans want to break from the past. But everything depends upon what kind of revolution they have. Only the liberals hold out the promise of an open, self-correcting, constantly self-reforming revolution. They pay far more attention to economics than do traditionalists or socialists. They believe democracy depends upon a growing, prosperous economy. They think the natural resources of Latin America offer a broad base for economic prosperity for all, especially at the bottom of the ladder.

During the past decade, nearly everyone has come to agree about the importance of democracy. Suffering under military dictatorships, the left has come to see that democracy is no "bourgeois illusion." Many conservatives have also been disillusioned by the bitter experiences of the last decade. But more clearly than most, the liberals recognize that political democracy without economic growth leads to a cycle of disillusionment. They have come to see that the survival of freedom in the polity depends on the enlargement of freedom in the economy, so that a truly creative era of economic growth can begin.

The key, the liberals believe, is an economy in which ordinary people will be, for the first time, free to choose and to act and to create. Not controlled by the traditional statism. Not dominated by socialist secret police.

1985

NOTES

INTRODUCTION: TOWARD A THEOLOGY FOR THE
WESTERN HEMISPHERE

1. Enrique Dussel, *Philosophy of Liberation* (Maryknoll, New York: Orbis Books, 1985), p. viii.

2. Jacques Maritain, *Reflections on America* (New York: Charles Scribner's Sons, 1958), p. 118. Maritain outlines the dynamism of the North American liberation philosophy: "The American body politic is, I think, the only one which was born independently of the various historical constraints (wars of subjugation, conquests, submission of the conquered to the conquerors, etc.), which in actual fact contributed to create human societies and played so great a part in its own prenatal conditions. The American body politic is the only one which was fully and explicitly born of freedom, of the free determination of men to live together and work together at a common task. And in this new political creation, men who belonged to various national stocks and spiritual lineages and religious creeds—and whose ancestors had fought the bitterest battles against one another—have freely willed to live together in peace, as free men under God, pursuing the same temporal and terrestial common good" (ibid., p. 168).

3. Jean-Jacques Servan-Schreiber points out the principal sources of modern wealth: "technological innovation; and the integrated combination of production factors that is the keystone of modern decision-making." He recognizes, further: "Behind the success story of American industry lies the talent for accepting and mastering change. Technological advance depends on virtuosity in management. Both are rooted in the dynamic vigor of American education. There is no miracle at work here. America is now reaping a staggering profit

from the most profitable investment of all—the education of its citizens." *The American Challenge,* trans. Ronald Steel, with a Foreword by Arthur Schlesinger, Jr. (New York: Avon Books, 1969), pp. 61, 83.

    4. See Howard J. Wiarda and Michael J. Francis in Michael Novak and Michael P. Jackson, eds., *Latin America: Dependency or Interdependence?* (Washington, D.C.: American Enterprise Institute, 1985).

    5. See Chapter 1, n. 46, *infra.*

    6. *We Drink from Our Own Wells* (Maryknoll, N.Y.: Orbis, 1984), p. xiii.

1. LOOK NORTH IN ANGER

    1. Chris Hedges, "Strife within Church 'Really War of Western Socialist Mores,'" *National Catholic Reporter,* 7 September 1984.

    2. "Friar Says Vatican 'Caricatures' Marxism," *New York Times,* 25 September 1984; and "Brazilian Priest Feels Exonerated After Vatican Trip," *Washington Post,* 22 September 1984.

    3. Gustavo Gutierrez, S.J., *A Theology of Liberation: History, Politics, and Salvation,* trans. Caridad Inda and John Eagleson (Maryknoll, New York: Orbis Books, 1973), p. 88.

    4. Philip Taubman, "The Speaker and His Sources on Latin America," *New York Times,* 12 September 1984. See also Ben Wattenberg, "When Maryknoll Talks, Tip Listens," *Washington Times,* 27 March 1986.

    5. Letter to *New York Times,* 13 September 1984.

    6. Vatican Congregation for the Doctrine of the Faith, "Instruction on Certain Aspects of the 'Theology of Liberation,'" *Origins,* 13 September 1984.

    7. In the Vatican's Instruction we are reminded that "the warning of Paul VI remains fully valid today: Marxism as it is actually lived out poses many distinct aspects and questions for Christians to reflect upon and act on. However, it would be 'illusory and dangerous to ignore the intimate bond which radically unites them, and to accept elements of the Marxist analysis without recognizing its connections with the ideology, or to enter into the practice of class struggle and of its Marxist interpretation while failing to see the kind of totalitarian society to which this process slowly leads.'" Ibid., p. 199, quoting *Octogesimo Adveniens,* 34.

    8. Leszek Kolakowski, *Main Currents of Marxism: Its Origin,*

Growth, and Dissolution, trans. P. S. Falla, vol. 3: *The Breakdown* (Oxford: Clarendon Press, 1978), p. 526.

9. See Arthur F. McGovern, S.J., *Marxism: An American Christian Perspective* (Maryknoll, New York: Orbis Books, 1980), Chapter 5, "Liberation Theology in Latin America," esp. p. 203.

10. See Robert McAfee Brown, "To Orbis, with Thanks," *The Ecumenist,* July–August 1978.

11. See Rich Carey, "Liberation Theology: Is the U.S. Next?" *National Catholic Reporter,* 10 September 1976, p. 4.

12. Ibid.

13. Ibid.

14. See Dom Helder Camara, "What Would St. Thomas Aquinas, the Aristotle Commentator, Do If Faced with Karl Marx?" *Journal of Religion* (Supplement) 58 (1978):183–184.

15. Juan Luis Segundo, "Capitalism—Socialism: A Theological Crux," in *Concilium 96: The Mystical and Political Dimension of the Christian Faith,* (1974); reprinted in Michael Novak, ed., *Liberation South, Liberation North* (Washington, D.C.: American Enterprise Institute, 1981), p. 22; page citations are to the latter version.

16. Moltmann, for example, has written that liberation theologians "only quote a few basic concepts of Marx. And they do this in such a general way that one learns only something about the fruits of the liberation theologians' reading and scarcely anything about the struggle of the Latin American people. In them one reads more about the sociological theories of others, namely Western Socialists, than about the history or the life and suffering of the Latin American people." "Open Letter to Jose Miguez Bonino," in Gerald H. Anderson and Thomas Stransky, eds., *Mission Trends No. 4: Liberation Theologies* (Glen Rock, New Jersey: Paulist Press, 1978), p. 77.

17. For texts of the Medellín documents, see Joseph Gremillion, *The Gospel of Peace and Justice: Catholic Social Teaching Since Pope John* (Maryknoll, New York: Orbis Books, 1976), pp. 445–476.

18. See Michael J. Francis, "Dependency: Ideology, Fad, and Fact," in Michael Novak and Michael P. Jackson, eds., *Latin America: Dependency or Interdependence?* (Washington, D.C.: American Enterprise Institute, 1985).

19. Quoted in Alan Riding, "Revolution and the Intellectual in Latin America," *New York Times Magazine,* 13 March 1983.

20. Gutierrez, *A Theology of Liberation,* pp. 273–274.

21. Segundo, "Capitalism—Socialism," p. 15.

22. McGovern, *Marxism,* p. 184.

23. This is a summary of Gutierrez's experiences recounted by José Míguez Bonino in a statement for Sergio Torres and John Eagleson, eds., *Theology in the Americas* (Maryknoll, New York: Orbis Books, 1976), p. 278; quoted in McGovern, *Marxism,* pp. 181–182.

24. Alfonso Lopez Trujillo, *Liberation or Revolution?* (Huntington, Indiana: Our Sunday Visitor, 1977), p. 101.

25. Medellín Documents, "Peace," 9(a), in Gremillion, *The Gospel of Peace and Justice,* p. 457.

26. Ibid., 9(e), p. 457.

27. Hugo Assmann, *Theology for a Nomad Church,* trans. Paul Burns (Maryknoll, New York: Orbis Books, 1976), pp. 45–46.

28. André-Vincent, O.P., "Les 'théologies de la libération,' " *Nouvelle Revue Théologique* 98 (1976):109–125; reprinted as "The 'Theologies of Liberation,' " trans. James McCauley, S.J., in James V. Schall, S.J., ed., *Liberation Theology in Latin America* (San Francisco: Ignatius Press, 1982), p. 194.

29. I have borrowed this formulation from James V. Schall, S.J., "Liberation Theology in America," in Schall, *Liberation Theology in Latin America,* p. 38.

30. François Hubert Lepargneur, "Théologies de la libération et théologie tout court," *Nouvelle Revue Théologique* 98 (1976):147–69; reprinted as "The Theologies of Liberation and Theology," trans. Msgr. Henry Cosgrove, in Schall, *Liberation Theology in Latin America,* p. 212.

31. Ibid., p. 220.

32. Ibid., p. 209.

33. Quoted in Schall, *Liberation Theology in Latin America,* p. 14. But consider Humberto Belli's account of his FSLN experience: "I was pleased to see these Christians coming closer to Marx and revolution. In no way did I experience any encouragement from them to consider the validity of Christian views. It was not we Marxists who had the identity crisis. They did. And the fact that they were moving in the direction of our philosophy was one more piece of evidence of the soundness of our philosophy. . . . There was no reciprocal process of conversion. Sandinista atheists were not becoming believers." Belli, *Breaking Faith: The Sandinista Revolution and Its Impact on Freedom and Christian Faith in Nicaragua* (Westchester, Illinois: Crossway Books, 1985), p. 26.

34. Eric Hobsbawm, "Religion and the Rise of Socialism," *Marxist Perspectives,* Spring 1978, p. 28.

35. Galbraith continues: "Raw materials and some tropical food products come from the poor countries to the rich. But the greatest suppliers of wheat, feed grains, coal, wood and wood pulp, and cotton fiber

are the two North American countries—the United States and Canada."
John Kenneth Galbraith, "The Defence of the Multinational Company," *The Harvard Business Review,* March–April 1978, pp. 85, 88–89.

36. "In the face of options between racial separation and full
community of rights, free international demand and supply and a balanced market (with an eye to the underprivileged countries) or capitalism and socialism, what is at stake is no mere analogy of the
Kingdom. What is at stake, in a fragmentary fashion if you like, is the
eschatological Kingdom itself, whose realization and revelation are
awaited with anguish by the whole universe." Segundo, "Capitalism—
Socialism," p. 22.

37. Peter Hebblethwaite, "The Gospel as a Handbook for Revolutionaries," *Religion and Freedom* (London), July 1978, p. 11.

38. "[A]lthough Marxist analysis does not directly imply acceptance of Marxist philosophy as a whole—and still less of dialectical materialism as such—as it is normally understood it implies in fact a
concept of human history which contradicts the Christian view of man
and society and leads to strategies which threaten Christian values and
attitudes.

"The consequences have often been disastrous, even though perhaps not always nor immediately. . . . Christians who have for a time
tended to adopt Marxist analysis and praxis, have confessed they have
been led bit by bit to accept any means to justify the end. There are
many instances today which still corroborate what Paul VI wrote in *Oc-
togesimo Adveniens* (n. 34): 'It would be illusory and dangerous . . . to
accept the elements of Marxist analysis without recognizing their relationships with ideology.' To separate one from the other is more difficult than is sometimes imagined." Pedro Arrupe, S.J., "Marxist
Analysis By Christians," *Origins,* 16 April 1981, p. 692.

39. Karl Marx and Friedrich Engels, *Manifesto of the Communist
Party,* trans. Samuel Moore (Peking: Foreign Languages Press, 1975),
p. 64; hereafter cited as *Communist Manifesto.*

40. Gutierrez, *A Theology of Liberation,* p. 91.

41. Segundo, "Capitalism—Socialism," p. 22.

42. Andre-Vincent, O.P., "The 'Theologies of Liberation,' " p.
192.

43. Segundo, "Capitalism—Socialism," p. 15.

44. "If one looks at the figures for the various countries of Latin
America, one finds a wide range of percentages of state-generated
GNP. It extends from about 35 to 40 percent (roughly equivalent to
our own) in some of the lesser developed countries, Honduras or Guatemala, for example, to 50 or 55 percent in the Dominican Republic

and to roughly 60 percent in Nicaragua. It further extends to about 65 or 70 percent in Mexico (with the nationalization of the banks and the various private concerns under the banks' domain) to about the same figure in Brazil, and to roughly 92 percent in Bolivia, according to the latest figures that I have seen. One could say that there is almost nothing left to nationalize in Bolivia." Howard J. Wiarda, "Economic and Political Statism in Latin America," in Michael Novak and Michael P. Jackson, eds., *Latin America: Dependency or Interdependence?* (Washington, D.C.: American Enterprise Institute, 1985), p. 6.

45. Marx and Engels, *Communist Manifesto,* p. 51.

46. "Necessity and violence, violence justified and glorified because it acts in the cause of necessity, necessity no longer either rebelled against in a supreme effort or accepted in pious resignation, but, on the contrary, faithfully worshipped as the great all-coercing force which surely, in the words of Rousseau, will 'force men to be free'—we know how these two and the interplay between them have become the hallmark of successful revolutions in the twentieth century, and this to such an extent that, for the learned and the unlearned alike, they are now outstanding characteristics of all revolutionary events. And we also know to our sorrow that freedom has been better preserved in countries where no revolution ever broke out, no matter how outrageous the circumstances of the powers that be, and that there exist more civil liberties even in countries where the revolution was defeated than in those where revolutions have been victorious." Hannah Arendt, *On Revolution* (New York: Penguin Books, 1965), p. 115.

47. Vatican Congregation for the Doctrine of the Faith, "Instruction on Certain Aspects of the 'Theology of Liberation,' " p. 203.

2. BUT DOES IT LIBERATE?

1. "It may be objected—why not give a more detailed account of the socialist model? Or why not speak of the possibilities of a model? Or why not speak of the possibilities of a moderate, renovated capitalism? There is one very simple reason for not doing this—we cannot foresee or control the universe of the future." Juan Luis Segundo, "Capitalism—Socialism: A Theological Crux," in *Concilium 96: The Mystical and Political Dimension of the Christian Faith,* (1974); reprinted in Michael Novak, ed., *Liberation South, Liberation North* (Washington, D.C.: American Enterprise Institute, 1981), p. 15; page citations are to the latter version.

2. Quoted in John Lofton, "Sharing, Caring and Tutu," *Washington Times*, 17 January 1986.

3. "For [Adam] Smith political economy was not an end in itself but a means to an end, that end being the wealth and well-being, moral and material, of the 'people,' of whom the 'laboring poor' were the largest part. And the poor themselves had a moral status in that economy—not the special moral status they enjoyed in a fixed, hierarchic order, but that which adhered to them as individuals in a free society sharing a common human, which is to say, moral, nature." Gertrude Himmelfarb, *The Idea of Poverty: England in the Early Industrial Age* (New York: Alfred A. Knopf, 1984), p. 63.

4. "[The bourgeoisie] has been the first to show what man's activity can bring about. It has accomplished wonders far surpassing Egyptian pyramids, Roman aqueducts, and Gothic cathedrals; it has conducted expeditions that put in the shade all former exoduses of nations and crusades." Again: "The bourgeoisie, during its rule of scarce one hundred years, has created more massive and more colossal productive forces than have all preceding generations together. Subjection of nature's forces to man, machinery, application of chemistry to industry and agriculture, steam-navigation, railways, electric telegraphs, clearing of whole continents for cultivation, canalization of rivers, whole populations conjured out of the ground—what earlier century had even a presentiment that such productive forces slumbered in the lap of social labor?" Karl Marx and Friedrich Engels, *Manifesto of the Communist Party*, trans. Samuel Moore (Peking: Foreign Languages Press, 1975), pp. 36, 39.

5. Robert N. Bellah summarizes the context: "That the Mosaic analogy was present in the minds of leaders at the very moment of the birth of the republic is indicated in the designs proposed by Franklin and Jefferson for a seal of the United States of America. Together with Adams, they formed a committee of three delegated by the Continental Congress on July 4, 1776, to draw up the new device. 'Franklin proposed as the devices Moses lifting up his wand and dividing the Red Sea while Pharaoh was overwhelmed by its waters, with the motto "Rebellion to tyrants is obedience to God." Jefferson proposed the children of Israel in the wilderness "led by a cloud by day and a pillar of fire by night." ' " See "Civil Religion in America," *Beyond Belief* (New York: Harper & Row, 1970), p. 188, n. 5. For related texts, see the anthology by Conrad Cherry, *God's New Israel* (Englewood Cliffs, New Jersey: Prentice-Hall, 1971).

6. "Second Draft of the U.S. Bishops' Pastoral Letter on Catholic

Social Teaching and the U.S. Economy," *Origins,* 10 October 1985, ¶¶36–62, pp. 261–264.

7. Maritain wrote that "these ideas and these aspirations [of the democratic state of mind] remained and will always remain essentially linked to the Christian message and to the action of hidden stimulation which this message exercises in the depths of the secular conscience of the world. That is why I said . . . that the democratic impulse burst forth in history as a temporal manifestation of the inspiration of the Gospel." Jacques Maritain, *Christianity and Democracy,* trans. Doris C. Anson (New York: Charles Scribner's Sons, 1950), pp. 57–58. See also the chapter entitled "Evangelical Inspiration and the Secular Conscience."

8. "[C]apitalism and capitalistic enterprises, even with a considerable rationalization of capitalistic calculation, have existed in all civilized countries of the earth, so far as economic documents permit us to judge. In China, India, Babylon, Egypt, Mediterranean antiquity, and the Middle Ages, as well as in modern times. These were not merely isolated ventures, but economic enterprises which were entirely dependent on the continuous renewal of capitalistic undertakings, and even continuous operations . . . the capitalistic enterprise and the capitalistic entrepreneur, not only as occasional but as regular entrepreneurs, are very old and were very widespread." Max Weber, *The Protestant Ethic and the Spirit of Capitalism,* trans. Talcott Parsons, with an Introduction by Anthony Giddens (New York: Charles Scribner's Sons, 1958), pp. 19–20.

9. "The earning of money within the modern economic order is, so long as it is done legally, the result and the expression of virtue and proficiency in a calling; and this virtue and proficiency are . . . the real Alpha and Omega of Franklin's ethic. . . . And in truth this peculiar idea, so familiar to us to-day, but in reality so little a matter of course, of one's duty in a calling, is what is most characteristic of the social ethic of capitalist culture, and is in a sense the fundamental basis of it. It is an obligation which the individual is supposed to feel and does feel towards the content of his professional activity. . . ." Weber, *The Protestant Ethic and the Spirit of Capitalism,* pp. 53–54.

10. Oscar Handlin, "The Development of the Corporation," in Michael Novak and John W. Cooper, eds., *The Corporation: A Theological Inquiry* (Washington, D.C.: American Enterprise Institute, 1981), p. 7.

11. Alexander Hamilton, James Madison, and John Jay, *The Federalist Papers* (New York: New American Library of World Literature, 1961), p. 322.

12. Abraham Lincoln, "Agriculture: Annual Address Before the

Wisconsin State Agricultural Society, at Milwaukee, Wisconsin, September 30, 1859," in Roy P. Basler, ed., *Abraham Lincoln: His Speeches and Writings* (New York: World Publishing Co., 1946), p. 501.

13. "Americans of all ages, all stations in life, and all types of disposition are forever forming associations. There are not only commercial and industrial associations in which all take part, but others of a thousand different types—religious, moral, serious, futile, very general and very limited, immensely large and very minute. Americans combine to give fetes, found seminaries, build churches, distribute books, and send missionaries to the antipodes. Hospitals, prisons, and schools take shape in that way. Finally, if they want to proclaim a truth or propagate some feeling by the encouragement of a great example, they form an association. In every case, at the head of any new undertaking, where in France you would find the government or in England some territorial magnate, in the United States you are sure to find an association." Alexis de Tocqueville, *Democracy in America*, ed. J. P. Mayer, trans. George Lawrence (New York: Doubleday & Co., 1969), p. 513.

14. See the author's *Freedom with Justice: Catholic Social Thought and Liberal Institutions* (New York: Harper & Row, 1984), Chapter 11, "The Communitarian Individual in American Practice."

3. A SHORT CATECHISM

1. See Denis P. Doyle, "Socialist Sweden Tries to Reinvent Philanthropy," *Wall Street Journal*, 27 August 1984.

2. "[T]his book contains no explicit analyses of the social, cultural and economic spheres of human existence. It does not employ the social disciplines of history, economics, sociology or political science. This may seem strange for any work on liberation theology. The decision not to enter this mode of reflection explicitly is largely due to my own lack of expertise in these disciplines." Roger Haight, S.J., *An Alternative Vision: An Interpretation of Liberation Theology* (Maryknoll, New York: Orbis Books, 1985), p. 3. See also Joyce A. Little's review of Haight's book: "Relativizing Catholicism," *Catholicism in Crisis*, January 1986.

3. Ibid., p. 16.

4. Ibid.

5. "During the period 1790–1830 factory production increased rapidly. A greater proportion of the people came to benefit from it both as producers and as consumers. The fall in the price of textiles

reduced the price of clothing. Government contracts for uniforms and army boots called into being new industries, and after the war the products of these found a market among the better-paid artisans. Boots began to take the place of clogs, and hats replaced shawls, at least for wear on Sundays. Miscellaneous commodities, ranging from clocks to pocket handkerchiefs, began to enter into the scheme of expenditure, and after 1820 such things as tea and coffee and sugar fell in price substantially. The growth of trade-unions, friendly societies, savings banks, popular newspapers and pamphlets, schools and nonconformist chapels—all give evidence of the existence of a large class raised well above the level of mere subsistence." T. S. Ashton, "The Standard of Life of the Workers in England 1790–1830," in Friedrich A. Hayek, ed., *Capitalism and the Historians* (Chicago: University of Chicago Press, 1954), p. 154. Paul Johnson writes that in Britain "in the nineteenth century, the size of the working population multiplied fourfold. Real wages doubled in the half-century 1800–1850, and doubled again, 1850–1900. This meant there was a 1600 per cent increase in the production and consumption of wage-goods during the century. Nothing like this had happened anywhere before in the whole of history." "Has Capitalism a Future?" in Ernest W. Lefever, ed., *Will Capitalism Survive? A Challenge by Paul Johnson with Twelve Responses* (Washington, D.C.: Ethics and Public Policy Center, 1979), p. 4.

6. The estimate for U.S. black persons' income (1985) is $188 billion, computed by Brimmer and Company, Washington, D.C. (Telephone inquiry, 13 January 1986). The World Bank's *World Development Report 1985* lists the gross domestic product of all nations (as of 1983); the cumulative GDP of Africa for 1983 was $349 billion.

7. Thomas Jefferson, "A Summary View of the Rights of British America," in *Thomas Jefferson,* The Library of America (New York: Literary Classics of the United States, 1984), p. 122.

8. Tocqueville observed that "For the Americans the idea of Christianity and liberty are so completely mingled that it is almost impossible to get them to conceive of the one without the other; it is not a question with them of sterile beliefs bequeathed by the past and vegetating rather than living in the depths of the soul." Tocqueville doubted "whether man can support complete religious independence and entire political liberty at the same time. I am led to think that if he has no faith he must obey, and if he is free he must believe." Alexis de Tocqueville, *Democracy in America,* ed. J. P. Mayer, trans. George Lawrence (Garden City, New York: Harper & Row, 1966; Anchor Books, 1969), pp. 293, 444.

9. John Courtney Murray, S.J., *We Hold These Truths* (New York: Sheed and Ward, 1960), p. 39.

10. "Puebla puts us on the track of further implications when it characterizes poverty here and now in Latin America as 'anti-evangelical.' There is no abstraction going on here, there is no playing with the gospel and with human beings, after the fashion of those who make poverty a sweet and tender ideal (which they are at great pains to avoid striving for).

"Puebla, like Medellín, not only does not use this ambiguous language about an 'ideal,' but explicitly rejects it, and continues to stress material poverty. The poverty in which the poor and oppressed of Latin America are living is contrary to the Christian message, and a denial of the God who reveals himself in the Bible. . . . It is knocking on the wrong door to wish to salvage the spiritual nature of the Christian message by trying to rid it of the clear and direct meaning of material poverty in the Bible as a determinate, concrete, human, social condition. On the contrary, a heightened consciousness of it is what most lucidly reveals the meaning of the proclamation of the kingdom of God." Gustavo Gutierrez, *The Power of the Poor in History,* trans. Robert R. Barr (Maryknoll, New York: Orbis Books, 1983), p. 140. Gutierrez first published this book in Spanish in 1979, but the essays in it date from 1969. This is significant because there is some evidence he has become less Marxist over the years.

11. "One of the most conspicuous economic miracles of the twentieth century developed in West Germany some years after World War II. Even there it was possible for an environment of economic freedom to be created, an environment that released an explosion of entrepreneurship. One cause was the comprehensive denazification process, the simple removal of the bureaucratic apparatus. The administrative organs of central control were more or less paralyzed."

Again: ". . . West German entrepreneurs, formerly shackled by central regulations, could shake off their bonds and begin an economic expansion such as no one at that time had dared to imagine. Once they had regained their freedom, nothing could stop them, neither bombed-out factories and installations nor the fact that machinery and equipment had been confiscated by the victorious powers. A manufacturing industry whose volume of production during the first six months of 1948 had measured 50 percent of its 1939 volume, achieved 130 percent of that 1939 volume, only three years later. And despite the fact that 8 million refugees flowed into West Germany between 1945 and 1950 with more to follow later, it was possible to reduce unemployment from 10 percent of the labor force in 1950 to 1 percent in 1960, while the number of workers increased from 14 to 21 million." Sven Rydenfelt, *A Pattern for Failure: Socialist Economies in Crisis* (New York: Harcourt Brace Jovanovich, 1984), pp. 13–14.

12. Although the World Bank 1985 report gives a figure of 96 percent of primary school-age children enrolled in school for 1982, Robert Wesson and David V. Fleischer write: "Only 40 percent of children went beyond first grade in 1980, the same fraction as in 1948, and only 17 percent finished sixth grade. Secondary schools, educating not for productivity but for status, prepare for a university education that only a tenth of their entrants receive." *Brazil in Transition* (New York: Praeger, 1983), p. 174.

13. Quoted in Dennis Smith, "Theologians on Economics in Latin America: A Struggle of the Gods," Religious News Service Special Report, 18 December 1985, p. 12.

14. See Council of Economic Advisors, *Economic Indicators*, July 1985, p. 13.

15. Remarks of Clarence J. Brown, Deputy Secretary of the Department of Commerce, at the first meeting of the National Commission on Jobs and Small Business, held in Washington, D.C., September 10–11, 1985.

16. Enrique Dussel defines domination thus: "Domination is the act by which others are forced to participate in the system that alienates them. They are compelled to perform actions contrary to their nature, contrary to their historical essence." Dussel, *Philosophy of Liberation*, trans. Aquilina Martinez and Christine Morkovsky (Maryknoll, New York: Orbis Books, 1985), p. 55.

17. Abraham Lincoln, "Annual Address Before the Wisconsin State Agricultural Society, at Milwaukee, Wisconsin, September 30, 1859," in Roy P. Basler, ed., *Abraham Lincoln: His Speeches and Writings* (New York: World Publishing Co., 1946).

18. José Miranda, *Communism in the Bible*, trans. Robert R. Barr (Maryknoll, New York: Orbis Books, 1982), p. 25.

19. Ibid., pp. 25–26.

20. Ibid., p. 26.

21. Ibid., pp. 26–27.

22. Ibid., p. 29.

23. Ibid., p. 28.

24. Ibid., p. 29.

25. See Alejandro Antonio Chafuen, *Christians for Freedom* (San Francisco: Ignatius Press, forthcoming).

26. Miranda, *Communism in the Bible*, p. 40.

27. Ibid., p. 55.

28. Ibid., p. 3. He disavows "Marxism"; see *Journal of Ecumenical Studies*, Summer 1985.

29. Ibid., p. 6.

30. Ibid., p. 73.

31. Ibid.

32. Ibid., pp. 73–74.

33. Sven Rydenfelt in *A Pattern for Failure* has thoroughly documented the economic crises experienced by socialist countries around the world, and in most of them the economic crisis is largely an agricultural crisis. He has also pointed out that while socialist rulers have almost always favored "the prosperous and the strong—the industrial workers, the police, the soldiers, the bureaucracy—and plunder[ed] the weakest members of the population, the peasants" (ibid., p. 120), "in the Western countries, governments, by setting prices *above* the market level, have used price control as an instrument to favor and protect their farmers. . . . Within a framework of governmental protection against competition from abroad, the farmers have, in fact, been able to function as free entrepreneurs with incentives so strong that they both work hard and develop their creative potential" (ibid., p. 162; emphasis in original).

34. Joseph Ramos, "Dependency and Development: An Attempt to Clarify the Issues," in Michael Novak, ed., *Liberation South, Liberation North* (Washington, D.C.: American Enterprise Institute, 1981), p. 61.

35. See Lay Commission on Catholic Social Teaching and the U.S. Economy, *Toward the Future: Catholic Social Thought and the U.S. Economy* (Washington, D.C.: Lay Commission, 1984), p. 72.

36. As Walter Lippmann has written of the democratic capitalist revolution, "For the first time in human history men had come upon a way of producing wealth in which the good fortune of others multiplied their own. . . . They actually felt it to be true that an enlightened self-interest promoted the common good. For the first time men could conceive a social order in which the ancient moral aspiration for liberty, equality, and fraternity was consistent with the abolition of poverty and the increase of wealth. Until the division of labor had begun to make men dependent upon the free collaboration of other men, the worldly policy was to be predatory. The claims of the spirit were otherworldly. So it was not until the industrial revolution had altered the traditional mode of life that the vista was opened at the end of which men could see the possibility of the Good Society on this earth. At long last the ancient schism between the world and the spirit, between self-interest and disinterestedness, was potentially closed, and a wholly new

orientation of the human race became theoretically conceivable and, in fact, necessary." *The Good Society* (New York: Grosset & Dunlap, n.d.), pp. 193–194.

37. Miranda, *Communism in the Bible*, p. 74.

38. See Stephen C. Schlesinger and Stephen Kinzer, *Bitter Fruits: The Untold Story of the American Coup in Guatemala* (Garden City, New York: Doubleday & Co., 1982).

39. Michael Novak, *The Guns of Lattimer: The True Story of a Massacre and a Trial August 1897–March 1898* (New York: Basic Books, 1978).

40. Joseph Cardinal Ratzinger with Vittorio Messori, *The Ratzinger Report: An Exclusive Interview on the State of the Church*, trans. Salvator Attanasio and Graham Harrison (San Francisco: Ignatius Press, 1985), p. 83.

41. The best source for international comparisons of religious habits and beliefs is the Princeton Religion Research Center, which publishes the newsletter *Emerging Trends*. See, e.g., the September 1985 issue for a review of belief in life after death and the March 1985 issue for a comparison of the frequency of moments of prayer and contemplation. In the latter, 85 percent of U.S. citizens say they "take some moments of prayer, meditation, or contemplation," a higher figure than found in the 13 other developed nations tested.

42. See Daniel Bell, *The Cultural Contradictions of Capitalism* (New York: Basic Books, 1976).

43. See James Q. Wilson, "The Rediscovery of Character: Private Virtue and Public Policy," *The Public Interest*, Fall 1985, pp. 3–16.

4. LIBERATION THEOLOGY AND THE POPE

1. Hugo Assmann spoke of a book at this meeting that is allegedly "a rigorous effort to unmask a part of the neoconservative scheme with which the imperial matrix threatens us [Latin Americans]": Ana Maria Ezcurra, *The Neoconservative Offensive: U.S. Churches and the Ideological Struggle for Latin America*, ed. and trans. Elice Higginbotham and Linda Unger (New York: New York Circus Publications, 1983).

2. For the text of Pope John Paul II's Opening Address see John Eagleson and Philip Scharper, *Puebla and Beyond: Documentation and Commentary*, trans. John Drury (Maryknoll, New York: Orbis Books, 1979), pp. 57–71.

3. For the history of the Conference of the Latin American Episcopate (CELAM) see Enrique Dussel, *History and the Theology of Liber-*

ation (Maryknoll, New York: Orbis Books, 1976), pp. 111–116; hereafter cited as *History*.

4. For the text of the Medellín documents see Joseph Gremillion, ed., *The Gospel of Peace and Justice: Catholic Social Teaching since Pope John* (Maryknoll, New York: Orbis, Books, 1976), pp. 445–476.

5. All of the quotations from Pope John Paul II that follow are from the text cited in n. 2, *supra*.

6. See Solzhenitsyn, "The World Split Apart," in Ronald Berman, ed., *Solzhenitsyn at Harvard: The Address, Twelve Early Responses, and Six Later Reflections* (Washington, D.C.: Ethics and Public Policy Center, 1980).

7. Alexis de Tocqueville, *Democracy in America*, ed. J. P. Mayer, trans. George Lawrence (Garden City, New York: Harper & Row, 1966; Anchor Books, 1969), pp. 444–445.

8. John Paul II, "The Church, the Oppressed and the Class Struggle," *Origins*, 6 September 1984, p. 179.

9. ". . . the person who works desires not only due remuneration for his work; he also wishes that within the production process provision also be made for him to be able to know that in his work, even on something that is owned in common, he is working 'for himself.' This awareness is extinguished within him in a system of excessive bureaucratic centralization, which makes the worker feel that he is just a cog in a huge machine moved from above, that he is for more reasons than one a mere production instrument rather than a true subject of work with an initiative of his own." John Paul II, *Laborem Exercens*, 15. For a text of *Laborem Exercens*, see *Origins*, 24 September 1981.

10. For example, Enrique Dussel writes: ". . . these concrete options must be made within *the framework of a grass-roots community* which is sincerely and authentically alive. Some sort of basic community, it seems to me, is an absolute necessity. Lay people probably ought to create communities of married couples on the grass-roots level, not to form little cliques for themselves but to serve each other and people around them. Priests and religious probably should form grass-roots communities of their own, suited to their particular nature but grass-roots communities nevertheless." *History*, p. 165 (emphasis in original).

11. A successful republic, the U.S. Founders thought, would require the widespread prosperity that freedom of opportunity brings. Thus Publius in *Federalist* No. 10 wrote that "the first object of government" should be the protection of "the diversity in the faculties of men, from which the rights of property originate." Alexis de Tocqueville agrees that a wide distribution of property enables American de-

mocracy to thrive: "The rich, on their side, are scattered and powerless. They have no conspicuous privileges, and even their wealth, being no longer incorporated and bound up with the soil, is impalpable and, as it were, invisible. As there is no longer a race of poor men, so there is not a race of rich men; the rich daily rise out of the crowd and constantly return thither. Hence they do not form a distinct class, easily identified and plundered; moreover, there are a thousand hidden threads connecting them with the mass of citizens, so that the people would hardly know how to attack them without harming itself. In democratic societies between these two extremes there is an innumerable crowd who are much alike, who, though not exactly rich nor yet quite poor, have enough property to want order and not enough to excite envy.

"Such men are the natural enemies of violent commotion; their immobility keeps all above and below them quiet, and assures the stability of the body social." *Democracy in America*, pp. 635–636.

12. *Rerum Novarum*, 14 (emphasis in original). For a text of *Rerum Novarum*, see William J. Gibbons, S.J., ed., *Seven Great Encyclicals* (Glen Rock, New Jersey: Paulist Press, 1963).

13. Tocqueville wrote that "Though private interest, in the United States as elsewhere, is the driving force behind most of men's actions, it does not regulate them all.

"I have often seen Americans make really great sacrifices for the common good, and I have noticed a hundred cases in which, when help was needed, they hardly ever failed to give each other trusty support.

"The free institutions of the United States and the political rights enjoyed there provide a thousand continual reminders to every citizen that he lives in society. At every moment they bring his mind back to this idea, that it is the duty as well as the interest of men to be useful to their fellows. Having no particular reason to hate others, since he is neither their slave nor their master, the American's heart easily inclines toward benevolence. At first it is of necessity that men attend to the public interest, afterward of choice. What had been calculation becomes instinct. By dint of working for the good of his fellow citizens, he in the end acquires a habit and taste for serving them." *Democracy in America*, pp. 512–513.

14. The crucial need democracies have for widespread prosperity is explained in n. 11 of this chapter. Tocqueville greatly feared what might happen if envy for equality ever outweighed respect for the rights of liberty. "I think democratic peoples have a natural taste for liberty; left to themselves, they will seek it, cherish it, and be sad if it is

taken from them. But their passion for equality is ardent, insatiable, eternal, and invincible. They want equality in freedom, and if they cannot have that, they still want equality in slavery." *Democracy in America*, p. 506.

15. "Per capita agricultural production in Africa declined by approximately 1.5 percent per year throughout the 1970's while it was growing at about 0.33 percent per year in developing countries as a group. Many African governments have been able to stay in power despite longstanding policies that discourage food production because they run one-party states that provide no way for the populace to compel change.

". . . First, agriculture is heavily taxed through a variety of techniques and consequently is discouraged. Price controls are used to force farmers to sell food to urban customers at ridiculously low prices, and a large portion of agricultural export receipts is diverted from farmers to the government through export taxes. Local currencies are badly overvalued, making imported goods cheap for city dwellers but also forcing down the price of food. . . . Governments of such countries typically insist on dominating all decisions in the economy through legal controls and state-owned enterprises, and vast numbers of people are employed to staff the resulting bureaucracies. Tax revenues fail to cover the costs of government agencies and the losses typically incurred by the state-owned businesses. . . . A dominant condition is that farmers are heavily taxed in order to subsidize an urban sector that consists largely of government employees. The resulting decline has left many African countries with serious food shortages and without sufficient agricultural exports to pay for vital imports. The recent drought has worsened these problems, but they were serious in years of good weather." Robert M. Dunn, Jr., "Africans vs. Food," *New York Times*, 20 July 1984.

16. Dunn points out that "India's farm sector provides an interesting contrast with Tanzania's. New Delhi's policies have long been basically pro-agriculture, and include large public investments in irrigation, and tax policies that strongly favor farmers. Despite a far worse population-to-land ratio than prevails in Africa, India has enjoyed sizable increases in food production during the last decade and is now self-sufficient in food in normal years." Ibid.

17. "In all cases of [onesidedly materialistic civilization], in every social situation of this type, there is a confusion or even a reversal of the order laid down from the beginning by the words of the Book of Genesis: Man is treated as an instrument of production, where he—he alone, independent of the work he does—ought to be treated as the

effective subject of work and its true maker and creator." John Paul II, *Laborem Exercens*, 7.

5. CREATION THEOLOGY IN LATIN AMERICA

1. Carlos Alberto Montaner, *Cuba, Castro, and the Caribbean: The Cuban Revolution and the Crisis in Western Conscience*, trans. Nelson Duran (New Brunswick, New Jersey: Transaction Books, 1985), pp. 1–2.

2. See Chapter 4, n. 17, *supra*.

3. Igor Shafarevich has remarked that Marx's "theory of value, a cornerstone of his political-economic theory, proved to be in complete contradiction to well-known facts of economic life! Concerning Marx's promises to present further evidence (or 'intermediary links') on the question, the Italian economist Loria wrote: 'I have justly asserted that this second volume with which Marx constantly threatens his opponents, and which, however, will never appear, was most probably employed as a cunning subterfuge in those cases where Marx lacked scientific arguments.' In the sixteen years that separate the publication of Volume I of *Capital* from his death, Marx did not offer a continuation of his study. In 1885, Engels published Marx's manuscripts as the second volume of *Capital*. In the preface, he mentions the contradiction cited above and remarks that 'because of this contradiction the Ricardo school and "vulgar economy" collapsed.' Marx, so Engels claimed, resolved this contradiction in Volume III, which was to appear in several months. Volume III appeared in 1894—i.e., nine years later. In his preface, Engels again returns to the 'contradiction' and quotes Loria in this connection. He points out that in the preface to Volume II, this question was 'publicly proposed' by him and that, therefore, Loria might have taken this into account. . . . But Engels does not mention his own promise that the contradiction would be resolved in Volume III, nor does he indicate the place where it is resolved." *The Socialist Phenomenon*, trans. William Tjalsma, with an Introduction by Aleksandr I. Solzhenitsyn (New York: Harper & Row, 1980), p. 211.

4. Böhm-Bawerk's first rebuttal of Marxist theory appeared shortly after the first volume of *Capital* appeared. See Eugen v. Böhm-Bawerk, *Capital and Interest: A Critical History of Economic Theory*, trans. William Smart (New York: Kelley & Millman, 1957), Book VI, Chapter 3, "Marx." After the third and final volume of *Capital* was published, Böhm-Bawerk wrote an essay conclusively demonstrating Marx's fail-

ure (and those of his apologists like Werner Sombart) to justify the labor theory of value. See *Karl Marx and the Close of His System* (Clifton, New Jersey: August M. Kelley, 1949). Thomas Sowell's description of the real-world refutation of the labor theory of value is so damning that it warrants quotation at length: "Once output is seen as a function of numerous inputs, and the inputs as supplied by more than one class of people, the notion that surplus value arises from labor becomes plainly arbitrary and unsupported. Factually, it is even worse off. The empirical implication of a special or exclusive productivity of labor would be that countries that work longer and harder would have higher outputs and higher standards of living. But the reality is more nearly the direct opposite—that countries whose inputs are less labor and more entrepreneurship tend to have vastly higher standards of living, including shorter hours for their workers.

"Nor is this simply a matter of having more physical capital to work with. Large transfers of physical capital to Third World countries, through nationalization and foreign aid, have often been only a prelude to the deterioration of that capital. Conversely, the apparently miraculous rise of the German and Japanese economies from the rubble after World War II demonstrated that physical capital is only a product of mental capital—organizational and scientific skills, discipline, experience, and habits of mutual cooperation. Despite the offhand assumption of Engels (and later, Lenin) that managing a business was only a trivial skill, countries where that skill is rare are almost universally sunk in poverty, even in the midst of rich natural resources, while countries where such skills are more abundant are typically prosperous, even when lacking most natural resources—Japan being the classic example. Similarly, racial and ethnic groups possessing such skills have at various times in history been reduced to destitution by hostile political decisions, only to rise rapidly to prosperity again at some other time or place—for example, the Jews in Europe and Chinese minorities scattered throughout Southeast Asia.

"For all Marx's intricate and ingenious elaboration of the implications of 'suplus value,' the original postulate on which it is all based was only the common and crude impression that goods are 'really' produced by those who physically handle production in a routine established by others. The early history of the Soviet Union provided the most dramatic empirical refutation of the Marxism assumption that management of economic enterprises is something to be taken for granted as occurring *somehow*. When economic incentives were drastically reduced or abolished in the heady egalitarian period following the Bolshevik revolution, the Soviet economy ground to a halt. Widespread hunger and a halt to vital services forced Lenin to resort to his 'New Economic Policy' that restored the hated capitalistic practices. The later nationalizing of all industry under Stalin and his successors did not restore egalitarianism. Quite the contrary. There were highly unequal rewards to management, including today whole systems of special privilege stores to which ordinary Soviet workers have no access. Moreover, the managers of Soviet industry have been disproportionately the descendants of the managerial class of earlier Soviet and czarist times." Sowell, *Marxism: Philosophy and Economics* (New York: William Morrow and Co., 1985), pp. 192–193 (emphasis in original). See also pp. 74–78, 113, 126–132, and 190–195.

5. "Under the influence of direct assault by economists like Böhm-Bawerk and Pareto, and even more importantly under the indirect assault of economists like Marshall who ostensibly dropped the labor theory of value on purely scientific grounds . . . there occurred in the late nineteenth and early twentieth centuries among Marxist economists a tendency to relax, qualify, modify and even abandon altogether the labor theory of value. The simple and most obvious course was outright abandonment, a course taken by such eminent 'Marxish' economists as Oskar Lange and Joan Robinson. . . . After all the labor theory of value never did apply to natural resources and *they* certainly enter into the valuation and allocation picture, and give rise to property income." James A. Yunker, *Socialism in the Free Market* (New York: Nellen Publishing Co., 1979), p. 159 (emphasis added).

6. See Herman Kahn, William Brown, and Leon Martel, *The Next 200 Years* (New York: William Morrow and Co., 1976); and Kahn, *The Great Transition* (Paris: International Chamber of Commerce, 1978).

7. See Octavio Paz, *One Earth, Four or Five Worlds: Reflections on Contemporary History*, trans. Helen R. Lane (New York: Harcourt Brace Jovanovich, 1985), Part Two, Chapter 2, "Latin America and Democracy."

8. Montaner, *Cuba, Castro, and the Caribbean*, p. 2.

9. "[T]he creative capacity of human beings is at the heart of the development process. What makes development happen is our ability to imagine, theorize, conceptualize, experiment, invent, articulate, organize, manage, solve problems, and do a hundred other things with our minds and hands that contribute to the progress of the individual and of humankind. Natural resources, climate, geography, history, market size, governmental policies, and many other factors influence the direction and pace of progress. But the engine is human creative capacity." Lawrence E. Harrison, *Underdevelopment Is a State of Mind:*

The Latin American Case (Lanham, Maryland: University Press of America, 1985), p. 2.

10. In a recent book greatly influenced by Montaigne, Judith N. Shklar writes: "Justice itself is only a web of legal arrangements required to keep cruelty in check, especially by those who have most of the instruments of intimidation closest at hand. That is why the liberalism of fear concentrates so single-mindedly on limited and predictable government. The prevention of physical excess and arbitrariness is to be achieved by a series of legal and institutional measures designed to supply the restraints that neither reason nor tradition can be expected to provide." *Ordinary Vices* (Cambridge: Harvard University Press, 1984), p. 237.

11. See the author's *Spirit of Democratic Capitalism* (New York: Simon and Schuster/American Enterprise Institute, 1982), Chapter 18, "A Theology of Development: Latin America," esp. the statistics cited on pp. 308–309.

12. Kirzner distinguishes in economic thought four separate stages of varying concern for the entrepreneur. "[T]he classical economists (with some notable exceptions such as J. B. Say, who continued the French tradition begun by Cantillon) did not recognize an entrepreneurial function distinct from that of the capitalist. For . . . [them] 'profit' meant the income share received by the capitalist, with no attempt made to distinguish pure interest separately from . . . pure entrepreneurial profit. . . .

"In the decades following the marginalist revolution, a vigorous literature emerged in which the entrepreneurial role was thoroughly discussed. During the 1880s and subsequently, entrepreneurship and entrepreneurial profit were the subject of doctoral dissertations and journal articles, including contributions by some leading neoclassical theorists . . . the second decade saw the fully elaborated theories of entrepreneurship developed by [Joseph] Schumpeter and by [Frank] Knight. . . .

"But the half-century that began about 1920 . . . saw economists paying scarcely any attention at all to analyzing the ways entrepreneurial activity affects the course of events in markets. To cite an often-quoted observation of Professor Baumol, the entrepreneur 'virtually disappeared from the theoretical literature.'

"The fourth stage . . . has thus far endured for only a very few years. . . . During these past few years economists have rediscovered the entrepreneur. . . ." Israel M. Kirzner, *Discovery and the Capitalist Process* (Chicago: University of Chicago Press, 1985), pp. 1–2.

13. Joseph Schumpeter, *History of Economic Analysis*, ed. Elizabeth

Boody Schumpeter (New York: Oxford University Press, 1954); Charles Gide and Charles Rist, *A History of Economic Doctrines: From the Time of the Physiocrats to the Present Day*, trans. R. Richards (London: D. C. Heath and Co., n.d.); Henry William Spiegel, *The Growth of Economic Thought*, rev. ed. (Durham, North Carolina: Duke University Press, 1983); Max Weber, *General Economic History*, trans. Frank H. Knight (New York: Collier Books, 1961); and Barry W. Poulson, *Economic History of the United States* (New York: Macmillan Publishing Co., 1981).

14. But for the stories of the fifteen failures see Sven Rydenfelt, *A Pattern for Failure: Socialist Economies in Crisis* (New York: Harcourt Brace Jovanovich, 1984), Part II, "Crises and Entrepreneurship in the East."

15. Eli F. Heckscher in *Dagens Nybeter,* 24 December 1951, quoted in Rydenfelt, *A Pattern for Failure,* p. 4.

16. Rydenfelt, *A Pattern for Failure,* p. 5, citing Eli F. Heckscher in *Dagens Nyheter,* 24 December 1951.

17. Paul Johnson, "Has Capitalism a Future?" in Ernest W. Lefever, ed., *Will Capitalism Survive? A Challenge by Paul Johnson with Twelve Responses* (Washington, D.C.: Ethics and Public Policy Center, 1979), p. 4.

18. Rydenfelt, *A Pattern for Failure,* pp. 6–8.

19. Ibid., p. 8.

20. Ibid., p. 9.

21. Edwin O. Reischauer, *Japan Past and Present,* 3rd rev. ed. (Tokyo: Charles E. Tuttle, 1969), p. 233.

22. See Rydenfelt, *A Pattern for Failure,* pp. 13–14.

23. C. Wright Mills criticizes seventeen central tenets of Marx's predictions in *The Marxists* (New York: Dell Publishing, 1962), Chapter 6, "Critical Observations." For example, the prediction that the "class structure" will become increasingly polarized and make revolution inevitable has been proven false, for "the polarization has not occurred; in the course of capitalism's history, the class structure has not been simplified into two classes. On the contrary, the opposite trend has been general—and the more 'advanced' the capitalism, the more complex and diversified has the stratification become." As for the material misery and alienation of the workers increasing, Mills writes: "Economic or material misery has not increased inside the advanced capitalist world. On the contrary, the general fact has been an increase in material standards of living. Wage-workers have generally improved their economic condition, decreased their hours of work, abolished such cruel practices as child labor . . . and, because of mechanization, have much less brutal, physical toil to do than workers did in the nine-

teenth century" (ibid., pp. 109–111). See also Sowell, *Marxism*, Chapter 10, "The Legacy of Marx."

24. Alvin Rabushka, *From Adam Smith to the Wealth of Nations* (New Brunswick, New Jersey: Transaction Books, 1985), pp. 166–167.

25. Ibid., p. 174.

26. See, e.g., the author's "Democracy and Human Rights," in Peter L. Berger and Michael Novak, *Speaking to the Third World: Essays on Democracy and Development* (Washington, D.C.: American Enterprise Institute, 1985).

27. The Polish priest philosopher Jozef Tischner has written: "What good does it do when a fisherman exceeds a quota if there is no place to store the excess fish? What good does it do when people build a steel mill if the steel produced in it is more expensive and of poorer quality than the steel available on the open market? This . . . kind of betrayal consists in condemning work to senselessness." *The Spirit of Solidarity*, trans. Marek B. Zaleski and Benjamin Fiore, S.J. (New York: Harper & Row, 1984), p. 86.

28. American writers have properly emphasized community. John Dewey, for instance, writes that "the reliance of liberalism is not upon the mere abstraction of a native endowment unaffected by social relationships. . . . There are few individuals who have the native capacity that was required to invent the stationary steam-engine, locomotive, dynamo or telephone. But there are none so mean that they cannot intelligently utilize these embodiments of intelligence once they are a part of the organized means of associated living." *Liberalism and Social Action* (New York: Capricorn Books, 1935), p. 52. For his part, Tocqueville thought association the most important practical discovery of Americans: "Nothing, in my view, more deserves attention than the intellectual and moral associations in America. American political and industrial associations easily catch our eyes, but the others tend not to be noticed. And even if we do notice them we tend to misunderstand them, hardly ever having seen anything similar before." He adds: "Among laws controlling human societies there is one more precise and clearer, it seems to me, than all the others. If men are to remain civilized or to become civilized, the art of association must develop and improve among them at the same speed as equality of condition spreads." Alexis de Tocqueville, *Democracy in America*, ed. J. P. Mayer, trans. George Lawrence (New York: Doubleday & Co., 1969), p. 517.

29. See Thomas J. Peters and Robert H. Waterman, Jr., *In Search of Excellence: Lessons from America's Best-Run Companies* (New York: Harper & Row, 1982).

6. BASIC CONCEPTS OF LIBERATION THEOLOGY

1. See Enrique Dussel, *History and the Theology of Liberation*, trans. John Drury (Maryknoll, New York: Orbis Books, 1976); hereafter cited as *History*. For the way I use *mythos, story,* and *horizon,* see my *Experience of Nothingness* (New York: Harper & Row, 1970); and my *Ascent of the Mountain, Flight of the Dove: An Invitation to Religious Studies,* rev. ed. (San Francisco: Harper & Row, 1978), esp. Chapter 2, "Autobiography and Story."

2. Ibid.

3. Enrique Dussel, *Philosophy of Liberation*, trans. Aquilina Martinez and Christine Morkovsky (Maryknoll, New York: Orbis Books, 1985); hereafter cited as *Philosophy*.

4. At the beginning of the first chapter of *History*, Dussel explains that "We shall try to interpret the crisis in which we now find ourselves as a Church and a culture, both in the world at large and here in Latin America itself. The crisis is so thoroughgoing that we must start with the very beginnings of mankind" (p. 1). See Diagram 1 in Dussel's *Philosophy* (p. 2.) for his view of center-periphery relationships.

5. "The experience of nothingness is an incomparably fruitful starting place for ethical inquiry. It is a vaccine against the lies upon which every civilization . . . is built. It exposes man as animal, question-asker, symbol-maker." Michael Novak, *The Experience of Nothingness*, p. 1.

6. Dussel, *History*, p. 141.

7. "It would be absurd to maintain that Marxism was, so to speak, the efficient cause of present-day Communism; on the other hand, Communism is not a mere 'degeneration' of Marxism but a possible interpretation of it, and even a well-founded one, though primitive and partial in some respects. . . . [I]t was Marx who declared that the whole idea of Communism could be summed up in a single formula—the abolition of private property; that the state of the future must take over the centralized management of the means of production, and that the abolition of capital meant the abolition of wage-labour. There was nothing flagrantly illogical in deducing from this that the expropriation of the bourgeoisie and the nationalization of industry and agriculture would bring about the general emancipation of mankind. In the event it turned out that, having nationalized the means of production, it was possible to erect on this foundation a monstrous edifice of lies, exploitation, and oppression. This was not itself a consequence of Marxism; rather, Communism was a bastard version

of the socialist ideal, owing its origin to many historical circumstances and chances, of which Marxist ideology was one. But it cannot be said that Marxism was 'falsified' in any essential sense. Arguments adduced at the present to show that 'that is not what Marx meant' are intellectually and practically sterile. Marx's intentions are not the deciding factor in a historical assessment of Marxism, and there are more important arguments for freedom and democratic values than the fact that Marx, if one looks closely, was not so hostile to those values as might at first sight appear." Leszek Kolakowski, *Main Currents of Marxism: Its Origin, Growth, and Dissolution*, trans. P. S. Falla, vol. 3: *The Breakdown* (Oxford: Clarendon Press, 1978), pp. 526–527.

8. Dussel questions whether Christians "can be Marxists in economics and Christians in their faith.

". . . If one moves from *Das Kapital* to other writings of Marx—e.g., *Misere de la philosophie, Die deutsche Ideologie,* and the manuscripts of 1844—one finds that a whole anthropology, ontology, and theology underlie his economics. Marx is a panontist, who affirms the totality as divine. This is a fact, it seems to me, and most critiques of Marx are superficial because they fail to take this into account." Dussel, *History,* pp. 133–134.

9. Ibid., p. 161.

10. Dussel writes that "If I want to know what average people think, I must de-culturate myself insofar as I am able. I must try to get into their world, so that I can dialogue with them in meaningful terms. I must enter a new novitiate, as it were, so that I can operate with hermeneutic and interpretative criteria that are more real and anthropological. We are just now beginning to do that." Ibid., p. 163.

11. In *The Open Church* (New York: Macmillan, 1962) I wrote about "nonhistorical orthodoxy," but in recent years the prevailing tendency seems to be "nonhistorical neodoxy": ". . . some theologians who have followed Vatican II are equally as nonhistorical as those who went before, although in a different way. For some of the newer activists, it is as if the world somehow started fresh just yesterday, or in any case about 1965. They have broken with the long, complex, historical traditions of the church. They have been so eager to 'update' the teachings of the church, and not only to read but to devour 'the signs of the times,' that they have lost their moorings in Newman, Bellarmine, Aquinas, Augustine, and the rest. No, nowadays they take their purest signals from Jurgen Habermas, Herbert Marcuse, and recent sociology. They are not so eager to be faithful to the past as to the new and up-to-date: *neodoxy.*" Michael Novak, *Confession of a Catholic* (New York: Harper & Row, 1983), p. 46 (emphasis in original).

12. See Carlos Rangel, *The Latin Americans: Their Love-Hate Relationship with the United States,* trans. Ivan Kats (New York: Harcourt Brace Jovanovich, 1977).

13. Hungarian poet Sandor Csori, at the 1986 Poets, Essayists, and Novelists writers' conference in New York, quoted in "Notable & Quotable," *Wall Street Journal,* 24 January 1985.

14. Dussel, *History,* p. 141.

15. Ibid., p. 133.

16. Ibid., p. 135.

17. Reinhold Niebuhr, *Christianity and Crisis,* 1969. See also Michael Novak, "Needing Niebuhr Again," *Commentary,* September 1972.

18. Dussel writes that "Ownership, such as the right to possess the other's product, is the counterpart in the dominator of the alienation in the dominated. In a consumer society it is the ownership of capital; in a bureaucratic society it is control of the functions that exercise power." *Philosophy,* p. 53.

19. Denis Goulet, *A New Moral Order* (Maryknoll, New York: Orbis Books, 1974), p. 83.

20. José Míguez Bonino, "Historical Praxis and Christian Identity," in Rosino Gibellini, ed., *Frontiers of Theology in Latin America* (Maryknoll, New York: Orbis Books, 1975), p. 279.

21. Alfredo Fierro, *The Militant Gospel,* trans. John Drury (Maryknoll, New York: Orbis Books, 1977), p. 102.

22. Ibid., p. 80.

23. Ibid., p. 114.

24. Quoted by Dennis Smith, "Theologians on Economics in Latin America: A Struggle of the Gods," Religious News Service Special Report, 18 December 1985. The story quotes Hugo Assmann using similar terminology.

25. Dussel, *Philosophy,* p. 51.

26. "Would anyone dispute that, apart from certain religious schools and certain colleges in the South and perhaps in Utah, the reigning ethos in American colleges and universities today is the anticapitalist ethos?

". . . The better—or, to be more precise, the more prestigious—the school, the more the ideas of anticapitalism tended to hold sway.

"From the schools to the culture at large: Joseph Schumpeter . . . had foreseen the process years before it had quite come about: 'Perhaps the most striking feature of the picture,' he wrote, 'is the extent to which the modern bourgeoisie, besides educating its own enemies, allows itself in turn to be educated by them. It absorbs the slogans of current radicalism and seems quite willing to undergo a process of conversion hostile to its very existence.' " Joseph Epstein, "The Education of an Anti-Capitalist," *Commentary,* August 1983, pp. 58–59.

27. Dussel, *Philosophy,* p. 145.

28. Ibid., p. 143.

29. Ibid.

30. Ibid., p. 144.

31. See Joseph Schumpeter, *History of Economic Analysis,* ed. Elizabeth Boody Schumpeter (New York: Oxford University Press, 1954), pp. 188–189.

32. Abraham Lincoln, "Agriculture: Annual Address Before the Wisconsin State Agricultural Society, at Milwaukee, Wisconsin, September 30, 1859," in Roy P. Basler, ed., *Abraham Lincoln: His Speeches and Writings* (New York: World Publishing Co., 1946), p. 494.

33. As Robert A. Goldwin has pointed out ("Rights versus Duties: No Contest," in Daniel Callahan and Arthur L. Caplan, eds., *Ethics in Hard Times* [New York: Plenum Publishing Corp., 1981]), the Constitution in its original form mentions the word *right* once, in Article I, section 8, ¶8: Congress shall have the power "To promote the progress of science and useful arts by securing for limited times to authors and inventors the exclusive right to their respective writings and discoveries."

34. See Oscar Handlin, "The Taxonomy of the Corporation," in Michael Novak and John W. Cooper, eds., *The Corporation: A Theological Inquiry* (Washington, D.C.: American Enterprise Institute, 1981), p. 23.

35. Quoted in Gerard Berghoef and Lester DeKoster, *Liberation Theology: The Church's Future Shock* (Grand Rapids, Michigan: Christian's Library Press, 1984), p. 13.

36. "The basic works of Marxism are utterly alien to the most fundamental characteristic of scientific activity—the disinterested striving for truth for its own sake. And although the scientist's duty is sometimes proclaimed, the truth, in practice, always remains a 'party truth'—i.e., it is subordinated to the interests of the political struggle." Igor Shafarevich, *The Socialist Phenomenon,* trans. William Tjalsma, with an Introduction by Aleksandr I. Solzhenitsyn (New York: Harper & Row, 1980), p. 207. See the entirety of Shafarevich's discussion of socialist teachings as scientific theory, pp. 203–213. See also Chapter 5, n. 3, *supra.*

37. Shafarevich, *The Socialist Phenomenon,* p. 207.

38. See Chapter 5, n. 3, *supra.*

39. See Chapter 5, nn. 4, 5, *supra*.

40. See Israel M. Kirzner, *Discovery and the Capitalist Process* (Chicago: University of Chicago Press, 1985).

41. Mill writes that "all accumulation involves the sacrifice of a present for the sake of a future good." John Stuart Mill, *Principles of Political Economy with Some of Their Applications to Social Philosophy*, edited, with an Introduction, by Sir William Ashley (London: Longmans, Green & Co., 1909; reprint ed., Fairfield, New Jersey: Augustus M. Kelley, 1976), p. 165. In a textbook edition of Mill's *Principles*, J. Laurence Laughlin elaborated on the desirability of sacrificing present for future goods: "This is the fundamental motive underlying the effective desire of accumulation, and is far more important than any other. It is, in short, the test of civilization. In order to induce the laboring-classes to improve their condition and save capital, it is absolutely necessary to excite in them (by education or religion) a belief in a future gain greater than the present sacrifice. It is, to be sure, the whole problem of creating character, and belongs to sociology and ethics rather than to political economy." Mill, *Principles of Political Economy*, abridged, with notes and introduction, by J. Laurence Laughlin (New York: D. Appleton and Co., 1888). See also the author's essay on Mill in *Freedom with Justice: Catholic Social Thought and Liberal Institutions* (New York: Harper & Row, 1984), Chapter 5.

42. See Paul Johnson, "Has Capitalism a Future?" in Ernest W. Lefever, ed., *Will Capitalism Survive? A Challenge by Paul Johnson with Twelve Responses* (Washington, D.C.: Ethics and Public Policy Center, 1979), pp. 4–5.

43. Ibid.

44. See Chapter 2, n. 9, *supra*.

45. See Julian Simon, *The Ultimate Resource* (Princeton, New Jersey: Princeton University Press, 1981); Shlomo Maital, *Minds, Markets, and Money: Psychological Foundations of Economic Behavior* (New York: Basic Books, 1982); and Warren Brookes, *The Economy in Mind*, Foreword by George Gilder (New York: Universe Books, 1982).

7. WHAT IS DEPENDENCY? WHO ARE THE POOR?

1. Carlos Alberto Montaner, *Cuba, Castro, and the Caribbean: The Cuban Revolution and the Crisis in Western Conscience*, trans. Nelson Duran (New Brunswick, New Jersey: Transaction Books, 1985), p. 4.

2. Gustavo Gutierrez, *The Power of the Poor in History*, trans. Rob-

ert R. Barr (Maryknoll, New York: Orbis Books, 1983), p. 48; hereafter cited as *Power*.

3. See Michael J. Francis, "Dependency: Ideology, Fad, and Fact," in Michael Novak and Michael P. Jackson, eds., *Latin America: Dependency or Interdependence?* (Washington, D.C.: American Enterprise Institute, 1985).

4. See Arthur F. McGovern, S.J., "Latin America and 'Dependency' Theory," in Michael Novak, ed., *Liberation Theology and the Liberal Society* (forthcoming), and *This World*, Spring/Summer 1986.

5. See Alvin Rabushka, *From Adam Smith to the Wealth of Nations* (New Brunswick, New Jersey: Transaction Books, 1985), Part II, "The Miracle Economies of Asia."

6. Francis, "Dependency," pp. 92, 95.

7. Gutierrez, *Power*, p. 186.

8. Francis, "Dependency," pp. 97, 99, 100.

9. Ibid., p. 98, quoting Tony Smith, "The Underdevelopment of Development Literature: The Case of Dependency Theory," *World Politics* 31 (January 1979):250.

10. "Far from the West having caused the poverty in the Third World, contact with the West has been the principal agent of material progress there. The materially more advanced societies and regions of the Third World are those with which the West established the most numerous, diversified and extensive contacts: the cash-crop producing areas and entrepot ports of South-East Asia, West Africa and Latin America; the mineral-producing areas of Africa and the Middle East; and cities and ports throughout Asia, Africa, the Caribbean and Latin America. The level of material achievement usually diminishes as one moves away from the foci of Western impact. The poorest and most backward people have few or no external contacts; witness the aborigines, pygmies and desert peoples."

Again: "Since the middle of the nineteenth century commercial contacts established by the West have improved material conditions out of all recognition over much of the Third World, notably in South-East Asia; parts of the Middle East; much of Africa, especially West Africa and parts of East and Southern Africa; and very large parts of Latin America, including Mexico, Guatemala, Venezuela, Colombia, Peru, Chile, Brazil, Uruguay and Argentina. The transformation of Malaya (the present Malaysia) is instructive. In the 1890s it was a sparsely populated area of Malay hamlets and fishing villages. By the 1930s it had become the hub of the world's rubber and tin industries. By then there were large cities and excellent communications in a country where millions of Malays, Chinese and Indians now lived much longer and better than they had formerly, either in their countries of origin or in Malaya.

"Large parts of West Africa were also transformed over roughly the same period as a result of Western contacts. Before 1890 there was no cocoa production in the Gold Coast or Nigeria, only very small production of cotton and groundnuts, and small exports of palm oil and palm kernels. By the 1950s all these had become staples of world trade. They were produced by Africans on African-owned properties. But this was originally made possible by Westerners who established public security and introduced modern methods of transport and communications. Over this period imports both of capital goods and of mass consumer goods for African use also rose from insignificant amounts to huge volumes. The changes were reflected in government revenues, literacy rates, school attendance, public health, life expectation, infant mortality and many other indicators." P. T. Bauer, *Equality, the Third World and Economic Delusion* (Cambridge: Harvard University Press, 1981), pp. 70–72.

11. Francis, "Dependency," p. 99.

12. Rabushka, *From Adam Smith to the Wealth of Nations,* pp. 138–139.

13. Octavio Paz, *One Earth, Four or Five Worlds: Reflections on Contemporary History,* trans. Helen R. Lane (New York: Harcourt Brace Jovanovich, 1985), p. 117.

14. See John M. Berry's article on U.S. trade: "Tide Turning Against U.S.," *Washington Post,* 18 December 1983.

15. Fernando Henrique Cardoso and Enzo Faletto, *Dependency and Development in Latin America* (Berkeley, California: University of California Press, 1979), p. xv.

16. Gustavo Gutierrez, *A Theology of Liberation: History, Politics, and Salvation,* trans. Caridad Inda and John Eagleson (Maryknoll, New York: Orbis Books, 1973), p. 81.

17. Hugo Assmann, *Theology for a Nomad Church,* trans. Paul Burns (Maryknoll, New York: Orbis Books, 1976), pp. 45–46.

18. Gutierrez, *A Theology of Liberation,* p. 87.

19. Gutierrez, *Power,* p. 45.

20. Gutierrez, "Teologia y ciencias sociales," *Christus,* October–November 1984.

21. Leonardo Boff, *Liberating Grace,* trans. John Drury (Maryknoll, New York: Orbis Books, 1979), p. 65.

22. Boff, *Liberating Grace,* p. 66. See also Leonardo Boff, *Jesus Christ Liberator: A Critical Christology for Our Time,* trans. Patrick Hughes (Maryknoll, New York: Orbis Books, 1978), pp. 276–277.

23. Boff, *Liberating Grace*, p. 66.

24. Ibid., p. 78.

25. See Chilcote and Edelstein, eds., *Latin America: The Struggle with Dependency and Beyond* (New York: John Wiley & Sons, 1974), p. 27.

26. McGovern, "Latin America and 'Dependency' Theory." See also Adam Smith, *An Inquiry into the Nature and Causes of the Wealth of Nations,* ed. R. H. Campbell, A. S. Skinner, and W. B. Todd, 2 vols. (London: Oxford University Press, 1976; reprint ed., Indianapolis, Indiana: Liberty Classics, 1981), Book III, "Of the Different Progress of Opulence in Different Nations."

27. See Hugo Assmann, "The Improvement of Democracy in Latin America and the Debt Crisis," in Novak, *Liberation Theology and the Liberal Society* (forth.) and in *This World*, Spring/Summer 1986.

28. Larry A. Sjaastad reports that, according to a study by the U.S. Federal Reserve, "Argentina's foreign debt grew $9 billion in 1980, a typical year in the period of heaviest borrowing, while foreign investment by Argentine residents rose $6.7 billion—nearly 75% of the increase in debt. That same year Mexico's foreign debt jumped $16.4 billion and assets held abroad by Mexicans increased $7.1 billion. Brazil's foreign debt rose $11.2 billion in 1980, and Brazilians managed to move $1.8 billion abroad despite very tight exchange controls. Venezuela's debt rose a mere $3.2 billion in 1980, but her residents acquired $4.7 billion in that year. For the entire period since the debt explosion began in 1973, residents of these four countries have acquired nearly $100 billion in foreign assets." "Where the Latin American Loans Went," *Fortune*, 26 November 1984, p. 195.

29. Raul Prebisch, "The Dynamics of Peripheral Capitalism," in Louis Lefeber and Liisa L. North, eds., *Democracy and Development in Latin America* (Toronto: CERLAC-LARU, 1980), p. 21.

30. See McGovern, "Latin America and 'Dependency' Theory."

31. Ibid.

32. See Paz, *One Earth, Four or Five Worlds,* Part 2, Chapter 2, "Latin America and Democracy."

33. McGovern, "Latin America and 'Dependency' Theory."

34. Ibid.

35. Montaner, *Cuba, Castro, and the Caribbean*, pp. 1, 2.

36. See Nancy Truitt, "Peru's Hidden Resources," *The Tarrytown Letter,* September 1985, pp. 8–9.

37. Quoted in ibid., p. 8.

38. Ibid.

39. John T. Cuddington, "Capital Flight: Estimates, Issues, and

Explanations," unpublished discussion paper for the World Bank (CPD), November 1985.

40. Gutierrez, *Power*, pp. 212–213.

41. Ibid., p. 193.

42. Ibid., p. 194.

43. Ibid., p. 195.

44. "[A]n option for the poor is an option for one social class against another. An option for the poor means a new awareness of class confrontation. It means taking sides with the dispossessed. It means entering into the world of the exploited social class, with its values, its cultural categories. It means entering into solidarity with its interests and its struggles." Ibid., p. 45.

45. Ibid., p. 200.

46. Ibid. See also pp. 194–197.

47. Ibid., p. 201.

48. This is the biographical blurb on the back cover of Gutierrez's *Power of the Poor in History*, published by Orbis Books.

49. See Gutierrez, *Power*, p. 187, e.g.

50. Ibid., p. 113.

51. Ibid., p. 186.

52. Ibid., p. 189.

53. Ibid.

54. Ibid., p. 176.

55. Ibid., p. 175.

56. Ibid., p. 215, n. 18.

57. Ibid., p. 187.

58. Ibid.

59. Ibid., p. 188.

60. Ibid., p. 190.

61. Ibid.

62. Ibid.

63. Ibid., p. 191.

64. See Karl Marx and Friedrich Engels, *Manifesto of the Communist Party*, trans. Samuel Moore (Peking: Foreign Languages Press, 1975), pp. 63–64; hereafter cited as *Communist Manifesto*.

65. Ibid., p. 46.

66. Quoted in Igor Shafarevich, *The Socialist Phenomenon*, trans. William Tjalsma, with an Introduction by Aleksandr I. Solzhenitsyn (New York: Harper & Row, 1980), p. 208.

67. Karl Marx, "Exposé of the Cologne Trial of Communists," quoted in Shafarevich, *The Socialist Phenomenon*, p. 223.

68. Quoted in ibid., p. 222.

69. Quoted in ibid., pp. 222–223.

70. Christian Marxists in Latin America have taken this distinction quite seriously. The Christians for Socialism's Draft Agenda, prepared for the Santiago, Chile, convention of April 1972, begins by recalling that "during his recent visit to Chile, Fidel Castro met with about 120 leftist priests and religious. On numerous occasions he reiterated that Christians 'are not merely tactical but also strategic allies' of Latin American revolution." The Draft Agenda goes on to say that in preparatory meetings "held so far we have gradually come to the idea that insofar as the internal objective of the convention is concerned, it will be attained through a close tie-up between three distinct stages." In the third stage "we will try to get a clearer picture of the operation of the 'Christian element' in the revolutionary process. We do not want to stay solely on the tactical level, drawing operational conclusions that are short-range in nature and directed to the immediate present. . . . We want our revolutionary praxis, viewed within the framework of the overall revolutionary process, to be an enriching component of revolutionary theory itself. This presupposes . . . strategic participation rather than mere tactical participation." Again: ". . . yet the tactical ally can turn into a strategic enemy. Given the existing ties between 'sociological Christianity' and capitalism, it often happens that groups which seem to be progressive or even leftist end up as strategic enemies of an authentic revolutionary process in the long run. It is along these lines, perhaps, that we must analyze postconciliar progressivism (Medellín in particular), the positions and accommodations of certain agents of the hierarchy, and the position of certain 'leftist' Christians." John Eagleson, ed., *Christians and Socialism: Documentation of the Christians for Socialism Movement in Latin America,* trans. John Drury (Maryknoll, New York: Orbis Books, 1975), pp. 19, 24, 26–27.

71. Marx and Engels, *Communist Manifesto,* p. 51.

72. Gregory Baum, *The Priority of Labor* (Mahwah, N.J.: Paulist Press, 1982).

73. See Gutierrez, *Power,* Chapter 3, "Liberation Praxis and Christian Faith."

74. "Beginning with the Bandung Conference of 1955, the term 'development' began to be used as the compendious expression of the aspirations of human beings today for more humane conditions of life." Ibid., p. 43.

75. Ibid., p. 44.

76. Ibid.

77. "[T]o offer food or drink in our day is a political action; it

means the transformation of a society structured to benefit a few who appropriate to themselves the value of the work of others. This transformation ought to be directed toward a radical change in the foundation of society, that is, the private ownership of the means of production." *A Theology of Liberation,* pp. 202, 273–76, 111–13.

78. "Today history is characterized by conflict which seems to impede [the] building of [human] brotherhood. There is one characteristic in particular which holds a central place: the division of humanity into oppressors and oppressed, into owners of the means of production and those dispossessed of the fruit of their work, into antagonistic social classes." Ibid., pp. 272–273.

79. "It is undeniable that the class struggle poses problems to the universality of the Christian love and the unity of the Church. But any consideration of this subject must start from two elemental points: the class struggle is a fact, and neutrality in this matter is impossible." Ibid., p. 273.

80. Gutierrez, *Power,* p. 44.

81. Ibid., p. 45.

82. Ibid.

83. See Milovan Djilas, *The New Class* (New York: Praeger, 1957); Bruno Rizzi, *The Bureaucratization of the World: The First English Edition of the Underground Marxist Classic That Analyzed Class Exploitation in the USSR,* trans., with an Introduction, by Adam Westoby (New York: The Free Press, 1985); and James Burnham, *The Managerial Revolution* (New York: John Day Co., 1941).

84. Gutierrez, *Power,* p. 45.

85. Eagleson, *Christians and Socialism,* p. 29.

86. Ibid., p. 28.

87. Ibid., p. 25.

88. Ibid., pp. 26–27. See also Chapter 7, n. 70, *supra.*

89. What follows is based on Chapter 10, "Liberation Theology in Practice," of my *Freedom with Justice: Catholic Social Thought and Liberal Institutions* (New York: Harper & Row, 1984).

90. See Chapter 5, n. 28, *supra.*

8. WHAT DO THEY MEAN BY SOCIALISM?

1. After recalling Marx and Engels' hatred for Marx's young works (they "willingly abandoned *The German Ideology* to the 'gnawings of the mice' ") Gertrude Himmelfarb writes that "In the present climate of opinion the early Marx is more congenial than the later:

'alienation' sounds more profound than 'exploitation,' and 'universal human emancipation' is more agreeable than the 'dictatorship of the proletariat.' By focusing on the young Marx, one can dissociate oneself not only from the Marxism that has become an instrument of tyranny, but also from the Marxist theories that have been so conspicuously belied by history: the polarization of classes and pauperization of the proletariat, the collapse of capitalism and universal triumph of Communism, the withering away of the state and emergence of a classless society." "The 'Real' Marx," *Commentary*, April 1985, pp. 40–41.

2. See Arthur F. McGovern, S.J., *Marxism: An American Christian Perspective* (Maryknoll, New York: Orbis Books, 1980) and Leszek Kolakowski, *Main Currents of Marxism: Its Origin, Growth, and Dissolution*, trans. P. S. Falla, vol. 3: *The Breakdown* (Oxford: Clarendon Press, 1978).

3. Octavio Paz, *One Earth, Four or Five Worlds: Reflections on Contemporary History*, trans. Helen R. Lane (New York: Harcourt Brace Jovanovich, 1985), p. 173.

4. Quoted in John Eagleson, ed., *Christians and Socialism: Documentation of the Christians for Socialism Movement in Latin America*, trans. John Drury (Maryknoll, New York: Orbis Books, 1975), p. 19.

5. Ibid., p. 21.

6. Ibid., p. 22. (emphasis in original)

7. Ibid., p. 23. (emphasis in original)

8. Ibid., p. 24. (emphasis in original)

9. Ibid., pp. 24–25.

10. Ibid., p. 25.

11. Ibid., pp. 25–26. (emphasis in original)

12. Ibid., p. 27.

13. Ibid., p. 28. (emphasis in original)

14. Ibid., pp. 28–29.

15. Ibid., p. 29. (emphasis in original)

16. Ibid., p. 191.

17. Joseph Cardinal Ratzinger with Vittorio Messori, *The Ratzinger Report: An Exclusive Interview on the State of the Church*, trans. Salvator Attanasio and Graham Harrison (San Francisco: Ignatius Press, 1985), p. 91.

18. For a discussion of Sandinista suppression of cultural liberty, see Pablo Antonio Cuadra, "Notes on Culture in the New Nicaragua," trans. Mark Falcoff, *Catholicism in Crisis*, November 1985, pp. 32–37; originally published in the August 1985 *Vuelta*, the Mexican journal edited by Octavio Paz.

19. Paz, *The Philanthropic Ogre* (New York: Evergreen Books, 1985).

20. Hilaire Belloc, *The Servile State*, with an Introduction by Robert Nisbet (1912; reprint ed., Indianapolis, Indiana: Liberty Classics, 1980).

21. Tocqueville devoted the concluding three chapters of *Democracy in America* to his fear of a new, soft despotism. He said it would stand over men as "an immense, protective power which is alone responsible for securing their enjoyment and watching over their fate. The power is absolute, thoughtful of detail, orderly, provident, and gentle. It would resemble parental authority if, father-like, it tried to prepare its charges for a man's life, but on the contrary, it only tries to keep them in perpetual childhood. It likes to see the citizens enjoy themselves, provided that they think of nothing but enjoyment. It gladly works for their happiness but wants to be sole agent and judge of it. It provides for their security, foresees and supplies their necessities, facilitates their pleasures, manages their principal concerns, directs their industry, makes rules for their testaments, and divides their inheritances. Why should it not entirely relieve them from the trouble of thinking and all the cares of living?" Alexis de Tocqueville, *Democracy in America* ed. J. P. Mayer, trans. George Lawrence (New York: Doubleday & Co., 1969), p. 692.

22. Alan Riding, "For Octavio Paz, A Solitude of His Own as a Political Rebel," *New York Times*, 3 May 1979, quoting from Paz's book, *The Philanthropic Ogre;* this article is hereafter cited as "Octavio Paz."

23. See Thomas Wilson, "Invisible Hands: Public and Private," in Horst Hanusch, Karl W. Roskamp, and Jack Wiseman, eds., *Public Sector and Political Economy Today* (Stuttgart and New York: Gustav Fischer Verlag, 1985).

24. Quoted in Alan Riding, "Octavio Paz."

25. Ibid.

26. Ibid.

27. John C. Cort, "Christ and Neighbor," *New Oxford Review*, January–February 1985, p. 22.

28. Ibid., quoting Gustavo Gutierrez, *A Theology of Liberation: History, Politics, and Salvation*, trans. Caridad Inda and John Eagleson (Maryknoll, New York: Orbis Books, 1973), pp. 272–273.

29. Cort, "Christ and Neighbor," p. 22, quoting Gutierrez, *A Theology of Liberation*, p. 284, n. 51.

30. Cort, "Christ and Neighbor," p. 30.

31. John C. Cort, "Reply," *New Oxford Review*, May 1985, p. 2,

quoting the proceedings of the April 1972 Convention of Christians for Socialism.

32. Cort, "Reply," p. 4.

33. Ibid. See Pius XI, *Quadragesimo Anno,* 64–68. See also the Frankfurt Manifesto, *The New International Review* 2 (Winter 1977):6–10.

34. Dussel says that "when you work for another person and come to depend not on work offered up to God but on work demanded by an employer for your daily bread, a kind of idolatry takes place. The institutionalization of this employee-employer relationship has resulted on [*sic*] the domination of one over another. Such domination is sin." Quoted in Dennis Smith, "Theologians on Economics in Latin America: A Struggle of the Gods," Religious News Service Special Report, 18 December 1985.

35. Michael Voslensky writes: "The nomenklatura is a class of privileged exploiters. It acquired wealth from power, not power from wealth. . . . [It] has some positive achievements to its credit, but it is becoming more and more parasitic. Its contribution to society is nil, and its stubborn desire for world domination involves the grave danger of world war." Again: "The essential feature of capitalist society is not privilege, but money; in real socialist society it is not money, but privilege. This makes the nomenklatura both arrogant and nervous, for it is aware of the reactions that the constant growth of its privileges rouse in the population." *Nomenklatura: The Soviet Ruling Class,* trans. Eric Mosbacher (New York: Doubleday, 1985), pp. 441, 240. See also Konstantin M. Simis, *USSR: The Corrupt Society: The Secret World of Soviet Capitalism,* trans. Jacqueline Edwards and Mitchell Schneider (New York: Simon and Schuster, 1982), esp. Chapter 2, "The Ruling Elite: Corruption, Legalized and Illegal."

36. Octavio Paz, *One Earth, Four or Five Worlds: Reflections on Contemporary History,* trans. Helen R. Lane (New York: Harcourt Brace Jovanovich, 1985), pp. 56–57.

37. Juan Luis Segundo, "Capitalism—Socialism: A Theological Crux," in *Concilium 96: The Mystical and Political Dimension of the Christian Faith* (1974); reprinted in Michael Novak, ed., *Liberation South, Liberation North* (Washington, D.C.: American Enterprise Institute, 1981), p. 13; page citations are to the latter version.

38. Ibid., p. 15.

39. "The Church, and every moral agent, should exercise a 're-serve' in deciding whether a concrete, actualized system does or does not serve the common good. The Church should not hold out for an

unattainable idea; it must be part of historical praxis, it does have to make here-and-now decisions to support a certain direction or not. But it is the very concreteness of these decisions that requires openness to new possibilities and rules out either-or decisions made in advance." McGovern, *Marxism*, p. 201.

40. Segundo, "Capitalism—Socialism," p. 15.

41. McGovern, *Marxism*, p. 201.

42. Ibid.

43. Ibid. (emphasis in original).

44. Ibid., p. 200, quoting Gustavo Gutierrez, "Liberation, Theology, and Proclamation," *Concilium 96: The Mystical and Political Dimension of the Christian Faith* (1974), p. 74.

45. Gustavo Gutierrez, *The Power of the Poor in History*, trans. Robert R. Barr (Maryknoll, New York: Orbis Books, 1983), p. 45; hereafter cited as *Power*.

46. Ibid. All quotations in this and the following paragraph are from this page.

47. Ibid., pp. 45–46.

48. Ibid., p. 46.

49. "[E]conomist Theodore Schultz ascribes responsibility for agricultural stagnation in poor countries to price controls. Excessively low prices have deprived peasants of the income and capital that would have enabled them to invest and modernize as farmers in the West have been able to do.

". . . In all socialist countries the peasantry, a remnant of capitalism, is treated as an outgroup, whose sole task is to produce cheap food for the ingroups in the cities; the status of the farmer in socialist states, in fact, corresponds to that of the serfs under feudalism." Sven Rydenfelt, *A Pattern for Failure: Socialist Economies in Crisis* (New York: Harcourt Brace Jovanovich, 1984), p. 15, citing Theodore Schultz, *Economic Growth and Agriculture* (New York: McGraw-Hill, 1968).

50. "We can see that all elements of the socialist idea . . . could be regarded as a manifestation of one basic principle: the suppression of individuality. It is possible to demonstrate this graphically by listing the more typical features that keep appearing in socialist theory and practice over two and a half thousand years . . . and then constructing a model of an 'ideal' (albeit nonexistent) socialist society. People would wear the same clothing and even have similar faces; they would live in barracks. There would be compulsory labor followed by meals and leisure activities in the company of the same labor battalion. Passes would be required for going outside. Doctors and officials would supervise sexual relations, which would be subordinated to only two goals: the

satisfaction of physiological needs and the production of healthy off-spring. Children would be brought up from infancy in state nurseries and schools. Philosophy and art would be completely politicized and subordinated to the educational goals of the state. All this is inspired by one principle—the destruction of individuality or, at least, its suppression to the point where it would cease to be a social force. Dostoyevsky's comparisons to the ant hill and the bee hive turn out to be particularly apt. . . ." Igor Shafarevich, *The Socialist Phenomenon*, trans. William Tjalsma, with an Introduction by Aleksandr I. Solzhenitsyn (New York: Harper & Row, 1980), p. 269. See the entire chapter ("Socialism and Individuality") for copious examples.

51. Gutierrez, *Power*, p. 46. (emphasis added)

52. Ibid.

53. Ibid., p. 47.

54. José Miranda, in the closing lines of *Marx and the Bible: A Critique of the Philosophy of Oppression*, trans. John Eagleson (Maryknoll, New York: Orbis Books, 1974), also describes liberation theology as a rebellion against the West: "God will be only in a world of justice, and if Marx does not find him in the Western world it is because he is indeed not there, nor can he be. As Freud attests, 'There is no longer any place in present-day civilized life for a simple natural love between two human beings.' All our rebellion against Western civilization and against its acute extreme called capitalism is the attraction exercised on us by a future world in which justice, authentic love, is possible."

55. See Arthur F. McGovern, S.J., "Latin America and 'Dependency' Theory," *This World*, Spring/Summer 1986, p. 120; and *Marxism*, Chapter 9, "Personal Reflections: Marxism, Socialism, the United States."

56. "In Michael Harrington's strategy of long-range vision and realistic approximations I found personally the kind of approach I had been looking for." McGovern, *Marxism*, p. 323.

57. See ibid., pp. 322–23.

58. See his "Marxism, Liberation Theology," *Logos* 5 (1984):15.

59. *"Developmentalism* thus came to be synonymous with *reformism* and modernization, that is to say, synonymous with timid measures, really ineffective in the long run and counterproductive to achieving a real transformation. The poor countries are becoming ever more clearly aware that their undevelopment is only the by-product of the development of other countries. . . . Moreover, they are realizing that their own development will come about only with a struggle to break the domination of the rich countries." Gutierrez, *A Theology of Liberation*, p. 26 (emphasis in original). "The question of social change is al-

ways a problem of scientific reasonableness and historical viability. All too frequently these factors contradict the humanitarian ideals of full and integral development. There are other more thoroughgoing reforms which are much more than developmentalism or refurbishings of the existing system. They are truly revolutionary reforms that pave the way for the gradual overthrow of a whole societal system." Leonardo Boff, *Liberating Grace*, trans. John Drury (Maryknoll, New York: Orbis Books, 1979), p. 78.

60. Ludwig von Mises, *Liberalism in the Classical Tradition*, trans. Ralph Raico, with a Foreword by Louis M. Spadaro (Irvington-on-Hudson, New York: Foundation for Economic Education and San Francisco: Cobden Press, 1985), pp. 7–8.

61. Ludwig von Mises, *Socialism: An Economic and Sociological Analysis*, trans. J. Kahane (Indianapolis, Indiana: Liberty Classics, 1981), p. 9.

62. Von Mises reminded his readers of this improvement in his preface to the second German edition; see ibid., p. 13.

63. Rydenfelt, *A Pattern for Failure*, p. 16.

64. Von Mises, *Socialism*, p. 6. He adds: "According to the Marxist conception, one's social condition determines one's way of thought. . . . [One] is not able to grow out of his class or to free his thoughts from the prescriptions of class interests . . . truth lies with the proletarian science only: 'the ideas of the proletarian logic are not party ideas, but the consequences of logic pure and simple.' Thus Marxism protects itself against all unwelcome criticism. The enemy is not refuted: enough to unmask him as a bourgeois" (ibid., pp. 18–19).

65. Himmelfarb points out that "both as historians and as party members, they had more reason than most to be aware of the highly publicized purges and trials of the 1930s, the executions and mass imprisonments, the precipitous changes in the party line requiring comrades to be Bolsheviks one week and Popular Fronters another, pro-war and anti-Fascist one day and anti-war and pro-German the next. (For almost two years, while their country was at war with Germany, British Communists had to defend the Hitler-Stalin pact.)" Gertrude Himmelfarb, "The Group: Bourgeois Britain and Its Marxist Historians," *The New Republic*, 10 February 1986, p. 35. The best work on this phenomenon is probably Paul Hollander, *Political Pilgrims: Travels of Western Intellectuals to the Soviet Union, China, and Cuba* (New York: Oxford University Press, 1981). Hollander has also written about this phenomenon in Latin America; see his "The Newest Political Pilgrims," *Commentary*, August 1985.

66. Von Mises, *Socialism*, p. 10.

67. Father McGovern, e.g., in his chapter on "Marxism, Social-ism, [and] the United States," writes that his critique "is directed against *concentration* of ownership, not private ownership as such. . . . American pride in the self-made person, and reward for personal re-sponsibility, hard work, and initiative, are not misplaced values, nor should they be equated with selfish individualism. Many parents have worked hard for the sake of their families, and have been generous and cooperative with others in the process." *Marxism*, p. 317. See also Michael Novak, *The Spirit of Democratic Capitalism* (New York: Simon and Schuster/American Enterprise Institute, 1982), Introduction and Chapter 1, "The Ideal of Democratic Capitalism."

68. "[A] system in which the workers, as producers, and not the consumers themselves would decide what was to be produced and how," would be, von Mises writes, "as little democratic as, say, a polit-ical constitution under which the government officials and not the whole people decided how the state was to be governed. . . . When we call a capitalist society a consumer's democracy we mean that the power to dispose of the means of production, which belongs to the en-trepreneurs and capitalists, can only be acquired by means of the con-sumers' ballot, held daily in the market-place. . . . True, there is no equality of vote in this democracy; some have plural votes. But the greater voting power which the disposal of a greater income implies can only be acquired and maintained by the test of election. That the consumption of the rich weighs more heavily than the poor is in itself an 'election result', since in a capitalist society wealth can be acquired and maintained only by a response corresponding to the consumers' plebiscite, and, once acquired, this wealth can be retained only if it is employed in the way regarded by consumers as most beneficial to them." Von Mises, *Socialism*, p. 11.

69. Even socialists have admitted the difficulties experienced in Yugoslavia. See, e.g., Robert Heilbroner, "A Feasible Vision of Social-ism," *Dissent*, Fall 1983; and Alec Nove, "Feasible Socialism?: Some So-cio-Political Assumptions," *Dissent*, Summer 1985. The latter writes: "Reverting to labor's role in managerial decisions in socialized enter-prises, one must recall two negative aspects of the Yugoslav experi-ence. One is the interest of the workers in not expanding the labor force, at a time of serious unemployment, because to do so could re-duce their incomes. The other is the worker's lack of long-term inter-est in 'their' enterprise, because it is in fact *not* theirs: they derive no benefit from working for it once they leave it, having no shares to sell" (p. 370; emphasis in original).

70. An example of the new interest in liberalism is Le Club de

L'Horloge, *Socialisme et Religion: Sont-Ils Compatibles?* (Paris: Editions Albatros, 1986).

71. Von Mises, *Socialism,* p. 13.

72. See McGovern, *Marxism,* Chapter 9, "Personal Reflections: Marxism, Socialism, the United States."

9. WHAT IS THE INNER WILL OF SOCIALISM?

1. Sven Rydenfelt, *A Pattern for Failure: Socialist Economies in Crisis* (New York: Harcourt Brace Jovanovich, 1984), p. 15.

2. "[A]s Bertrand Russell once put it, [Marx's] aim was far more the unhappiness of the bourgeoisie than the happiness of the proletariat." Henry William Spiegel, *The Growth of Economic Thought,* rev. ed. (Durham, North Carolina: Duke University Press, 1983), p. 477.

3. Leszek Kolakowski, *Main Currents of Marxism: Its Origin, Growth, and Dissolution,* trans. P. S. Falla, vol. 3: *The Breakdown* (Oxford: Clarendon Press, 1978), pp. 525–526.

4. George Bernard Shaw, *The Intelligent Woman's Guide to Socialism and Capitalism* (New York: Brentano's Publishers, 1928), p. 470.

5. See Michael Novak, *The Spirit of Democratic Capitalism* (New York: Simon and Schuster/American Enterprise Institute, 1982), Chapter 12, "Income Distribution and Race." For the most recent income statistics available, see U.S. Internal Revenue Service, *Individual Income Tax Returns 1983.* The latter reports (see Table 1.1) that less than two-thirds of one percent of all tax returns reported income of $100,000 or more.

6. Calculated from *Individual Income Tax Returns 1983,* Table 1.1.

7. Aleksandr I. Solzhenitsyn, Introduction to Igor Shafarevich, *The Socialist Phenomenon,* trans. William Tjalsma (New York: Harper & Row, 1980), p. vii.

8. See Shafarevich, *The Socialist Phenomenon,* pp. 197ff.

9. Gustavo Gutierrez, *The Power of the Poor in History,* trans. Robert R. Barr (Maryknoll, New York: Orbis Books, 1983), p. 202; hereafter cited as *Power.*

10. Solzhenitsyn, Introduction, p. viii.

11. Ibid., p. ix.

12. See Shafarevich, *The Socialist Phenomenon,* pp. 142, 151.

13. See ibid., pp. 132–151.

14. Quoted in Dennis Smith, "Theologians on Economics in

Latin America: A Struggle of the Gods," Religious News Service Special Report, 18 December 1985.

15. Quoted in Shafarevich, *The Socialist Phenomenon*, p. 147.

16. Quoted in ibid., pp. 148–149.

17. Ibid., p. 150, quoting from G. Otruba, *Der Jesuitenstaat im Paraguay: Idee und Wirklichkeit* (Vienna: n.p., 1962), p. 146.

18. Ibid., p. 151, quoting from Montesquieu, *The Spirit of the Laws*, Book 4, Chapter 6.

19. Ibid., quoting Voltaire, *Essay on Rights*.

20. "The Jesuits' enemies, the anti-clerical writer Asara in particular, reproached them for having starved the Indians and burdened them with work. But the impression gained from Jesuit sources seems more convincing and logical: hunger-free existence, rest every Sunday, guaranteed dwelling and a cloak. . . . Yet this almost successful attempt at reducing hundreds of thousands of people to a life as lived in an ant hill seems far more terrible a picture than that of a hard-labor camp." Ibid., p. 150; ellipsis in original.

21. See ibid., pp. 152–192.

22. See Chapter 8, n. 50. Walter Berns explains that "those who now demand the equal distribution of material goods will inevitably come to demand (and in some cases have already demanded) an equal right to the happiness these goods are supposed to bring. . . ." To illustrate this point, he then cites Allan Bloom's critique of John Rawls: "Rawls, because he substitutes the equal right to happiness for the equal right to life, must equalize not only the conventional primary goods but also the natural ones. The latter is harder to envisage (apart from the salutary work of geneticists who, Rawls believes, might one day improve our progeny). One thinks of Herodotus' account of the Babylonian law by which all the marriageable girls were auctioned off; the beautiful ones brought high prices from the rich and voluptuous men; the city used the money so derived to provide dowries for the ugly girls; thus making the naturally unattractive attractive. Nature's injustice to the unendowed is what the thoroughgoing egalitarian must rectify. The redistribution of wealth is hardly sufficient, for, as we all know, the most important things are those 'that money can't buy.'" Berns, "Does the Constitution 'Secure These Rights'?" in Robert A. Goldwin and William A. Schambra, *How Democratic Is the Constitution?* (Washington, D.C.: American Enterprise Institute, 1980), pp. 76–77, citing Allan Bloom, "Justice: John Rawls vs. the Tradition of Political Philosophy," *The American Political Science Review* 69 (June 1975):654.

23. "The future banner of international revolution, the red flag,

made its modern debut in Paris during riots and demonstrations after the funeral of a popular general, Maximilien Lamarque, on June 5, 1832. In a nocturnal scene worthy of his own melodramas, Victor Hugo unfurled the red flag that night on the barricades in the Rue de la Chanverie and lit a torch beside it. . . ." James H. Billington, *Fire in the Minds of Men: Origins of the Revolutionary Faith* (New York: Basic Books, 1980), p. 159.

24. Robert L. Heilbroner, "What Is Socialism?" *Dissent* 25 (Summer 1978):346–348.

25. Shafarevich, *The Socialist Phenomenon*, p. 218, quoting Piatakov's article "The Proletarian Revolution and the Renegade Kautsky" from J. Eibl-Eibesfeldt, *Grundriss der vergleichenden Verhaltensforschung* (Munich: n.p., 1967), p. 148. Recall also Arthur Koestler's classic tale *Darkness at Noon*, trans. Daphne Hardy (New York: Bantam, 1966): " 'The Party can never be mistaken,' said Rubashov. 'You and I can make a mistake. Not the Party. The Party, comrade, is more than you and I and a thousand others like you and I. The Party is the embodiment of the revolutionary idea in history. History knows no scruples and no hesitation. Inert and unerring, she flows towards her goal. At every bend in her course she leaves the mud which she carries and the corpses of the drowned. History knows her way. She makes no mistakes. He who has not absolute faith in History does not belong in the Party's ranks' " (p. 34).

26. Speaking of the Tristan myth, Denis de Rougemont writes: "The love of love itself has concealed a far more awful passion, a desire altogether unavowable, something that could only be 'betrayed' by means of symbols such as that of the drawn sword and that of perilous chastity. Unawares and in spite of themselves, the lovers have never had but one desire—the desire for death! Unawares, and passionately deceiving themselves, they have been seeking all the time simply to be redeemed and avenged for 'what they have suffered.' . . . In the innermost recesses of their hearts they have been in the throes of *the active passion of Darkness.*" *Love in the Western World,* trans. Montgomery Belgion, rev. ed. (New York: Pantheon, 1956), p. 46 (emphasis in original).

27. Shafarevich, *The Socialist Phenomenon*, p. 275, quoting from T. Büttner and E. Werner, *Circumcellionen und Adamiten* (Berlin: n.p., 1959), p. 140.

28. Shafarevich, *The Socialist Phenomenon*, p. 276, quoting *Michail Bakunins sozial-politischer Briefwechsel mit Alexander Ivanovitsch Herzen* (Stuttgart: n.p., 1895), pp. 361, 363.

10. THE CONSTITUTION OF LIBERTY

1. See Enrique Dussel, *Philosophy of Liberation* (Maryknoll, New York: Orbis Books, 1985), pp. 18–19, 93; hereafter cited as *Philosophy*. "The first proximity, the immediacy before all other immediacy, is nursing. Mouth and nipple form a proximity that feeds, warms, and protects. The hands of the child that touch the mother do not yet play or work. The little feet have not walked or gone deeply into farness. The mouth that sucks has not yet launched speeches, insults, or benedictions; it has not bitten someone it hates or kissed a beloved. Nursing is the immediacy anterior to all farness, to all culture, to all work; it is proximity anterior to economics; it is already the sexual, the pedagogical, and the political. The proximity of nursing is nevertheless eschatological: it projects itself into the future as does the ancestral past; it calls like an end *and* a beginning. And it is unique no matter how often repeated" (ibid., p. 18). See also the quotation in n. 2, *infra*.

2. "The parents are responsible for [the child's] distinctive alterity; they listen with devotion to the child's cry, protest, and juvenile criticism. If there is no castrating father, there is no castrating mother, and the son is defined not as phallus, potentially an enemy, but as mouth-hands-feet that attaches himself in order to obtain nourishment. Thus he does not address the woman in her clitoral-vaginal openness but in her nourishing, protective, soft, and warm maternal breasts. In the nipple-mouth proximity, the child, fulfilled, not repressed, slowly and surely starts on the road of alterity that will take it to adult sexuality and politics." Ibid., p. 93.

3. Ibid., p. 8.

4. Paz writes: "All these reflections can be summed up in a few words: in its simplest and most essential expression, democracy is dialogue, and dialogue paves the way for peace. We will be in a position to preserve peace only if we defend democracy." He believes Latin Americans must "recognize that the defense of democracy in our own country is inseparable from solidarity with those who are fighting for it in totalitarian countries or under the tyrannies and military dictatorships of Latin America and other continents. By fighting for democracy, dissidents are fighting for peace—fighting for all of us." Octavio Paz, *One Earth, Four or Five Worlds: Reflections on Contemporary History*, trans. Helen R. Lane (New York: Harcourt Brace Jovanovich, 1985), p. 212.

5. See Carlos Rangel, *The Latin Americans: Their Love-Hate Relationship with the United States*, trans. Ivan Kats (New York: Harcourt

Brace Jovanovich, 1977), esp. "Democracy and Marxism-Leninism," pp. 272–274.

6. Ibid.

7. Dussel, *Philosophy*, p. vii.

8. See Michael Novak, *The Experience of Nothingness* (New York: Harper & Row, 1970).

9. Nietzsche asked himself again and again: "What does nihilism mean?" He answered: "The aim is lacking; 'why?' finds no answer." Friedrich Nietzsche, *The Will to Power*, ed. Walter Kaufmann (New York: Random House, 1967), p. 9.

10. See Judith Shklar, *Ordinary Vices* (Cambridge: Harvard University Press, 1984), esp. Chapter 1, "Putting Cruelty First."

11. See St. John of the Cross, *Ascent of Mount Carmel*, trans. E. Allison Peers (Garden City, New York: Doubleday & Co., 1958).

12. See Richard John Neuhaus, *The Naked Public Square: Religion and Democracy in America* (Grand Rapids, Michigan: William B. Eerdmans, 1984).

13. Reinhold Niebuhr, *Moral Man and Immoral Society* (New York: Charles Scribner's Sons, 1932), p. xx.

14. Even a man as wise as Aristotle cautioned himself to be humble when considering politics. At the beginning of his *Nicomachean Ethics* he wrote: "The same exactness must not be expected in all departments of philosophy alike. . . . The subjects studied by political science are moral nobility and justice; but these conceptions involve much difference of opinion and uncertainty. . . . We must therefore be content if, in dealing with subjects and starting from premises thus uncertain, we succeed in presenting a broad outline of the truth: when our subjects and our premises are merely generalities, it is enough if we arrive at generally valid conclusions." Aristotle, *The Nicomachean Ethics*, with an English translation by H. Rackham (Cambridge, Massachusetts: Harvard University Press, 1926), I, ii, 1–4.

15. Friedrich Hayek has made this argument in a famous essay; see "Why I'm Not a Conservative," in Hayek, *The Constitution of Liberty* (Chicago: Henry Regnery, 1960).

16. See Alvin Toffler, *Future Shock* (New York: Random House, 1970).

17. See Thomas Sowell's masterful *Knowledge and Decisions* (New York: Basic Books, 1980).

18. Liberation theologians insist on one sort of openness to history. Segundo, e.g., insists upon a "sensibility" of the left defined thus: "the conquest of that which is still without form, of that which is still unrealized, of that which is still in a state of utopia." Juan Luis Se-

gundo, "Capitalism—Socialism: A Theological Crux," in *Concilium 96: The Mystical and Political Dimension of the Christian Faith* (1974); reprinted in Michael Novak, ed., *Liberation South, Liberation North* (Washington, D.C.: American Enterprise Institute, 1981), p. 22; page citations are to the latter version. Liberals call for a different openness, that of the entrepreneur who "owes his very existence and his function to the unpredictability of his environment and to the ceaseless tides of change that undergird that unpredictability." Israel M. Kirzner, *Discovery and the Capitalist Process* (Chicago: University of Chicago Press, 1985), p. 41.

19. By contrast, Thomas Wilson paraphrases Smith and argues that " 'By minding his own business and getting on with his own particular job, a person frequently promotes the welfare of society more effectively than when he tries to conduct his affairs in such a way as to allow for all the complex and often barely discernible implications for the society in which he lives.' . . . If the pursuit of 'self-interest' really means the pursuit of objectives that are sufficiently restricted to be comprehensible and manageable, then behaviour of this kind becomes an obligation." Wilson, "Invisible Hands: Public and Private," in Horst Hanusch, Karl W. Roskamp, and Jack Wiseman, eds., *Public Sector and Political Economy Today* (Stuttgart and New York: Gustav Fischer Verlag, 1985), p. 15.

20. See Chapter 8, n. 35, *supra.*

21. Wilson, "Invisible Hands," p. 15.

22. See Chapter 5, n. 5, *supra.*

23. William Shakespeare, *King Henry V*, Act I, scene 2.

24. Adam Smith, *An Inquiry into the Nature and Causes of the Wealth of Nations,* ed. R. H. Campbell, A. S. Skinner, and W. B. Todd, 2 vols. (London: Oxford University Press, 1976; reprint ed., Indianapolis, Indiana: Liberty Classics, 1981), 1:456; hereafter cited as *The Wealth of Nations.*

25. Ibid.

26. Wilson, "Invisible Hands," p. 15.

27. "The State authorities should leave to other bodies the care and expediting of business and activities of lesser moment, which otherwise become for it a source of great distraction. It then will perform with greater freedom, vigor and effectiveness, the tasks belonging properly to it, and which it alone can accomplish, directing, supervising, encouraging, restraining, as circumstances suggest or necessity demands. Let those in power, therefore, be convinced that the more faithfully this principle of 'subsidiarity' is followed and a hierarchical order prevails among the various organizations the more excellent will

be the authority and efficiency of society, and the happier and more prosperous the condition of the commonwealth." Pius XI, *Quadragesimo Anno*, 80. For a text of *Quadragesimo Anno*, see William J. Gibbons, S.J., ed., *Seven Great Encyclicals* (Glen Rock, New Jersey: Paulist Press, 1963).

28. Entrepreneurship "consists in the function of securing greater consistency between different parts of the market. It expresses itself in entrepreneurial alertness to what transactions are in fact available in different parts of the market. It is only such alertness that is responsible for any tendency toward keeping these transactions in some kind of mutual consistency." Kirzner, *Discovery and the Capitalist Process*, p. 61.

29. The conventional economist's view, "which sees the capitalist economy as a system of markets at or near equilibrium, is not merely a *simplified* view of capitalism but also a *distorted* view. This view is distorted in perceiving, as the salient feature of capitalism, its being at all times close to the fully coordinated state—when in fact the salient feature of capitalism is surely to be found, rather, in the ceaseless market agitation generated by the continual discovery of *failures* in coordination." Ibid., p. 156 (emphasis in original).

30. "Americans are not more intelligent than other people. Yet human factors—the ability to adapt easily, flexibility of organizations, the creative power of teamwork—are the key to their success. Beyond any single explanation, each of which has an element of truth, the secret lies in the confidence of the society in its citizens. This confidence often seems rather naive to Europeans, but America places it both in the ability of its citizens to decide for themselves, and in the capacity of their intelligence." *The American Challenge*, trans. Ronald Steel, with a Foreword by Arthur Schlesinger, Jr. (New York: Avon Books, 1969), pp. 222–223.

31. See Daniel J. Boorstin, *The Discoverers: A History of Man's Search to Know His World and Himself* (New York: Random House, 1985); and Page Smith, *The Rise of Industrial America* (New York: McGraw-Hill, 1984). See also Nathan Rosenberg and L. E. Birdzell, Jr., *How the West Grew Rich: The Economic Transformation of the Industrial World* (New York: Basic Books, 1986).

32. Smith, *Wealth of Nations*, p. 26.

33. Smith writes: "Though the state was to derive no advantage from the instruction of the inferior ranks of people, it would still deserve its attention that they should not be altogether uninstructed. The state, however, derives no inconsiderable advantage from their instruction. . . . An instructed and intelligent people besides are always

more decent and orderly than an ignorant and stupid one." He adds: "The expence of the institutions for education and religious instruction, is likewise, no doubt, beneficial to the whole society, and may, therefore, without injustice, be defrayed by the general contribution of the whole society." Ibid., pp. 788, 815.

34. Lay Commission on Catholic Social Teaching and the U.S. Economy, *Toward the Future: Catholic Social Thought and the U.S. Economy* (Washington, D.C.: Lay Commission, 1984), p. 58.

35. "For the mass of men the idea of artistic creation can only be expressed by an idea unpopular in present discussions—the idea of property. The average man cannot cut clay into the shape of a man; but he can cut earth into the shape of a garden; and though he arranges it with red geraniums and blue potatoes in alternate straight lines, he is still an artist; because he has chosen. The average man cannot paint the sunset whose colours he admires; but he can paint his own house with what colour he chooses; and though he paints it pea green with pink spots, he is still an artist; because that is his choice. Property is merely the art of democracy. It means that every man should have something that he can shape in his own image, as he is shaped in the image of Heaven." G. K. Chesterton, *What's Wrong with the World* (London, 1910), p. 47.

11. EPILOGUE: THE SECOND VATICAN INSTRUCTION ON LIBERATION

1. Congregation for the Doctrine of the Faith, "Instruction on Christian Freedom and Liberation" (Vatican City: Vatican Polyglot Press, 1986), 73; hereafter cited as "Christian Freedom and Liberation."

2. See Joan Frawley, "New 'Liberation' Document Praised," *National Catholic Register*, 20 April 1986.

3. See E. J. Dionne, Jr., "New Vatican Effort on Theology Seen," *The New York Times*, 4 April 1986.

4. Ibid.

5. "Christian Freedom and Liberation," 31.

6. Ibid., 76

7. Joseph Cardinal Hoffner, "Economic Systems and Economic Ethics," *Catholicism in Crisis*, June 1986, p. 12.

8. In fact, the disciplines of the liberal society exceed those of the traditionalist society. Consider this passage from a recent study of liberal virtues inspired by Montaigne: "Since the eighteenth century,

clerical and military critics of liberalism have pictured it as a doctrine that achieves its public goods, peace, prosperity, and security by encouraging private vice. Selfishness in all its possible forms is said to be its essence, purpose, and outcome. This, it is said now as then, is inevitable once martial virtue and the discipline imposed by God are discarded. Nothing could be more remote from the truth. The very refusal to use public coercion to impose creedal unanimity and uniform standards of behavior demands an enormous degree of self-control. Tolerance consistently applied is more difficult and morally more demanding than repression. . . . One begins with what is to be avoided, as Montaigne feared being afraid most of all. Courage is to be prized, since it both prevents us from being cruel, as cowards so often are, and fortifies us against fear from threats, both physical and moral. . . . The alternative then set, and still before us, is not one between classical virtue and liberal-self indulgence, but between cruel military and moral repression and violence, and a self-restraining tolerance that fences in the powerful to protect the freedom and safety of every citizen, old or young, male or female, black or white. Far from being an amoral free-for-all, liberalism is, in fact, extremely difficult and constraining, far too much so for those who cannot endure contradiction, complexity, diversity, and the risks of freedom." Judith Shklar, *Ordinary Vices* (Cambridge: Harvard University Press , 1984), pp. 4–5.

9. See Alejandro Antonio Chafuen, *Christians for Freedom*, with an Introduction by Michael Novak (San Francisco: Ignatius Press, forthcoming).

10. Ludwig von Mises, *Human Action: A Treatise on Economics*, 3rd rev. ed. (Chicago: Henry Regnery, 1966).

11. Friedrich A. Hayek, *The Constitution of Liberty* (Chicago: Henry Regnery, 1960).

12. Cardinal Hoffner, "Economic Systems and Economic Ethics," p. 15.

13. Wilhelm Roepke, *The Humane Economy: The Social Framework of the Free Market*, trans. Elizabeth Henderson (Chicago: Henry Regnery , 1960). Roepke writes (p. 6): "A government which, in peacetime, relies on exchange control, price control and invidious confiscatory taxation has little, if any, more moral justification on its side than the individual who defends himself against this sort of compulsion by circumventing, or even breaking, the law. It is the precept of ethical and humane behavior, no less than of political wisdom, to adapt economic policy to man, not man to economic policy.

"In these considerations lies the essential justification of ownership, profit, and competition. But—and we shall come back to this later—they are justifiable only within certain limits, and in remembering this we return to the realm beyond supply and demand. In other words, the market economy is not everything. It must find its place within a higher order of things which is not ruled by supply and demand, free prices, and competition."

14. Cardinal Hoffner's twelve preconditions for a humane economy may be summarized thus (from pp. 15–16): (1) Material goods should be sufficient not only for basic needs but also for the development of a refined cultural life. (2) The market economy must not lead to consumerism. (3) Striving for economic success must be complemented by the social aims of economic activities. (4) Steps should be taken to prevent overcentralized power; unavoidable natural monopolies should be regulated. (5) The economy must be considered as less than the highest goal of human beings and society. (6) Capital and labor do not contradict each other but call for cooperation between partners and the participation of employees in capital formation. (7) Decision-makers must be willing to see technical progress occur harmoniously, not in crisis-ridden leaps. (8) Business enterprises must be structured on an appreciation of human dignity. (9) International competition does not sufficiently care for the poor nations of the world; worldwide regulative measures are necessary. (10) Employment must be safeguarded; national and international agencies have considerable responsibilities in this area. (11) Technical progress must not be allowed to spoil the biosphere. (12) Modern industrial states have, by means of social insurance, adjusted their nations' income. "However, the trend towards an all-providing state is disquieting. Catholic social teachings advocate, for the sake of human beings themselves, a strengthening of self-responsibility and a rejection of welfare-statism. In the long term, a nation cannot spend more than it has earned by its labors."

15. Alexander Cairncross, "The Market and the State," in Thomas Wilson and Andrew S. Skinner, eds., *The Market and the State: Essays in Honour of Adam Smith* (Oxford: Oxford at the Clarendon Press, 1976), p. 113.

16. See John Emerich Edward Dalberg-Acton, *Selected Writings of Lord Acton*, vol. 1: *Essays in the History of Liberty*, ed. J. Rufus Fears (Indianapolis, Indiana: Liberty Classics, 1985), esp. "The History of Freedom in Christianity." In that essay Acton quotes St. Thomas Aquinas and says that his language "contains the earliest exposition of the Whig theory of the revolution. . . . And it is worth while to observe that

[Thomas] wrote at the very moment when Simon de Montfort summoned the Commmons; and that the politics of the Neapolitan friar
are centuries in advance of the English stateman's" (p. 34).

17. "Christian Freedom and Liberation" (no. 73) reiterates the
great value attached to the principle of subsidiarity precisely because
subsidiarity enables associations and other mediating structures to
flourish: "By virtue of the [principle of subsidiarity], neither the State
nor any society must ever substitute itself for the initiative and responsibility of individuals and of intermediate communities at the level
on which they can function, nor must they take away the room necessary for their freedom."

18. See Michael Novak, "The Quintessential Liberal: John Stuart
Mill," in *Freedom with Justice: Catholic Social Thought and Liberal Institutions* (New York: Harper & Row, 1984), esp. pp. 97–100. Mill writes
that "when the 'sacredness of property' is talked of, it should always be
remembered that any such sacredness does not belong in the same degree to landed property. No man made the land. It is the original inheritance of the whole species. Its appropriation is wholly a question
of general expediency. When private property in land is not expedient, it is unjust. . . . Even in the case of cultivated land, a man whom,
though only one among millions, the law permits to hold thousands of
acres as his single share, is not entitled to think that all this is given to
him to use and abuse, and deal with as if it concerned nobody but himself. . . . The rents or profits which he can obtain for it are at his sole
disposal; but with regard to the land, in everything which he does with
it, and in everything which he abstains from doing, he is morally
bound, and should, whenever the case admits, be legally compelled to
make his interest and pleasure consistent with the public good." *Principles of Political Economy*, abridged, with Notes and a Sketch of the History of Political Economy, by J. Laurence Laughlin (New York: D.
Appleton and Co., 1888), pp. 173–174.

19. "Christian Freedom and Liberation," 84: "[A proper work
culture] will affirm the priority of work over capital and the fact that
material goods are meant for all."

20. Abraham Lincoln, "First Annual Message to Congress, De-
cember 3, 1861," in *Abraham Lincoln: His Speeches and Writings*, ed. Roy
P. Basler (New York: World Publishing Co., 1946), p. 633. See also
"Annual Message to Congress, December 3, 1861," in ibid.

21. The Lay Commission on Catholic Social Teaching and the
U.S. Economy closed its lay letter on this very note: "[W]e humbly pro-
pose as a motto for the Church in this new age, not solely Justice and
Peace, but Liberty, Justice and Peace. The Liberty of voluntary coop-

eration. The Liberty of providence. Liberty under law, Liberty suffused with moral purpose. Liberty, in the end, is the contribution of the experience of the United States to the social teaching of the Catholic Church: LIBERTY AND JUSTICE FOR ALL." *Toward the Future: A Lay Letter* (Washington, D.C.: Lay Commmission on Catholic Social Teaching and the U.S. Economy, 1984), p. 80.

22. Cardinal Hoffner, "Economic Systems and Economic Ethics," p. 14.

23. Ibid., p. 15.

24. Ibid.

25. Arthur F. Burns, "The Condition of the World Economy," *The AEI Economist*, June 1986, p. 4.

26. "Christian Freedom and Liberation," 60.

27. Ibid., 1.

28. Ibid., 78.

29. John Paul II writes: "It is not difficult to see that in the modern world the sense of justice has been reawakening on a vast scale. . . . The church shares with the people of our time this profound and ardent desire for a life which is just in every aspect. . . . And yet it would be difficult not to notice that very often programs which start from the idea of justice and which ought to assist its fulfillment among individuals, groups and human societies, in practice suffer from distortions. Although they continue to appeal to the idea of justice, nevertheless experience shows that other negative forces have gained the upper hand over justice, such as spite, hatred and even cruelty.

"In such cases, the desire to annihilate the enemy, limit his freedom or even force him into total dependence, becomes the fundamental motive for action. . . .

"Not in vain did Christ challenge his listeners, faithful to the doctrine of the Old Testament, for their attitude which was manifested in the words: 'An eye for an eye and a tooth for a tooth.' . . . It is obvious, in fact, that in the name of an alleged justice (for example, historical justice or class justice) the neighbor is sometimes destroyed, killed, deprived of liberty or stripped of fundamental human rights. The experience of the past and of our own time demonstrates that justice alone is not enough, that it can even lead to the negation and destruction of itself, if that deeper power, which is love, is not allowed to shape human life in its various dimensions." *Dives in Misericordia*, 12, in *Origins*, vol. 12, no. 26.

30. "Christian Freedom and Liberation," 76.

NAME INDEX